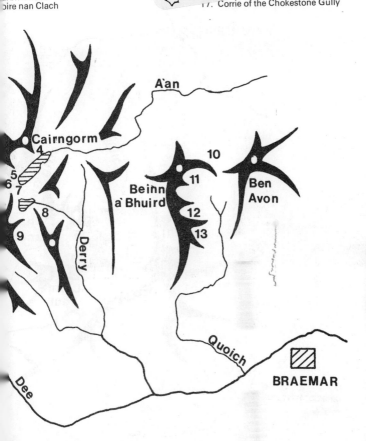

STEVE SECKINGER

ell's Lum Crag
helter Stone Crag and Cairn Etchachar
reagan a'Choire Etchachan
oire Sputan Dearg
arbh Choire
bire nan Clach

YO-CHV-766

oire Dnaidh
17. Corrie of the Chokestone Gully

A'an

Cairngorm
4

5
6
7
8
9

Beinn
a'Bhuird

10
11
12
13

Ben
Avon

Derry

Quoich

Dee

BRAEMAR

Climber's Guide to The Cairngorms

A Comprehensive Guide

Allen Fyffe   Andrew Nisbet

The Scottish Mountaineering Trust

First published in Great Britain in 1985
by The Scottish Mountaineering Trust

Copyright © by The Scottish Mountaineering Trust

ISBN 0 907521 12 6

Front cover—*P. Whillance and P. Botteril on the 1st ascent of Naked Ape; 2nd pitch: Creag an Dubh Loch. Photo by Rab Anderson.*

Rear cover—*Pinnacle Gully; Shelter Stone Crag. Photo by Mark Diggins.*

Filmset by Advanced Filmsetters (Glasgow) Ltd
Printed by Brown, Son & Ferguson, Ltd, Glasgow
Bound by James Gowan, Glasgow

CONTENTS

DIAGRAMS

INTRODUCTION

This is the fourth in the new series of SMC guides, but has been written in an updated style. In order to abandon the unpopular selective nature of the previous three, while still covering a large area, the compromise of full descriptions for the good routes and a summary of grade and line only for the poorer ones has been adopted. A comprehensive list of routes at the back combines first ascent details with a reference to further information for the routes not fully described.

The route descriptions themselves have also been modernised. Individual pitch technical grades for routes of Very Severe grade and above are now widely accepted and these routes should be no exception. Such detail has only recently been collected so many of the technical grades are based on a limited opinion. But a start is necessary now to improve accuracy in the future. The traditionalists may consider such intricacy unsuitable for the Scottish mountains but modern opinion requires the spirit of mountaineering to be combined with rock climbing technicality.

Winter gradings have also been modified, though the difference is less obvious. With modern methods route length *per se* is not such an important factor and the harder routes in particular have been graded mostly on technical difficulty (also seriousness, though many of these routes are adequately protected). To reflect the increase in top standards, albeit much slower than in summer, grade VI has been introduced. This has been somewhat tentative, as shown by several routes given V/VI. This grade VI is set harder than the liberal VI used in non-SMC publication for the western ranges.

The guide covers the whole Cairngorms, an area once intended for five volumes. Of these, three were written over ten years ago and the Braeriach volume did not appear; the last guide to Braeriach is now almost 25 years old. Lochnagar and Creag an Dubh Loch were updated in 1978 but here has seen the greatest activity in recent times, with the Dubh Loch developing into Scotland's finest mountain cliff for hard rock and Lochnagar at the forefront of rising winter standards. This is not forgetting the Shelter Stone Crag, which has also played its part in recent Cairngorm history.

The rock is an "honest granite" (to quote Mac Smith), generally sound away from the gullies, and of an overlapping slab structure. Most of the climbing has short technical sections interspersed with good rests, and the lack of accommodating holds usually requires an active brain as well as brawn. Friction is an important part of the particular climbing style and the full impact of new sticky boots has yet to be felt. This is the first Cairngorm guide to assume that pegs are not carried in summer, but nut and Friend protection is much better than reputed.

In winter the climbing can be as much on rock and frozen vegetation as on snow and ice, particularly away from the gullies. Good névé is less common here as the area receives less freeze and thaw than the West Coast. This however can give consistent conditions for fairly long periods (though it may not always be good). The approaches to the more remote cliffs can be very arduous in winter and fitness plays a major role in success and safety. The use of ski as a means of approaching these cliffs can be an advantage.

It will be obvious how much we have relied on the work of previous guidebook authors. Particular mention must be made of Greg Strange and Dougie Dinwoodie's recent guide to Lochnagar and Creag an Dubh Loch, from which large sections have been taken. The older guides have been important too, those by Allen Fyffe, Greg Strange and Bill March. The foundations had, of course, been built previously by Mac Smith's two volume masterpiece of 1961, which turned the Cairngorms into a major climbing ground and established many of its legends and traditions.

ACKNOWLEDGEMENTS

Our thanks go to many friends who have contributed so enthusiastically to this project:

Greg Strange, Dougie Dinwoodie, Murray Hamilton, Rob Archbold, Ged Reilly, Rab Anderson and Kenny Spence for criticism of the text.

Roy Bremner, for his excellent diagrams and Kenny Spence for his magnificent cliff diagrams of the northern crags.

To all those who contributed slides and photographs so willingly.

Mungo Ross, for help with photographs. Mrs. Marian Burrows-Smith, Carolyne Lucas, Mrs. Margaret Sinclair and Mrs. Sheila Riach for typing the manuscript.

Norman Keir and Raymond Simpson, for permission to re-use their diagrams of Creag an Dubh Loch and Lochnagar.

Brenda Nisbet for help with proof-reading.

Alf Robertson, whose early work got this project off the ground.

To all those who contributed information, opinions on routes and grades and enough material to put together a graded list, particularly Rab Anderson, Rob Archbold, Bob Barton, Geoff Cohen, Dave Cuthbertson, Dougie Dinwoodie, Brian Findlay, Murray Hamilton, Steve Kennedy, Brian Lawrie, Graeme Livingstone, Colin MacLean, Neil Morrison, Guy Muhlemann, Ged Reilly, Alf Robertson, Alasdair Ross, the staff at Glenmore Lodge, Greg Strange and Pete Whillance.

NOTES ON THE USE OF THE GUIDE

CLASSIFICATION OF ROUTES

Summer

For rock climbs the following grades have been used:

> Easy   Moderate   Difficult   Very Difficult   Severe
> Hard Severe   Very Severe   Hard Very Severe   Extremely Severe

The Extremely Severe grade has been subdivided into E1, E2, E3, E4, E5, etc., in keeping with the rest of Britain.

In this guide for the first time technical pitch gradings are given for routes of Very Severe and above. Some routes have all the relevant pitches graded, others have only the crux pitch so described. An attempt has been made to make these technical grades consistent with those used in other areas bearing in mind the unique nature of Cairngorm granite climbing. As a rough guide the following technical grades equate to these adjectival grades:

> 4b   Mild Very Severe*   4c   Very Severe
> 5a   Hard Very Severe   5b   E1
> 5c   E2   6a   E3
> 6b   E4, E5

> * Mild Very Severe is not used in this guide. Very Severe 4b generally indicates this grade.

Generally a technical grade below that expected from the adjectival grade would indicate a sustained or poorly protected route. A higher technical grade would indicate a short and generally well-protected crux section.

As many of the routes in this guide have received very few repeat ascents, particularly since the introduction of technical grades, these grades should be regarded as guides not gospel, and a basis for a more accurate work.

Winter

For winter climbs Grades I to V have been used with the addition of Grade VI, but any specific route length requirements have been dropped.

Grade I—Uncomplicated, average-angled snow climbs having no pitches normally. They may, however, have cornice difficulties or dangerous runouts.

Grade II—Gullies which contain either individual or minor pitches; or high-angled snow with difficult cornice exits. The easier buttresses under winter conditions.

Grade III—Gullies which contain ice in quantity. There will normally be at least one substantial pitch and possibly several lesser ones. Sustained buttress climbs, but only technical in short sections.

Grade IV—Steeper than Grade III and of higher technical difficulty. Vertical sections may be expected on ice climbs and buttresses will require a good repertoire of techniques.

Grade V—Climbs which are difficult, sustained and serious. Also well-protected technical desperates. They may not be possible in poor conditions.

Grade VI—Routes of exceptional overall difficulty. Several contenders for Grade VI have been given V/VI.

Split grades, e.g. II/III indicate difficulty in assignment, either due to variable amounts of ice or a borderline grade. Routes are graded for average to good conditions, and this is based on observation and experience. These gradings, however, remain an approximation because conditions can vary rapidly. A good cover of firm snow and ice will ease the difficulties whereas a poor build-up will make ice routes more difficult.

With present day ice climbing techniques there can be an apparent difference in difficulty between ice climbs and buttress climbs of the same grade. This disappears with experience of Cairngorm climbing. As a rough guide, however, the following gives the summer grade and how it generally translates into winter on buttress routes. Gullies do not translate and open face routes are normally harder than buttresses,

Moderate	II or III	Difficult	III
Very Difficult	IV	Severe	IV, occasionally V
Hard Severe	V	Very Severe	V or VI

Style

Rock climbs are graded for parties not carrying pegs. The damage caused by pegs is well documented. Only a few routes require peg protection and certainly not the classics. As peg runners have been used extensively until recent times, however, the quality of nut protection has not been fully assessed, but unless mentioned, all the routes should be possible without their use. It is to be hoped that any necessary pegs will be left *in situ*; in this way pegs will soon become unnecessary. It is assumed that a modern range of nuts will be carried. Any ascent involving bolts will be ignored.

Many parties use chalk and few of the routes above E2 have been climbed without. Routes of a lower grade are almost always climbed without; this is to be encouraged.

Many of the Extremely Severe routes of the 80's have been inspected and cleaned on abseil, often involving extensive gardening and wire brushing, however, these routes have been graded for an on-sight lead.

Summer ethics should be applied to the use of pegs for aid in winter. The use of aid will be a lesser achievement than a free ascent. Pegs are still necessary, however, for safe anchors on the majority of winter routes, even routes as easy as Grade II. Parties should attempt to limit their use on popular rock routes.

Left and Right
The terms "left" and "right" refer to a climber facing the direction being described, i.e. facing the cliff in route descriptions, facing downhill in descents.

Pitch Lengths
Pitch lengths are in metres, sometimes rounded to the nearest 5 m. The lengths are usually estimates rather than measurements. 45 m ropes are sufficiently long for the Cairngorms, although 50 m is popular especially for harder winter climbs. Where lengths greater than 45 m are given, this does not indicate moving roped together, merely belay where required.

Recommended Routes
Recommendations are given only in the text. Many routes have not had sufficient ascents to justify the three star system of recommendation, upon which newcomers would rely too heavily. It is hoped that future guides will have sufficient information to allow its use.

First Ascentionists
The year of first ascent is given in the text. The full date and first ascentionists are listed cliff by cliff in chronological order at the back of the guide. The original aid is also listed, usually with first free ascent. Details of variations are given under the parent route.

Winter ascents are listed separately from their corresponding summer route, with different forks of gullies also listed separately. Aid eliminations in winter are not generally noted.

Litter and Vandalism

Litter is a continuing problem at popular camping sites and bothies despite a slow improvement in recent years. Common examples with false justifications are empty bottles and surplus food in bothies, and orange peel. A spare polythene bag allows easy removal of rubbish to bins in the valley. In the end, justified complaints by landowners can lead to access problems. Please cooperate by not leaving any traces behind you.

In recent times, vandalism to bothies has provoked threats from landowners to close them. Though hopefully not due to climbers, it is as well to be vigilant.

Mountain Rescue

In case of accident requiring rescue or medical attention, telephone 999 (police). This will usually mean a return to habitation except that there is a public telephone at Derry Lodge (NO. 041934). Give concise information about the location and injuries of the victim. Try to leave someone with the victim. In a party of two with no one nearby there will be a difficult decision to make. If you decide to go for help, make the victim comfortable and leave in a sheltered, well-marked place. It is often better, however, to stay with the victim.

There is a first aid box in the corrie of Lochnagar (NO. 251857) on a small flattening about midway between the Loch and the right side of Central Buttress (cairn). Its contents vary but there is often a casualty bag.

Maps

The maps recommended for use are the Ordnance Survey 1:50,000 maps. Sheet 44 entitled Ballater covers the Southern area of this guide and Sheet 36 entitled Grantown and Cairngorm covers the Northern area. This is also partly covered by Sheet 43 entitled Braemar. The 1:25,000 Outdoor Leisure Map entitled High Tops of the Cairngorms is also very suitable for the Northern section of this guide.

AVALANCHES

Every year avalanches occur in the Cairngorms, sometimes with tragic results. Climbers venturing into the hills in winter should acquaint themselves with the principles of snow structure and at least the elements of avalanche prediction. There are several suitable books on the subject. A knowledge of what to do if involved in an avalanche, either as a victim or observer, may help to save lives. A knowledge of first aid and artificial resuscitation is an obvious necessity.

Avalanches are classified by certain criteria which are:

Type of breakaway—either single point (loose) or whole area (slab).

Position of sliding surface—either full or partial depth.

Humidity—wet or dry.

Less important are the track form which can be confined or unconfined depending on the terrain and the form of movement, which can be airborne or flowing.

The main types of avalanche encountered in the Cairngorms are:

Powder:

Most common during or immediately after snowfall in calm conditions these avalanches can be confined in gullies or on open slopes. They are almost invariably partial depth as the cover of fresh snow slides on a harder base. Uncommon on steep slopes as the snow slides off before it can reach dangerous proportions. The most common occurrence of this general type is in spin-drift avalanches in gullies which can be very unpleasant but rarely large enough to be very dangerous.

Wet snow:

Most common during periods of thaw, especially in the spring when the snow becomes saturated with water which weakens the bonds between the snow layers. Often start near rocks which are heated by the sun so causing more melting. These can vary from small slow moving surface slides to huge full-depth wet slab avalanches such as the one that occurs most years on the Great Slab in Coire an Lochain. The breakaway can be either single point or slab and it can be confined or unconfined.

Slab:

By far the most common and certainly the most dangerous type of avalanche. They are formed by the build-up of wind-damaged snow crystals in a sheltered area such as lee-slopes but can occur anywhere wind-blown snow can accumulate. Slab often has a dull, chalky appearance and breaks up into angular blocks; it may creak or boom when walked on or when probed with an axe shaft. They can vary from soft slab to the more treacherous hard slab which appears solid. It can attain depths of several metres with break-offs in excess of a kilometre in length. After a period of snow with accompanying wind, the usual situation in this area, these may be found on lee slopes and in particular below cornices.

To be able to predict the probability of a slope avalanching with a degree of accuracy requires considerable data and scientific application; to give a rough assessment of the risk presented by a slope is, however, something much more easily undertaken if the main factors causing avalanches are considered.

Avalanches occur when the bond between snow layers, or the ground, fails, or when the bonds between the crystals themselves fail. The cause of this can be due to internal or external factors.

The greater the amount of fresh snow the higher the risk remembering that accumulations of wind-blown snow can be considerable even when little or no snow has fallen. Weather, particularly wind direction, over the previous few days is very important.

Slopes between 22° and 60° can avalanche but wet snow avalanches can occur at lower angles. The most prone to avalanche however are slopes between 30° and 45°. Fractures commonly take place on the convex part of a slope.

There is a period of high risk during and in the 24 hours after a snowfall. The colder the weather the longer this will persist as settling of the snow cover is slowed down.

Cornices are a danger during periods of thaw; the fracture line is often further back than one would expect.

A snow pit can give a large amount of information concerning a slope's stability. The pit is dug down to the level of the ground or at very least through the top layers and the layers making up the snow cover inspected. This is done in a safe situation on a similar slope to the suspect one. The adhesion of the layers to each other (and the ground) is of prime importance and this is related to the relative hardness of these layers. This can be roughly assessed on a 1 to 5 scale depending on what can be pushed into the layer—fist, fingers, single finger, pencil, knife. The greater the difference, the greater the risk. In particular, look for very weak layers such as those that may be formed by powder snow or the collapse of very weak layers. Very hard icy layers are also significant as they provide a good sliding surface. If the top layer is suspected of being slab, a simple test is to stamp on the snow above the pit. The easier that angular blocks of snow break away the higher the risk. This information will only apply to a slope of the same altitude and aspect as the one on which the pit is dug.

If an avalanche slope must be ascended or descended, go straight up or down, rather than diagonally. If it must be crossed, cross as high up the slope as possible as burial from above is usually to a greater depth. Use available shelter or rock outcrops, move one at a time, trail an avalanche cord but first make sure that there is absolutely no alternative.

If involved in an avalanche:

If caught by an avalanche try at once to jump clear or, by holding on to your axe or anything else, delay being swept away. Once under-way, try to "swim" and remain on or as near the surface as possible; keep your mouth closed, especially in powder and as the snow slows down try to create a breathing space in front of your face. As debris slows try to break free, especially in wet snow which hardens rapidly after coming to rest. If still trapped try to remain calm and you will use less oxygen.

If you are a witness to an avalanche accident, prompt action can save lives, as the sooner the victim is found the greater the chance of survival; over 80% if dug out immediately but only 10% after three hours. Immediately search the avalanche debris for survivors—this is vital. Mark the last known point of the victim and his disappearance point as this may give clues as to where he may be buried. Keep quiet in case there is anyone shouting in the burial area and continually look out for clues such as clothing, etc. Continue searching until assistance arrives.

If a victim is found clear out the air-way and give E.A.R. if required then treat other injuries. Remember immediate searching can save lives.

GEOLOGY

The area covered in this guide consists of two roughly circular granite masses. That of Lochnagar and Creag an Dubh Loch in the south and the main Cairngorm massif in the north. These large granite plutons were formed about 500 million years ago during the Caledonian orogeny, when they formed the roots of a vast mountain chain. These were, with wind, weather and time, worn down to below sea-level and covered with sediments. About 50 million years ago these rose again to form a great flat plain which was eroded to reveal the old mountain roots which, because of their resistant nature, were left higher than the surrounding area.

The present day appearance of the Cairngorms is one of a high plateau with gently rolling slopes. This shape was produced by a period of tropical and sub-tropical weathering during the Tertiary period. It was then modified by the action of ice during the Quaternary period. These ice-sheets and local glaciers were selective in their erosion and left us pre-glacial features such as the rounded hills and tors but also gouged out great troughs such as the Lairig Ghru and Loch A'an and the many corries that cut into these mountains. It is these glacial features that give the area its climbing potential.

The rock itself is a remarkably homogeneous granite. It is generally coarse grained and pinkish in colour when freshly exposed but weathering to grey. The three joint systems are regular and approximately at right angles to each other. Because of the uniform nature of the rock there has been little to encourage preferential weathering giving many cliffs their massive appearance. The majority of gullies are the lines of small vertical faults or crush lines and again many of them are of poor and shattered rock. Typical of Cairngorm granite is its "woolsack" appearance due to its vertical joints and sheeting, a type of joint which roughly parallels the surface and becomes thicker with depth, probably due to pressure release as a deeply buried rock was revealed by erosion. These rounded blocks are seen in many cliffs but most notably in No. 4 Buttress of Coire an Lochain.

The rock may also be cut by pegmatite or aplite veins. The former consists of large crystals and the latter are veins of very fine rock. Several routes use these veins which sometimes weather to give a ladder of tiny square holds. Occasionally, cavities in these veins contain crystals of quartz, which may be tinted with impurities to give it a smokey yellow to dark brown colour, the semi-precious Cairngorm stones that lured the first explorers onto these cliffs. Gas pockets or druses which may contain crystals can also be found in places.

HISTORY

LOCHNAGAR AND CREAG AN DUBH LOCH
(modified from notes by D. Dinwoodie and G. Strange)

The earliest known visitors to the cliffs were the quartzdiggers and botanists on Lochnagar. In the earliest explorations of the SMC Lochnagar naturally attracted attention. The mountain was accessible and its bold cliffs clearly visible to the traveller through the glen. The more secluded Dubh Loch cliffs were found disconcertingly smooth and left untouched.

The first way made up the cliffs, in 1893, was a snow climb, Black Spout by the left hand branch. The earliest rock climb was Tough-Brown Traverse in 1895, the outcome of a bold assault on the massive buttress in the middle of the crags. Raeburn attempted a number of lines with scant success, the main reward being the great central gully now named after him. This was a popular climb in later years until the best pitch was obliterated by rockfall in 1940. The remaining major gully was of more evil character—the disintegrating Douglas–Gibson. The SMC's efforts in this oppressive gash did little to foster enthusiasm for Cairngorm granite. By 1902 five attempts had been made, three by Raeburn. An abseil inspection (the start of a modern trend?) was even made in 1902 and the upper gully reported as "not being impossible".

Scottish climbing virtually died out in the years around the Great War and for almost two decades Lochnagar was abandoned to enjoy the same peace as Dubh Loch. Exploration was resumed by two members of the Cairngorm Club, Symmers and Ewen, the first of the local campaigners. The climbs of this pair have gained notoriety rather than popularity, an unfair reflection on their enterprise. Performing heroics on loose rock and vegetation they climbed most of the remaining gullies and chimneys, and three major buttresses. Symmers also made the first recorded climb on Creag an Dubh Loch, the South-East Gully (1928).

Symmers and Ewen had been aware of the better possibilities on Lochnagar, naming such features as Parallel and Eagle Buttresses and examining the line of Eagle Ridge. The field was left open, however, to Dr. J. H. B. Bell, whose outstanding climb was the aforesaid Eagle Ridge. Building on a previous skirmish (Eagle Buttress) and the work of Scroggie and Ferguson of Dundee, he completed his Lochnagar masterpiece in 1941. It remains a milestone in Cairngorm history, the only earlier climb of comparable quality being the remote and unsung Cumming–Crofton Route on Mitre Ridge. Other examples of Bell's pioneering skill were Parallel Buttress and the hard Direct Route on Tough-Brown Ridge. Bell, like Symmers, paid the odd visit to Dubh Loch and made the first important climb there, the difficult Labyrinth Route (1941).

Soon were to come the first probes of a new generation (partly inspired by his climbs and writings), namely, the various bands who were to make up the Aberdeen School of the fifties. At this time entire untouched corries and crags abounded all over the vast Cairngorm region and the number of existing climbs would soon be doubled. In the early years of this era the easier breaks between the bare faces were climbed at Dubh Loch, and the remaining classical lines on Lochnagar. Sutherland and Brooker led off with Route One on the Black Spout Pinnacle, last of the great Lochnagar buttresses to fall. In 1952 an eight-man party stormed the last of the classical lines, Parallel Gully B. The leader was Tom Patey, the most energetic explorer of the day.

The time was now ripe for the breakthrough on the bolder "impossible" faces. It was obvious that these would provide the best climbing. The first of the big climbs was the huge intimidating corner of Vertigo Wall, climbed by Patey, McLeod and Will. Forced in the same year as Sassenach on Nevis (1954), Vertigo does not compare technically but must have been a similar psychological undertaking. Climbed in nails and bad conditions it was an inspired achievement. Astonishingly, attempts were later made to climb an even more frightening line on the gully wall, while the slabbier frontal face remained virgin. This was the very exposed line of slab-shelves leading high up into The Giant. On the boldest attempt Dick Barclay and Sticker Thom free climbed up into the corner only to find themselves trapped. Friends on the plateau threw down ropes and hauled them to safety. Their pegs were to baffle the Squirrels on their subsequent direct ascent.

Perhaps even more important than Vertigo was Jerry Smith's Pinnacle Face on Lochnagar the following year. Using rope-soled shoes he threaded the big slab-apron avoided by Route One. Pinnacle Face was the first of the "overlapping slab" routes which provide much of the best modern climbing, particularly south of the Dee. It proved that the smooth open faces ran to better holds than appearances suggested. The next year Bill Brooker and Ken Grassick, wearing Vibrams, repeated Pinnacle Face and continued up the steep Black Spout face to make The Link. This success was an eye-opener for Brooker and a clear indication of the great possibilities open in the Cairngorms. In 1958, with Dick Barclay, he applied this knowledge to Central Gully Wall and made the first open face route there, Waterkelpie Wall. The big Waterkelpie climb was paralleled by Ronnie Sellar's impressive Citadel on Shelter Stone Crag the same year. As the fifties drew to an end, the energy of the Aberdeen movement seems to have fizzled out, just as great things were being achieved. Mac Smith's guide was written at this time, winding up the era and stamping the Cairngorms as one of Scotland's main climbing areas.

The end of this campaign coincided with the arrival of the first modern invaders, the Edinburgh climbers. Jimmy Marshall had already plundered Parallel Gully B in the winter of 1958. The next year, in the unlikely month of November, he turned up at Dubh Loch to climb the Mousetrap, later to become the trade route at Dubh Loch, a line unaccountably missed by the locals who failed to find an entry into the recess. As far as exploration is concerned a lull fell over the whole region in the early sixties. In 1964 a new generation of Aberdeen and Edinburgh men started tentative probes at Dubh Loch, soon to be joined by Dundee climbers. Jim McArtney provided Waterkelpie Wall with a long direct start. Later he was to open up Eagle's Rocks and do early work on King Rat and Goliath. Jim Stenhouse and Brian Lawrie finally answered the stark challenge of the Central Slabs with Dinosaur. Better pegs and PA's had taken some of the sting out of the naked slabs. The following year Dave Bathgate and the Squirrels climbed the long-sought Giant, an epic ascent requiring many pegs. Lochnagar was forgotten in the Dubh Loch boom, apart from efforts on the forbidding Tough-Brown Face, which was opened up by two young Aberdonians, Mike Forbes and Mike Rennie, with Mort and Crypt (1967). At Dubh Loch Brian Robertson led the technical Blue Max, a direct ascent of the Central Slabs. The most important event of the year, however, was an English intrusion; the Barley brothers forced a most impressive line up the middle of the impregnable-looking Broad Terrace Wall. Shrouded in mystery for a number of years, Culloden remains one of the harder Dubh Loch routes.

In 1968 Rennie's partly artificial Cougar was also impressive, a bold and committing climb up the most intimidating part of Central Gully Wall. Meanwhile the great plum of King Rat fell to Allen Fyffe and John Bower at a surprisingly reasonable standard. Activity reached its height in June 1969 when the three classics of Black Mamba, False-face and Goliath were climbed on the same day by rival teams. Fyffe and John Grieve stayed on for another four routes that week, including Pink Elephant. Predator, Sword of Damocles, Dubh Loch Monster and Gulliver fell in another short spell in 1970 and with these rapid developments a new guide was written by Fyffe, the most active pioneer of these years. Ian Nicolson's bold on-sight lead of the Red Wall of Gulliver had produced the hardest pitch in the new guide.

In the seventies, Creag an Dubh Loch became the most popular summer crag in the Cairngorms. While the climbing was at last being appreciated, the place had sadly lost much of its mystique. Exploration shifted towards the dripping Broad Terrace Wall, while aid was being whittled away on the established lines. Most active pioneers were Dougie Dinwoodie and Bob Smith. This pair and others of the Etchachan Club also dispelled the myth that Lochnagar had little to offer in summer with a series of fine routes on the Tough-Brown Face and the Black Spout Pinnacle, culminating in the magnificent Black Spout Wall (1976). Dougie Dinwoodie and Greg Strange's guide appeared in 1978.

A new era, focussing on the monolithic walls of Creag an Dubh Loch, started in 1977 when Dave Cuthbertson and Murray Hamilton made free ascents of Cougar and Giant. (It was not known at the time that Giant had been freed previously by Nick Estcourt in 1974.) Four consecutive wet summers delayed the onset but Murray Hamilton's Sans Fer (E4, 1979) was the start. The fine summer of 1982 saw Pete Whillance, Murray Hamilton and others produce six excellent routes of E3 and above, starting with the first E5, Slartibartfast on the False Gully Wall. The remaining five routes were on the Central Gully Wall, with pride of place going to Whillance's The Naked Ape (E5) and Hamilton's Ascent of Man (E4), both on the long-admired "impossible" wall between Giant and Cougar. These routes proved that the seemingly blank steeper walls did run to holds which the modern armoury could exploit. Gardening on abseil was a crucial factor which combined with the jump in technical ability.

The pattern continued in 1983 as more participants caught on to Creag an Dubh Loch's great potential. Flodden (E5) and Range War (E4) were climbed on the overhanging wall left of Culloden while Voyage of the Beagle (E4) and Perilous Journey (E5) started the criss-crossing of lines on the "Cougar Wall". Yet another E5 was added here in 1984, as well as three more to the False Gully Wall, including Graeme Livingstone's The Improbability Drive, probably the hardest on the cliff. Just as significant were several on-sight repeats, including Ascent of Man, Sans Fer, Slartibartfast and The Naked Ape.

These routes have established Creag an Dubh Loch as Scotland's best mountain crag, poised for a new increase in popularity if the good summers continue.

WINTER

It is not inappropriate that the first recorded ascent of Creagan Lochnagar was made under winter conditions. This was in March 1893 when Douglas and Gibson climbed the left hand branch of The Black Spout. The previous day they had made an audacious attempt at the gully now named after them but were turned back below the 60 m headwall; 57 years were to elapse before the gully was eventually climbed under winter conditions.

Apart from the classic Raeburn's Gully by Symmers and Ewen in 1932, few notable climbs were recorded before the Second World War. This is quite surprising considering the level of achievement attained elsewhere. Things were to change after the War. In the space of a single decade, from 1948 to 1958, snow and ice climbing on the mountain progressed from the ascents of easy gullies to the climbing of some of the most difficult face and buttress routes in the country. During these golden years the NE Corrie of Lochnagar was the new crucible of modern winter climbing in Scotland. Each new season seemed to produce climbs of greater difficulty. Giant's Head Chimney, Douglas–Gibson Gully, The Stack, Polyphemus Gully and Eagle Ridge all represented significantly more serious and psychologically harder undertakings. Although there were a number of local climbers involved with these developments, Brooker, Patey and Taylor were probably the most active. Their $4\frac{1}{2}$-hour ascent of Eagle Ridge proved how well they had mastered the art of climbing snow-covered rock. It was during the mid fifties that Patey and Smith commenced work on the climbers' guide to Lochnagar and the Cairngorms (edited by Smith) and at the same time devised the now widely accepted 5-grade system of categorising winter climbs.

By 1958 ideas were changing and a new force emerged from Edinburgh in the shape of a crampon-shod Jimmy Marshall. Marshall's ascent of Parallel Gully B in icy conditions not only grieved the local climbers but represented a breakthrough in pure ice climbing by clearly demonstrating the advantages of crampons over nailed boots for climbing ice. Local climbers took advantage of a good winter in 1959 to climb the first big winter routes on Creag an Dubh Loch. Sellars, Annand and Jerry Smith climbed Labyrinth Route and

Brooker climbed Labyrinth Edge; the obvious potential of the Dubh Loch had at last been realised.

Lochnagar went into the sixties with all its major gullies and buttresses climbed. In later years several important climbs were made; notably Grassick, Light and Nicol's ascent of Pinnacle Face—the swansong of the tricouni tricksters—but ironically a route of modern conception and difficulty, repeated only twice until the eighties. Apart from Pinnacle Face technical standards rose very little beyond those of the golden years. Crampons with front points became the accepted footwear, but it was not until the early seventies that the technique of front-pointing steep ice began to supercede the tradition of step cutting. Once mastered, the new technique enabled ice climbs and climbs involving frozen turf to be ascended in faster times and more and more parties began to tackle the harder routes. In 1970 Bower and Simpson climbed the difficult Bower Buttress in the Hanging Garden and recorded the first winter route on Eagle's Rocks. Two years later James Bolton made his bold ascent of Labyrinth Direct thus creating the most difficult gully climb of its time in the country. The new technique had at last been successfully applied to a long-standing problem. The mid seventies saw further climbs in the Hanging Garden and a rapid development of the water courses on Eagle's Rocks as worthwhile ice climbing alternatives to the main Dubh Loch faces.

The mid seventies saw a great increase in the number of winter climbers, with Lochnagar particularly popular. Confidence in the new techniques was growing slowly and the hard routes began to see regular ascents with Eagle Ridge the major testpiece. For those with exploratory ideas there was much to be climbed on pure ice; further climbs were made in the Hanging Garden and a rapid development of the watercourses on Eagle's Rocks as a less serious ice-climbing alternative. Norman Keir was more forward-thinking and determined efforts on the ice-glazed slabs of Pink Elephant with Dave Wright (1975) cost an involuntary bivouac but showed the way ahead. Influenced by Keir's audacity, Andrew Nisbet and Alfie Robertson adopted a more clinical approach in a two-day ascent of the formidably steep Vertigo Wall in 1977. Although not a technical advance, a psychological barrier had been broken and all the big VS routes were now winter targets. The technical advance came soon with John Anderson's ascent of The Link (1979), the first grade V/VI.

January 1980 saw excellent conditions on the Dubh Loch and the influx of Edinburgh climbers. Pink Elephant was the first of three great routes to fall in a week; the Aberdonian's answer was Goliath. The long-sought Mousetrap was the third, and Murray Hamilton, Alan Taylor and Kenny Spence had achieved the first route on the front face of the Central Gully Wall. By March the exceptional conditions had shifted to the Black Spout Pinnacle and there were repeats of Pinnacle Face and The Link, as well as first ascents of the prominent line of Pinnacle Grooves and the desperate Epitome by visiting Polish climber Jan Fijalkowski, along with Aberdonian Bob Smith.

Three mediocre winters, a switch in emphasis to rock climbing, and the deaths of three of the keenest pioneers, John Anderson, Bob Smith and Brian Sprunt, limited activity until 1984, a comeback year. The start was Arthur Paul's ascent of Psyche. Axe torquing, which had become increasingly important as harder rock climbs had been attempted in winter, was taken a step further by ascents of the big HVS layback cracks of Nymph (Colin MacLean) and Pantheist (Dinwoodie, Nisbet).

NORTHERN CAIRNGORMS

The first climbing ground opened up in the Cairngorms was Gleann Einich, being accessible from the railway line. After an ascent of Pinnacle Ridge by Harold Raeburn in March 1902, the SMC held an Easter meet in Gleann Einich in 1902 and climbed several routes. Though of poor quality, they remained popular till the early fifties. The only good rock in the jungle of vegetation was provided by Robert's Ridge, climbed in 1938 by J. H. B. Bell and party, including E. E. Roberts on his 64th birthday.

Apart from early exploration by Raeburn, including Pygmy Ridge (1904) and Raeburn's Buttress (1907), Coire an t-Sneachda and Coire an Lochain remained virtually untouched until the thirties and the Loch A'an basin until the fifties. The exception was the Clach Dhian Chimney which repulsed at least three attempts, one involving a fatality, until its ascent by W. S. Thomson in 1947.

The northern two corries are best known in winter and early exploration took place in winter as well as summer. E. M. Davidson and A. Henderson were most active with winter ascents of Aladdin's Couloir descending by The Couloir, and The Vent (1935). Development was slow in the forties (Savage Slit in 1945) and early fifties (Left Branch of Y-Gully, 1952) until Tom Patey climbed many of today's best known winter routes in 1958 and 1959, including Aladdin's Buttress, Fiacaill Couloir, Central Crack Route and Western Route, all solo.

Exploration of the Loch A'an basin by the Aberdeen group, usually approaching from Braemar, began slowly in the early fifties with I. M. Brooker's ascents of Deep Cut Chimney (1950) and Hell's Lum (1952) and Ken Grassick and H. Bates' ascents on the loose main face of Cairn Etchachan in 1952–53. The first winter route, Scorpion (1952), with its now notorious "sting in the tail", was climbed in epic style by the powerful team of Ken Grassick, Graeme Nicol, Tom Patey and Mike Taylor and was one of the earliest Grade V's. In the mid fifties Tom Patey climbed six routes on the Upper Tier of Cairn Etchachan and several more routes appeared on Stag Rocks, Mac Smith being most active.

In 1957 and 1958 Ronnie Sellars and G. Annand visited Hell's Lum Crag (Brimstone Grooves, Hellfire Corner and Devil's Delight) as well as climbing The Citadel, first route on the main bastion of the Shelter Stone Crag and a major breakthrough. Big routes were done in the winter too, with Route Major and Sticil Face in 1957. The Coire Cas ski road was opened in July 1960. Now that the easiest approach had switched to Aviemore, the area became popular with visitors from all parts of Scotland. Summer activity continued steadily into the sixties; two of the plums, The Clean Sweep (1961) and The Needle (1962) were picked up by Robin Smith. The Needle was the first Extreme in the Cairngorms and set a standard which could not be matched by the Aberdonians, whose greatest feats were always in winter (Sticil Face being no less an achievement). These incursions by Edinburgh climbers set up Loch A'an as a more cosmopolitan climbing area; the Aberdonians continued to dominate elsewhere. The Shelter Stone Crag remained at the forefront of rock climbing difficulty in the late sixties, surpassing even Creag an Dubh Loch which was also under intensive development. Rab Carrington's The Pin and Ken Spence's Steeple (both 1968) were followed up by Haystack (Carrington and Ian Nicolson, 1971), the hardest route in the Cairngorms until recently. Also at this time, during preparation of a new guide to the area by Bill March, locally based climbers were very active. Glenmore Lodge instructors such as March and John Cunningham and Aviemore cobbler George Shields, led this group and between 1968 and 1971 climbed over 30 new routes in the area and established Stac an Fharaidh as a fine slab-climbing cliff.

In winter the Northern Corries were by now fairly well developed but the Loch A'an basin comparatively neglected. Activity resumed in the late sixties with March particularly busy picking off some of the more obvious lines such as Raeburn's Buttress. At this time John

Cunningham was developing his front point technique using ice daggers on steeper ice. This culminated in 1970 with The Chancer, a fine icicle climb on Hell's Lum Crag. Later that winter Chouinard visited the area and introduced his curved picks. Cunningham and March immediately took these up and went on to produce some fine routes such as Salamander and Devil's Delight.

By the late seventies however, explorers were forced onto the steeper snowed up rocks of Cairn Etchachan, Shelter Stone Crag and Stag Rocks. On the latter Gordon Smith was particularly active climbing several hard lines. The real plums though fell to Edinburgh climbers. Hamilton, Spence and Taylor climbed Postern with one bivouac to produce the area's first Grade VI. Spence and Hamilton then went on to climb the even more impressive Citadel. This sought after route is now the most serious winter undertaking in the area with its crux high up and retreat unappealing.

Recent times have also seen development on the rock climbing front. Several VS and HVS routes have been done by Fyffe, Barton and others on Stag Rocks, the Upper Tier of Cairn Etchachan and Hell's Lum Crag, the latter now being one of the best cliffs for medium grade routes in the Cairngorms. But the Shelter Stone Crag continues to be the area's main attraction with its selection of very difficult routes on the Central Slabs, of which Pete Whillance's Run of the Arrow takes pride of place, while the "Big Three" on the Main Bastion continue to draw the crowds.

CREAGAN A'CHOIRE ETCHACHAN, SPUTAN DEARG, BEINN A'BHUIRD

These cliffs are in the remote plateau area most accessible from Braemar. They have never achieved the popularity of the big cliffs of Shelter Stone, Lochnagar or Creag an Dubh Loch, nor have the accessibility of the Northern Corries or Loch A'an. Consequently development has been fairly recent and almost exclusively by Aberdonians.

Before 1948 activity was confined to easy snow climbs on Beinn a'Bhuird and to the Mitre Ridge, the focus of pre-war attention and at 200 m high, the only feature to rival the bigger cliffs. Determined efforts resulted in ascents of the ridge and Cumming–Crofton Route on the same day in July 1933. Only Eagle Ridge could rival these for difficulty in the pre-war period. Two further routes in the Mitre Ridge area were climbed by Armed Forces in training during the War.

Early guides had described the rock of Etchachan as "rather frag-mentary" and Sputan as "not suited for climbing, the rocks being rounded and devoid of holds". Once the post-war move was made out from the gullies on to the buttresses and faces, these descriptions were quickly proved wrong. Sputan, with its clean juggy rock and fine low grade buttresses, was the first to attract attention. After Pinnacle Buttress and the excellent Crystal Ridge were climbed in the summer of 1948, a further eight routes, including most of the main buttresses, followed in 1949. Main activists were Bill Brooker, J. Tewnion and Mac Smith. In the fifties Brooker, Smith, Tom Patey and others, including the "Kincorth Club" (Freddy Malcolm, Alec Thom, Dick Barclay) moved away from Sputan and began to develop Etchachan and the Beinn a'Bhuird corries. Standards were rising and by 1956 most of the obvious lines up to mild VS had been climbed. Important climbs were Hourglass Buttress (1953), Squareface (1953) and The Carpet (1955). In September 1955, Patey and John Hay made a move on to the Crimson Slabs, the first attempt on one of the smooth Cairngorm faces. The result was The Dagger, hardest route in the Cairngorms at that time. Hay returned to the slabs the following year to put up the companion route, Djibangi. These routes opened up great possibilities and became the major test pieces in the area for almost a decade. Also from 1956 were Talisman and another test piece, Amethyst Wall. A temporary lull fell over this area and in 1961 Mac Smith's climbers guide to the Cairngorms was published.

Such had been the level of activity in the early fifties that further development required a rise in standards. This was to come in the mid-sixties, with the emergence of a new generation. They called them-selves "The Spiders" and included John Bower, Mike Forbes, Brian Lawrie and Mike Rennie. VS routes became commonplace as PA's replaced boots, although Ronnie Kerr's very early first ascent of Sheath (1961), perhaps the earliest HVS in the Cairngorms, was achieved in boots. Although Beinn a'Bhuird was largely neglected, several fine routes were established at Sputan, like Grey Slab and Terminal Wall (1963) and McArtney's free finish to Amethyst Wall (1964). Meanwhile at Etchachan in 1966, Mike Forbes and Mike Rennie made the impressive ascent of the oft-tried Stiletto, the fore-runner of a new rise in technical standards. A few months later they climbed the popular Scabbard.

In the period 1970–72 there was a new burst of activity before the publication of Greg Strange's guide to the area in 1973. Strange, along with Dougie Dinwoodie, Brian Lawrie and others of the Etchachan Club, tidied up many of the good VS lines. Since 1973 rock climbing standards have risen relentlessly and although the classic routes of Etchachan and Sputan have remained popular, attention has switched to the bigger, steeper cliffs. Beinn a'Bhuird has steeper rock and emerged from neglect in the mid-seventies. Although always a rock climbing backwater, development by members of the Etchachan Club (including Greg Strange, Rob Archbold, Norman Keir, Gordon Stephen and Andrew Nisbet) has been steady since that date. The West Face of the Mitre Ridge has become established as a fine modern face, with several recent routes, including Slochd Wall (free, 1979) and The Empty Quarter (1983).

WINTER

In the fifties, the standards of winter climbing were advancing rapidly, as well as the growing attitude that all rock climbs were potential winter climbs. Many of the buttresses as well as the gully climbs received ascents by the Aberdeen climbers, although the remoteness kept progress at a lower pace than summer. The south-facing Sputan was rarely visited and many of the best routes on the icy Etchachan were left for the crampon-shod later generations, apart from The Corridor (Freddy Malcolm and Alec Thom, 1954). The Garbh Coire of Beinn a'Bhuird gave the best routes such as Mitre Ridge, by Brooker and Patey in 1953 and S.E. Gully, by Ronnie Sellars and G. Annand in 1959.

Development was slow for a period but revived in the late sixties by the Spiders, now in crampons but still step-cutting. John Bower and Jim McArtney were particularly to the forefront, with McArtney on ice (Djibangi, 1965) and Bower on technical winter rock, The Carpet and Hourglass Buttress (1970) being several years ahead of their time. With the advent of front-pointing, ice-climbing was suddenly in vogue and the icy Etchachan became popular. New ice routes included Carmine Groove (1974) and The Dagger (1977). Equally popular were the remote and serious Garbh Coire, with Flume Direct (1974), East Wall Direct (1974) and Crucible Route (1978). Only in the late seventies did technical winter rock re-emerge, one of the first and hardest being Cumming–Crofton Route by Dick Renshaw and Greg Strange in 1977. This was the year when powder lay deep and unchanged for 3 months and their round trip to the Mitre Ridge and back took over 24 hours. The Ridge itself was repeated in 1974 and twice more in 1977, becoming established as a classic Grade V.

CAIRNTOUL–BRAERIACH AMPHITHEATRE

The Cairntoul–Braeriach amphitheatre is the most remote of all the great Cairngorm climbing areas. Not only has its development been the slowest but an air of mystery has always been encouraged by its devotees. Strangely enough the first recorded scramble in the Cairngorms was the tracing of the source of the River Dee to the plateau above Garbh Choire Dhaidh in 1810. At the turn of the century, A. W. Russell made several visits to Coire Bhrochain climbing the West Gully (summer) in 1898 and the East Gully (winter) in 1901. Until the Second World War, visits were very occasional and almost always confined to Coire Bhrochain, with ascents made of the Black Pinnacle (1911) and Braeriach Pinnacle (1931). The only significant venture away from Coire Bhrochain was A. H. Hendry's ascent of The Chokestone Gully in 1937, also the first winter route of any difficulty on Braeriach.

There was sudden activity from 1940–42 with the start of exploration of Garbh Choire Mor by the Tewnions and further routes in Coire Bhrochain by W. T. Hendry and others, as well as the first route in Garbh Choire Dhaidh. Activity ceased again until the great age of Cairngorm exploration in the fifties, but here it was less pronounced than the more accessible areas. Garbh Choire Mor was opened up with four of the main buttresses, including Sphinx Ridge, climbed by Mac Smith and Kenny Winram in 1950–53. The two following years saw the first three routes on the main slabs of Garbh Choire Dhaidh, including The Great Rift. By 1955 most of the obvious lines had been climbed, except for a few steeper buttresses, and with little scope for modern face routes, summer exploration slowed and has never been more than sporadic since. 1955, however, saw the start of regular winter climbing on Braeriach but ascents were still occasional and confined to the more accessible Coire Bhrochain until 1964.

The winter potential was still enormous and the building of the Garbh Coire bothy in 1967 by the Aberdeen University Lairig Club eased the access problem and helped to soften the hostile reputation. Leading activist Jerry Light did battle with the giant cornices and put up a fine series of winter routes including The Great Rift (1965) with Nicol and Phoenix Gully (1967). A series of April visits by Raymond Simpson, Greg Strange and others established this as the best time to reduce cornice problems and they climbed many of the best remaining lines including the very hard Bugaboo Rib (1970). Since 1970 development has reverted to sporadic, mainly in winter but including three very fine steep ice lines in the modern vein, Vulcan (1975), White Nile (1977) and Ebony Chimney (1982).

Visits to Braeriach remain very rare and confined to those with a wish for exploration rather than technical difficulty. Consequently, few of the routes in the Amphitheatre have had many ascents and in winter about half are unrepeated, including the last three named.

LOCHNAGAR (NO. 2485)

CAC CARN BEAG   1155 m

Lochnagar is understandably one of Scotland's most famous mountains. Its distinctive outline rises gracefully above a complicated mass of lower hills and wooded slopes and provides a noble mountain landscape for all residents and travellers on Royal Deeside.

The greater part of the climbing on the mountain is situated in the magnificent north-east corrie, which in its embodiment of all aspects of corrie form and scenery is unrivalled in this country. The cliff front extends for 1½ km, reaching a height of 230 m and encircling the loch which has given its name to the mountain. It is split by great gullies into many important buttresses giving long, natural routes. Lochnagar's infamy attributed to its vegetation and loose rock is not altogether unfounded. Considerable areas of cliff are grassy and with few exceptions the gullies are loose. However, the rock-climbing Aberdonian would rightly defend his "citadel of vegetatious granite", for on the steep, clean faces and ridges of the buttresses are to be found climbs of the highest calibre.

In winter the buttresses and gullies excel. In this country only Ben Nevis has a comparable concentration of outstanding winter climbs of all grades. Conditions are particularly reliable, and even when doubtful some of the buttresses offer safe alternatives. Its deep enclosure protects the snow from the effects of a thaw and shelters the climber from strong south or west winds. The main criticism is that powder may lie unchanged throughout January and February. But the classic buttress climbs are only a little harder, and perhaps more intricate under powder, progress being reliant on grass instead of snow or ice.

Approaches to the North-East Corrie of Lochnagar

Lochnagar, lying wholly in the Royal Estate of Balmoral, has restrictions placed on the use of approaches to the corrie from Deeside, but the route from Glen Muick gives unhindered access at all times.

There is a Ranger/Naturalist Service at Spittal of Glen Muick where full access information is available. Telephone Ballater 55434. Camping is prohibited near the picnic site at Spittal Wood in order to prevent the growth of large-scale car-borne camping or caravanning. During August and the stalking season, movement should be along the recognised paths. This instruction applies to almost any deer forest during the season.

From Spittal of Glen Muick (Large car park)
Reached from Ballater by 15 km of motor road (often blocked by snow in winter) or from Braedownie in Glen Clova by the Capel Mounth path (10 km walking).

From the car park walk through the wood past the visitor centre, turn immediately right (signpost) and follow private unsurfaced road across the Muick to T-junction beside out-building of Allt-na-giubh-saich Lodge. A path follows a fence westwards from the southern end of this outbuilding. Take this path which leads through pine trees to join a bull-dozed landrover track. This is followed all too obviously out of the pines and up the open hillside to the Muick/Gelder col. Here the path branches off the bulldozed track to the left and is well marked to the summit plateau. Leave this main path beyond the spring known as Foxes' Well and go over the col between Meikle Pap and Cuidhe Crom to descend into the corrie. Distance 7 km.

Descents
In summer the universal descent to the corrie floor is by the main (right) branch of the Black Spout. If the Spout is snow-filled, follow the corrie edge and descend beyond the West Buttress. In winter either branch of the Spout can be descended with care but the main branch is recommended as the cornice is almost always easily passed on the left (looking down). The normal winter descent is to follow the cliff edge back to the Meikle Pap col (beware of cornices). In stormy weather, a foolproof but longer descent can be made via the Glas Allt and Loch Muick. From any point near the cliff top, head south (if at the top of the West Buttress, beware of the Black Spout which cuts into the plateau). Gentle slopes soon lead into the upper basin of the Glas Allt, which is followed to Loch Muick.

LOCHNAGAR: NORTH-EAST CORRIE

SOUTHERN SECTOR
The corrie has two sectors of differing aspect. The Northern with its great amphitheatre of buttresses and gullies forms the main climbing arena. The Southern sector forms a wide bay with a frieze of rock under the plateau. The line of demarcation is Central Gully, an open chute sending its screes to the lochside on the left of Central Buttress, the first major buttress on the Glen Muick approach.

At the back of the Southern sector is a short prominent scree chute, the Red Spout. On the left of the Spout, rising like a steeple beyond some indeterminate ribs, is Sunset Buttress, Very Difficult. The obvious gully in the right flank of the buttress is Sunset Gully (III by the left fork). The only other recorded climb between this and the Meikle Pap col is Jacob's Slabs, Difficult, which lie on the isolated piece of rock high under the plateau rim near the top of the "Ladder" section of the tourist path.

To the right of the Red Spout the rocks gain in stature as they approach Central Gully, presenting a trio of buttresses. The leftmost is indeterminate. The central is the Cathedral, named so for its regular architecture, four slender buttresses or ribs 100 m high, divided by chimneys and grooves. Towards its left end is an impressive mummy-shaped tower, right of which is Transept Route, Severe. The broken groove line immediately left of the mummy-shaped tower gives Transept Groove, IV, finishing by the deep chimney of Transept Route. The obvious deep chimney near the right end of the Cathedral is III.

The division between the Cathedral and the right buttress is Forsaken Gully, II. The right buttress is Sinister Buttress, the largest of the trio and descending lower into the corrie than Cathedral. The rib right of Forsaken Gully is Forsaken Rib, III. Direct Route, Severe, is based on a prominent chimney cleaving the lower buttress slightly right of centre. The steep wall left of Direct Route gives a technical winter problem, IV/V. Terrorist, IV, is another winter line, just right of Direct Route and joining it for a pitch. On the right side of Sinister Buttress is Gully Route, Moderate, which starts some way up Central Gully. Central Gully itself is I.

CREAGAN LOCHNAGAR

NORTHERN SECTOR

The great semi-circle of cliff beyond Central Gully is entirely continuous but for ready identification a division of the buttresses into four natural groups is made, the groups being determined by the three largest gullies cutting through the cliff. The gullies, whose positions may be pinpointed in thick weather by their great scree or snow fans, are from left to right;

Douglas–Gibson Gully: a straight-cut gash between high walls. It is bounded on the left by a trio of buttresses forming the distinctive "Shadow" group, to the right of Central Gully. Snow lies longer here than elsewhere in the corrie and a tongue usually lasts into July.

Raeburn's Gully: lies in the far western recess of the corrie and is inconspicuous from most viewpoints because of its slanting course. Its screes, however, can be seen joining those of—

The Black Spout: unmistakeable; a wide corridor slanting right and scree-filled to the plateau.

The standard place for gearing-up is the first aid box, on a platform below the screes of the northern sector. The following are magnetic bearings from the box to major routes. For winter use, it should be noted that all the direct approaches cross regular avalanche paths.

Central Buttress (initial gully)	190°
Shadow Buttress A, Original Route	214°
Parallel Gully A	258°
Raeburn's Gully	278°
Black Spout	286°

SHADOW BUTTRESS GROUP

The group is composed of three buttresses left of Douglas–Gibson Gully. Central Buttress, whose rocks can be traced to the lochside, is on the left.

Shallow Gully, ill-defined, separates Central from Shadow Buttress A which is easily recognised by its prominent curving band of grass/snow (The Spiral Terrace) starting low down below large overhangs. Rightmost is Shadow Buttress B, narrow and well-defined by steep walls dropping to Douglas–Gibson Gully on the right and Polyphemus Gully on the left. Its base lies at a higher level than that of Shadow A and in the angle formed between them is Shadow Couloir, a bay into which fall the chimneys (Shadow Chimney and Giant's Head Chimney) and buttressing ribs of Shadow Buttress A.

1   Central Buttress   300 m   Moderate   (1928)

The easiest of the major buttresses and the first in the file. The left flank is composed of easy-angled grassy ledges; but the steep slabby face dropping into Shallow Gully has continuous rock in its lower reaches.

The best route starts up an introductory gully leading left from the foot of Shallow Gully. At its top traverse right as soon as practicable and climb the crest to two gendarmes set on a level arete. From here about 120 m of scrambling leads to the plateau. The climb on the whole is spoiled by the ever-present easy ground on the left. (Diagram p. 36.)

Winter II (1948)

A good introduction to the Lochnagar buttresses and a safe choice in powder conditions, although take care with the snow slope under the plateau. Numerous easy possibilities on the left flank, but follow the summer line to get the most out of the climb.

2   Mantichore   60 m   E1   (1976)

A short but good and sustained climb. Just above the start of the introductory gully of Central Buttress ordinary route there is a steep rippled slab bounded on its right by a groove. The line ascends this slab then follows the right-hand twin groove above.

An easy ramp leads via a little groove up on to the rippled slab. Climb the slab to its apex. Step down on to a moss ledge and belay (25 m, 5b). Move up to a higher ledge, then step right and climb a tapering slab-flake into a V-groove. Continue up the groove to near its top, move left then go up to a grass ledge below a square-cut roof. Go up left to easy ground (35 m, 5b). (Diagram p. 36.)

3   Centrist   140 m   IV   (1974)

A direct winter ascent of the right face of Central Buttress. It gains the normal buttress route at the gendarmes, from where one can follow the ordinary route to the plateau or descend ledges on the left to return to the corrie floor.

Start just right of the lowest rocks about 20 m left of Shallow Gully. Climb a shallow groove and over a chokestone, then going up into a big groove with an overhang at its top. Avoid this on the left (crux) and continue curving leftwards up ramps until an easier groove leads rightwards to the crest just before the gendarmes. (Diagram p. 36.)

Between Centrist and Mantichore is Patey's Direct Route, a line of shallow grooves leading to the crest below Centrist, Hard Severe, IV. A vague line of grooves left of Shallow Gully, including an obvious V-groove and ending beside a prominent square tower, gives Sciolist, IV.

4   Shallow Gully   300 m   III/IV   (1959)

The shallow depression between Central Buttress and Shadow Buttress A. A good climb when in condition, but not being recessed, it fills up less readily than the major gullies, and is therefore variable in standard. Difficulties are confined to the lowest 60 m, after which snow leads to the upper slopes of Central Buttress. Very Difficult in summer, with bad rock and vegetation. (Diagram p. 36.)

5 Shadow Rib 280 m IV (1970)

This is the slabby rib immediately right of Shallow Gully and separated from the original route on Shadow Buttress A (via the Spiral Terrace) by large overhangs.

Go up the introductory gully of Original Route and diverge left on to the rib to belay in an obvious cave. Move out left and climb a series of grooves to a ridge overlooking Shallow Gully (45 m, crux). Go up the ridge then traverse right below a wall to a short awkward flake crack which gives access to a ledge returning left. Where the ledge ends make an exposed step round a corner then go up left and climb an easy gully to a small col on the upper crest. Climb the crest, as for Original Route, to the plateau. Difficult (or Severe direct) and vegetatious in summer. (Diagram p. 36.)

6 Shadow Buttress A, Direct Route 250 m V (1984)

This is a direct winter route on Shadow Buttress A, taking a ramp which cuts through the steep lower buttress. Starting at the cave, follow Shadow Rib for 10 m until possible to break right up an awkward short slab into the bottom left corner of a roofed recess. Leave the recess immediately by a steep corner to a belay overlooking Shadow Rib (30 m). Curve up and right to a ledge system, then go up to enter the base of the ramp by a wild move up a short wall (30 m). Climb the ramp and a prominent V-groove to reach the apex of the lower buttress (40 m). Continue up the easier crest, soon joined by the normal route, to the plateau.

7 Shadow Buttress A, Original Route

300 m Moderate (1932)

Very vegetated and rarely climbed, but interesting mountaineering. Follow the introductory gully leading to the Spiral Terrace which provides a lush promenade below the prow of the buttress to a high balcony overlooking Shadow Couloir. From the high end of the balcony climb a narrow rib immediately alongside Shadow Chimney (crux, summer and winter). Some parties have turned upwards too soon from the Spiral Terrace and found extra difficulty, particularly in winter. Diverge left initially then go right by short pitches to a causeway on the crest leading to a small tower under the plateau. (Diagram p. 36.)

Winter III (1949)

A first-class mountaineering route, following the summer route. Also a good choice for a strong party in poor conditions.

On the left side of the Shadow Couloir are two short routes which give variation starts to Shadow Buttress A, Original Route. The prominent chimney leading past the crux of Original Route is Shadow Chimney, Very Difficult, III. The rocks on its left give Bell's Route, Moderate, III, joining Original Route at the balcony on the Spiral Terrace.

8 Giant's Head Chimney Direct   200m IV   (1972)

Giant's Head Chimney is the right-hand of the Shadow Couloir chimneys. Polyphemus Gully, which is inconspicuous from most angles and is the dividing line between Buttress A and Buttress B, branches from the chimney a short distance up (the branch banks out in winter). Giant's Head Direct is a very fine route with an exposed, technical crux. Climb the narrow, lower chimney with one ice pitch, usually short, to a large overhang. Traverse left across the overhang (crux) to a belay. Enter the shallow upper chimney and follow it to a snow bowl. From this gain the Giant's Head Arete on the right which leads to the crest of Shadow Buttress A and the top. Very Difficult in summer.

9 Giant's Head Chimney   220m IV   (1950)

Another fine climb, a little easier than the Direct version.

Climb the chimney to the overhang and move right to belay as for the Direct. Follow a terrace round the corner on the right into a trough. The initial 30m of the trough may contain much ice and in these conditions gives a superb exposed pitch. Higher up the trough becomes an easy snow scoop. Here, more difficult climbing may be sought by moving right on to the "Feathered Arete" which leads to the plateau beside the tower of Multiple Chimneys. Very Difficult and unpleasant in summer.

10 Polyphemus Gully   200m IV   (1953)

An excellent gully, one of the best in Scotland. Similar in standard to Zero Gully on Ben Nevis and South Post Direct on Creag Meagaidh. Good rock belays. The gully cuts deeply into the left side of Shadow Buttress B and must be reached by a traverse on steepening snow from the base of Giant's Head Chimney. There are two big pitches separated by 60m of steep snow. The upper pitch can be climbed directly on ice above a cave or in thinner conditions, either by a little corner on the right or an obvious V-groove on the left followed by a traverse right. The cornice is often huge but can usually be outflanked by a traverse right on to Shadow Buttress B. (Diagram p. 36.)

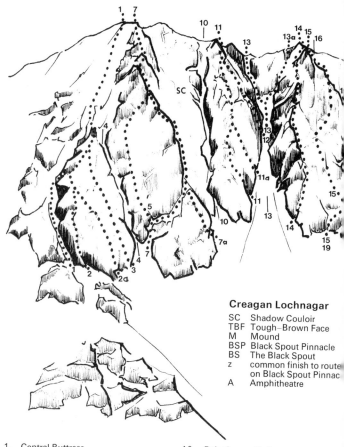

Creagan Lochnagar

SC   Shadow Couloir
TBF Tough–Brown Face
M   Mound
BSP Black Spout Pinnacle
BS   The Black Spout
z   common finish to route
     on Black Spout Pinnac
A   Amphitheatre

1. Central Buttress
2. Mantichore
2a. Central Buttress Direct
3. Centrist
4. Shallow Gully
5. Shadow Rib
7. Original Route: Shadow Buttress "A"
7a. Bell's Route: Shadow Buttress "A"

10. Polyphemus Gully
11. Bell's Route: Shadow Buttress "B"
11a. Original Route: Shadow Buttress "
12. Penumbra
13. Douglas–Gibson Gully
13a. Right Fork
14. Eagle Ridge
15. Eagle Buttress

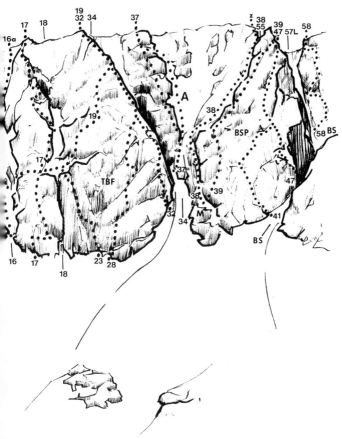

16. Parallel Gully "A"	37. Scarface
17. Parallel Buttress	38. Pinnacle Gully 1
18. Parallel Gully "B"	39. Grovel Wall
19. Tough–Brown Traverse	41. Pinnacle Face
23. Crypt	47. Route 1
28. Mort	55. Pinnacle Gully 2
32. Tough–Brown Ridge Direct	57L. Left-Hand Branch (Black Spout)
34. Raeburn's Gully	58. The Stack

Two variation finishes have been made on the left wall of Polyphemus Gully above its lower pitch. A prominent tower cleft by a V-
chimney can be seen high up on the left under the plateau. Multiple
Chimneys, Difficult, IV, leaves the gully immediately above the pitch
and heads for and climbs the V-chimney. The Tower Variation, IV,
leaves higher up and follows the first corner on the right of the Tower.

SHADOW BUTTRESS B
Shows classical buttress form—a steep lower section built on broad
austere lines, leading to easier angled ground before tapering to a
narrow crest at the top.

11 Bell's Route 200 m Severe (1941)
A fine line, but with bad rock and vegetation. Start just inside the foot
of Douglas–Gibson Gully where a grassy break leads leftwards to
the centre of the buttress.

Go up a crack on the right until two teeth are encountered below a
vertical wall. From a perch on the left tooth, "flit quickly across a
holdless wall to grasp a flake handrail"—Severe. The flake is loose.
Beyond this, ascend a groove to a belay and cairn on a large platform
at the top of the steep section. Scrambling now follows until the final
rocks steepen below the plateau. Here, the best way is on the left.
(Diagram p. 36.)

Winter IV

A rewarding climb, typical of the best winter buttresses. The steep
lower section is open to variation. The Original Route (Severe in
summer), which starts inside Douglas–Gibson Gully about 10 m
above Bell's Route and follows shallow grooves to the crest, is the
easiest. Bell's Route was the line of the first winter ascent; other
parties have climbed between these two. Above this, enjoyable climbing up the crest leads via snow aretes and short steps to the steeper
summit rocks. The cornice is occasionally the crux.

12 Penumbra 110 m IV (1972)
This interesting line follows the larger corner running from the narrows of Douglas–Gibson Gully to the top of Shadow Buttress B. From
the point where D–G Gully suddenly narrows, climb the obvious
discontinuous corner for three pitches to the cornice. Sometimes

necessary to traverse left below this to exit on the true crest of Shadow Buttress B. (Diagram p. 36.)

13 Douglas–Gibson Gully 200 m IV (1970)
The great gully between Shadow Buttress B and Eagle Ridge. An historically important climb. Although it has lost much of its original aura of impregnability, the gully still provides a fine climb in impressive surroundings. It is perhaps unique among Lochnagar's major climbs in that it reserves all its defences to the final 60 m, the last obstacle of which may be a huge unavoidable cornice. A great fan of snow forms below the gully and can avalanche.

Under normal conditions straightforward snow with perhaps one short pitch leads up through the narrows to the foot of the top wall. Move left and climb a groove to a small rock fault above until possible to move left into an easier snow runnel leading to the cornice. Poor protection. The route is also good early in the season when there is much ice and a smaller cornice.

When free from winter's icy grip, it is a death-trap. The upper wall is totally rotten and the whole gully wet, Very Severe. The first ascent was solo, by C. Ludwig in 1933 and described as "unjustifiable"! (Diagram p. 36.)

The Forks
Three other forks diverge from the base of the top wall. All are harder than the normal route (left fork) and about 60 m.
1 Right fork, IV (1973). Runs up the Eagle Ridge side of the top wall. Severe in summer.
2 Central fork, V (1984). Requires good conditions. An icicle forms at the base of the top wall. The icicle was climbed, then an icy groove to a bulge passed on the right (not by the obvious chimney). A hidden, right-trending line led to the finish.
3 Far-left fork, IV (1980). Traverse left and slightly up into a far-left gully with a huge chokestone.

PARALLEL BUTTRESS GROUP
Between Douglas–Gibson Gully and Raeburn's Gully. First from the left is Eagle Buttress. The narrow, soaring crest on its left edge is Eagle Ridge, from which huge undercut walls plunge into Douglas–Gibson Gully. To the right of Eagle Buttress, cleaving the central cliff, are Parallel Gullies A and B. Parallel Gully B commences as a thin 80 m

chimney before funnelling outwards in its upper reaches. Sandwiched between them is flat-fronted Parallel Buttress which tapers to a slender ridge near the plateau. Tough-Brown Ridge, massive and forbidding, fills the angle between Gully B and Raeburn's Gully. Its frontal face, the Tough-Brown Face, provides some of the finest rock climbs in the area.

14 Eagle Ridge 250 m Severe (1941)

One of the finest climbs in the country, and very popular. The ridge dries quickly after rain. It can be climbed in the wet but is much harder and the small amount of vegetation makes its presence felt.

Start just inside the screes of Douglas–Gibson Gully and climb the first obvious 20 m groove. Easier climbing follows up a shallow gully bending right to a short chimney leading on to the buttress face. Regain the crest in 30 m by a choice of routes leftwards. The crest is rounded and inclines easily to a slabby nose where the way rounds a corner on the right. From here it goes up a 10 m inset corner to the crest once more.

Here the ridge steepens in a rugged 15 m tower. Swing up into a recess on the right, then continue up steep rock and slightly left to gain a splendid sentry box. The next pitch follows a smooth arete and finishes up a little corner to a ledge on the crest (do not go further right here). Follow the crest over the "Whaleback" for 20 m to a ledge and belay at mid-height in a short slab corner, the top of which ends in an airy knife-edge forming the crest.

The vertical 4 m wall against which the knife-edge abuts is traditionally the crux, although many find the Tower as hard. Climb it by a crack on the left to reach another level arete. Climb the crest to a projecting square-cut overhang. Swing up on to the coping slab above and from some cracked blocks, mantleshelf into a V-recess. Finish up the final slabs which dip into D–G Gully. (Diagram p. 36.)

Winter V (1953)

The Queen of Lochnagar's winter climbs. Viewed from the corrie floor, the ridge sweeps up majestically in a series of alluring snow crests and intimidating walls. In calm weather and with firm snow a technically reasonable climb may be enjoyed; but the grade V is reserved for more traditional conditions, when the ridge becomes a big undertaking. The Tower provides the winter crux. Some parties have avoided the summer crux section by climbing further right of the crest. This should not be missed, however, as it provides an exciting problem, one of the highlights of the climb. For the final pitch a corner on the right of the summer route is usually taken.

15 Eagle Buttress 250m IV (1956)
The buttress holds snow well and is often in condition. With poor protection and a crux near the top, the route has seen a number of accidents in recent years.

Start about mid-way between Eagle Ridge and Parallel Gully A. For about 120m the climbing is straightforward up to the head of a central snow scoop. The line of least resistance then veers rightwards to below the steep upper wall. Here a ledge leads right to three parallel V-grooves overlooking Gully A. Climb the central groove (crux). Turn leftwards and follow the edge close to Gully A, joining it at the very top. Difficult in summer. (Diagram p. 36.)

16 Parallel Gully A 270m II/III (1948)
An extremely variable climb which may have several long ice pitches or completely bank out into a snow chute. Enjoyable climbing with continuous interest, particularly early in the season or in lean conditions. The direct first pitch can give as much as 30m of sustained ice; but can be avoided by a traverse-in over Eagle Buttress. There is a shallow chimney in the gully bed above. It can be climbed but it is better to go left on ice to a long stretch of snow leading past a narrow, minor gully on the right to a bifurcation. A rising traverse to the left gains entry to the left fork (often the crux). The left fork is straightforward to the cornice, which is taken on the left. (Diagram p. 36.)

Variations:

(1) Right fork (1958): at the bifurcation, the steep and more direct Right Fork is III/IV.
(2) 1930's Route, IV (1978): close to the summer line, Severe. It follows the narrow, minor gully on the right to a cul-de-sac on the side of Parallel Buttress. Move left on to the buttress, which leads steeply to the top. The cul-de-sac is thought to have been climbed direct in excellent conditions.

17 Parallel Buttress 280m Severe (1939)
There is a fair amount of vegetation, but it does not lessen the climb's character. A pleasant climb in dry conditions. Start up a wide groove just right of Gully A. Enter it from the right and finish at a grassy corner. Above are twin grooves (these form the variation start: start in

the right groove and transfer to the left—Very Severe, 4b). Instead, move right along a ledge into a defined chimney. Straddle this and exit on to a ledge on the right. Slant right up two recessed corners to a big flake, from where easy ground slants left to the grassy section where Tough-Brown Traverse crosses.

Work up easy ground until forced by the great slabby face of the buttress to move right to the edge of Parallel Gully B. Gain a shelf overlooking the gully and climb it to its end, almost in the gully (30 m). Move left on to the face and ascend the right-hand of two faults for 30 m to a ledge girdling the buttress—"The Necklace". From the centre of the ledge either climb a groove and recess to the crest above or move right and climb the crest directly. Continue up the crest via a pointed block to a platform below the Tower. Gain a small ledge up on the left then climb the shallow groove above for 3 m to a large jammed spike (crux). There is a large ledge beyond the crest on the left but continue up and right to the top of the Tower. Scrambling to the plateau. (Diagram p. 36.)

The variation start and the left edge of the buttress above, joining the normal route just below the Tower, gives an alternative route of Very Severe, 4c standard, grade V in winter.

Winter   V   (1956)

An excellent climb. Continuously interesting climbing all the way to the plateau. As with Eagle Ridge, consolidated snow will considerably ease the difficulty. The most likely points of difficulty are the defined chimney in the lower section, the ramp overlooking Parallel B, the initial moves above the Necklace and the Tower, which may require a point of aid. At the jammed spike on the Tower, move left on to a sloping snow shelf which one follows until it is possible to return to the crest behind the Tower. A graceful snow arete leads to the plateau.

18   Parallel Gully B   280 m   Very Severe   (1952)

When dry, this is one of the best climbs on the mountain. It is quite uncharacteristic of a Cairngorm gully, both in appearance and in the quality of the rock which is clean and sound. Continuity of the gully is broken by two large grass bays, the lower of which is the scoop crossed by Tough-Brown Traverse.

The first section is narrow 80 m chimney which starts from the screes as a steep crack, normally wet. When dry it gives a good pitch, Very Severe, 4c. Otherwise start well to the left and enter the chimney after 15 m. Follow the chimney to the scoop (4b).

Above the scoop the true line of the gully continues easily to a large rounded chokestone which bars further progress. This section of the climb, up to the second grass bay, is taken on the right of the gully bed. From the belay at the back of the scoop climb up and rightwards for a long pitch to a ledge about 10 m below a large overhang. Immediately above, on the left, is a 4 m groove—"The Contortion Groove". Climb this and exit left on to a sloping ledge (4b). Work up leftwards to gain the second bay. From here the big pitch above is loose and an easy ramp leading rightwards is vegetated so it is better to take a horizontal ledge leading out leftwards from the back of the bay on to Parallel Buttress. Continue by this route, including the fine Tower pitch. (Diagrams pp. 36 and 44.)

Winter IV/V

An outstanding climb. The gully is climbed direct throughout. The left-hand start is usually easier and gives access to the chimney, which is sustained but well-protected. Entry to the top pitch is blocked by a bulge, sometimes easier on the left side. An alternative here is a groove on the right which leads to the top of Tough-Brown Ridge.

TOUGH-BROWN RIDGE

The massive buttress left of Raeburn's Gully. It presents a forbidding facade of steep boiler-plate slabs, known as the Tough-Brown Face, which taper gradually upwards to form a defined ridge. The true crest of the buttress commences near the foot of Raeburn's and follows the extreme right end of the frontal slabs before merging with the upper ridge. The first attempt to climb the buttress resulted in a devious line outflanking the lower slabs by starting on Eagle Buttress and gaining the ridge in its ledged upper half. This is the Tough-Brown Traverse, the first recorded rock climb on the mountain. In 1941 the true crest was climbed directly from the foot of Raeburn's to produce Tough-Brown Ridge Direct. For another 25 years the slabs of the Tough-Brown Face remained inviolate. Then, in 1967, two of the more obvious features on the face, Crypt and Mort, were climbed by the same party and the aura of impregnability had been dispelled.

19 Tough-Brown Traverse 300 m   Very Difficult   (1895)
Nowadays it has little interest as a summer route, consisting mostly of short walls and grassy ledges. However, it serves as an exit route, either upwards or in descent, from the Tough-Brown Face.

Tough–Brown Face

Start on Eagle Buttress some distance left of the initial pitch of Gully A. Traverse into Gully A above the pitch. Continue to traverse right and upwards over the easy section on Parallel Buttress to the grassy scoop above the chimney of Gully B. Use a short chimney to gain the Great Terrace, which runs across the buttress above the Tough-Brown Face. There is a network of possible lines above the Great Terrace. The original route leaves the Great Terrace about 10 m before its upper end by climbing a short wall to a ledge. Continue rightwards up a slab ramp which is soon left by a horizontal ledge to the left. A zig-zag course then leads to the crest. (Diagrams pp. 36 and 44.)

Winter   III   (1952)

One of the classics of the mountain. With successful route finding the line of the pioneer summer ascent is technically straightforward but many parties trend too far right at the Great Terrace and encounter more difficult climbing near the crest of the buttress. In fact, a fairly direct line may be followed from the left end of the Great Terrace (close to Gully B) up to join the obvious ramp ascending from the upper bay of Gully B.

The route should not be underestimated in poor weather or late in the day as retreat is very difficult.

TOUGH-BROWN FACE

This great wall of slabs, dominating the lower half of the Tough-Brown Ridge, is one of the finest rock faces in the Cairngorms. The face is more vegetated than Creag an Dubh Loch, though largely confined to ledges. Those used to the pre-cleaned lines of the Dubh Loch may consider the climbing a little dirty. Sustained technical climbing is a characteristic of all routes on the face.

The most prominent feature on the face is a pair of corners (slightly offset and one above the other) situated left of centre and trending slightly leftwards towards the scoop of Parallel Gully B. This is the line of Crypt.

All the lines eventually lead to easy ground on the upper buttress where Tough-Brown Traverse can be ascended or descended. From Mort and routes to its right, the quickest descent is to abseil into Raeburn's Gully. From the top of these routes, traverse right until overlooking the initial groove of Backdoor Route. Descend easily rightwards on vegetation (i.e. away from Backdoor Route). After about 15 m there is a sling on a block and a peg, from which a 45 m abseil down a steep wall reaches the scree fan of Raeburn's Gully. The following four routes end at the scoop on Parallel Gully B, from where descent of Tough-Brown Traverse is the easiest option. Route lengths are to the Great Terrace.

20 Nymph   90 m   Hard Very Severe   (1974)

The less prominent left-hand of twin cracklines, running parallel to and approximately 3 m right of the chimney of Parallel B. A fine direct line; the first move is by far the hardest.

Start 10 m right of the initial crack of Parallel B. Climb an obvious line of stepped corners slanting left and climb on up to a good belay (shared with Psyche) 5 m below the obvious corner-crack (35 m, 5b to start). Climb the corner. Break left over a bulge where the corner curves right towards Psyche and follow subsidiary corner to small ledges (30 m, 5a, Psyche belays here and crosses left). Climb up right for a few feet and back left by flakes and layback round a bulging nose. Climb straight up and left to the top (25 m, 5a). (Diagram p. 44.)

Winter   VI   (1984)

The summer route was followed closely, except that the initial 5b corner was banked up. Very little ice was present except on the ledges. A fair amount of ice has been known to form, particularly in the corner of pitch 2. Three rests on axes were taken to place protection on this pitch; the whole route was well protected. The bulging nose on pitch 3 (Arthur's Bulge) had a little ice on top but was still the technical crux (as with Psyche).

21 Psyche   90 m   Hard Very Severe   (1972)

This is the more prominent right-hand twin crackline lying midway between Parallel B and Crypt. The climb's *raison d'être* is a magnificent flake crack easily recognised by a prominent white scar near its top. The climb is strenuous and the fastest to dry on the face. Start just left of Crypt.

Follow lower, left-trending grassy fault for about 25 m, then climb straight up to belay 5 m below and left of the crack (35 m, 4c). Gain the corner on the right and after 3 m step into the crack (or step left higher up—easier). Climb past an optional belay at jammed blocks to the white scar. Climb the scar for 5 m, break left on to a ledge and go up left to a belay ledge (35 m, 4c). Nymph goes up round a small bulge here. Traverse to the edge of Parallel B, then go up and climb a bulge. Easier to the top (20 m, 4c). (Diagram p. 44.)

Winter V/VI (1984)

The summer route was followed, stepping left into the flake crack as high as possible (pitch 2) and using the optional belay, until reaching the point where Nymph crosses. Nymph was followed to the top, the bulging nose providing the crux. Several falls were taken here, hence it has been named Arthur's Bulge. Climbed under powder, but it is not an ice-holding line. Well protected.

22 Sylph 90 m Hard Very Severe (1978)

The thin line of cracks and grooves between Psyche and Crypt. The finger cracks are superb.

Start up a left trending groove system just right of the similar starting grooves of Psyche (40 m, 4c). Belay under the big Psyche crack. Just right of the big cracks are twin finger cracks. Climb these to the top of a detached block. Avoid a blank section above by traversing right under a small roof on to the rib of Crypt. Step back left into the groove above and climb it to an awkward pull-out at the top. Move up and step left to pull over a roof by a flake-crack (the continuation of the big Psyche crack). Continue up the rib above past the left side of a big roof to belay as for Crypt (40 m, 5b). Finish up Crypt (10 m).

23 Crypt 80 m Hard Very Severe (1967)

Follows the two main corners left of the centre of the face. The long second pitch is superb.

Climb the grassy right-hand corner to exit left on to belay ledge (30 m, 4b). Traverse the ledge to the left-hand corner. This is usually wet and mossy, so step left and follow a layback crack to move back into the corner (optional belay). Climb the corner until below an overhung grass ledge, move out left on to the rib and climb this to regain the corner above an overhang (it is also possible but messy to climb the corner all the way to the overhang and move left underneath it). Belay on a grass ledge below a second overhang (40 m, 5a). Move left from below the overhang and climb up clean rock (common to Nymph) to the top (10 m). (Diagrams pp. 36 and 44.)

Winter V (1979)

In good conditions, ice forms down the left-hand corner and down the slabs left of the summer start. Climb this ice, enter the main corner direct (crux, avoided in summer) and follow the corner system to the scoop of Parallel B. On the first ascent (but not the two subsequent) the ice on the lower slabs was absent and the route was started by the first pitch of Psyche followed by a long traverse right (one tension move) to reach the base of the corner. The first pitch of the summer route is another alternative.

24   The Outlands   100 m   E3   (1981)
A fine direct route, straight up the cliff in the line of the first Crypt corner. The crux is technical but protection is always good.

Climb the first pitch of Crypt (30 m, 4b). Continue straight up the corner over a bulge and up on to the top of the great Dirge flakes. Continue up the groove as for Dirge to the grassy ledge, then move right as for this route and up on to the grassy ramp where there is a good stance (30 m, 5b). Dirge goes rightwards up the ramp. Instead, climb directly up the short wall above the belay to gain a good flake crack. Step down left and across on to a small slab-ramp running up to the overhangs. Move left round the bulge and up into a diagonal crack (crux) in the upper slab. Go up this then move up left and back right by a finger-flake and up to grassy belay ledges (20 m, 6a). Continue straight up the slab to gain the final groove which slants up right to Tough-Brown Traverse (20 m, 4c). (Diagram p. 44.)

25   Tough-Brown Integral   140 m   E1   (1975/1983)
A constructed line based on the start of Dirge (E1, 5a, not described) and including most of Post Mortem. The fine crux section of Post Mortem is missed, but this is often wet. The Integral gives a natural line, sustained and inescapable, and uses the maximum height of the cliff.

Start just right of the first Crypt corner at a shallow open corner. Go up this and over a bulge at 10 m, move right and up to a tiny ledge. Follow the obvious horizontal traverse right and climb up to belay under an obvious 10 m corner (35 m, 5a). Climb the corner and go up to a good belay ledge (10 m, 5a). (From here Dirge goes up into a damp slanting cleft then down left under a bulge to join The Outlands. It rejoins the Integral/Post Mortem two pitches on.) For the Integral, traverse right along a narrow rising footledge to join Post Mortem in the crackline leading to the perched block (30 m, 5b). Continue with Post Mortem to the top (25 m, 5b; 40 m, 5a). (Diagram p. 44.)

26   Post Mortem   130 m   E2   (1970)
A direct line up shallow cracks in the centre of the face. A superb route, very sustained, generally good protection, but the crux may be bold without peg runners. Unfortunately, it is slow to dry.

Start at a large, pointed block 10 m up and below the centre of the face. Go up the obvious groove just on the left, then up right by a grass ledge to belay on the Terrace (a long, upper grass ledge) — (35 m, 4c). A better, alternative start is the first pitch of Nevermore (5a).

From the left end of the Terrace climb a short ramp leading left-wards. Step left into a groove and follow it for 5 m (crux) until possible to traverse left to a resting place. Climb a short slab under a roof and traverse back right to regain the crackline above the groove. Follow the crackline, now a corner, passing a roof, to belay on a perched block (30 m, 5b). Climb the corner above the block, step right underneath a roof into a second corner, climb this and step back left to an awkward rest under a bulge. Climb the crack above to jammed flakes and work out leftwards to reach a large ramp (Dirge joins here). Belay in a grassy niche (25 m, 5b). Follow the ramp for 5 m to a break, descend rightwards to a lower ramp, make an awkward move round a corner and climb upwards to gain the continuation of the main ramp. Follow cracks in the ramp to its top and make a big step up round a block (40 m, 5a). The way on to the upper Terrace of Tough-Brown Traverse is now obvious as a line of flakes leading leftwards (20 m). From here it is more satisfying and probably quickest to go to the plateau. (Diagram p. 44.)

27 Nevermore 115 m E2 (1981)
Takes a line up into the prominent triangular niche high up in the centre of the face between Post Mortem and Mort. Start at the large pointed block (same as Post Mortem). 5 m to the right of this, make a mantleshelf move up left on to a shelf. Continue up more shelves, then detour out right into a crackline (the lower continuation of the crack-line of Crazy Sorrow, usually wet). Return left, finishing up a shelf to the Terrace (35 m, 5a). Follow Mort for 10 m to the downward point-ing tooth and move left round this to a recess. Move up and pull over the bulge. Go straight up the crackline to exit on to the next grass ledge left of twin cracks of Mort, and move left down the ledge to belay in a recess under the groove system running down from the big niche (20 m, 5c). Gain the groove above from the right rib and climb it up on to a grassy patch below a mossy leaning corner. Climb the corner into the niche, which has good cracks but a sloping floor (20 m, 5b). A direct continuation is taken up the crackline above the left side of the niche. The direct exit from the niche is very hard (only climbed on tight rope so far) but the same can be achieved by a fine sequence of moves on its immediate left. Climb a shallow groove

above, step out left at the top, move up, then exit out left by a flake on to the ramp of Post Mortem (20 m, 5c). Finish up Post Mortem (20 m, 5a). (Diagram p. 44.)

A direct second pitch, independent of Mort, is planned but gardening is not yet complete.

28   Mort   145 m   E1   (1967)

This is the impressive crackline slanting rightward from near the centre of the face. At about 45 m it breaks through a prominent roof beside a large downward-pointing tooth of rock. A classic companion to Post Mortem, only a little easier but with shorter difficulties. Both routes are highly recommended though still a little dirty (not having been cleaned on abseil). Post Mortem is perhaps slightly better.

The first pitch is common with Post Mortem (35 m, 4c). An alternative, cleaner first pitch is the start of Nevermore (5a). Climb steeply up for 10 m to the right side of a downward pointing tooth of rock in a roof. The roof is cut by twin cracks. Climb over the bulge and up the right-hand crack to a poorly protected mantleshelf (crux section). To the left is a well-defined rib. Go up the right side and pull up left on to the top. Climb the left-hand crack above to a grassy ramp. Go up this 5 m to belay (35 m, 5b). There are now two ways to enter the continuation groove. The lower and easier is to traverse immediately left under a small roof. The upper alternative is cleaner but harder and poorly protected; go up the ramp to its top, up left over a bulge and traverse precariously back left to rejoin the line. Continue up to a grass trough and belay by a big perched block (40 m, 5a or 5b). (Diagrams pp. 36 and 44.)

29   Crazy Sorrow   115 m   E3   (1982)

The next crackline right of Mort. The crux section is short and well-protected. An independent first pitch following this crackline has been gardened but not climbed since it is almost never dry.

Start by the first pitch of Nevermore to the Terrace and belay at the right side of a block, just left of a huge standing block with a gap behind it (40 m, 5a). From the top of the smaller block, move left and up to the crux roof (seldom completely dry under the roof). Surmount the roof up into the crackline (possible belay) and follow it to reach a grass ramp, belay at the top (35 m, 6a, just right of the grass ramp of Mort)—junction with Rolling Thunder. Finish by this route, starting by a traverse right under a roof (5b). Hopefully a direct finish from the belay (without going under the roof) will be possible. (Diagram p. 44.)

The following two routes approximate to parallel, left-slanting cracklines between Crazy Sorrow and the right edge of the buttress (Tough-Brown Direct). The cracklines pass either side of a large white scar, which is just below the long ledge which slants down leftwards from the crux of Tough-Brown Direct. The line of the left-hand crack meets the line of Crazy Sorrow (which slants slightly right) high up. This section of cliff is more vegetated than further left and completely dry conditions are required to appreciate the good rock present.

30 Rolling Thunder 95 m E1 (1982)
This route approximates to the left-hand crackline, climbing up to the scar and passing it on the right, then going diagonally left. Start 15 m from the right end of the lowest terrace (approach from right) below a narrow, jutting roof.

Climb the crack on the left of the roof and work up and left by cracks to a small terrace. Go right under a small roof to a horizontal crack and gain a crack which leads to the next terrace right of a huge block (25 m, 5b, crux). Move back right, up a short corner and continuation crack to the scar. Move right a few metres then trend back left to the long ledge (20 m, 4c). Climb the fine diagonal crack going left and, when it ends, continue left, then up to below a right-slanting roof (junction with Crazy Sorrow). Traverse right under the roof to gain a grassy trough (20 m, 5b). From here it is possible to escape right to the crest of the ridge, but a very fine pitch through the final walls has been made. Go left round an edge, gain a higher slab, cross the overlap above, then continue via cracks and corners to easy ground (30 m, 5a). (Diagram p. 44.)

31 Tough-guy 105 m Very Severe (1980)
The route is based on the right-hand intermittent crackline, at the right edge of the front face before it curves round towards Tough-Brown Direct. Start at the right end of the lowest terrace, adjacent to the scree fan of Raeburn's. Vegetated.

Follow a series of cracks punctuated by grassy ledges to finish on the long ledge a few metres right of the scar (60 m, 4b). Climb the wall above, well right of the diagonal crack of Rolling Thunder and to the left of two thin vertical cracks, using flakes and small ledges leading up left (crux). Cross a rake leftwards (this rake is the escape below the

final pitch of Crazy Sorrow and Rolling Thunder) and continue diagonally left via large cracked blocks to a stance some 10 m below
another white scar (30 m, 5a). Trend up left into a grassy trough
(15 m). (Diagram p. 44.)

32   Tough-Brown Ridge Direct   250 m   Very Severe   (1941)
This climb takes the easiest line on the extreme right hand side of the
Tough-Brown Face, then follows the ridge above. Most of the
climbing is vegetated and quite straightforward which is unfortunate,
because the only Very Severe pitch is a good one.
   Start just inside the scree shoot of Raeburn's Gully. A short wall,
then a slabby ledge passing right leads to a long grassy groove sloping
up to the left. At the top make a sharp right traverse to a pile of huge
blocks. The next pitch goes left by a flake-crack and then a short slab
traverse ends at a wall above (45 m). Here, steep slabs rise in three ill-
defined steps and bar access to easy ground above. Climb the slabs to
the second step, then move round the edge on to a short vertical wall
and pull up to a rounded ledge. Continue up slabs to belay on ledges
above (20 m, 4c). Much easier climbing leads up the ridge to the
plateau. (Diagrams pp. 36 and 44.)

Winter   IV   (1969)

The steep 60 m initial section will be very hard without a build-up of
hard snow. Follow the summer line to the terrace below stepped slabs
(45 m). Instead of climbing the slabs, move round to the right and
pass below the short vertical wall to a miniature arete poised above
Raeburn's Gully. Climb the groove above the arete or step down to the
right beyond the arete and climb a wall. A version of the summer line
may also be possible. Each route leads to easier ground. Finish up
grooves left of the prominent groove of Backdoor Route or traverse
right into Backdoor Route.

33   Backdoor Route   220 m   III/IV   (1954)
An enjoyable climb with good situations, unjustifiably neglected. Just
right of the crest of Tough-Brown Ridge a prominent groove system
descends in a direct line to a point immediately below the bend in
Raeburn's Gully. The first pitch, a big corner, is the crux. Either climb it
direct or (easier) traverse left after 10 m of the corner, then up across
slabs and slant up right to gain its top. Follow the groove system
above to reach the crest about 50 m below the plateau. Difficult in
summer.

34 Raeburn's Gully 200 m II (1932)

An excellent climb early in the season when much ice may be present. The gully fills quickly in the course of a normal winter leaving one ice pitch. There is often a very large cornice which may necessitate a steep traverse to the top of Tough-Brown Ridge. (Diagrams pp. 36 and 44.)

Note: In the past there have been many accidents in Raeburn's caused either by climbers starting an avalanche or being hit by one. The gully has a large catchment area, including the corniced rim of the Amphitheatre, and for this reason, it is probably more prone to avalanche than other gullies in the corrie. Apart from the Black Spout, Raeburn's Gully is the easiest way to the plateau in winter and climbers usually make a bee-line for it, determined on making an ascent regardless of conditions—sometimes with unpleasant consequences.

Variations:
   (1) Lemmings Exit, III (1977)—an obvious fault on the left wall well right of and parallel to Backdoor Route, starting just above the bend and below the ice pitch of Raeburn's.
   (2) The Gutter, Very Difficult, III (1954)—a steep offshoot of Raeburn's breaking the right wall above the easy intermediate section and about 80 m from the top.

35 Raeburn's Gully via The Clam

200 m   Hard Severe   (1954)

The Clam is the thin impressive slit on the Scarface (right) wall of Raeburn's Gully. A unique formation, providing a strenuous route of character. There is some loose rock but little vegetation. Recommended as an expedition in wet weather, as the waterwashed rock does not become slippery, but not for the purist. Graded for wet conditions (normal). There is some rockfall danger.

From the scree-tongue, Raeburn's Gully provides wet slabs and scree up to two massive chokestones. These are not very difficult and beyond them is a sandy recess. The crux of the gully (and the whole route) follows. Climb the left wall on small holds and return to the gully bed. A little higher is a cave in the right wall. The huge boulders jammed in the gully immediately above form the winter crux, but are straightforward in summer. 30 m above the boulders is the start of the Clam.

Surmount huge blocks to a square recess on the right, then pass over a short wall into the slit. The scenery is remarkable, with choke-

Black Spout Pinnacle

M   Mound
S   Springboard
BS   The Black Spout
z   common finish to routes
      on Black Spout Pinnacle
38.   Pinnacle Gully 1
39.   Grovel Wall
40.   Katsalana
41.   Pinnacle Face
42.   Fools' Rib
43.   Pinnacle Grooves
44.   Pantheist
45.   The Nihilist
46.   Epitome
47.   Route 1

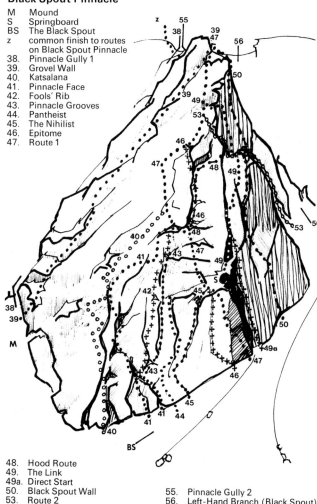

48.   Hood Route
49.   The Link
49a.   Direct Start
50.   Black Spout Wall
53.   Route 2

55.   Pinnacle Gully 2
56.   Left-Hand Branch (Black Spout)

stones jammed far out between the walls. From near the back, chimney up and outwards for 10 m to a tiny bracket providing a welcome resting place on the very edge of the slit. There is a flake belay 2 m up a slab on the outside. From the flake return directly into the narrow upper chimney. Thread the chokestones on the inside "with an exit akin to that of a cork from a bottle". Easy to the plateau.

Winter   IV   (1977)

Short and fierce. The upper chimney, above the flake belay, was climbed on the outside (good conditions). The route might be easier in lean conditions, when the upper chimney would not be blocked.

36   The Straight-Jacket   100 m   V/VI   (1980)
Visible in summer as a prominent chimney-crack high on the Scarface wall of Raeburn's. A desperate inch-by-inch struggle. Icy conditions required.

   Immediately above the crux ice pitch of Raeburn's Gully, cut back right and up to a ledge below the chimney (20 m). In summer one can get inside the chimney but in winter it is off-width (10 m). Immediately above the chimney is a steep corner. Climb it and exit right on to a slab (10 m). Traverse left and climb a spiral shelf leading to the upper rib of Scarface (45 m). Easy to the plateau. Very Severe, 4c, but usually wet and requiring aid in summer.

BLACK SPOUT PINNACLE GROUP
Between Raeburn's Gully and the Black Spout. Scarface, first buttress in the group, frowns down on Raeburn's Gully, its face marked by a great rockfall. Between the upper rib of Scarface and the Pinnacle is the Amphitheatre, a large grassy bowl with small ribs under the plateau.

   The Pinnacle itself, a massive wedge-shaped structure, culminates in a true peak cut off from the plateau by a narrow col. The pinnacle is demarcated by Pinnacle Gullies 1 and 2, which run up to the col from either side. Pinnacle Gully 1 starts from the Mound, a rock-island at the foot of Raeburn's Gully and round the back is Pinnacle Gully 2, an offshoot of the left Branch of the Black Spout. From the col to the plateau is 30 m of easy rock.

   From a rock-climbing point of view, the Pinnacle's only rival is the Tough-Brown Face. The Pinnacle has two distinct areas of interest, namely the lower slabs and the Black Spout Wall. The lower slabs form an apron of continuous rock which starts beside the Mound and stretches upwards for about 100 m until the angle eases and the rock becomes broken and vegetated towards the summit of the Pinnacle. Moving up rightwards into the Black Spout the slabs become progressively steeper and merge with the very steep Black Spout Wall. This 150 m wall is roughly triangular-shaped; with the Black Spout at its base and the two sides formed by the limits of steep rock.

Climbs started on the lower slabs do not lead naturally on to the upper Black Spout Wall but tend to veer leftwards on to easy ground. The solution is the Springboard, a large platform of vegetated ledges about 35 m above the Black Spout and a thoroughfare between the lower slabs and the Black Spout Wall. From the Springboard three lines of weakness fan upwards. From left to right these are followed by Route 1, Hood Route and the Link. Any of these climbs may be used to reach the summit after completing a route on the lower slabs. Alternatively, abseil from the Springboard into the Black Spout or reverse the first pitch of Route 1 (Mild Severe).

37   Scarface   170 m   IV   (1972)
Starts on the right wall of Raeburn's Gully, marginally above the bend and climbs a shallow depression into the Amphitheatre. At certain times, particularly towards the end of the season, or after a long thaw, the depression becomes very icy and thus provides a fine direct climb.

Climb the ice as directly as possible to the Amphitheatre. The summer line (Severe) follows the rib on the left but the best winter line is to continue easily up the left edge of the Amphitheatre, then climb an ice groove (the leftmost of the three faults above the Amphitheatre) and exit left on to the final few metres of the rib. (Diagram p. 36.)

38   Pinnacle Gully 1   200 m   III   (1951)
The gully slanting from the Mound to the col behind the Pinnacle. Only the final section up to the col shows true gully formation; lower down the climb follows a diagonal fault which leads towards the Amphitheatre (when followed into the Amphitheatre and by the right hand fault above, it gives Amphitheatre Route, III). A safe choice in powder snow.

Gain the top of the Mound from the base of the Pinnacle. Go left and climb a chimney slanting left followed by broken ground. At a point about 40 m from the base of the chimney, traverse back right across a slab above a cave, climb a short chimney and exit right to easier ground. Two pitches, mostly snow, lead to the col, a fine exposed knife-edge of snow. From the col to the plateau is easy apart from an amusing little rock step. Moderate and very vegetated in summer. (Diagrams pp. 36 and 54.)

A route has also been made between Amphitheatre Route and Pinnacle Gully 1, leaving the diagonal fault above the Pinnacle Gully 1 traverse and finishing by a big corner left of the upper gully of Pinnacle Gully 1 (III and good in lean conditions).

39 Grovel Wall 200m IV (1977)
The route is often in condition when other pinnacle routes are clear of snow. A fairly direct line is followed from the Mound to the Pinnacle summit. From the left edge of the Mound climb diagonally rightwards for 20 m, then cut back left and straight up to a short overhanging wall. Avoid this on the right and climb a line of grooves and shallow chimneys parallel to Gully 1 to the Pinnacle summit. Severe and very vegetated in summer. (Diagrams pp. 36 and 54.)

The French Connection is a desperate direct start to Grovel Wall (winter). The first 15 m is common to Winter Face; then it takes a groove leftwards to join Grovel Wall low down.

The frontal slabs of the Pinnacle are complex and the lines of the two summer routes are difficult to pick out from below. The start of Pinnacle Face is the best landmark.

40 Katsalana 130m E1 (1982)
Start 10 m down from and left of Pinnacle Face. Climb a prominent left-trending groove passing left of a pale scar to reach a recess marked by twin water streaks (30 m, 5b). Continue up a corner, then go right and traverse left to reach a fault line (taken by Winter Face— see Pinnacle Face in winter). Follow the fault via a big flake to the large grass stance at the end of pitch 2 of Pinnacle Face (30 m, 4b). Climb the left-hand crack of Pinnacle Face, traverse left below a bulge and go up right on good holds. Make a delicate traverse right then continue up and right to a belay ledge beside a spike (40 m, 5a). Climb up right round a rib and continue with one awkward move to easy ground on Route 1. (Diagram p. 54.)

41 Pinnacle Face 100m Very Severe (1955)
A classic route with some fine climbing. It follows a natural but not too obvious line covering a fair area of the impressive lower slabs. Sustained at 4b.

Start at the corner of the Black Spout about 10 m above the lowest rocks. Two grooves slant left on to the face; either may be used to start. The shallow left-hand one starts as an awkward wall, then up the groove to a short chimney at 20 m. The V-shaped right-hand groove, again awkward at the start leads in 10 m to a delicate left traverse into the other line. Continue via the chimney, then by cracks trending leftwards to a belay (35 m). Climb a few feet to a corner and pull on to the right-hand slab. Work leftwards up a slabby fault to a large grass stance (25 m). Continue left a short distance to two cracks. Climb either crack, finishing at the top of the right-hand crack. Continue up the right-hand crack, then traverse right on flakes to a niche (25 m). Climb the steep corner above to a ledge (10 m). An easy traverse right on grass ledges leads to Route 1 about 30 m above the Springboard. (Diagrams pp. 36 and 54.)

Winter   V   (1966)

A demanding climb of great quality. The climb has been made entirely on snow and ice but usually mixed climbing will be encountered. There will be short, very technical sections if done free in thin conditions. The line is open to some variation but all choices are hard.

The summer line is followed for the first two pitches. Thereafter, climb a groove right of the summer line then traverse right to easier ground near the Springboard (the usual line, common to Winter Face). If conditions allow, climb as directly as possible upwards to the Pinnacle summit (near pitch 3 of Katsalana).

Winter Face, V, starts just left of the lowest rocks and works up and right to a fault-line which crosses Pinnacle Face (summer) at the end of the latter's second pitch. Unfortunately this fine line appears to require an exceptional build-up of snow at the start.

42 Fool's Rib   80 m   Hard Very Severe   (1976)
This is a direct version of Pinnacle Face, following the rib just left of Pinnacle Grooves. Climb the right-hand starting groove of Pinnacle Face and step right at the top. There is a groove directly above, which hugs the left side of the rib. Climb into the groove and up to a short corner under an alarming detached flake. Climb the corner and the flake and go up steeply to small ledges (35 m, 5a). Continue up left under the bulge of the rib for 5 m. Pull out right on to the rib and climb it directly to belay on a grass ledge below and right of the steep final corner of Pinnacle Face (35 m, 5a). Move out right on to a flake edge

and traverse diagonally up to the grass ledge at the end of Pinnacle Face (or traverse right to easy ground). (Diagram p. 54.)

43 Pinnacle Grooves   70m   Very Severe   (1975)

This route follows a direct line of grooves starting from the foot of Pinnacle Face and ending at easy ground on Route 1 just above and left of the Springboard. Excellent, well protected climbing.

Climb the right-hand starting groove of Pinnacle Face. At its top move right, then go left and up to a large downward pointing flake. Layback up its left side to step into a smooth groove on the left. Climb the groove to a grass stance and belay (30m, 5a). Continue up the groove to a grass ledge on the right (15m, 5a). Step left, then go up for about 10m until a series of grass ledges lead right to easy ground above the Springboard. (Diagram p. 54.)

Winter   V   (1980)

An excellent route climbed in good conditions with ice in the back of the groove. 1NA was used at the downward pointing flake.

44 Pantheist   55m   Hard Very Severe   (1978)

A worthwhile climb, particularly the second pitch. It follows the obvious groove just right of Pinnacle Grooves. Start 5m right of the initial groove of Pinnacle Face by obvious cracks which lead by a square slot to a ledge. Move right up a little slab over a bulge then break left and back up right to belay in a grassy niche (25m, 5a). Traverse left and climb the big groove to the Springboard (5a). (Diagram p. 54.)

Winter   VI   (1984)

It provides two very hard pitches of contrasting styles, the first on slabs and bulges, the second by the steep corner-crack. Each can be eased by the presence of ice, but good conditions on both pitches is unlikely. On the only ascent to date, the ice was of the eggshell variety and only a little help. Protection was adequate but strenuous to place (2 rests on axes on pitch 2).

A line different from summer was taken in the middle section of pitch 1. From the ledge above the square slot, the winter line went higher and further left (near Pinnacle Grooves) before making a descending traverse right under a bulge to join the summer route (which then reclimbs the bulge and takes another bulge rightwards to the belay).

45 The Nihilist   45 m   Hard Very Severe   (1976)
This excellent route packs a lot of climbing into its 45 m. Near the foot
of the Black Spout a large smooth wall lies directly below the Springboard. This climb follows a diagonal line up rightwards, close to the
left edge of the smooth wall, then ascends the prominent twin grooves
above to reach the Springboard.

Start 10 m right of the V-groove of Pinnacle Face/Pinnacle
Grooves, immediately left of the smooth wall. Climb up to obvious
holds and make a difficult move left before swinging up on to a large
ledge. From a higher ledge gain a steep narrow slab with bulging wall
above and traverse right to reach an apparently desirable mantleshelf
ledge. Continue up rightwards eventually to gain the main grooves
where it is necessary to descend a few feet to belay (25 m, 5b). Ignore
the dirty groove on the left. Make a long stretch to reach steep cracks
above an obvious hooded overhang. Relatively easy climbing now
leads up rightwards to a hard exit on to the ledge of the Springboard
(20 m, 5a). (Diagram p. 54.)

Variation Start (harder):

15 m right of the start of Nihilist is an obvious V-groove with a flat
bottom. Climb up into the groove and up it continuing straight up to
join the normal route at the large ledge (10 m, 5b).

46 Epitome   150 m   Hard Very Severe   (1977)
A direct line of variations based on Route 1. The climb takes the
prominent groove beneath the Springboard, to the left of the first pitch
of Route 1, then follows the central fault and the hanging crack left of
the roof skirted by Hood Route.

Traverse in leftwards to the foot of the prominent groove, then
follow it to the Springboard (30 m, 4c). Scramble up to the start of
Hood Route and climb its first pitch to belay on the large grass ledge
(60 m). Go diagonally left and climb the big hanging crack (crux).
Near the top move left to a ledge on the arete then climb a delightful
slab mantleshelf to gain easier ground on Route 1 (20 m, 5a). Continue to summit via Route 1.

An easier (Very Severe, 4c) but inferior variation avoids the hanging
crack by swinging round the arete on the left from the top of a large
downward-pointing block and rejoining Epitome just below the
mantleshelf. (Diagram p. 54.)

Winter VI (1980)

A desperate technical problem climbed in good conditions with a lot of ice, which formed to the right of the hanging crack of summer. The first pitch was hard also.

47 Route 1 200m IV (1956)
A classic winter climb. Continuously interesting with particularly fine situations. The first pitch is the crux. Start in the Black Spout, beyond a vertical groove (Epitome) in the steep smooth wall below the Springboard. Climb a prominent slabby ramp passing an overlap (very hard when no ice). Traverse left 3 m above the overlap and gain the Springboard via a short wall (also hard). Go up ledges above, then traverse left into the left-hand fault. Follow the fault out on to the front face. Here one can continue leftwards but the better line goes up rightwards starting by a big flake to gain the crest at a point overlooking the fork in the Black Spout. A wall and an arete lead to the Pinnacle summit. Hard Severe in summer. (Diagrams pp. 36 and 54.)

48 Hood Route 90m Hard Very Severe (1976)
The central fault above the Springboard, passing the very large roof on the right. From the Springboard, scramble up easy grass ledges to where Route 1 traverses left. Continue up the fault to big ledges below the prominent hanging crack of Epitome (60m). Climb up right on to a slab edge and up the left side of a big flake. Go up to a point below the left side of the roof. Move awkwardly down right on to a ledge and go along this for 5m to huge flakes stacked under the roof. Pull strenuously up right on to a slab where good holds lead up to a belay stance at the end of the Route 2 traverse (30m, 5a). The groove of Route 2 leads to easy ground and the top of the Pinnacle. (Diagram p. 54.)

49 The Link 120m Very Severe (1956)
As the name suggests, this route connects Route 1 and Route 2. Initially it follows the right-hand fault above the Springboard then takes a slightly contrived line up across the Route 2 traverse to finish left of the summit crest. The "trade route" on the upper pinnacle; good sustained climbing.

Start at the top right side of the Springboard in the rightmost of the three faults. Enter a V-groove by a short, awkward right traverse. Climb groove to stance on rib on right (20m). Make a few moves up the rib then step back into the groove and climb it to below a prominent triangular overhang. Move up and right round a huge block to a small recess under an overhang. Climb the overhang then follow a good crack slightly right to a stance behind another huge block (30 m, 4c). Now a big vegetated groove slants left (taken in winter) and a prominent crack continues right. Follow the crack and near its top move out left. Go leftwards (crossing Route 2) to a steep groove, climbed to a large overhang. Pass this on the right, using a rotating block (4c). One can escape by swinging up and traversing left between two overhangs but it is better to climb the overhang above by good cracks (5a). (Diagram p. 54.)

Direct Start   Very Severe

This pitch takes a line right of Route 1 (avoiding the grass ledges of the Springboard) and provides an independent start to The Link (although most parties start with one of the routes below the Springboard). Just right of the start to Route 1 there is a recess with a steep vegetated groove above. Scramble to the foot of this groove and climb obvious parallel cracks in short chimney on left. Continue up leftwards over vegetation; then steep slabs lead to the stance on the rib 20 m above the Springboard (30 m, 4c).

Winter (Link Face)   V/VI   (1979)

A superb, exposed climb. Extremely hard but can become very icy and a little easier. Commencing with the first pitch of Route 1, the line followed the summer route beyond the overhang above the recess, then took the big groove slanting left to join Route 2.

Winter (The Link Direct)   V/VI   (1984)

This ascent started up the vegetated groove immediately right of the direct start to The Link, climbed the groove to an exit on to slabs, then tensioned left to join the direct start. This was followed, then The Link (summer line) to join and finish by Route 2.

50   Black Spout Wall   170 m   E3   (1976)

This route climbs the formidable wall above and to the right of the start of Route 1 and the direct start to The Link. Higher up it finishes by cracks in the steep gable wall above the traverse of Route 2. Now free and one of the best routes in the Cairngorms; low in its grade and with excellent protection. It is recommended that pegs are carried for the belay at the end of pitch 1. There is a great overhung recess in the middle of the wall. The route follows the obvious crackline in the pillar to the left.

Traverse along a small ledge to gain a deep crack and climb this on to a block at 15 m. Climb the strenuous bulge above and continue up a smooth dwindling groove, and up to a big peg (visible from the Spout). Climb back down to the lip of the overhang and swing left on to the base of an undercut ramp. Climb the ramp and the overhang at the top and up to better holds. The only good stance is a sloping ledge lower on the right. Move across the wall and down a leaning corner to the ledge (40 m, 5c).

Climb into and up the corner above over a bulge into the groove above and climb this to exit out left to ledges close to The Link (30 m, 5c). Climb out and up rightwards by slabby shelves to gain the arete above the great overhangs. Go up the arete to the little ridge at the top of the chimney-crack of Route 2 (40 m). To the left is the "Inhospitable Crack" which goes up leftwards to join the direct finish to The Link and directly above is a forking crack system. This is climbed by the long right fork to gain the apex of the wall (25 m, 5b). Climb the crest to the top of the pinnacle (35 m). (Diagram p. 54.)

The following two one-pitch routes take obvious lines up the steep wall right of Black Spout Wall and below the initial chimney of Route 2. Both are slow to dry out.

51 The Vault 35 m   E1   (1982)
The left-hand chimney line. Climb a stepped wall up into the base of the wide chimney, which has poor rock in the back. Move up the chimney and exit left on to a flake formation to finish up a crack and groove line (5b).

52 Drainpipe Crack 35 m   E2   (1982)
The right-hand line. A fine jamming crack, which provides one of the best pitches on Lochnagar. Sustained and strenuous up the crack into a recess under the final overhangs (possible belay). Surmount the overhang (crux) to gain the right-hand crack leading to the top (5c).

Above the fork in the Black Spout a large grass ledge cuts into the right-hand side of the Black Spout Wall. Route 2 and Twin Chimneys Route start from this ledge.

53   Route 2   120 m   Severe   (1953)
One of the few good routes below Very Severe. Very exposed. From the large grass ledge climb the prominent chimney-crack slanting left and ending at a little ridge projecting from the steep gable wall (35 m). Descend vegetated ledges leftwards for 5 m and make a long traverse left into a big groove (taken by The Link in winter). Climb the groove for 5 m to belay on large ledges (25 m). Easy climbing leads to Route 1 and the summit (60 m). (Diagram p. 54.)

Winter   IV   (1962)

A serious climb, top end of its grade. The chimney-crack often contains ice and may be quite straightforward but the traverse will always be hard and sustained. A magnificent situation.

54   Twin Chimneys Route   100 m   IV   (1961)
Follows a prominent chimney system fairly direct from the fork in Black Spout to the summit of the pinnacle. An impressively steep line. Very Difficult in summer.

Between Twin Chimneys Route and Pinnacle Gully 2 is Slab Gully, Difficult, III.

55   Pinnacle Gully 2   90 m to the plateau   II   (1932)
The short prominent gully running up behind the Pinnacle from the Left-Hand Branch. Popular; the chokestone in lean conditions has stopped many parties. Moderate in summer. Loose, but a good way to the top of the Pinnacle. (Diagrams pp. 36 and 54.)

56   The Black Spout   250 m   Easy
The great scree corridor separating the main face from the West Buttress. The right branch has no pitches. The left branch, hidden from the corrie floor, has one pitch—a huge chokestone with a small time-honoured through route. Recommended to hillwalkers but beware of old hard snow in early summer. The main branch is used summer and winter as a descent route for climbers. (Diagram p. 54.)

Winter   I   (1893)

The chokestone soon becomes buried and both branches are then straightforward snow, the left branch slightly steeper and with occasional cornice difficulty. Attractive scenery.

57 Crumbling Cranny 60m Easy (1926)

A wide chimney cutting into the right wall of the Left Branch almost opposite Pinnacle Gully 2 and providing a steep, though dirty scramble finishing under a rock bridge under the plateau. (Diagram p. 36.)

Winter II (1913)

A short snow chute, usually with a huge cornice, requiring tunnelling (or avoided on the right, harder). Surprisingly popular.

58 The Stack 150m Hard Severe (1952)

The buttress between the two branches of the Black Spout, following a line of chimneys high on the face overlooking the Left Branch. An enjoyable though not classic route with an intriguing variety of pitches. The crux is almost Very Severe; the rest is sustained but no more than Very Difficult.

Start just below the pitch in the Left Branch. Zig-zag cracks in a slab lead to a steep wall 20m up on the right. Climb the wall by a strenuous corner (crux), then above this step off a block and keep passing right until a grass platform is reached. Scramble leftwards over vegetation to belay at the base of an obvious chimney blocked by jammed boulders. A few feet up the chimney move left and follow a narrow ledge provided with a continuous handrail downwards for 10m. Return to the right by two short cracks to an alcove above the jammed boulders. Follow the chimney directly ahead for a further 10m to a large bollard. Step boldly off this on to a sloping shelf on the right, then climb a short wall to a grass platform. Move left and climb slabs and walls leftwards to the plateau. (Diagram p. 36.)

Winter IV (1952)

Short and sustained with an intimidating appearance. The climb is usually very icy (it has been climbed without touching rock) and due to its high situation often comes into condition before other routes in the corrie. The first platform may be gained either by the first pitches of the summer line or by a much shorter route up an icefall which forms just to the left. Above follow the summer route, the move from the bollard on to the shelf possibly requiring an aid peg. In good conditions the whole fault can be climbed directly (avoiding the descending traverse and the bollard move). Early in the season, especially by the summer start, the route may feel V. Recommended.

On the left wall of the Main Branch, an icefall forms, the White Spout, III.

WEST BUTTRESS

The final section of cliff, right of the Black Spout. At each end of its defined part, two buttresses extend unbroken to the screes—on the left is Black Spout Buttress on the edge of its gully and on the right, West Rib whose left flank plunges into the deep West Gully. Between these buttresses the lower face is indeterminate—mixed rock and grass up to the Midway Terrace from which the climbs on the upper face originate. Set in the middle of the upper face is Gargoyle Chimney, a thin slit leading to a high amphitheatre. On the right above the amphitheatre is the Gargoyle, a small but prominent feature jutting from the plateau rim. Late in the winter season it catches the sun, resulting in poor conditions.

59   Black Spout Buttress   250 m   Difficult   (1908)

The best of the easier routes in the corrie. The line on the lower buttress is heavily vegetated and may be avoided by traversing on from the Black Spout opposite its fork.

The integral route starts at a chimney-fault at the top of a grass slope about 10 m right of the Black Spout. Climb the chimney then scramble for about 60 m to a level arete marking the end of the lower section. Above the arete a ridge of piled blocks leads to a deceptively difficult 3 m chimney. Easy climbing leads to a 5 m wall started at the centre and finished at an awkward corner on the right. A steep 10 m wall now bars the way. Taken direct it is a fine pitch on good holds. Above, follow a ledge on the left and regain the crest leading without difficulty to the top.

Winter   III   (1949)

A good winter climb which is quite hard if climbed directly. It comes into condition with the first snow and is a good choice under powder. The lower buttress should not be missed as it is much improved under snow. The steep 10 m wall at the top is usually evaded by a peculiar right traverse to a recess at the head of a flanking gully (Western Slant). Return left as soon as possible to the crest.

The vague gully close to the right flank of Black Spout Buttress is Western Slant, II. On its right and immediately left of Causeway Rib there is a vegetated depression which occasionally forms a prominent icefall, West End, IV. Causeway Rib is the rib bounding Gargoyle Chimney on its left. It gives a pleasant climb both in summer, Very Difficult, and winter, IV.

60 Gargoyle Chimney 120 m III/IV (1952)

The prominent thin chimney in the middle of the Upper Face, which gives an excellent pitch, sometimes a 30 m ice pitch. Above this, go up and left on snow to a steep finish, sometimes with a difficult cornice. Difficult in summer.

Gargoyle Direct, Very Difficult, follows a complex line based on the rib left of West Gully. The second pitch takes a diversion into the shallow gully right of Gargoyle Chimney. A rockfall on this second pitch has spoilt the route as a rock climb—Causeway Rib is now a better choice for this part of the buttress. A genuinely direct version of Gargoyle Direct is Dod's Diversion, Hard Very Severe, which takes a direct crackline on the rib for pitch 2 (5a) and gains the plateau by the obvious steep crack finishing a few feet left of the Gargoyle block (5a). In winter, either the summer route or the shallow gully can be followed, IV.

61 West Gully 250 m IV (1948/1966)

A good winter gully. The lower section soon ices up and provides an ideal introduction to steep ice climbing. The upper gully, although impressive, is relatively straightforward. The final chimney (direct) up to the plateau may be difficult if the blocks are uncovered. An easier alternative is the left branch, an easy snow slope after an initial steepening. Difficult in summer.

Below the final chimney of West Gully three prominent chimneys cleave the right wall. Only the central one (Shylock's Chimney, a back and knee Very Severe) is worth the excursion from the plateau via the easy left branch of West Gully. The left chimney is Difficult; the right is a tight Severe.

The buttress to the right of West Gully is West Rib, Very Difficult in summer and IV in winter. It can be good in winter but rarely has consolidated snow. The shallow gully to the right of West Rib is Gelder Gully, II.

A girdle traverse has been made from The Black Spout (starting up Route 2) to Central Buttress. Much of the climbing is very vegetated (Severe). Though equally pointless in winter, it gives good climbing and was done in two separate days, starting up Pinnacle Gully 2 (IV).

COIRE NA SAOBHAIDHE (NO 247865)

This is the shallow corrie directly below the summit of Lochnagar. It is separated from the main North-east Corrie by the West Ridge (i.e. the ridge on the west side of the main corrie). The back wall of the corrie consists of an area of waterwashed slabs. A slanting 50 m fault (Moderate) forms the junction between easy-angled slabs on the right and steeper foliated slabs on the left. An obvious water course runs down the centre of the steeper section. This gives a climb of about Severe in summer and a good, short ice climb in winter (100 m, II/III).

COIRE LOCH NAN EUN (NO 230854)

This large western corrie of Lochnagar has very little continuous rock, but the prominent Stuic Buttress, a scramble in summer, gives a worthwhile climb under snow, I.

CNAPAN NATHRAICHEAN (NO 224888)

This northern outlier of Lochnagar (approx. 3 km south-west of Gelder Shiel) reveals two exposures of slab on its north-east flank. The lower western slabs (just above the Ballochbuie Forest) are heavily vegetated, but near the centre there is a column of water-washed rock which gives an interesting ice climb, The Plaid, II/III.

Close under the Cnapan's summit there is a more attractive area of fairly clean slab known as the Sleac Ghorm. Five slab routes, each around 100 m in length have been climbed. The prominent straight corner on the left side of the slabs is Green Mamba, Severe. The crackline just left of it is Bushmaster, Very Severe. The obvious curving corner to the right of Green Mamba is Boomslang, Very Severe. The overlapping slabs to the right of Boomslang (just right of a clump of young trees) give The Padder, Severe, while The Grass Snake, Severe, follows overlapping slabs well to the right, left of an easy, grassy corner.

In winter this slabby face largely banks out under a heavy build-up, but early in the season it may provide an accessible alternative to the unconsolidated higher areas. Four routes have been climbed, II or III, following obvious groove-lines on early season ice, as well as the broken ribs left of the main section, II.

EAGLE'S ROCKS (NO 2384)

These slabby rocks belong to Lochnagar; a long discontinuous band of cliff high on the White Mounth escarpment, opposite Creag an Dubh Loch. The main feature of the rocks is a big waterfall away to the left. Also prominent is the open and easy-angled Diagonal Gully near the right end.

The rocks are too high above the loch to become the playground they might have been but are nevertheless a useful alternative to the main cliff. The climbs are short and light-hearted following natural lines on sound granite. Those climbs which are not watercourses usually dry much quicker after heavy rain than the bigger Dubh Loch routes. In addition, the place has a south-facing aspect and catches a good deal of sun—a point worth bearing in mind in cold weather or in the afternoon, when the sun has left the main cliff.

In winter the drainage lines generally ice up readily, no snow being required. Early in the season after a hard frost a number of fine icefalls form. Though shorter, they offer comparable quality to Hell's Lum in early season, but their relative inaccessibility has limited popularity to Aberdonians. Later in the season, some of the routes partially bank-out with snow and the crag's sunny aspect can wreak havoc with the ice.

THE GREEN SLAB

This is the obvious slab not far left of the Waterfall, recognisable by the pink central fault of Bumble, Very Difficult. The quickest summer descent lies immediately down the left (west) side, but this is tricky at the bottom. Alternatively go further left to easy slopes. The slabs left of the pink fault of Bumble give Jade Pavement, Very Difficult. In the course of a normal winter the slabs soon disappear under snow. When not banked out it may be sheathed in snow and ice. It has been climbed by two separate lines based on Bumble, II.

62   Green Slab   90 m   Hard Severe   (1968)

The route goes up the clean slabs right of Bumble, with a good pitch through and above the halfway wall. Not well protected.

Go up the slab and an obvious corner just right of Bumble to ledges below the steep halfway wall. Move up left on to a ledge and up and across right along the wall using flakes (crux). Move on right and climb an overlap to finish up cracked slabs.

THE WATERFALL CLIMBS

The waterfall cascades down a large slabby buttress which tapers up to the right. After a dry spell, the longer the better, the left side of the main stream can be climbed, Severe. The best descent lies down broken ground immediately alongside the fall on its left (west) side.

In winter enormous amounts of ice form here. In very cold conditions the waterfall can freeze completely (unusual) and the whole buttress disappear under ice. The winter descent back to the start of the routes is either awkward or long. One can make an easy descent away to the left (beyond the Green Slab) or the right (climb up and over the plateau edge and descend Diagonal Gully). The short but harder descent is Green Gully, which lies between the corner of Lethargy on the right and an ice curtain draping a vertical outcrop on its left wall. Although Green Gully can be grade I with a large build-up the best line of descent is difficult to find and worth grade II.

63 The Waterfall 150 m II (1974)

Continuous low-angled ice to the left of the flow of water. Escapes are available to the left. The direct line, when frozen, would give a steeper variation. Severe in summer, by the left side of the main stream.

64 Spectrum 110 m Very Difficult (1971)

The obvious line of corners and grooves right of the Waterfall and immediately right of black overhanging walls. When dry (slow), the best route of its standard on Eagle's Rocks. Start at the first obvious break well up right from the foot of the fall and climb up into a corner leading to a recess below a dark slanting crack (45 m). Climb the short, steep wall right of the recess and follow slabs up rightwards to belay at the base of a big V-groove (30 m). Climb the groove to the top, turning the final part on the left (straight up is Very Severe). A better finish is the fine crack in the rib on the right (Hard Severe).

Winter III (1971)

A sustained climb on continuous water ice. Distinguished by the big V-groove near the top which gives a fine finish. Just to its right is another groove system which would give a shorter but not too separate line.

Just left of the grassy fault of Green Gully is a patch of clean hued slab which gives Stratus, Very Severe, 4c, in summer but banks out with snow and low angled ice in winter.

THE MID-WEST BUTTRESS

This is the left hand of two large zones of rock set roughly in the centre of the cliff. It is the highest and most continuous section and is recognisable by the pink watercourse corner of Lethargy to the left and several obvious groove lines to the right. Descent is by Green Gully or by Diagonal Gully away to the right (see The Waterfall section).

The rib between the grassy bank of Green Gully and the corner of Lethargy gives Nimrod, Very Severe, 4c.

65 Lethargy 120 m   Hard Severe   (1967)

The obvious corner on the left of the buttress. Usually a watercourse but pleasant when the flow decreases. Follow the corner as directly as possible (but start 5 m right of it) to a point where escape left is apparent. The Green Gully descent lies below. Finish up the steep 5 m left-hand corner above.

Winter II/III (1970)

The corner forms a continuous ribbon of ice early in the season but later tends to bank out. Above the corner, take the escape left, climb the summer finish or follow the Direct, IV, the prominent steep icefall above the corner.

66 Indolence 140 m   Very Severe   (1967)

The first of the crack and groove lines right of Lethargy. Although it is a drainage course, the line can be followed up the dry right side all the way. Good climbing. Start at a grassy fault forming the left margin of a big slab (10 m right of Lethargy corner).

Climb the fault or start by padding up the big slab, (4c) for about 60 m to a big overlap. Break through this by a 5 m corner and overhang just right of the watercourse. Continue up cracks right of the upper gully, then follow a narrow rib and crack on the right to the top.

Winter III (1976)

The watercourse forms a fine icefall, the best part of which does not bank out. Very early in the season, before the slabs below the upper gully form ice, the best combination is the first pitch of Lethargy followed by an easy traverse right across the grassy trough to reach the upper icefall of Indolence.

67 Nomad's Crack 150 m Very Severe (1967)
The next and best defined groove line right of Indolence. Better in winter. Climb slabs to a prominent V-chimney. Climb the chimney and slabs to a wide V-groove system. Follow this to the top (usually wet).

Winter IV (1976)

A good sustained climb via the summer line, on a narrow ice ribbon throughout. The first slabs soon bank out. Slow to come into good condition.

To the right of Nomad's Crack are two obvious corners. The left is Taboo, Very Severe, 4c; and the right is Abstention, Very Severe. A prominent icefall forms high on the summer line of Abstention, IV.

THE MID-EAST BUTTRESS
This face is roughly triangular in shape and lies up and left of some broken slabs lining the left bank of Diagonal Gully. The most prominent feature is the big inverted L-shaped corner of Gibber set in the central pink slabs. Diagonal Gully is the obvious descent, summer or winter.

68 Sliver 150 m III (1974)
This is an obvious winter line running up the right side of the broken ground between the Mid-West and Mid-East buttresses. A fairly continuous line of water ice will reliably be found.
    Flamingo, Hard Very Severe, 5a, goes up the rocks to the left of the big corner of Gibber.

69 Gibber 120 m Very Severe (1969)
Climbs the big inverted L-corner which provides the best pitch on Eagle's Rocks when dry (rare). Start at the lowest continuous rocks and work up and across left to a belay near the edge (45 m). Go up the slabby ramp on the right and up a short corner in a steep wall to a belay ledge. Climb up left into the base of the big corner and follow up and right round the roof to gain a glacis (5a). Easier rocks lead to the top.

Winter 130 m III/IV (1977)

In winter a sliver of ice forms which approximates to the summer route. The big corner may be seriously unprotected if the crack in the back is inaccessible. The amount of ice present is very variable, hence the split grade.

Right of the Gibber corner are three grooves. Whisper, Very Severe, 4c, III/IV, takes the middle groove.

70 Shiver 150m III (1976)
This is the icefall which forms on the rocks right of the slabs of Whisper and the big corner of Gibber. There are no obvious escapes but variation is possible. On the first ascent the icefall was abandoned after 30m in favour of a line trending up rightwards.

LIKELY STORY SLAB
This is the greenish disc of overlapping slab to the right of the lower part of Diagonal Gully. It is the most readily accessible of the climbing zones, dries very quickly and receives much sun. It provides fine climbing reminiscent of the Etive Slabs, including the poor protection. The easiest descent is to traverse into and down Diagonal Gully but in dry weather a devious way can be made on the right (east).

A short hard route has been made on the extreme left edge of the slab (Hard Very Severe, very artificial). A right to left girdle traverse (Severe) goes between the two main overlaps.

71 The Stretcher 80m E1 (1975)
In the centre of the lower slabs is an obvious corner above featureless slabs, the line of A Likely Story. The Stretcher finds a way up slabs left of this. The protection is poor without pegs and the grade allows for this. Start at a curious white trickle mark near the lowest left corner of the slab.

Climb to the first overlap, move left along the lip and up a tiny corner just left of a scoop (Fraud Squad). Belay on left (20m, 5a). Move about 5m right over slabs and up to reach a short crack running back left to the main overlap. Climb the crack and the double overlap direct, then trend slightly right and back left to reach a belay ledge under a sharp nose in the big upper overlap. An easier indirect version of this pitch is to traverse left after the double overlap, then go up to the belay (40m, 5a). Climb the overlap just right of the nose and go up right to gain a grassy crack leading to heather (20m).

72 The Fraud Squad 70m E2 (1984)
A direct line just right of The Stretcher. Better climbing than The

Stretcher but escapable (not too obviously) on to it. Start just right of the white trickle mark.

Climb direct to the first overlap (reaching it as for A Likely Story). Traverse left for 3 m through the overlap (briefly joining The Stretcher) and climb a scoop with horizontal quartz bands. Exit left from the top of the scoop, return right above it for 2 m and climb directly up the slab to a crack which penetrates the main overlap just right of a V-notch (30 m, 5b). Climb the crack through the double overlap and go slightly right to follow a blind pocketed crack (or the slab on its immediate right) to the base of a thin curving flake. Above this traverse left to belay near The Stretcher (30 m, 5b).

Go through the upper overlap to the right of The Stretcher, just left of a good thread. Go up mossy cracks to belay (10 m, 4c).

73   A Likely Story   80 m   Hard Very Severe   (1968)
A little gem, the best and most popular on Eagle's Rocks. Dries very quickly. Start in the middle of the lower slabs.

Go up slightly left to an overlap, move 2 m right and cross the overlap to climb up to an obvious corner which leads to a belay ledge (30 m, 4c). Go up by a flake to gain the corner above and follow this up to make a delicate right traverse under an overlap into a notch. Pull through the overlap and go up to belay in a triangular depression (20 m, 4c). Traverse left along a slab below a steep wall and go up an obvious crack in the slab to finish (30 m, 4b).

A much harder variation to the first pitch goes left through the first overlap (as for Stretcher/Fraud Squad), then traverses back right and up to climb the left rib of the Likely Story corner (5a).

74   Prohibition   90 m   Hard Severe
Takes the obvious line of cracks and grooves just right of the centre of the slab. Start near the lowest right corner of the slab and climb straight up the slab and up by a big blunt flake. Move up and right into the crack system (this point can also be reached from the right). Continue up the crack system to the upper overlap. Climb over this into a long shallow corner which leads to the top.

75   Nameless   60 m   Severe   (1968)
Climbs the right side of the slab. Start up an obvious left-leaning corner and the bulge above (20 m). Go straight up the slab above via

an open scoop, cross an overlap and finish up slabs or traverse left to the shallow corner of Prohibition.

PLATEAU BUTTRESS
Up right from Likely Story Slab is a curious lattice work of slab. Higher still under the plateau is a little brown buttress housing a small waterfall. This forms a prominent icefall in winter, The Drool, III/IV. Flanker's Route, Very Difficult, takes the rocks right of the waterfall, skirting a steep section which is climbed by Vanguard, Hard Very Severe, 5b.

CREAG AN DUBH LOCH (NO 2382)

The Dubh Loch is set in a high secluded valley between the extensive White Mounth plateau of Lochnagar (1155 m) to the North and the cone-topped plateau of Broad Cairn (998 m) to the South.

Creag an Dubh Loch is the huge Broad Cairn precipice guarding the loch. At three-quarters of a mile in length and 300 m in vertical height, it is the biggest cliff in the Cairngorms. With over 60 routes Very Severe and above, including 37 Extremes, and many of these routes of outstanding quality, Creag an Dubh Loch has more on offer to the harder climber than any other Scottish mountain cliff. Of lesser importance are Eagle's Rocks, the jumble of sprawling slabs high on the north side of the valley.

The usual Glen Muick approach is an attractive one. It passes by the Royal Lodge of Glas Allt Shiel, sheltered by a dark pinewood near the head of Loch Muick, then continues up the side of a rough birch-strewn glen, down which cascades the burn from the Dubh Loch. The cliffs are over 8 km from the car park.

The rock at Dubh Loch is as good as any in the region; a very sound grey or pink granite typified by a roof-tile formation of colossal glaciated slab. Progress is generally dependent upon well-defined crack lines with tenuous slabby linkages where these fade out. The earlier routes took the major faults of the cliff in the more broken and vegetated areas between the open faces. Few of these are worthwhile climbs and there are better crags in the Cairngorms for lower grade routes.

Creag an Dubh Loch faces north-east and several days of dry weather are needed for it to dry out after a long wet spell (although some of the steepest routes dry faster). During a good summer, individual days of rain may have little effect on the drainage and the cliff can dry quickly. The cliff catches the sun till midday so an early start is worth the effort.

The climbs on Eagle's Rocks are relatively trivial but pleasant nevertheless. Facing south the climbs generally dry more quickly than those of the main cliff.

Winter

The Dubh Loch is a lonely and intimidating place in winter, the cliffs taking on an impressive scale. There are some very fine and serious climbs here but with the cliff base at about 700 m, Creag an Dubh

Loch is less frequently in condition than the higher winter cliffs. Certainly, Lochnagar is a much more reliable choice when conditions are doubtful. In prime conditions, however, the cliff is one of the best and iciest in the Cairngorms.

Prediction of prime conditions, however, has perplexed even the closest observers. A spell of very cold weather freezes the springs at their source and even a day's thaw can strip the cliff bare. Deep powder in the valley is usually an indication of poor conditions. The Hanging Garden area is more reliable and the best conditions form later in the season; after heavy snow followed by thawing and freezing.

Eagle's Rocks are higher and often draped with fine icefalls. These give entertaining exercises in pure ice-climbing and a reliable alternative to disappointing conditions on its larger neighbour.

Access

1 *From Spittal of Glen Muick* (large car park)

Reached from Ballater by 15 km of motor road. In winter the last 5 km across the moor is frequently blocked. From the car park, follow a private unsurfaced road to a farm. Just past the farm the Lochnagar road breaks off to the right. Continue straight on towards the south-east side of Loch Muick, ignoring the left fork to Glen Clova via the Capel Mounth path. Just before the loch, a small path leaves the road on the right and follows the shore to the north-western side. The bridge at the outflow of Loch Muick is absent (1984) and a shallow wade is necessary. Alternatively take a slight detour via the bridge on the Lochnagar path. Another road leads along the north-west shore to the Glas Allt Shiel. Continue up a good path to the Dubh Loch, which has small paths on both sides. The halfway point is marked by the Stulin, a waterfall tumbling from the hidden Lochan Buidhe. 8 km. This is by far the easiest route.

2 *From Callater* (The Braemar approach)

Leave the Perth-Braemar road 3 km south of Braemar and follow a private, rough road for 5 km to Callater Lodge. A path starts up the hillside just before the lodge, slants over the slopes of Creag an Loch and contours the southern shoulder of Carn an t-Sagairt Mor. Continue down the Allt an Dubh Loch. 11 km.

3 *From Glen Clova*

This approach is sometimes used by climbers from the Dundee

area. From the road-end at Braedownie continue up the glen to the woods at Bachnagairn in Upper Glen Esk (an attractive place). Cross a footbridge over the falls and climb a zig-zag path to the plateau. Follow the path to two shacks known as Sandy Hillock Huts. Follow a bulldozed track until it peters out under the summit cone of Broad Cairn and break right to contour between the summit slabs and lower outcrops to the Dubh Loch. In bad weather it is best to make for the Head of Corrie Chash. Leave the path here and go north-west over the shoulder to the Allt an Dubh Loch. The outcrops are easily passed. 8 km.

Accommodation
In summer visitors camp at Dubh Loch where there are good sites at both ends. There are also a number of howffs in the boulders under the crags. None of them is totally waterproof.

CREAG AN DUBH LOCH

The cliff is a straight face split into two main sections by Central Gully. The eastern, left-hand section is the higher. It contains the very steep Broad Terrace Wall high on the left, and the great sweep of Central Slabs on the right. These are subdivided by the prominent couloir of Labyrinth Groove which snakes up past the high amphitheatre of the Hanging Garden.

The western, right-hand section is dominated by the big slab-face of Central Gully Wall. Its top right extension is the steep, tilting False Gully Wall which forms the left flank of the broken North-West Buttress curving round to the right.

At opposite ends of the entire face are South-East and North-West gullies with their smaller terminal buttresses.

Descents
Summer: Central Gully is the usual, toe-crushing descent. When snow-filled in early summer, Central Gully Buttress is a useful alternative. Go down the easy crest and cut down leftwards into lower Central Gully; the obvious line ends at a short slabby ramp. This is often greasy and there is an easier line 10 m higher, a small ledge leading horizontally left to a short wall of blocks at the bottom. The way is not obvious at first acquaintance. The north-western end of the cliff can also be descended; this is easy but care should be taken to go beyond the last outcrops. After finishing a climb on the left side of the

cliff, one can take the easy hollow well to the left of South-East Buttress (or descend the buttress itself).

Winter: Central Gully is the usual descent and certainly the easiest in poor visibility. The cornice is usually avoidable on the left side of the gully. A little easier but longer, one can descend at either end of the cliff, giving small outcrops a wide berth. When there is a good build-up of snow, South-East Gully gives an interesting descent, usually with a steepening near the bottom.

SOUTH-EAST BUTTRESS
This is the broken buttress at the left end of the cliff. The ordinary route goes up the easy right-hand ridge overlooking South-East Gully. The obvious discontinuous snow-ramp trending left to right up the left side of the buttress is Eastern Ramp, II. The most obvious feature of the frontal face is a big, roofed dièdre taken by Dogleg. The steep grooved wall just to the left of the dièdre is Rock Island Line, Very Severe, 5a. Just left of Rock Island Line is a vague corner system which gives an unnamed winter route, III.

76 Friends Essential 30 m   E2   (1983)
An obscure wee crack on the slabby wall on the left-hand side of South-East Buttress, well left of Eastern Ramp where the wall is highest. The crack is prominent and stepped and the difficulty eases with height (6a).

77 Dogleg 150 m   Hard Very Severe   (1977)
A good route, but rarely climbed because of longer routes nearby. Low in the grade. It takes the big roofed dièdre, climbed using a hanging chimney leading up towards the left end of the roof. Start below and left of the line of the chimney at a pair of cracks, a boulder ledge and spike belay.

Climb the cracks to reach a slab ramp winding rightwards to the mouth of the chimney. Belay on flakes (5a). Airy bridging leads to within 4 m of the roof. Traverse rightwards, including a 2 m descent, to a blaeberry stance (4b). Go up almost to the roof and step over a rib, down a few metres, then swing up round the next undercut rib (in line with the right end of the roof) to gain a system of steep cracks ahead. Climb these to a branch leading to a big ledge (5a). Tackle the wall behind the belay on the right, cross over a slot and slant rightwards up a slabby ramp in some 60 m to the top. (Diagram p. 84.)

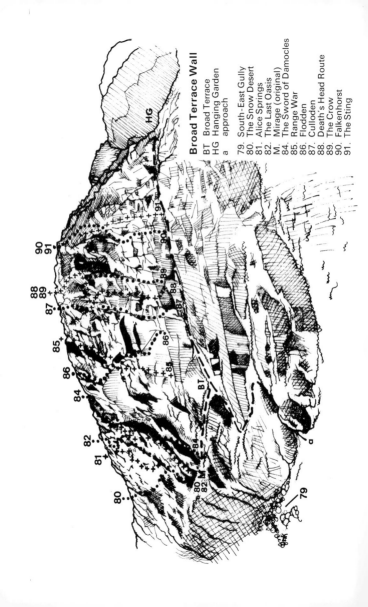

Broad Terrace Wall

BT Broad Terrace
HG Hanging Garden
a   approach

79. South-East Gully
80. The Snow Desert
81. Alice Springs
82. The Last Oasis
M.   Mirage (original)
84. The Sword of Damocles
85. Range War
86. Flodden
87. Culloden
88. Death's Head Route
89. The Crow
90. Falkenhorst
91. The Sting

78 South-East Buttress 200 m Moderate (1930)

Takes the crest overlooking the gully. Mostly a grassy scramble with a slab corner pitch at the start, on the gully side of the crest. A start not far to the left can also be made (best line in descent). (Diagram p. 84.)

Winter II (1948)

A pleasant route which should always be climbable. Easy after the first pitch, the left-hand start being the least awkward in soft snow.

79 South-East Gully 200 m I/II (1947)

A popular climb, sometimes the only one in condition on the cliff. An ice pitch near the bottom soon banks out. A disintegrating Difficult in summer. (Diagrams pp. 80 and 84.)

BROAD TERRACE WALL

This is the dark, menacing crag high on the left side of the cliff. It is set at a savage angle, particularly in the centre where a smooth wall leans out over the Grass Balcony, a long ledge unvisited until 1982. To the right the face sustains a fierce angle until the boundary edge of Bower Buttress is reached. Climbs on this section follow parallel crack lines. Despite its forbidding appearance, the rock here is more amenable with numerous blocks, flakes and deep cracks. All the climbs of this face are memorable, particularly for their high grip factor. Bounding the left of the steep wall is the huge fault of The Sword of Damocles, conspicuous even from the head of Loch Muick. Further left the face is more slabby and curves round before petering out in the hanging jungle above South-East Gully. Here is the lesser fault of The Last Oasis.

The wall was left alone till 1967 when Culloden was forced up the frontal face. Since then it has been less frequented than the Central Slabs or Central Gully Wall, partly due to its atmosphere and partly because it is the last section of cliff to dry, usually taking till July. The section from The Sword of Damocles leftwards is particularly slow.

Access is via the Broad Terrace, the grassy promenade under the frontal face. To reach it zig-zag up the left side of the broken lower crags by luxuriant vegetation, starting near the foot of South-East Gully. This is also the start of the left-hand routes, the wall dropping into the gully being repulsive and overhanging.

80 The Snow Desert 300 m IV (1977)

A natural winter line working up the broken rocks overlooking South-East Gully. It is exposed and open to some variation.

Start by the zig-zag approach to the Broad Terrace and traverse left to the foot of the left-hand of the two big faults, The Last Oasis. Above and to the left lies a hanging snowfield. The pioneers reached this by climbing a full rope length up Last Oasis and traversing left over a ramp. At the left end of the snowfield is an obvious broken chimney. This was climbed for some way and an exit made left, from where a difficult horizontal traverse led to easier ground and so to the plateau. (Diagram p. 80.)

81   Alice Springs   95 m   E2   (1983)

Tucked away at the top left corner of the Broad Terrace Wall, this is a good line on perfect rock, though rarely dry. It takes the crackline in the centre of the slabby wall left of Last Oasis.

Start up Last Oasis and follow the fault easily for 20 m to belay below a steepening. Climb the corner above (as for Last Oasis), then step left on to rib and follow a thin crack leftwards to ledges. Climb the prominent finger crack above to ledge, belay on right (40 m, 5c). Move up 3 m into the base of a corner, step right on to rib and reach a crackline on the right. Follow this and groove to top (35 m, 5b). (Diagram p. 80.)

82   The Last Oasis   130 m   Very Severe   (1972)

This is the less prominent left-hand one of the twin faults, and a watercourse. When dry, however, it provides a delightful climb, the easiest on the wall.

Follow the pink fault for almost 90 m. Move right at the top below bulges to belay under a short pale groove behind a detached block. The groove is taken by Mirage and leads up into the upper fault of Damocles. Instead climb up left over a bulge to ledges (4c). The big precarious blocks above can be climbed direct but the best way is to traverse left 5 m, then go up and back right above the flakes. Finish up a leftward slanting groove to the plateau. (Diagram p. 80.)

Winter   V   (1980)

Occasionally the watercourse of Last Oasis forms a tremendous ice-fall. Usually this is in mid–late season when thaw and freeze starts drainage from old snow on the plateau. At this time of the year the route receives a lot of sun so a very early start is required. There is always ice early in the season but in recent years it has been very thin, although the route may still be possible.

When present, the icefall rears up to a final 15 m of vertical ice. On the only ascent to date this direct finish was avoided by the summer line on the left (1PA, 1NA).

83   Mirage (variations)   120 m   Hard Very Severe (1976/1982)

Mirage (original) takes a line between The Last Oasis and The Sword of Damocles, starting up the left rib of Damocles. The route described is a natural line with excellent sustained climbing.

Start up the steep wall to the left of the easy chimney of Damocles, by a series of small ledges and a crack leading directly to the base of the big corner of Damocles (15 m, 5b). This pitch makes a good direct start to Damocles. Climb the big corner to the large belay ledge on the left (20 m, 5a), and junction with Mirage (original). Climb directly up the edge overlooking Damocles for 10 m to gain a good flake-crack. Traverse this left then up a prominent corner-crack on to a ledge (20 m, 5a). Move left, pull over a bulge and return right as soon as possible on to the wall above. Mirage (original) continues via the short pale groove above and joins Damocles. Instead, go left over the bulge (as for Last Oasis) and follow Oasis to the top (4c).

84   The Sword of Damocles   140 m   E1   (1970)

The right-hand fault above South-East Gully is a huge corner system, the most obvious line on the whole wall. It gives a very strenuous climb of great character. The top chimney is very slow to dry out and repulsive when wet.

Start up an easy chimney next to a steep wall. Traverse left along the wall to a ledge at the base of a big corner. Alternatively, climb the first pitch of Mirage (variations). Climb this fine corner to a belay ledge on the left (35 m, 5a). Continue up the corner above to a large flake to belay below the hanging chimney (20 m, 4c). Climb the chimney direct to big ledges at the top. There is a dubious block half way up (15 m, 5b). Move right and go up a short corner on to a white slab. Climb the chimney on the right (hard and mossy) or left (as for Mirage original) (5a). Finish up giant steps and broken ground to the top. (Diagrams pp. 80 and 84.)

Variation (5b):

This variation is useful when the top chimney turns out to be wet. From the belay ledge under the hanging chimney, climb the first big bulge until past the first old bolt. Now traverse the left wall on to the edge. Move up the arete and traverse left to the short pale groove of Mirage. Go up this to the big ledge above the chimney.

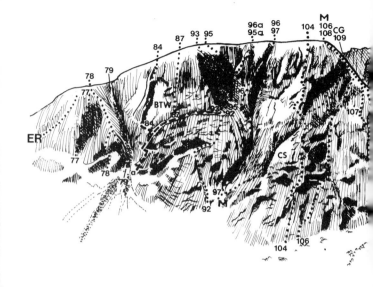

Creag an Dubh Loch

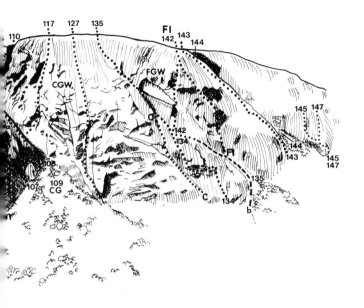

85 Range War 110m E4 (1983)

This and the following route climb the appallingly steep wall between Sword of Damocles and Culloden, crossing at the Pinnacle. A superb climb with a strenuous but well-protected crux section. Start by scrambling up the big corner right of the Sword of Damocles, then traverse right and up a short wall (Severe) to reach a short corner midway between Damocles and Culloden (and about 15m left of Flodden).

Climb the short corner. Climb to a roof, pull over the roof and so up and left to obvious jammed block/spike. Continue up and left to the Grass Balcony. Climb to the top of a Pinnacle on the right (45m, 5c). Climb cracks in the overhanging wall above to reach a niche below a roof. Traverse right under the roof and pull into the corner above. Follow the corner up into a recess, pull out left and continue up the corner till the angle eases (35m, 6a). Continue in the same line to the plateau (30m, 4c). (Diagram p. 80.)

86 Flodden 135m E5 (1983)

Takes a stunning diagonal line on the wall, crossing the previous route. Climbed over two days. Scramble up left, then traverse right to a point 15m left of Culloden, below a left-leaning corner which is the start.

Climb the corner to where it leans. Climb a flake with more difficulty to a resting place. Step up and move left across the wall to gain a crack; climb this to belay below a large roof (40m, 6a). Gain the crack round the left side of the roof, climb it to ledge above, traverse this to faint crack and climb it and scoop above to the right end of the Grass Balcony. Traverse left to a nut and peg belay in a corner (15m, 6a). Traverse left round a corner and climb a crack to the top of a pinnacle (10m, 5a, common to Range War). Traverse left off the top of the pinnacle and move up to a position under the left-hand end of a roof. Step left and follow a ramp passing a flake to step down from its top to a poor resting place. Climb the slim groove above and move left across a slab to gain a corner; follow this steeply to belay (25m, 6b). Climb the corner behind the belay and move left. Follow the easiest line to the top (45m, 5a, scrambling after 10m). (Diagram p. 80.)

87 Culloden 130m E3 (1967)

A superbly positioned climb. To the right of the smooth impending wall are two big roofs one above the other. Culloden takes the first line to the right of these, a distinctive feature being a big V-groove halfway up.

The highest ledge of Broad Terrace contains some piled blocks at the highest point. Start down left from these blocks and climb up left on to a big obvious platform to belay. Continue straight up grooves, cracks and a flaky wall to move right on to the top of a monster flake (45 m, 5a). Climb the overhanging crack above and the big hanging groove to belay ledges (25 m, 5c). Go straight up the shallow grooves above for 10 m to a bulge avoided on the left and leading to a small perch (20 m, 6a). Continue up a short groove and up greasy walls to the top (35 m). (Diagrams pp. 80 and 84.)

88 Death's Head Route 155 m E1, 2PA (1976)

This route and the following one take twin parallel cracklines right of Culloden. They pass to either side of a black rectangular roof over halfway up the wall. Very sustained and breathtaking exposure. Start at the piled blocks on the upper ledge of the Broad Terrace.

Traverse left along the wall left of the blocks and go up to a ledge. Climb the crackline direct to a belay ledge under a long corner-crack (20 m, 4b). Climb the corner and the overhang above to a ledge. Here is a peculiar block weathered like a man's face. Climb up this and the wide crack above to move out right and up big flakes to reach the right end of the monster Culloden flake (30 m, 4c). Move up right to a short overhanging corner in the barrier wall. Use a peg and another over the lip to gain a steep hanging corner running up to the black roof. Move up the corner until just below old peg, then swing left and up the rib to gain a horizontal flake-crack. Hand traverse this left on to a slab at the top of the big groove of Culloden. Step left over the groove to belay ledges (35 m, 5a, crux). Here Culloden goes straight up. Return awkwardly up right and go easily along slabs on to the top of a huge grass-topped block (15 m, 5a). Climb the short wall above (5b) and zig-zag up big blocks to reach another big block on the left. Drop down left and finish up stepped walls (55 m). (Diagram p. 80.)

89 The Crow 150 m E2 (1976)

Another high quality route. Start at the same point as Death's Head Route at the piled blocks on the upper ledge.

Climb straight up the steep wall immediately left of the blocks and then up easier ground to belay below a wide crack (15 m, 5b). The original, easier start went right from the blocks and back left. Gain the crack using a big flake on the left and go up it for a few metres to reach for a flake handrail on the right. Go up a flake and an overhang to step right and up another flake to belay on top (30 m, 5b). This is just right of the monster Culloden flake. Move up over a bulge under the barrier wall. Move up a shallow corner forming the right side of a scoop, then swing up right and up the left side of a prominent jutting flake to a belay ledge. This ledge is tucked under a big jutting rib, a prominent feature of the line (10 m, 5b). From the left end of the ledge climb the wall above until it is possible to traverse right on to a slab topping the rib. Step back left and go up a bulging wall past the right edge of a black roof. Go up to the black corner above and swing left on to the edge. Climb the bulging crack above to gain grass and the huge block of Death's Head Route (35 m, 5c, crux). Finish up this route (55 m, initially 5b). (Diagram p. 80.)

90 Falkenhorst   140 m   E1   (1973)
Right of the Crow is another crackline which peters out. This route takes the next crack system in the pink rocks to the right. Start at a short left-trending ramp left of the pinkest rock.

Go easily up a short steep slab then move back left to a short overhanging groove. Climb the groove and go straight up, then horizontally right along a narrow ledge to a corner. Climb the corner and escape left. Traverse left then go up a corner to a large platform on the left. Belay at a big flake beside the upper ledge (40 m, 5a). Move back right and climb a thin crack in a pink wall and so up to a ledge on the crest. Traverse right and go up to belay in a niche formed by a huge detached flake (15 m, 5b, crux). Move back down and climb an overhang on the right. Continue rightwards and up beyond a poised block to a good ledge and belays (10 m, 5b). Easier ground on the right edge has now been reached and there is a choice of line. Go up a short way to a rock shelf below a wet corner. Climb two short walls on the right of the corner to a grass ledge. Go right and back left to a large grass platform directly above the corner (30 m). Trend left up an obvious fault over monstrous blocks, then go straight up to the top (45 m). A more direct line can be made using the finish of the Sting. (Diagram p. 80.)

91 The Sting   130 m   Hard Very Severe   (1975)
This is the rightmost of the prominent crack systems on the wall. The rock on the first pitch is waterwashed and distinctly pink but beyond this becomes increasingly mossy. Start right of Falkenhorst under a prominent, triangular, overhanging groove.

Climb the groove at the right-hand side, taking an overlap to reach the apex of the groove. Climb the overhang and continue up the crack above to a sloping grassy ledge. Belay on another ledge immediately above (25 m, 5a). Follow the main groove to a ledge on the left, climb over huge blocks then continue up the groove to a larger ledge. Climb a deep crack at the left corner of the ledge to another ledge and belay (35 m, 4c). Easy ground is now visible on the right. Junction with Falkenhorst. Traverse horizontally left for 5 m to a shallow mossy groove and climb this to easier blocky ground (4c). Climb short cracks and huge blocks slanting leftwards for two pitches (70 m, many possible variations). (Diagram p. 80.)

THE HANGING GARDEN

This is the lofty basin on the right of Broad Terrace Wall. It is bounded on the right by the big curving couloir of Labyrinth Direct, which is blocked by a formidable cul-de-sac just above the level of the Garden. The Garden is a grass slope surrounded by steep walls some 120 m high. The rock climbing is wet and sometimes vegetatious and loose—no routes are described. In full winter conditions, however, the Garden comes into its own—an exposed snowfield with ice-plastered walls. The winter climbs are difficult and serious with unique situations and scenery. Belay cracks can be hard to come by and ice screws may be found invaluable. Retreat down Broad Terrace would be awkward in the dark.

Starting by the zig-zag rakes near the foot of South-East Gully, the traverse of the Broad Terrace provides an intricate but easy approach into the Garden. In good conditions the lower half of Labyrinth Direct gives a better and more direct approach to the Garden, III.

92 The Aqueduct 120 m IV (1975)

In favourable conditions, a steep icefall flows from the Garden directly over the tiered rocks below, providing a hard, poorly protected entry into the Garden. Very Difficult and a watercourse in summer. (Diagram p. 84.)

Ariadne, Very Severe (4c), climbs the rocks between the Aqueduct and Labyrinth, heading for a prominent groove high up.

93 Bower Buttress 150 m IV (1970)

Entering the Garden from Broad Terrace, a prominent edge is rounded, forming the border between the Garden's left wall and the vertical rocks of Broad Terrace Wall. This is the general line of the climb. In good conditions the entire climb is on ice and of outstanding quality. It is, however, also good and only a little harder under powder.

The route is open to variation. Climb grooves in the crest slanting leftwards to a big ledge (the Gallery). Follow ice-choked cracks trending slightly right to enter a shallow gully which is taken to snow slopes under the cornice (avoided on left). A harder line further left has been taken above the Gallery, finishing up the brink of Broad Terrace Wall (the final part of Falkenhorst). (Diagram p. 84.)

94 Yeti 140m IV (1975)
Between Bower Buttress and the prominent gully of Hanging Garden Route is an impressive set of slabby ramps. These are a major drainage line in summer and can become sheathed in ice. The Aqueduct forms in similar conditions and makes a good introduction. An exposed, serious route (ice screws required for protection and belays?). In prime conditions the Yeti icefall splits into two low down, the minor branch descending into the Hanging Garden Route chimney (both branches have been climbed).

95 Hanging Garden Route 300m IV (1959/1977)
An excellent climb, normally the first of the big routes to come into condition. The left fork is now a classic, being a more obvious line of ice and with superb situations.

Follow the initial couloir of Labyrinth and move left to enter the Garden. Follow the gully at the top of the Garden to an imposing triangular buttress which splits the route into its two forks. Take a belay (usually ice screws) underneath and just left of the point of the triangular buttress.

Left Fork: Go up the groove above until a steep wall forces a leftward traverse across an exposed, iced slab to reach snow under the cornice (avoidable on left). Very unpleasant Severe in summer.

Right Fork: From the pedestal move down and to the right to gain a stepped icy fault which leads up and rightwards to a difficult (occasionally impassable) cornice, climbed on the right.

An alternative line from the top of the Garden, taking a fault just right of the gully, provides a more logical start to the Right Fork but is inferior. The original summer ascent (Very Difficult) took the Right Fork on tolerably clean, sound rock, but usually very wet (several variations possible). (Diagram p. 84.)

Between Hanging Garden Route (Right Fork) and Labyrinth Left Hand is a vegetated buttress cut low down by two shallow faults. The left one is the start of Labyrinth Buttress, IV/V, which finishes close to Hanging Garden Route (Right Fork). The right one is the line of Labyrinth Route, Hard Severe, which finishes up the rib left of the big corner of Labyrinth Left Hand (variation).

96 Labyrinth Left Hand 300 m IV (1979)

A fine climb, the closest line to the Direct which is seldom in condition. Climb the lower Labyrinth couloir and go leftwards towards the Hanging Garden. On the left of the Direct is a big, roofed slab usually sheathed in ice and from this slab an icefall forms towards the extreme right edge of the Hanging Garden. The exact line taken depends on the length of the icefall; reach its base from the left. The slab can be gained even if the icefall is absent (as on the first ascent) by a short, overhanging cleft (very hard, 1NA). Climb the slab up rightwards to enter the easy upper reaches of the Direct. (Diagram p. 84.)

Variation 80 m IV (1983)

This variation gives a better finish if conditions and the cornice allow. About 20 m up the slab, a big corner runs up leftwards to the cliff top. Follow this in two long pitches to the cornice, climbed on the immediate left.

97 Labyrinth Direct 300 m V (1972)

This is a hard ice climb, one of the most demanding in the Cairngorms, and with negligible protection. The hardest pure ice climb in the country at the time of its first ascent. The Labyrinth couloir is followed direct throughout. After the initial ice pitch, easy snow leads to the difficult upper section. Follow a steep groove to the cul-de-sac (40 m). This is turned on the left wall by 10 m of vertical ice (crux). A steep groove continues for another 30 m before the angle eases for the final 40 m to the plateau. There is a tolerable belay in the cul-de-sac if rock is visible. The route is harder than the Minus Gullies on Ben Nevis or Smith's Gully on Creag Meagaidh but is less often in condition— four ascents known up to 1984. (Diagrams pp. 84 and 92.)

THE CENTRAL SLABS

This is the huge sweep of granite in the centre of the cliff—over 300 m of cracked and overlapping slab. The angle is just too steep for friction

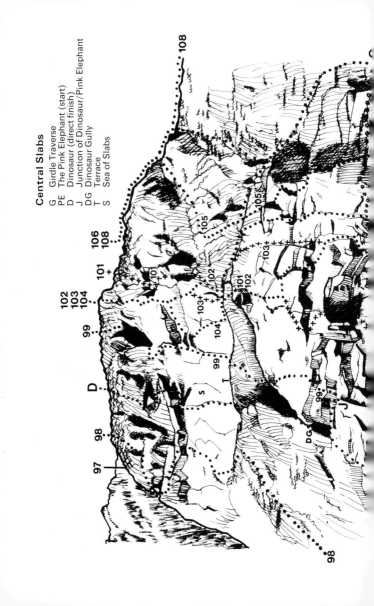

Central Slabs

G   Girdle Traverse
PE The Pink Elephant (start)
D   Dinosaur (direct finish)
J   Junction of Dinosaur/Pink Elephant
DG Dinosaur Gully
T   Terrace
S   Sea of Slabs

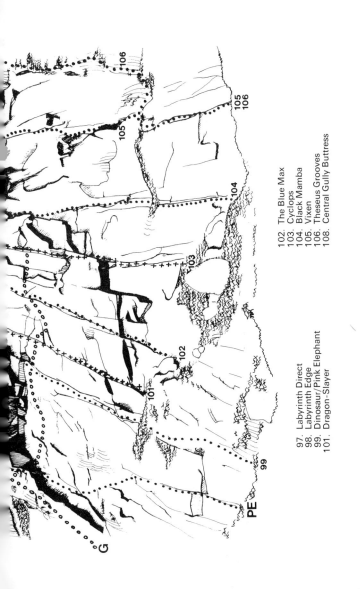

106

105
106

105

104

103

102

101

99

PE

G

97. Labyrinth Direct
98. Labyrinth Edge
99. Dinosaur/Pink Elephant
101. Dragon-Slayer

102. The Blue Max
103. Cyclops
104. Black Mamba
105. Vixen
106. Theseus Grooves
108. Central Gully Buttress

climbing and the routes must follow the natural lines. Nevertheless, the style is delicate and enjoyable, with the overlaps providing variety.

Continuity of the climbs is broken by a terrace system at mid-height, effectively dividing the routes into two distinct halves. Routes are interchangeable at this point and it is possible to traverse off right on to Central Gully Buttress. This escape makes the slab climbs less serious than the more committing routes of Central Gully Wall.

The Central Slabs have a very complex system of shallow cracks, grooves and overlaps. It is possible to cross from one route to another at some places. The pioneers often followed devious lines (e.g. Yakaboo, not described); the routes have been rationalised on the lower slabs to follow natural direct lines. Except for Black Mamba, which follows the easiest line, the routes are necessarily slightly contrived but have superb climbing on perfect rock. Many parties find difficulty routefinding above the Terrace.

98 Labyrinth Edge 300 m Severe (1951)
Takes the left edge of the slabs. The line is irreproachable with fine situations. The climbing is on vegetation and not recommended.

Start at the bottom of the Labyrinth Couloir. Work up rightwards by a grassy fault line for 20 m to below big corners. Traverse right 10 m and return left to a fern-filled bay above the corners. Alternatively (the winter line), reach the bay by climbing the grassy right bank of the Labyrinth Couloir for a short way.

Continue by an easy grassy line up rightwards until an exit to the left leads to a big groove. Go up this to a platform. Continuing up right, one emerges on to the left side of the Sea of Slabs. Climb straight up these by a ribbon of grass-choked crack (or a crackline to the right—Very Severe) to exit by a cleft in a line of overhangs at the top. Jump down to a ledge on the left. Now either continue left and climb straight up the steep Lower Tower or bypass it by the short awkward wall on the right. Continue up to the Fang, an upstanding tooth of rock on the edge. Turn this on the left wall overlooking Labyrinth Direct. The Upper Tower lies above. Traverse along a ledge to reach a hidden chimney round the right side. Climb out by the right wall of this and finish up broken ground. (Diagram p. 92.)

Winter IV (1959)

A good climb, possible in most conditions. The summer route is generally followed, passing the Lower Tower on the right. The Upper Tower is normally the crux and has been climbed on both the right side (as in summer) and by the left flank overlooking Labyrinth Direct (more direct, but harder).

Mammoth, III/IV, takes a diagonal line from the foot of the Labyrinth Couloir via the Dinosaur Gully to the halfway terrace and away rightwards to finish on Central Gully Buttress.

99 Dinosaur/Pink Elephant   330 m   Very Severe

(1964/1969)

The lower tier of Dinosaur and the upper tier of Pink Elephant provides the best route on the left side of the main slabs; sustained at 4c. The sections omitted by the combination are the lower part of Pink Elephant, which is good but very contrived, and the upper part of Dinosaur, the original route on the main slabs, which traversed into and finished up Labyrinth Edge (although there is now a worthwhile direct finish—Very Severe, 5a).

Dinosaur starts up a crack system to below the main overlap in the lower slabs, then escapes left and up its gully to the terrace. Start at the lowest rocks and climb broken cracks to a grass rake. Alternatively, scramble up the rake from the right to left. Follow the main crack system above (5 m left of the thinner crack of Dragon Slayer/Blue Max original start) to a stance 5 m below the long lower overlap (40 m). Surmount the overlap above and go up the slab over an awkward bulge. Go on up slightly higher to follow a toe-traverse leftwards (it is a mistake to go too high here). Step up left then slightly down left into the obvious shallow corner. Climb this using the left rib to belay on top of a big flake (40 m). Now follow Pink Elephant (Dinosaur goes left into the Dinosaur Gully). Go up to a grassy niche and climb the bulging corner above. Break right over a big left-slanting overlap on to slabs and follow the obvious line up into the Dinosaur Gully. Follow this by its right branch to the Terrace under the Sea of Slabs.

There is an obvious corner on the right side of the Sea of Slabs. Climb this to belay under bulges (20 m). Continue up the grooves above, through an overhang by a short bulging slot, and up slabs to belay (45 m). Climb a tapering slab leading up left on to the right end of a big grass ledge below the upper overhangs. Traverse rightwards on to a slabby knife edge to drop into the big upper groove (slow to dry). Climb the groove negotiating a steep step by the left wall to regain the groove. Finish up the groove or the rocks on the left. (Diagram p. 92.)

100   The White Elephant   330m   V   (1980)
A winter ascent of Pink Elephant. The upper tier, via the big groove, is more often in condition than the fickle lower tier. The line described gives a magnificent route taking a thin icefall emanating from the big groove and occasionally reaching the foot of the cliff. This tends to be in condition early in the season after a wet Autumn and a long spell of temperatures just below freezing (but not very cold weather).

Climb direct over the lower overlap to enter the Dinosaur Gully. Follow this (via its right branch) or by ice on the slabs on the right to below the Sea of Slabs. The continuation line of ice flows from the big upper groove directly into the corner of the summer line at the right side of the Sea of Slabs. Follow this ice to the top.

Upper Tier only: it is common for the upper tier to be attractively icy while the lower tier, which is more susceptible to thaw, is bare. The upper tier icefall can be reached by starting up Labyrinth Edge and moving right to the Terrace (III). Grade IV/V overall (variable).

In good conditions at the end of a big winter, the Sea of Slabs may be iced over. They can then be climbed directly, followed by a traverse right to enter the big groove (III/IV).

An esoteric traverse line, Trunk-line, IV, has been made from the Hanging Garden down into the Labyrinth Couloir, out over its right wall (crux) to the base of the Sea of Slabs. These were iced and climbed to a finish up the big groove of The White Elephant.

101   Dragon Slayer   300m   Extremely Severe, E4   (1972)
This route takes the most direct line on the lower slabs, with a very hard and poorly protected 10m through the main overlap. Above the Terrace it follows either of two obvious corners round the right edge of the upper slabs. The Mouth section on the lower slabs is slow to dry.

Scramble to the top of the grass rake past a large block. The route starts up the crackline 5m right of the more obvious Dinosaur crack system (the original start to Blue Max is here too). Climb the crackline direct to belay on a tiny ledge under the lower overlap (40m, 4c). Surmount the overlap directly above and continue straight up the crackline to belay under the great V-mouth in the main overlap (30m, 4c). Climb over a small overlap into the Mouth, up the groove at the back and out across the left wall. Go up slabs to a poor stance below the next overlap (25m, 6b). Go up left and up a bulging crack to slabs. Go right up these to a belay ledge (35m, 4c). Follow the obvious line to the Terrace.

Scramble up to the right edge of the upper slabs. Round the edge is an obvious long corner. This is below and left of a great pink dièdre (the alternative finish). Climb the longer corner direct to a sloping ledge below a layback corner. Turn this on the left and go up slabs to belay 10 m higher (40 m, 5a). Above are two V-grooves (the Quartz corner of Blue Max is also close on the left). Climb the right-hand groove, then slant right to easier ground (30 m, 5b). (Diagram p. 92.)

Alternative Finish   40 m   E3   (1983)

This is an alternative finish above the Terrace, climbing the great pink dièdre (5c). A fine, sustained finish if dry (very rare).

102 Blue Max   300 m   Hard Very Severe   (1967)
This route gives very fine and sustained climbing although contrived in line on its crucial section. It breaks through the main overlap at a distinctive rockfall scar. Scramble up the grass rake to a large block.

Climb the crackline straight above the block over a difficult bulge. Continue up cracks and move up right into a long corner to belay (40 m, 5a). The original start followed the first 10 m of Dragon Slayer, then trended right to the same belay (easier). Climb the corner to small ledges and go on up to make a thin traverse right over a smooth slab to belay under the main overlap (35 m, 5a). Break through the overlap above by a rightward traverse across the wall immediately above a recent rockfall scar then go up cracks to belay (25 m, 4c). This is the crackline taken by Cyclops. Abandon it by a leftward traverse to below a huge diamond-shaped block in the next overlap. Climb the block by its right side to the upper bulge. Surmount this to gain a groove and go straight up this to the next bulge. Step right and go over the bulge by a crack which twists back into the groove. Continue up the groove to belay on the rib above. This is a superb pitch (40 m, 5b, crux). Continue up the rib then go straight up the succeeding crack and corner to a roof. The continuation corner is blank. Turn the roof on the right by cracks leading to a small ledge. Go up the walls on the left for 10 m to a good belay ledge. Scramble up to the right edge of the upper slabs.

Near the right edge the most obvious feature is a big crescent-shaped groove with a crack in the back (taken by Cyclops). Turn it on the right by a smaller groove (or by a wide V-groove round the right edge) to a union below short twin grooves. Climb the left hand groove and continue up slightly left by a short cleft and cracks above to a grass stance below an obvious nose (40 m, 4b). Climb up just right of the nose then go up and left over a slab to the base of the Quartz corner. Climb the corner for 5 m and exit right on to the rib. Continue up the rib to gain grassy grooves and go up these to belay (45 m, 4b). Finish up the big groove on the right, traversing the right wall to reach broken ground (25 m). (Diagram p. 92.)

103   Cyclops   300 m   Very Severe   (1973)
Takes a straight line of cracks up the lower slabs using the wall of Blue Max to pierce the main overlap. A fine direct line, better pitches than Black Mamba, but harder.

At the bottom of the grass rake of Dinosaur is a tongue of slab encircled by a ring of grass. Start at the top of this. Climb the left-hand of twin parallel cracks right of a large brown corner to pull on to a hanging flake from the right side. Go up the edge to belay under a small overlap (30 m, 4c, crux). Climb the bulge above and follow the obvious crack to a scoop with a constricted groove above. Climb the groove over a grass plug and up to a stance (35 m, 4b). Go straight up through the overlap by traversing rightwards across the wall immediately above the rockfall scar (Blue Max) and continue up the crackline to belay above a second overlap (35 m, 4c). Follow the continuation fault to belay level with the large pointed block of Black Mamba to the right (30 m, 4b). Climb directly up cracks in pink, waterwashed rock to the Terrace. The route takes the big obvious crescent-shaped groove near the right edge of the upper slabs (4c), finishing by Blue Max (see description for Blue Max). (Diagram p. 92.)

104   Black Mamba   330 m   Very Severe   (1969)
The classic on the slabs. Very sustained at 4b with some moves close to 4c. To the right of the grass ring of Cyclops is a grass ledge 20 m up the slabs. Start from a grass base at a low point in the slabs.

Climb a delicate, shallow crackline to reach the left end of the grass ledge (20 m). Climb directly up the crack system above to gain a long corner system. Climb this to pull out left at the top on to a belay stance under the main overlap (45 m). Climb the overlap using the cracked groove on the right and follow cracks to belay ledges. Step round a big flake and go up cracked slabs to gain a shallow gully containing a large pointed block. Continue up easy slabs leftwards to the Terrace. Scramble up to the right edge of the upper slabs. The obvious crescent-shaped groove is taken by Cyclops. Climb up and diagonally left under small bulges left of the Cyclops groove to gain a pink rib and slabs above. Belay close to Pink Elephant. Traverse back rightwards to gain the crackline of Blue Max which leads up to a grass stance under an obvious nose. Finish up Blue Max. (Diagrams pp. 84 and 92.)

Winter   V/VI   (1984)

The summer line was followed to the Terrace. The first two pitches were well-iced but above the main overlap there was very little ice and much clearing of slightly consolidated snow was required. A long arduous route with the crux at the top.

From the Terrace, the White Elephant icefall (starting up iced slabs between Pink Elephant and Black Mamba summer lines) was climbed for 40 m to belay under a large overhang. A traverse right, then up a corner-groove and capping bulge led to slabs and a belay below the Quartz Corner (30 m). The Quartz Corner was climbed to its top (1 PA at the final overhang). Ice then led to easier ground on the right (45 m).

105 Vixen 140 m E1 (1977)
Takes a line of grooves and cracks near the right edge of the lower slabs. A worthwhile climb, particularly if combined with the top half of Dragon Slayer which makes a logical continuation. Start about 15 m right of Black Mamba.

Climb a shallow pink corner to the middle of the first grass ledge of Black Mamba (20 m). Go up the obvious deep groove above, then slightly rightwards into a smooth left-facing corner. Climb it till forced on to its right rib, then continue up to belay under a wall, the extension of the main overlap (40 m, 5b). Climb the wall directly and go up walls above to belay below slabs which steepen to wall angle on the right (30 m, 5a). A series of cracklines are visible above; take the left one which slants rightwards and steepens at the top. Exit left and go up a short slab and a small square corner (a good landmark from the ground)—25 m, 4c. Climb straight up the slab above to broken ground (25 m). (Diagram p. 92.)

A low girdle of the slabs below the main overlap has been made, Hard Very Severe, 2 PA.

106 Theseus Grooves 300 m III (1969)
A good popular winter line. Difficulty will vary according to conditions but protection will always be hard to find. Bordering the slabs on the right is a line of grassy grooves and snow basins which trend right

on to Central Gully Buttress. Very Difficult in Summer. (Diagrams pp. 84 and 92.)

The large section of cliff right of the Slabs and Theseus Grooves is scrappy and tiered, but some climbing has been done. Nemesis, Very Severe (4c) is a direct line of reasonable quality on the left, and Minotaur, Severe, less direct. There is one reasonable winter climb, Centaur.

107   Centaur   300 m   III   (1970)
Follows the chimney and ledge system which slants left below the crest of Central Gully Buttress. Start in a bay 30 m from the corner of Central Gully. Climb either of two wide grooves and continue to the bay at the top of the fault. Above is a steep, prominent icefall which provides a good direct finish, IV. The normal route goes diagonally left and follows obvious ledges left below a deep chimney (Minotaur) to a wide corner. Climb this, exiting left and return up right to the crest of Central Gully Buttress. (Diagram p. 84.)

108   Central Gully Buttress   300 m   II   (1955)
The easy-angled ridge bordering the left side of Central Gully. The crest is straightforward but the first pitch, starting at the base of Central Gully, will be tricky unless there is a good build-up. Difficult in summer. (Diagrams pp. 84 and 92.)

109   Central Gully   300 m   Easy
This is the corridor running through the cliff, remarkable for its scale and spectacular right wall. It is not a rock climb but large blocks choking the bed make the ascent quite agreeable for hillwalkers. (Diagram p. 84.)

Winter   I   (1933)

Entertaining. The cornice is usually avoidable on the left.

CENTRAL GULLY WALL
This is the great convex face forming the right side of Central Gully. Magnificent in its monstrous bulk, it is a wall to rank alongside any in Britain.
There are two major facets, the 250 m frontal slab face and the shorter but forbiddingly steep wall impending over the gully. At the bend in the face between these two facets is a transitional zone—a

maze of roofs and hanging slabs taken by Cougar. These extend over a tremendous overlapping wall guarding the mouth of the gully and containing five of the most impressive routes in the country. Routes on the frontal face generally follow big, raking crack lines while the gully wall is cleaved by three great corner systems.

The climbing is of a uniformly high quality and climbers venturing on to the less well-known routes will not be disappointed. At the top of most of the climbs there remains a scrambly finish up a chaotic region of blocks and greenery below the rim. After prolonged rain, weep continues to ooze down from this area for several days; if a line has big wet streaks it is usually a waste of time embarking on it. The section from the Naked Ape to Vampire is probably quickest to dry; The Giant, The Israelite, and Gulliver are slowest. Mousetrap and The Wicker Man are also quick.

At the top of Central Gully is a short but very steep wall arrayed with sharp hanging aretes. This section is separated from the main wall by the fault of Sabre Cut and contains two climbs, Four Corners Route, Very Severe, 1 PA, about 35 m above Sabre Cut, and Sabre Edge, Hard Severe, the left arete of Sabre Cut and containing a unique move off a pinnacle.

110 Sabre Cut 80 m IV (1957)
Although short, this will normally give a steep hard climb. The cornice is often big and could pose serious problems. Severe in summer. (Diagram p. 84.)

111 The Wicker Man 150 m E3 (1982)
Below the fault of Sabre Cut is the corner system of Vertigo Wall. The route takes the conspicuous crackline in the centre of the wall left of Vertigo Wall. A fine climb with a short and very safe crux. Should become popular. Start as for Vertigo Wall.

Climb up for 5 m to a grassy bay below a leftward trending groove. Follow the left wall and rib of the groove to a ledge and belay at a large perched block (30 m, 5a). Step right and climb thin cracks in a faint groove to a ledge below a small, square-cut overhang. Climb the thin, right-hand crack into a sentry box, then up the wall above to a ledge. Up the obvious corner-crack to a belay on the right (35 m, 6a). Continue up the corner and slabby groove above exiting right at the top. Up grass ledges for 5 m to belay at a large embedded flake (25 m, 5a). Move left around the corner and follow easy ledges leftwards and then back diagonally right to reach a belay below the bulging headwall (30 m). Move up right on to a glacis and climb the overhang at its narrowest point to reach a rightwards slanting groove. Climb the crack on its right to the plateau (30 m, 5b). (Diagram p. 108.)

112   Vertigo Wall   160 m   Very Severe, 1 PA   (1954)
This is the huge recessed scoop below Sabre Cut, easily recognised by the scar of a big rockfall which removed one of the original belay platforms in 1957. A climb of considerable character and well named.
   Start at a large block in the gully bed up from the true line of the corner. A grassy shelf leads rightwards on to the face. From near its left end climb straight up for 5 m to gain a traverse line which leads right to a grassy recess below an obvious 5 m crack (25 m). Climb the crack to a platform and move up right on to a big detached block. Traverse right, then pull up blocks on the left to gain a shelf and continue rightwards up stepped slabs to belay under a black 5 m chimney (40 m). The chimney is invariably wet and slimy (4c, 1 PA). Above this an overhang forces a detour right for some 10 m, then up and back left into the true line of the corner. It is wise not to belay under the creaking flake so climb up left to a poor belay ledge (30 m). Climb the slab above to the impending headwall and traverse right along the alarming creaking flake into a shallow corner. Move up and across the wall on the right then finish with a pull-up to the top (25 m, 4b). Easier to the plateau (40 m).

Winter   V   (1977)

An outstanding mixed route by the summer line. A rather unsatisfactory single ascent has been made using eight points of aid and a bivouac. It should go free in a day, though at a high standard.

113   Bombadillo   135 m   E3   (1982)
Follows grooves in the nose of the buttress formed between the corner systems of Vertigo Wall and Goliath. An improbable line with good sustained climbing. Quite necky in places but with a short and well protected crux.
   Start as for Goliath by traversing easily right for 15 m across slabs to a grass ledge and peg belay. Step down and right, then go up to gain the slab above. Climb the slab and shallow groove to exit left by a rock scar to ledges. Move right and climb a slab rightwards, then go up a hidden flake-crack to gain a niche. Move left and pull up into a prominent V-groove. Climb this and continue up to a large ledge.

Belay 5 m right along the ledge (45 m, 5c). Climb the broken wall rightwards to a ledge below an overhanging groove. Hand traverse left across a steep wall and pull up onto the slab above (poor peg runner). Traverse delicately back right to the groove and a welcome peg runner; climb the groove to where the angle eases (crux). Follow an obvious leftward slanting ramp line to the arete, move left to a crack, then up to a ledge and belay (40 m, 6a). Up a vague crack above the belay for 5 m, then traverse right to an obvious thin crack. Follow this till a good ledge leads right onto the arete. Up the arete to the top (35 m, 5b). Scramble to the plateau.

114   The Israelite   125 m   E4   (1982)

Climbs the smooth waterworn groove above the initial traverse slab of Goliath; the groove provides a long and particularly fine pitch but is slow to dry. Start as for Goliath; traverse right across slabs to a small stance and peg belay below the groove line (25 m).

Climb the slab above, then slightly leftwards till a traverse right can be made to a crack leading up to an overlap. Climb the overlap on the right to enter the main groove and follow it direct to where the angle eases. Traverse right to the belay of Goliath (45 m, 6a). Go up the obvious thin crack in the centre of the slab to a large ledge and belay below the huge corner (20 m, 5a). Climb the corner direct to the top (35 m, 5b). Scramble to the plateau.

115   Goliath   150 m   Hard Very Severe   (1969)

This route breaks through the guarding walls and slabs between the great corners of Giant and Vertigo to finish up the big diagonal slab corner in the upper cliff. It is one of the best routes at Dubh Loch, unusually varied with mainly slabby climbing in an impressive position.

Up the gully from the Giant is a vertical wall with a vast wedged block. The direct start goes up here. For the normal line, start up on the left and climb diagonally rightwards, then traverse rightwards across slabs to belay on the right below a small corner in the steep wall above (40 m, 4b). Climb the steep corner and move up to a shelf (crux). Step left and continue up the fault line to a belay on the right (40 m, 5a). Go across the slab on the left and up to a ledge leading left to a huge slab. Climb the slab for 10 m, move on to its right edge and so up to a stance about halfway up the great corner (40 m, 4b). Traverse right to finish up fine cracks splitting the slab (30 m). Scrambling to the plateau.

Direct Start   35 m   Hard Very Severe

A good start with a unique pitch up the vast, wedged block. Originally aid; but now free. Start 10 m left of the block. Traverse right on to a grass ledge (or gain the same ledge from below on the right). Hand traverse right and mantleshelf to gain the block. Chimney up the back and belay on top (20 m, 5a). Go left up a flake and pull over a bulge to gain slabs at the start of the second pitch of the normal route (15 m, 4c).

The Shelf Variation   30 m   Hard Very Severe

After the 10 m corner above the first pitch, continue rightwards up the slabby shelf to a wall at the top. Climb this to reach the belay stance on the normal route (5a).

Winter   V/VI   (1980)

A superb exposed route, mostly on ice. It does not often come into condition and requires a long spell of temperatures just below freezing (at a rough estimate, about a month). In very cold weather, the springs freeze at their source. The chosen line will depend on the ice but will always take the Goliath Icicle as the first pitch.

  Climb the initial slab and a steep finger of ice (Goliath Icicle) which forms in the groove of The Israelite, left of Goliath's summer line. Traverse right to meet the summer route and follow this up and back left to the stance halfway up the great corner (20 m). The route followed on two ascents to date traverses horizontally across the slab below the cracks of summer (peg handhold to start) with a short descent to pass under an overlap and a short rise again to reach easy ground. Continue to belay above the slab (30 m). Easy to the plateau.

116   The Goliath Eliminate   130 m   Hard Very Severe
Sustained high quality climbing. Climb the Direct Start to Goliath (35 m, 5a, 4c) then the crux of Goliath normal route (10 m, 5a). Take the Shelf Variation (5a) but instead of returning left to Goliath, go up and right to the final corner of Giant. This is reversing a section of the Catwalk. Climb the final corner of Giant (30 m, 5a). Scramble to the plateau.

117   The Giant   100 m   E3   (1965)
A climb of great character. It climbs the lowest of the three great

corner systems, an impressive slash in the fiercest section of the wall. It has a short desperate crux, poorly protected at the time of writing as the protection peg is very rusty.

Climb easily rightwards up a sloping ramp to the foot of the first corner (belay). Go up cracks above to the base of two parallel grooves. Swing up on to a flake in the left-hand groove and climb this to a ledge (20 m, 5b). Make sure the belay is bombproof, as the stance is awkward and the protection dubious above. Above are another set of twin grooves which are the crux. Climb the left one, using the peg in the right one for protection. Above, the grooves go left and up a vertical flake-crack to a big ledge and belays (20 m, 6a). Climb over blocks to a groove with a steep slab on the left. At the top of the groove, below an impending wall, move left on to the slab and go up and left to a grass ledge. Traverse back right to step on to an over-hanging nose. Climb the crack above, go left, then up to a big platform below the impressive final corner (30 m, 5a). Climb the corner, then easier ground to a grass ledge (30 m, 5a). Scramble to the plateau. (Diagrams pp. 84 and 108).

118   The Naked Ape   130 m   E5   (1982)

A magnificent route which finds a line up the big arete right of the Giant and offers bold climbing in an impressive situation. Peg runners were placed while climbing and left *in situ*.

Start below a groove leading directly up to the main corner system of the Giant. Climb the groove and where it forks keep right up a flake-crack to reach a ledge and belay at the top of the initial ramp of the Giant (35 m, 5b). Above the belay is a smooth groove right of Giant. Climb its left-hand rib, then step across it to reach a peg runner on the right at 10 m. Move up right on to the steep slab, traverse right to the arete and step up to a peg runner. Continue traversing right along an obvious foot ledge and step up to a good ledge and belay (junction with Ascent of Man and Voyage of the Beagle) — (30 m, 6b). Follow the leftward slanting slabby corner to a niche below a roof and place a runner in the lip. Climb delicately down leftwards to a good foothold near the arete. Step up left and climb a break in the overhang to gain a sloping ledge. Up a short steep wall (peg runner) to a ledge and belay in a niche (25 m, 6a). Climb the overhanging crack above to a large ledge. Step up right and climb cracks to enter a groove system. Follow this to a grassy terrace at its top (40 m, 5c). Scramble up right to the plateau. (Diagram p. 108.)

119   The Ascent of Man   125 m   E4   (1982)

Climbs the obvious groove and crack-line in the huge steep wall between Giant and Cougar. A fine natural line, the scene of previous attempts. Climb a crack for 3 m and traverse right along a ledge to gain the lower groove. Follow this up and traverse left across a slab to regain the crack. Climb this to a break in the roof (old peg runner) and pull into the groove above which is followed to a hanging peg belay *in situ* (30 m, 6b). Step up and move across right to gain a subsidiary groove (if wet, climb the arete on its left, returning to main groove as soon as possible—6a, unprotected). Climb this and move left to climb a crack which leads to a leaning wall. Step up left (this is where The Naked Ape belays at the top of its second pitch), climb the short crack above and hand traverse right into a groove. Belay at the top of this groove (30 m, 5c). Climb the short corner above to reach the traverse line of the Prowl, follow this up left along a slab and down into a recess occupied by a large detached block (junction with The Naked Ape)—(35 m, 5a). Step back up right and climb cracks to enter a groove which is followed to a grassy terrace (35 m, 5a). Scramble off right. (Diagram p. 108.)

120   Perilous Journey   125 m   E5   (1983)

Climbs the face not far right of Ascent of Man to gain an obvious hanging crack leading up on to Cougar below its last pitch. Below Ascent of Man is a big overhanging alcove. The route starts up a break in the bulge just up the gully from this.

Swing up right to a jug on top of a peculiar boss of rock, then surmount the bulge. Move up right and up a crack to easier slabs. Climb an overlap and go up to a detached block in an open corner. Climb up here to a good thread belay (20 m, 5c). Climb the slabby wall directly above the belay to gain a slab-shelf (the last runners for the next hard section are here but protection can be improved by making a detour leftwards along a creaking flake under the shelf and up to a jug where more runners can be arranged, then coming back to the original point). Make a hard mantleshelf move above the shelf on to a smaller shelf. Go left and step up delicately to reach good flake holds leading up to peg belays on the big slab running along hereabouts (20 m, 6b).

Step down left and traverse the lip of the slab past a poor peg runner to an evil sloping perch at the end. Swing left round the overhanging nose and make hard moves across left and up past a peg runner (in place). Climb up and step right to follow a vague groove system, then twin cracks up a wall to stance and peg belay (good nut up on arete to

left)—(30 m, 6b). Move up left round the arete into the groove of
Ascent of Man. Go up this for a short way then go on up to make an
awkward move across a slab rightwards to reach the hanging crack.
Climb the crack and go up to belay on top of the great blocks of
Cougar (25 m, 5b).

Climb a shallow, recessed corner as for Cougar, then leave Cougar
leftwards up a shelf (as for Prowl). Climb a bulging nose past a spike,
then go up slightly right then left to join the left traverse of Cougar just
below the rounded spike. Finish as for Cougar, traversing left along a
bulge and up to easy ground (30 m, 5b). (Diagram p. 108.)

121   Cannibal   140 m   E5   (1984)

Starts at a prominent cracked arete approx. 10 m down from Perilous
Journey and 15 m up from Voyage of the Beagle. This is just right of
the large overhung alcove.

Climb the crack just left of the arete till moves can be made round
the arete into another crack. Climb this till it fades and step left to gain
a crack on the crest. Climb this steeply to a stance on the slab above
(30 m, 5c). Move up left and gain holds which lead to a peg runner
below the roof. Pull out right until a crack above the roof leads to a
stance and peg belay on a higher slab (10 m, 6a). Move up to gain a
left-slanting corner and climb this to a roof. Traverse left to a loose
flake. Climb the crack behind to a recess (peg runner) and pull over its
right wall on to Cougar Slab. Belay as for Cougar, at the right end of
the Slab (30 m, 6b). Above and slightly right is a stepped corner.
Climb the first step, then swing right on to the arete and move up till
the corner can be regained. Continue up the corner and pull out right
below a steep nose. Climb the wall right of the nose to gain a short
crack and pull on to a block on top of the nose. Follow a slab left
below a roof to a stance (40 m, 6b). Climb the crack above. Scramble
to top (30 m, 5a). (Diagram p. 108.)

122   Voyage of the Beagle   160 m   E4   (1983)

This voyage takes the very prominent diagonal line under Cougar to
link with the top pitches of Naked Ape. Offers slabbier climbing than
the other recent routes on this wall.

Start 5 m left of Cougar at a groove. Climb a flake-crack on the right
to gain the groove. Follow the groove, initially with difficulty, then
more easily up the continuation to a small, square-cut ledge. Move left
across wall, then regain corner. Step down left and gain a crack
leading back into the fault which leads to nut belay on start of slab

Central Gully Wall

SC Sabre Cut
V top of Vertigo Wall
b top of Bombadillo
g top of Goliath/The Israelite
r Red Wall (Gulliver)
a access to Falseface
s Sans Fer main crack

111. The Wicker Man
117. The Giant
118. The Naked Ape
119. The Ascent of Man
120. Perilous Journey
121. Cannibal
122. Voyage of the Beagle

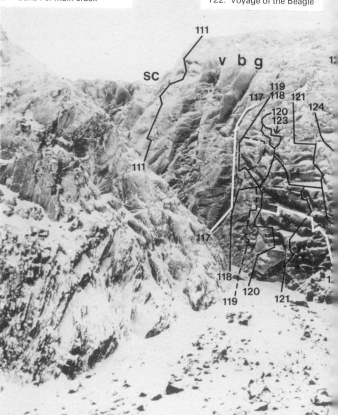

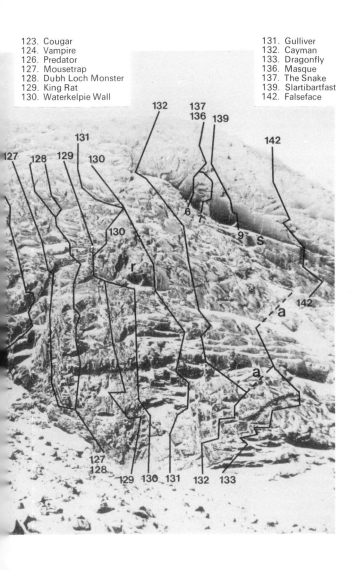

(40 m, 6a). Climb across the slab to old pegs and nut belay (15 m, 4c).
Step down to gain lower slab (runners on upper slab). Cross slab to
arete, step left round arete and climb straight up to enter groove (on
Ascent of Man). Climb this to its top (to protect the second it is
advisable to split ropes and return right on upper slab to place runner).
Move left to gain a groove leading to the stance on Naked Ape at the
end of its second pitch (40 m, 6a). Follow Naked Ape to the top
(25 m, 6a; 40 m, 5c). (Diagram p. 108.)

123 Cougar 135 m E2 (1968)

The Central Gully Wall below Giant soars up for about 100 m in a
series of monolithic slabs and roofs. This magnificent climb takes a
curving line of dièdres near the right end of the wall, then cuts in over
the main section by the huge, hanging Cougar Slab to thread the maze
of roofs above. The climbing is exposed and intimidating despite good
protection, and very sustained. The three hard pitches are borderline
5b/5c.

The route starts at the top of a big grassy mound with embedded
blocks, at the foot of Central Gully. The start is common to Vampire
and Predator. Make a short right traverse into the initial corner and
climb it (often wet) into a notch. Continue up left and work up on to a
good ledge under an overhang (30 m, 4c, common with Vampire).
Follow cracks leading up left over a bulge and go up the steep corner
line above to a belay on the Cougar Slab (40 m, 5c). Traverse the slab
left by a crack and step down into a recess below a short overhanging
corner-crack. Climb this (very strenuous) and continue leftwards by
great flakes to belay under a short, impending recessed wall
(35 m, 5c). Climb the wall to gain a girdling slab (the Prowl) under the
final bulging band. Move right and mantleshelf on to a block. Above is
a crack with a protruding stone. Climb it to reach an overlap. Make a
left traverse under the overlap bridging a slight gap. Continue
traversing left to reach a good rounded spike. From this make a step up
and traverse left along a bulge until possible to move up then left to
belay under a roof on a good ledge (30 m, 5c). Scramble to the
plateau. In case of rain, a 45 m abseil from the base of the overhanging
crack (Cougar Slab) will just reach the gully bed (50 m abseil from top
of crack). (Diagram p. 108.)

124 Vampire 180 m E1 (1972)

A sustained route, one of the best on the cliff. Climb Cougar for 30 m
to belay under the overhang (4c). On the right the bulge is split by an

overhanging crack with a jammed flake at its base. From the jammed flake, pull rightwards round the bulge and climb the corner above to a grass ledge with a good stance just above (40 m, 5a). The big corner above can be climbed directly but is dirty (E3, 5c). It is better to step back down, then up on to slabs on the right. Go diagonally rightwards up slabs and a bulge to reach a ledge after 20 m. Make a toe traverse left across a tiny dwindling ledge, go up a corner to bulges and break out left by a short wall and slab to gain a grassy belay stance (40 m, 5b, poor protection). Move left up a slab and climb a short recessed corner. Climb the slot above and go up the slab to exit right (5b). (Alternatively, move right and climb a steep crack to the same point—5c; or start up the crack and move left above the slot—5b.) It is now easy to go left to broken ground, then right to the plateau but good climbing is continued by trending rightwards and following the final two pitches of Raptor to the easy ground (4c)—originally climbed as a continuation to Vampire. (Diagram p. 108.)

125 Raptor 215 m E1 (1981)

An eliminate line between Vampire and Predator. Climb the Direct Start of Predator to belay under the short wall (5a). Climb the wall, go up the slab (as for Predator), then traverse left over the top of the slab below a steeper slab. Climb up the centre of the slab until a horizontal traverse right leads on to the block-strewn ledge of Predator (35 m, 5b, crux). Return up left across a slab and climb the slabby wall above by a crack leading on to a slab. Move up left to join Vampire at the bulge of its slab section. Go diagonally right as for Vampire to belay before the traverse (45 m, 5b). Continue directly up the groove above to reach another blaeberry stance (20 m, 5a). Move on up slabs and straight up a bulging wall section of a big overlap to a ledge. Layback directly over the lap above and up slabs to a belay ledge (20 m, 5b). Move left round cracked blocks and work fairly directly to easy ground in two pitches, climbing not far left of a grass-choked groove (4c).

126 Predator 180 m Hard Very Severe (1970)

The obvious black crack system right of Vampire corner, the leftmost of the big frontal crack systems. A sustained route in a fine position; low in its grade.

Start at the top of the mound the first 10 m being part of Cougar/Vampire. Make a short right traverse into the corner and climb it (often wet) to a ledge on the right. Climb the short vertical crack above to gain a shelf leading away up right to a grass ledge (35 m, 4b). Climb the short wall above and go up a slab to the foot of an overhanging crack in a red wall. Traverse right to breach the wall by a shorter overhanging crack to gain the corner above (often wet). Climb up the corner and swing out left and across a slab to a block-strewn platform on the left (30 m, 5a). Climb the bulging crack above to move right on to a slab. Continue up through the roof and climb the crackline to belay above the left end of the prominent Bow-Roof of Catwalk (30 m, 5a). Follow cracks to below roofs, climb a smooth scooped corner and move right across a slab to belay in a recess (40 m, 4c). Climb cracks through another overlap and so to easy ground (45 m). (Diagram p. 108.)

Direct Start   25 m   Hard Very Severe

Slightly harder than anything on the normal route. Start up a break in the wall down right from the ordinary start to gain a shelf, then a higher shelf. (These shelves lead right towards the Mousetrap recess, the higher being the line of the winter ascent of Mousetrap.) Climb twin cracks in the vertical wall above to gain the normal route (5a).

127 The Mousetrap   180 m   Very Severe   (1959)

A fine natural line, well protected and a classic, the easiest way up the frontal face. It uses the obvious grassy recess right of the grassy mound above the foot of Central Gully. This leads up to the big crack system right of the black Predator crackline.

At the lowest point of the frontal face is the big King Rat recess. Start up left from this at a deep easy groove leading up to an array of cracks. Climb the groove and traverse left over a slab and up to belay below the left of the main crack (35 m). Move up right and climb the wide crack (4c, crux), or more easily use the rib on the right before moving back left, and so to the recess above. Continue up the recess to belay near the top (45 m). Climb the steep flake-corner on the left, move up to gain cracks and follow these for two long pitches to reach easier ground. (Diagrams pp. 84 and 108.)

Winter   V/VI   (1980)

Climb the first short corner of Predator using 1 PA, then traverse right round a shelf under the twin cracks of Predator Direct Start. Continue rightwards, then up to the grassy recess of Mousetrap. Thereafter, follow the summer route.

The Kraken, Hard Very Severe, 5a, starts up Mousetrap, climbs cracks right of Mousetrap crux and exits out of the top right side of the recess to join Dubh Loch Monster.

128 Dubh Loch Monster 200 m E1 (1970)

Takes the line of the thin solitary crack to the right of the Mousetrap/Kraken cracks and some way left of King Rat system. An excellent climb although escape is possible on to Mousetrap. Very sustained at 5a, with one move of 5c.

Start just below and right of the easy groove of Mousetrap. Climb cracked slabs to belay under a conspicuous chimney break (30 m, 4b). Climb the chimney (crux), then continue up an awkward wall and on up the crackline to belay under a big overhanging notch (40 m, 5c). Move left and climb the arete returning right to a big ledge (10 m, 5a). Follow the cracks above to a double bulge. Climb the first bulge, move right 2 m and climb the second with difficulty. Go up slabs to belay under short wall (25 m, 5a). Move left to a break (junction with Kraken) and climb this to gain the slab above. Move left 2 m and pull over a short wall into a corner. Follow the corner for 5 m, then the rib on the right over two bulges, the second being turned on the left. Move right to a belay ledge (5a). From here there are two finishes (Dubh Loch Monster and Kraken). Climb slabs diagonally rightwards to a crack at the right end of an overlap. Go up the crack then up a steepening corner. Follow the crack above to easier ground. The Kraken finish is to climb up and slightly left to gain a corner which leads to a ledge going leftwards to below an overhanging groove. Go up the groove and left to awkward cracks which lead to a belay. Climb a cracked slab above to easier ground. (Diagram p. 108.)

129 King Rat 220 m E1 (1968)

This is the fine crack system running straight up the frontal face. From below the line is dominated by a big roof 50 m up, sometimes climbed with 2PA (in place, Very Severe). Start close to the left wall of the big recess at the lowest point of the face directly below the big roof.

Climb the steep rocks at the back of the recess for some 15 m, then traverse the left wall using flakes to a ledge on the open face (a more direct line continues straight up the recess to the slabs below the roof, 5a). Climb straight up the crackline to a big grass ledge (40 m, 4b). Move right from the ledge and go up cracked slabs to a shallow cave under the roof. Move awkwardly up left into a corner and up this to a ledge (20 m, 5b). Now follow the general line of the cracked ribs above for about 50 m until under a short vertical wall. Go leftwards up slabs to belay under the short leaning corner of Waterkelpie Wall (4b). Climb the corner to ledges (10 m, 4b). The obvious line trending up right is Waterkelpie. The roof directly above must be turned on the left. Climb a short wall to gain a slab under the roof. Surmount the bulge some 3 m left of the roof and traverse a narrow slab rightwards above the roof and up to belay ledge (30 m, 4c). Move into the upper crack system and follow it in two pitches to grass ledges (4b, 4a). Scramble away left and up to the plateau. (Diagram p. 108.)

130 Waterkelpie Wall   240 m   E1   (1958/1964)

A meandering route up the centre of the frontal face, but it has some good pitches. In the middle of the face is the Red Wall of Gulliver overlooking the left end of the Caterpillar, a long grass ledge. The lower section takes a vague line straight up to the left end of the ledge system. A circuitous line left and back right leads to the continuation crack of the Red Wall cracks.

Start at the right side of the King Rat recess and climb a rather unpleasant grassy fault to a rockfall scar. Move left under the rockfall scar and over alarming hollow flakes, then up the second corner left of the scar to slabs. Climb up the slabs to a vertical corner immediately right of the King Rat roof (45 m, 5a). (The unpleasant start to this pitch involving the fault and hollow flakes can be avoided by starting up King Rat and where that route traverses left, continue straight up and slightly right to regain Waterkelpie—5a).

Climb the vertical corner to a belay ledge (10m, 5b, crux). Climb up right to a terrace and go straight up cracks to the left end of the Caterpillar ledge system (35 m, 4c). Work left over pink slabs ignoring an obvious break. Go left and up a slab to belay below a short leaning corner (15 m, 4b, common with King Rat). Climb this to ledges and follow the obvious line up right to a barrier bulge with prominent old pegs (20 m, 4b). Climb the double bulge (5b) and traverse away right over slabs to gain the line of the chimney-crack above the Red Wall. Follow it to the top in two pitches. Left-hand variations (better quality but perhaps 5a) are possible if the crack is wet (as for Gulliver). (Diagram p. 108.)

131 Gulliver   240 m   E2   (1970)

A direct line right of Waterkelpie, taking in the steep Red Wall, which is sustained and strenuous, substantially harder than anything on the rest of the route. Apart from the Red Wall, the route is a little disappointing in quality. Slow to dry.

Start directly below the Red Wall at the lowest point of the face, just right of the King Rat recess and the grassy fault of Waterkelpie. Trend rightwards up broken slabs and cracks. Climb an awkward bulge and go up the slab above to traverse horizontally right to belay under two tiered corners (35 m, 5a). Climb the two tiered corners and traverse left over detached blocks on the lip of the overhang to shelves (40 m, 5a). Move right and up a bulging wall to ledges below tiered walls (10 m, 5a). Climb the walls using the obvious heathery break and go up slabs to ledges under the Red Wall (45 m, 4b). Climb parallel cracks in the Red Wall (20 m, 5b). Continue up cracks above over a bulge to belay under the chimney-crack of Waterkelpie Wall (40 m, 4c). Climb slabs and corners to the left for a long pitch to reach easier ground (5a). Alternatively finish up the Waterkelpie crackline, the natural way when dry. (Diagram p. 108.)

132 Cayman 270 m E2 (1977)
A good direct line right of Gulliver. It reaches the left end of the Caterpillar, which is the grass runnel slanting leftwards into the face towards the Red Wall of Gulliver. Above the Caterpillar it breaks through the long roof right of the Red Wall to follow an obvious crack system. The start, originally the Bower–Lang Route, just Hard Very Severe (5a), can be used as an approach to Falseface.

In the middle of the rocks below the Caterpillar is a big curving roof. The route starts by a rising traverse line above this roof. Start just right of the lowest part of the frontal face, close to the start of Gulliver.

Go straight up cracked slabs, then up and right into a shallow, left-facing corner. Exit out right to small ledges (20 m, 4c). Traverse right and go up by a shallow corner to exit right on to a slab. Make a thin traverse right for 5 m to gain a small ledge leading up into a short corner (20 m, 5a). (Access to Falseface is from here—traverse right, up and over a big jutting nose and rightwards via short walls to grassy ground in the Caterpillar; two pitches—4c). For Cayman, traverse right 5 m, climb the wall above, then trend left up slabs and up the right side of a big slabby plinth to gain the right end of a ledge (4c). Climb the awkward recessed wall above and go up short walls to belay (35 m, 5b). Traverse rightwards up the steep wall above using flakes and go left by two detached blocks to the Caterpillar (25 m, 4c). Above is a roof. In the centre is a downward pointing flake shaped like an alligator's head. Climb left up big flakes into a corner, then move right and up over the roof using the alligator's head. Continue up the crackline above surmounting a hard bulge at the top (crux).

Go up to a belay ledge on the right, occupied by big flakes (10 m, 5c). Go up through the obvious notch above to follow a groove to grassy belay ledges (20 m, 4c). Continue up the pink groove above, alongside a big smooth slab (20 m, 4c). Climb up right, then left by slabby rocks to belay under a big steep chimney (30 m, 4c). The line of False Gully has been joined. The original ascent finished by this route, which takes the left arete of the chimney. The chimney itself would give a good finish but is often wet. Instead, move up right on to the right arete of the chimney passing a small spike. Continue up thin cracks to step right into a groove and move left to reach a ledge. Go up and right across a perched block to climb the right edge of a groove and its continuation, stepping right just below the top to a good belay ledge (40 m, 5a). Move up left and scramble to the top. (Diagram p. 108.)

133 Dragonfly 90 m   Hard Very Severe   (1981)
Climbs up rightwards below the big curving roof of Cayman. Start about 10 m right of Cayman, below and right of a rowan sapling. Go up rightwards over the first overlap. Continue up right, then traverse left and break through short walls. Traverse right, then climb up and left to belay at a spike, below and just right of the left end of the curving roof (30 m, 4c). Traverse horizontally right across a slab to a grass patch. Move further right, then go straight up to an overhang (10 m, 4c). Continue traversing below the roof, then climb an obvious corner to a pedestal (5a). Trend leftwards and up on to the Caterpillar.

The Caterpillar itself is mainly grass but includes a short slab, Very Severe (4c), IV with 4PA on the only winter ascent. (Diagram p. 108.)

134 Sous les Toits 110 m   E1, 1PA   (1976)
Good sustained climbing, suitable for a second route of the day or as an approach to Falseface. The route weaves a way up the subsidiary buttress on the right of Caterpillar Crack. Start up in a grassy bay at the right side of the buttress. Climb the obvious steep chimney, continue up, then work up leftwards to traverse left on to a stance under a jutting nose. Abseil from a peg on to the hanging slab on the left and so to a belay (20 m, 5a). Traverse the slab to the far end, go round the corner and up left by a delicate slab under a bulge. Break up over the wall above on the right side of an overhang and move up right to a recess. Pull straight over the roof above to a slab belay under more

roofs (30 m, 5b). Turn these on the right, then go up and left to the lip of the left-hand roof. Go up the slim ramp above and swing right to a stance below the final roof (10 m, 5a). Turn this by a corner running up the right side then go away up and left to grass and belay under a short wall (40 m, 5a). Climb the wall to the grass of False Gully.

The above is the description of the first ascent, which used peg belays (not in place). On the only other ascent, without pegs, a belay was taken before the descent and all the difficulties were climbed on a very long second pitch. There were rope-drag problems and the final belay was very poor. Subsequent ascenders are advised to split this pitch at any suitable point. (Diagram p. 84.)

FALSE GULLY WALL

This is the tilting left wall of the rounded North-West Buttress. It lies high on the right above the frontal face of Central Gully Wall and above False Gully, an intermittent terrace slanting left to peter out in the upper rocks.

The distinctive feature of the wall is a smooth and very steep central section containing the two hardest routes, Slartibartfast and The Improbability Drive. At the right side of the smooth area are the thin cracklines of Sans Fer and Iron in the Soul. The smooth area is bounded low down to the right by the very prominent leaning corner of Falseface, and on the left by the corner lines of Masque and The Snake. The routes are usually reached via False Gully but a route on the lower tier can be conveniently included.

135 False Gully 200 m   IV/V   (1964)

An interesting and unusual winter route. The crux is right at the top from where retreat might be difficult. Follow the fault for several pitches until it peters out into a ledge. There is a shallow chimney above. Either climb it and gain the left arete (peg for tension) which is followed to easier ground; alternatively, continue leftwards by a hard move to another ledge. From the left edge of this, tension leftwards to snowy ledges which lead away left to the top. In excellent conditions, which are very rare, one could imagine this route becoming quite easy. Hard Severe in Summer. (Diagram p. 84.)

136 Masque 60 m   E2   (1983)

This is the left-hand and deeper of two corner lines which bound the smooth section of wall at its top (left) end. Start below the steep leaning corner at the left end of a grassy terrace.

Climb the leaning corner to a roof, pull out left and climb a crack to a ledge (20 m, 5c). Climb up twin right-slanting cracks above to a roof. Step right and climb a fault to enter a grassy groove which leads to the top (40 m, 5b). (Diagram p. 108.)

137   The Snake   65 m   E3   (1984)
Starts up the right-hand and shallower of the two corners. Another good line but poorer protection than Masque.

Start up the corner, then move out slightly right and up to the top of a big flake. Step up past the flake and move right to flakes on the arete (the left edge of the smooth wall). Go up the flakes to gain a sloping shelf. Step right and climb a bulging wall to gain another shelf. Step right again and go up a short corner past a spike to exit left at the roof on to a belay ledge (peg 5 m up on the left) — 30 m, 5c. Go up past the belay peg and traverse left round the edge and across horizontally into a jam-crack in slabs. Climb this for 5 m to join the crackline of Masque. Finish up Masque (35 m, 5b). (Diagram p. 108.)

138   The Improbability Drive   60 m   E6   (1984)
The main pitch of this route climbs the wall left of Slartibartfast. Sustained and fierce with limited protection; nevertheless the E6 grade is provisional. Start 10 m left of Slartibartfast, just right of an obvious crack.

Climb rightwards up little foot shelves using diagonal cracks, then go up the wall to gain a horizontal break. Go straight on up the wall to a semi-resting place at the next break. Climb the twin cracks directly above, using mainly the left-hand crack (crux). Belay peg in place on slab above (the left side of the Slartibartfast niche) — (20 m, 6c). Climb directly up the bulge just left of the belay and go up slightly right to climb the third roof of Slartibartfast's second pitch. Belay here or on ledge on right rib (10 m, 5c). Climb the obvious groove on the right rib, then veer slightly right and make awkward moves up a notch into the niche of Sans Fer. Stride across the black gunge usually flowing down here and finish as for Sans Fer (if too wet, move back left below the notch and rejoin the final cracks of Slartibartfast) — (30 m, 5c).

139   Slartibartfast   80 m   E5   (1982)
Takes the most prominent crack and groove line in the centre of the smooth wall, some 30 m left of the obvious leaning corner of False-face. High quality climbing taking a fine line. The first pitch is very

serious. Start from a slanting grass terrace, below a crack in the middle of the smooth wall.

A ledge on the wall, just right of the crack, gives access to a small groove. Climb the groove until it peters out (nut runner up on right), then up and left across the wall to gain the crack. Follow the crack and shallow corner, moving right at the top to belay on sloping ledges. (20 m, 6b). Climb the obvious corner, containing three small overhangs and belay on a slab above (20 m, 6a). Continue in the same line via steep cracks to the top (40 m, 5c). (Diagram p. 108.)

140   Sans Fer   145 m   E4   (1979)

This route and Iron in the Soul offer fine climbing but are not good lines as pitches on each can be interchanged and escapes made. The highlight of Sans Fer is a fine crack on the smooth wall right of Slartibartfast. Start 10 m left of the leaning corner of Falseface in the middle of the face.

Climb a niche and slab, heading for a prominent finger crack; climb this to a sloping stance and belay as for Falseface (40 m, 5b). Walk left 10 m to the base of a crack in the wall. Climb the crack (20 m, 6b). Traverse left 5 m to a groove and climb this to rest under a bulge. Continue over the bulge, then up grooves slightly right, then left to belay on a ramp (40 m, 6a). Traverse up left on the ramp to a niche and exit left through the roof. Traverse left, then up into another niche. Continue straight up through a roof to reach easy ground and a block belay (45 m, 5b).

141   Iron in the Soul   80 m   E4   (1984)

Starts up the next crack right of Sans Fer's main crack, shares a belay, then takes the continuation of the Sans Fer crack (Sans Fer goes left). More sustained but not as well protected as Sans Fer. Reach the start by climbing the first pitch of Sans Fer or walking along the terrace, passing under Slartibartfast and Sans Fer's main crack.

Climb the crack direct on to a shelf, then go up and left negotiating two bulges to traverse the slab left to Sans Fer's belay (20 m, 5c). Climb the bulge above the belay and go up cracks and up a corner-crack slightly left under the next bulge. Layback right and up over the bulge to follow a flake-crack curving up and left in a slab. Go on up a short corner to belay on the ramp of Sans Fer (30 m, 6a). Above are mossy cracks. Move left up the ramp and climb a short cleaned crack. Step right and follow more cracks and blocks to easy ground (30 m, 5a).

142 Falseface 90 m E1 (1969)
A first-class climb, varied and exposed, top end of the grade. Best approached by climbing Sous Les Toits (E1), Dragonfly (HVS) or the start of Cayman (HVS). From a point in False Gully below the big obvious corner, climb up slightly rightwards to gain a grass shelf leading into the corner (Very Difficult).

Climb this big leaning corner (strenuous) to reach a sloping ledge and belay on the left (5b, crux). Climb on up the short wall above and move right into a hidden chokestone chimney which is climbed to a ledge on the left below an overlap. Gain a sloping ledge above, surmount the overlap (prominent old peg) and traverse right across the overhung slab to good holds. Climb up and back left to a series of grooves and follow this to a big ledge (5b, belay at far end). Move back left and climb up into a big steep corner. Go up this until near the top, then go along the right wall and up by a detached flake to ledges and easier ground (5a). Finish up broken ground to the plateau. (Diagrams pp. 84 and 108.)

Once on easier ground, an obvious ramp can be seen leading left. This is the ramp joined by Sans Fer. By following the ramp, one can take in the last pitch of Sans Fer (5b).

The hidden chokestone chimney can be reached by a fault which slants in from the right (4c), but this misses out the best pitch. Well to the right of Falseface is a short line, starting in a prominent slanting fault and following a corner and wall (Coon's Yard, E1, 5b, 1 PA in wet).

NORTH WEST BUTTRESS
This is the broad, broken buttress at the right end of the cliff; its left side is False Gully Wall and its right side borders North-West Gully. The left edge overlooking False Gully Wall is the disappointing False Impression, Very Difficult. It has a direct finish, Very Severe, on the left. Mistral, IV, is a winter line following an obvious line of grooves just right of False Impression.

143 North-West Gully Arete 200 m II (1967)
The broken ridge on the left of North-West Gully. It should always be climbable in winter. The easiest way lies up the right side of the crest. Grassy and moderate in summer. (Diagram p. 84.)

144 North-West Gully 200 m II/III (1952)
A classic winter gully, often in condition. The entry slabs form a big

icefall avoidable on the left but better climbed direct. Moderate in summer. (Diagram p. 84.)

NORTH WEST GULLY BUTTRESS

The rocks to the right of North-West Gully are very broken but low down is a pleasant plaque of pink slabs. This little buttress has three enjoyable climbs, good for a second route of the day. Unfortunately, they are no quicker drying than the bigger routes.

145 The Strumpet 60 m Very Severe (1974)

Takes the deep crack splitting the big flake-whaleback on the left. The buttress is undercut and the route starts at an arete on the right, the lowest point of the buttress. Climb the arete for 5 m and traverse left to belay under an obvious corner (20 m). The corner is taken by Late Night Final. Work left to gain a groove leading to a ledge under the whaleback (20 m). Climb a thin crack leading to the main crack on the crest and climb this to a good stance below easy ground (5a). (Diagram p. 84.)

146 Jezebel 50 m E3 (1984)

A short direct line with a friction crux. Between The Strumpet and Late Night Final is a smooth slab with twin parallel cracks. Start immediately below these.

Climb the overhanging wall and go up (crossing Strumpet) to climb the left-hand of the twin cracks, moving left into a scoop after 3 m. Climb this and the big corner above to belay below a wide crack (25 m, 6a). Climb this crack and the corner above, then move up left to easy ground. Belay up on right (25 m, 5b).

147 Late Night Final 60 m Hard Severe (1969)

Climb the first pitch as for Strumpet and follow the big corner to a stance at the top (40 m). Continue up cracks above to an overhanging corner in a steep wall. Go up this to a grassy niche, then move right and up to the top (20 m). (Diagram p. 84.)

Girdle Traverses

There are two girdle traverses of the Central Gully Wall. Unlike other girdles in the Cairngorms, these follow fairly natural lines and give good climbing, though not recommended for an early visit to the cliff.

148 Catwalk 400 m Hard Very Severe (1969)

Most of the climbing is about Mild Very Severe standard, but there is one hard, well-protected move. Climb the Caterpillar and traverse to its left end under the Red Wall. Continue along pink slabs and up to a stance next to the short leaning corner of Waterkelpie. Traverse left to a break in a leaning wall (common to Kraken and Monster). Go up this and move left along a narrow slab to reach a crackline (Mousetrap). Climb the crack for a short way to a slab stance above. Traverse left below the prominent bow-roof (5b) and up to a good stance (Predator). Climb the cracks and corner above for 20 m and move left to a stance beside a small curved roof. Move left round cracked blocks then along the lip of the roof. Go up cracks to gain grassy ledges (escape to the plateau is apparent here). Follow the ledges leftwards to belay by a large block level with the base of the final corner of Giant. Traverse left under this corner and descend a groove to traverse left again into Goliath. Finish up Goliath.

149 The Prowl 420 m E1 (1978)

A very sustained girdle at a lower level than Catwalk. Increasingly impressive situations with a memorable pitch leading into Giant.

Go up Caterpillar Crack to a bare slab. Step left and work up then down and away across sustained pink slabs to belay on the jutting nose of Dragonfly/Bower–Lang Route (5b). Continue at the same level below an overlap and go up a short groove on the right side of a slabby plinth (Cayman) to a belay ledge (4c). Go left along the ledge and up a bulge (Gulliver) to easy ledges (4c). Go along these then down slightly left to a ledge—5 m above the roof of King Rat. Go up King Rat for 5 m then go left by small ledges into the crackline of the Monster (4b). Go up this to the overhanging notch and exit left into the Mousetrap recess (4c). Go up Mousetrap for 10 m then move down left into the overhanging cracks on the red wall of Predator. Climb Predator to a point some 5 m above the break in the roof (5a). Traverse left (not obvious) to step down on to a ledge on Vampire slab, 10 m below the toe traverse (5a). Climb along the toe traverse and up and left to the next stance (5b). Traverse the big slab on the left to hand-traverse a block and step down on to the small girdling ledge of Cougar (5a). Go along this joining the Ascent of Man and round a nose to belay on a hanging green slab (4c). Move up the slab and climb a bulging wall to gain a higher slab tucked under the roof. Go left along this then climb down a little arete to gain a huge recess occupied by a big detached block (5a, common with The Ascent of Man). Swing up the arete on the far side and move left to an airy belay perch (5a). A fine flake-crack below leads sensationally into Giant corner in 10 m (4c). Climb leftwards to an old peg in a slab and climb the overhang above to step left on to Goliath's Shelf Variation (5a). Finish up Goliath.

BROAD CAIRN BLUFFS

The bluffs come into view on the left about half a mile before the Dubh Loch on the approach from Loch Muick. They form the 60 m left wall of an open green shoot (or easy angled snow gully in winter) going up to the last step in the flat ridge of Broad Cairn before the rise to the summit cone.

The obvious narrow gash is Coffin Chimney, Difficult, III, and the buttress on its right is Rake's Rib, Difficult, III. The front of the buttress facing the valley gives Yoo-Hoo Buttress, III, a pleasant climb when icy, but it is a good monitor of conditions on Creag an Dubh Loch. Those seeing it icy should hurry onwards.

150   Funeral Fall   50 m   IV   (1974)

Above Rake's Rib forms a very prominent icefall which catches the eye from the last stretch of the path before the Dubh Loch. Good for a short day or in bad weather.

Lower down the south side of the glen, about half a mile up from Loch Muick, an intriguing, isolated, diamond-shaped slab is obvious from the Dubh Loch path and gives a good short climb—Solitaire.

151   Solitaire   35 m   E1   (1983)

Start at the toe of the minor buttress below the main slab. Pull left over initial overhang, then step right and climb shallow groove over bulge and up past block to belay below steep cracked slab (10 m, 5a). Climb cracks up left, then move right and straight up to top (25 m, 5b).

GLEN CLOVA

Glen Clova is the long, narrow valley of the River South Esk where it penetrates the South-East Cairngorms. In this area south of the Lochnagar—Broad Cairn range schists and gneiss replace granite, grass replaces heather and the character of the mountains changes. The cliffs become rather vegetated and the rock climbing deteriorates, the exception being the Red Craig (NO 2975) a line of outcrops rather Lakeland in character, on the east side of Glen Clova overlooking the public road shortly before it terminates at Braedownie. The Red Craig is fully described in the guide "North-East Outcrops" and is not duplicated here. The higher corries, however, (such as Corrie Fee and Winter Corrie), give good winter climbing in the lower grades. Despite the lack of top quality routes, the crags here have always been popular due to the area being the only winter climbing ground immediately accessible from Angus and Dundee.

BASSIES (HILL OF STRONE)

The large gully directly behind the Whitehaugh Bothy (NO 300743) is Whitehaugh Gully, I/II. One mile south-east of the Winter Corrie of Dreish is a stream which joins the River South Esk at NO 296745. Midway up the open hillside of Bassies, this stream issues from a gully (Hogmanay Gully, III). The corrie between this hillside and the Winter Corrie is Corrie Farchal. The gully in the middle of the craggy backwall of Corrie Farchal is Farchal Gully, II/III.

WINTER CORRIE OF DREISH (NO 278744)

This is the high cupped corrie on the left side of the glen opposite Braedownie. On its right side lies a conical outlying buttress, the Scorrie. The rocks in the corrie are very broken, offering little in the way of good rock climbing, though the back wall rises for almost 250 m. In winter, however, there are several gullies which offer fair ice climbing. As they are mainly water courses, ice may form here as early as November and as this corrie is higher than Corrie Fee, the routes come into condition faster. The following gullies provide interesting winter climbs (described left to right).

152   The Waterfall   60 m   II/III
The icefall (waterfall) high on the left of the face. On the left of the corrie below The Waterfall, there sometimes forms a fine two pitch icefall, IV.

153   Central Gully   120 m   II
The obvious deep gully right of The Waterfall, and in the centre of the corrie.

154   Easy Gully   120 m   I
A prominent straight gully. A straightforward snow climb and a good approach to Dreish. Right of Easy Gully is the highest section of cliff, the most prominent feature being Diagonal Gully, which cuts centrally through the steep lower section of the face (the Main Buttress) and opens out at mid-height into a grassy slope, the Basin.

155   Backdoor Chimney   200 m   II/III
Left of the Main Buttress is the wide Backdoor Gully. From the back wall where this bends right is the deep Backdoor Chimney.

156   Backdoor Gully   200 m   II
As mentioned above, this gully cuts deeply behind the Main Buttress emerging at the top of the Basin.

157   Diamond Slab   III/IV   (1980)
A chimney and steep slab to the left of Diagonal Gully. A good climb.

158   Diagonal Gully   200 m   III
The best route in the Winter Corrie. In the centre of the Main Buttress is a 30 m icefall coming from a rightward sloping chimney. Climb the icefall and chimney to the Basin. From the top of the basin, climb the chimney containing a chokestone behind a pinnacle on the right. Follow the snow slope on the left to the top.

159   Pinnacle Gully   120 m   II
The first deep gully right of Diagonal Gully. It leads to the Basin.

160   The Shute   120 m   I
The obvious wide snow gully at the right side of the cliff.

161   The Scorrie: Y Gully   250 m   I/II
The obvious Y-shaped gully.

162   The Scorrie: Y Gully, Left Hand Branch   250 m   II/III
The deep, well-defined gully on the left.

CORRIE FEE OF MAYAR (NO 2574)

This corrie on the north-east flank of Mayar is the finest feature of the district for scenery and mountain atmosphere, but although its cliffs are high (200 m) and most of the rock steep, its buttresses are too vegetated to provide continuous climbing in summer. Under snow, however, this area gives the longest and best winter climbs in the Glen Clova area.

The corrie has two walls meeting at the Fee burn waterfall at its head. The south, which is the finest, extends inwards from the Shank of Drumfollow; the North from the headland of Craig Rennet.

CORRIE FEE: SOUTH WALL
From left to right there are five gullies; A, B, Look C, D and E. A, B, D and E are well-defined, Look C less so.

163   A Gully Buttress   200 m   I/II   (1972)
Left of A Gully is a large triangular buttress, which provides the route. Start just right of steep rocks at the base of the buttress and traverse diagonally left to the crest.

164   A Gully   200 m   I
The gully on the left corner of the cliffs. Uniform snow slope.

165   A-B Integrate   200 m   II
On the right of A-gully there is an easy angled 100 m corner which contains ice early in the season.

166   A-B Intermediate   200 m   II/III
This lies midway between A and B Gullies. Start at an obvious ice pitch, then a shallow gully and small pitches rightwards to the Upper Chimney, exiting near the top of B Gully Chimney.

The deep-cut B Gully is the best defined of the gullies. About 60 m up B Gully, B Gully Chimney breaches the left wall. B Gully Buttress is formed between the two; it culminates high up in a pinnacle with a great flake on the left shoulder at the top. The left branch of B Gully runs up to a col behind this pinnacle.

167   Central Route   250 m   II   (1975)
Start at A-B Intermediate. Climb ice pitch, then groove above to large snow basin. Climb groove rightwards for two pitches until forced to descend into B Gully Chimney.

168   B Gully Chimney   150 m   III   (1962)
A good ice climb, recommended. It follows the chimney which breaks left out of B Gully. Can be combined with Look C Gully (see below). Difficult in Summer.

169   B Gully Buttress   150 m   III   (1915)
Climb the buttress direct from its base at the bottom of B Gully Chimney. Moderate in Summer.

170   Shelf Route   165 m   III
Starts in B Gully 30 m below and left of B Gully Chimney. Traverse left, climb a shelf parallel to B Gully, cross B Gully Chimney and up to join B Gully Buttress below the pinnacle.

171   B Gully   200 m   II   (1915)
Recommended. Generally contains at least one ice pitch, although it can be avoided by climbing up right. The left branch is the obvious deep chimney high up containing several chokestones.

172   Look C Gully   200 m   III/IV   (1953)
Probably the best route in Corrie Fee. Requires a good freeze to come into condition. The steep, shallow gully in the left section of the largest mass of rock, Central Buttress. The lower half of this route is a prominent, steep icefall, climbed to the upper section of the gully, which is easy angled and uninteresting.

By climbing up and left above the steep section and descending a small gully into B Gully, this route can be combined with B Gully Chimney to give 200 m of excellent and continuous climbing.

173   Wet Knees   200 m   III/IV   (1972)
Follows a direct, though discontinuous line of chimneys breaching the steep rock bands immediately right of Look C Gully.

174   The Wild Places 200 m   III/IV   (1980)
Follows a line of ice grooves leading to the obvious overhung niche in
the centre of the face between Look C Gully and Romulus and Remus
(Central Buttress). Start directly below the niche in a right slanting ice
groove. Hooker's Joy (Moderate) is a herbaceous summer route
following a similar line.

175   Romulus and Remus   190 m   Very Difficult   (1946)
A route comprising of two sections on the right of Central Buttress.
Very scrappy.

176   D Gully   200 m   I
Straightforward snow. It runs up the right side of Central Buttress.

177   Diamond Buttress   60 m   Severe
On the right of D Gully are two pyramids; the upper and leftmost is
Diamond Buttress. Probably the best rock route in Corrie Fee.

178   The Pyramid   60 m   IV   (1975)
The lower of the two pyramids. Very Difficult in summer.

179   E Gully   I
A short, open runnel high up at the end of the face.

180   The Comb   60 m   IV   (1973)
The small isolated buttress high up on the extreme right of the face,
just right of E Gully and some 300 m left of the waterfall. Difficult in
summer.

181   The Girdle   III   (1970)
A left to right girdle, starting in B Gully.

CORRIE FEE: NORTH WALL
There is only one climb, a dark rift only seen when one is close under it
on the approach from the north side of the corrie. This is Slanting
Gully, III, which lies well inside the corrie near the waterfall. Other
lines have been done here, but are scrappy and have not been recorded.

GLEN DOLL: CRAIG RENNET (NO 251757)

Glen Doll is the glen carrying the southern headstream of the River

South Esk and leading to the Clova-Callater watershed. The path which goes up the glen is known as Jock's Road. Craig Rennet is OS spot height 745 m at the northern tip of Corrie Fee and is a fine impressive feature, grade II. The first, shallow gully inside Glen Doll from the Craig Rennet point is North Gully, I. Further right is the deeply set Glen Doll Gully, which generally gives one good ice pitch, grade II.

GLEN DOLL: CRAIG MAUD (NO 239768)

Between Glen Doll Gully and Craig Maud is the Dounalt escarpment, which offers little climbing. Craig Maud is a buttress 200 m high (scrambling) flanked by Curving Gully, I, on the left and North Gully, I, on the right.

GLEN DOLL: CAIRN DAMFF
On the north side of Glen Doll, opposite Craig Maud and just short of the point where Jock's Road rises more steeply to the plateau, lies Maud Buttress, Very Difficult.

JUANJORGE (NO 265795)

This most curiously named cliff lies above the main (northerly) head-water of the South Esk river. It is on the flanks of Sandy Hillocks about three miles from Braedownie and a mile short of the gorge, waterfall and larches of Bachnagairn. As seen from the glen the rocks rise steeply in smooth slabs on the right of a small hanging corrie at the back of which the rocks are even steeper. The principal mass is on the left of the corrie and is hemmed in on the left by the scree-filled West Gully.

Low on the left of the crag is a steep 30 m wall of excellent granite. Two high quality modern routes have been recorded (for full descriptions see the North-East Outcrops guide); Roslin Riviera, E3 6a, climbs a groove on the toe of the wall, then the prominent, left-slanting diagonal crack above. Ladies of the Canyon, E3 6a, climbs scoops in the wall 5 m right of Roslin Riviera.

Two older routes have also been recorded; Diagonal Crack (Severe and lichenous) which start from West Gully well up the left flank of the principal rock mass, and Gimcrack Gully (Difficult) which is a well-defined gully a little nearer Bachnagairn and starting low down.

CRAIG OF GOWAL (NO 235805)

This retiring hill lies $1\frac{1}{2}$ km south-west of Broad Cairn. The climbing is on the East Face, which lies above the Burn of Gowal, a tributary of the River South Esk (upstream from Juanjorge). The rock is granite and must be very close to the southern frontier of the Lochnagar intrusion. A visit from Dubh Loch seems pointless and would involve subsequent reascent. The climbing is best reached by the pleasant walk up Glen Esk from Clova.

The face is mostly broken and vegetated but there is a cleaner strip of slab near the centre (the Gowk climbs this). Left of the cleaner strip is an obvious gully slanting left, grade II. Left of the gully is a smaller buttress which gives Slipup, III/IV, starting by the prominent steep icefall in its lower rocks (crux).

182   The Gowk   200 m   Hard Very Severe   (1968)

A pleasant route, although those making a special visit to this remote cliff with the sole aim of completing the route may be disappointed. The band of clean rock is narrow; the original line used a point of tension (now free).

Start at the lowest rocks and find a way up slabs in some 60 m to reach a prominent overhang barring the whole slab. Break through this on good holds and follow a slab and whaleback to a ledge and block belay. Traverse down left to a small ledge below a small overlap, then continue delicately left (5a) to another ledge. Climb the short wall and slab above to belay. Climb the crack in the broken wall to the left, then go directly up the slab to a small overlap. Traverse right and break through the overlap via a rounded flake. Continue by short wall and slabs to belay below the huge terminal overhangs. Traverse right under these and climb a damp corner to a 5 m crack. Go right across sloping ledges on the wall and up a short slab to the top.

Winter   IV   (1979)

In winter the slabs become sheathed in water ice, giving a fine sustained climb near the summer line.

183   The Skiver   200 m   III   (1975)

Takes the shallow recess immediately to the right of the Gowk slab, starting almost at the same point. Climb to a snow basin, then up a shallow gully leading to a large rock wall. Climb this direct, or detour to the left, depending on the build-up.

GLEN ISLA: CAENLOCHAN GLEN

The crags of Caenlochan and Canness Glens belong to Glas Maol and Cairn of Claise. Access is usually via Glen Isla although it may be nearer to come over the summit of Glas Maol. While steep in places, these are mostly broken and too vegetated for good rock climbing. The only rock climbs recorded are on the face below Druim Mor (973 m), known locally as Craig Herrich (NO 190772), a top attached to Cairn of Claise. The cliff is seen high up on the north side of Caenlochan about one mile above the junction of the streams. Craig Herrich Buttress, Difficult, follows a central rib just to the right of a scree fan and culminating at a notch half-way up the cliff. Between Craig Herrich and the Caderg on its right is a Y-gully which has been climbed several times in winter. Other easy snow climbs have been done in this area.

Almost 1 km south-east of the summit of Glas Maol there is a corner of the Caenlochan Glen, just to the north-west of the ruined shack (NO 175761) on Little Glas Maol (961 m). From this corner an easy gully rakes down beneath the undercut base of a north-facing buttress. The only obvious weakness in this overhanging wall is a prominent ramp slanting right to reach a couloir between two large rock ridges. This is The Ramp, II/III. The East-facing broken cliff on the left (facing down the easy gully; NO 175765) has several ice runnels and vegetated rock. The ice forms early in the season and is quite reliable. The central runnel climbed direct is grade II/III.

GLAS TULAICHEAN: NORTH COIRE (NO 056767)

There is a slabby, south-facing belt of rock some 80 m high in this corrie. Six routes, graded from Moderate to Very Difficult have been climbed. "The rock is clean, solid, compact mica schist with quartzite intrusions, and provides pleasant, fairly easy climbing." Rumour has it that this description is optimistic.

GLEN THAITNEICH: CREAG DALLAIG (NO 083757)

On the west face of Creag Dallaig is a small rock face with a pinnacle climbed by J. N. Collie in 1908. From the top of the pinnacle, one can continue up a sharp arete to the top of the crag.

GLEN CALLATER: CORRIE KANDER (NO 186808)

This fine little corrie lies on the south side of Glen Callater, a 3 km walk beyond the head of the loch. It can also be reached from the Glenshee road (A93) by skirting Carn an Tuirc on its north side. The corrie contains an inky lochan dominated by grassy crags of schist. These are too broken for summer climbing but provide good grade I snow routes over 200 m long. There is little scope for harder routes but high on the left flank is an obvious curving recess which gives a grade III climb, with several good but avoidable ice pitches.

On the north-east spur of Carn an Tuirc, running out from Coire Kander and facing down towards the head of Loch Callater there is a burn running through a small gorge. This produces an icefall some 150 m high, with some fine ice scenery (Snip-snip, III).

GLEN CALLATER: CREAG AN FHLEISDEIR
(NO 197828)

This little crag is wrongly marked on the OS map as Creag an Fhir-shaighde, its local name (and on old maps) is Creag an Fhleisdeir. It lies on the north side of the glen about 1 km beyond the head of Loch Callater (8 km from the Braemar Road). It is broken, but in the centre lies a compact slab buttress. An obvious gully runs up the left side. This is Central Slabs Cleft, Severe. In winter it gives a good ice climb early in the season (100 m, III). The crag terminates at its eastern end in a gully which gives a grade I in winter.

About 2 km beyond Creag an Fhleisdeir, on the same hillside, lies Creag Leachdach. It consists of broken slabs, but pleasant pitches could probably be climbed.

SOUTHERN LAIRIG GHRU

BEINN BHROTAIN: THE DEE FACE

Towards the River Dee the mountain presents a continuously steep slope but little in the way of continuous rock. There are three sections of cliff.

The southern section is marked at its right end by a wide and easy-angled grass and scree chute. A little to the left is a defined gully (Green Gully, Moderate, I) which offers a direct route from Derry Lodge to the summit of the mountain. Near the centre of this section is a recess with steep rocks on its left and slabs either side. The left-hand slabs are quite short and interspersed with patches of vegetation. They contain several narrow rock bands (dykes) which rise diagonally left across smooth slabs and two of which, despite appearances, give amusing and unusual climbs. Both are hardest at the start and unprotected without pegs (peg runners used on Brodan's Dyke).

184 Brodan's Dyke 95 m Very Severe (1983)
Follows the leftmost dyke, which is very narrow. Start at the lowest point of slabs and climb twin dykes up left over a bulge (4c). Continue on the main upper band to belay at the top of a heather slope below a small overlap (30 m). Climb slightly right of the belay to heather, then continue up the next section of band to reach ledges with a belay up on the right (35 m). From the left end of the ledges follow the band up round and across a grassy fault to finish up waterwashed slabs with an exit left.

185 Klonedyke 65 m Hard Very Severe (1984)
Climbs the rightmost dyke which is immediately right of a wider dyke. Start by an awkward scramble to a poor belay just below and left of the start of the dyke (on the wider dyke). Climb straight up the slab to reach the base of the thin dyke. Follow the dyke to a long grass ledge—good, small wire belay just to the left (45 m, 5a). Continue up the dyke (20 m, 4b). Exit on the left (30 m scrambling).

The central section is a large area of glaciated slabs containing a conspicuous inverted V-overlap. Unfortunately, the slabs are penetrated at mid-height by great swards of vegetation. These slabs have been climbed at the highest point of continuous rock (in the centre) to give a 300 m Very Difficult route of reasonable quality; good situations at the start and finish but easy-angled in the middle.

The northern section has nothing to offer the climber. There is a short gully high on the nose between the Dee Valley and Glen Geusachan and heavily vegetated patches of slab on either side.

BEINN BHROTAIN: CARN CLOICH-MHUILINN

On the north slopes of Carn Cloich-mhuilinn (NN 968907) is a band of slabs about 60 m high. These are climbable in several places at about Severe. A few short problems are possible but don't merit a special visit.

BEINN BHROTAIN: COIRE CATH NAM FIONN
(NN 951933)

This corrie forming the north-west face of Beinn Bhrotain is one of the most secluded spots in the Cairngorms. High on the left at the entrance is Fingal's Buttress, composed of steep slabby rock on its left and centre; on its right it throws down ribs into a scree-filled amphitheatre. From the corrie floor a crack can be seen rising in three short sections up the edge where the ribs and slabs meet. This is Tiered Cracks, 100 m, Very Difficult, of doubtful quality.

The rest of the face to the Bhrotain-Monadh Mor col is composed of vegetated buttresses with two defined gullies giving good grade I climbs. A Gully is the left-hand and steeper; B Gully is on the right.

THE DEVIL'S POINT (NN 976952)

This striking headland which contributes in no small measure to the great character of the Lairig Ghru is in spite of its fierce appearance most disappointing to the climber. Much apparently attractive ground is in fact unstable vegetation and loose rock. The whole face may be wandered over save at the northerly belt of slabs topped by its huge overhangs. Even these are less steep than they look. Passing the right-hand end of the overhangs is the poor quality Corrour Slabs, Difficult, II.

In winter the mountain improves and after heavy snow is a magnificent spectacle. The natural lines, however, are not sufficiently steep to give other than grade I climbs, though these are good. The four best defined lines are (a) the open chimney below the south end of the huge overhangs (see above), continuing past the overhangs to steep slopes and ribs above. (b) South-East Gully: at the south end of the Dee face is an open depression striking up to the summit. (c) South-West Gully: just inside Glen Geusachan. It has steeper rocks on its left edge (South-West Arete, Difficult). (d) Geusachan Gully: the large gully well to the left of South-West Gully. It is more defined than the others and cuts back diagonally to the summit.

The mountain continues westwards into Glen Geusachan as a great wall of slab, of minimal interest to the climber. The only feature hereabouts is the Devil's Cave, perched in the midst of the slabs, two thirds up the face in a steep wall facing up the glen. It is hidden from the Dee approach and is reached by turf ledges from the west. The first recorded visit was in 1929. Since then visits have been rare but it has been used as sleeping quarters by seekers after the unusual.

CARN A' MHAIM: THE PALETTE (NN 986966)

High up on the face opposite Corrour bothy are short ribs and slabs offering problems up to 30 m. Further north is the Palette, an un-mistakeable patch of slab, aptly named from its shape and colour.

The left side of the Palette is barred high up by a big overlap penetrated only by Gadd's Route at a prominent nose. At its right end it becomes more broken and here Medium-Rare goes through. On the right side of the Palette and lower down is a smaller overlap system which forms an inverted-V. Tickled Pink goes through the left arm of this V and Pink Dwarf at the apex. The characteristic feature of the Palette is a set of parallel pink streaks low down. These provide the three right-hand routes with excellent crux pitches of unprotected padding. Unfortunately most of the slab is less smooth and the routes have long easy sections.

186 Gadd's Route   150 m   E1   (1955)
Rockfall has altered the lower part of the route. A very prominent white corner has been created. Go up slabs to the foot of the corner. Climb the right-hand rib of the corner using grassy cracks (5a). (Alternatively, the corner itself should give a fine pitch, probably easier but with some loose material.) Continue directly up slabs and up an overlap to a prominent cracked nose at a weakness in the big overlap (4c). Surmount this by the short overhanging corner (con-taining an old ring peg) on the right (5c). Continue up slightly right to

a heather patch and climb the final overlap to gain the easy upper slabs. Here it is convenient to traverse off right.

187   Medium-Rare   115 m   E1   (1984)

Right of the white corner is a fine sheet of slab with several water-washed pink streaks. The route takes a very straight line including the left-hand pair of streaks. The bottom of the slabs has a prominent crescent-shaped overlap.

Start up past the left end of this overlap and go rightwards to belay below the left-hand pair of streaks (25 m). Climb either streak (right is slightly easier), then go straight up slabs to belay at the left end of a small overlap (45 m, 5b). Climb a shallow right-facing corner (just left of a steep slab and streak in line with the lower streak), then go right under a small overlap, back left and up slabs to a system of short corners at the right end of the big overlap. Slant left up the left-hand corner, then right across a slab to easier slabs. Finish up these (45 m).

188   Tickled Pink   105 m   Hard Very Severe   (1981)

The route takes the less steep right-hand streak above the right end of the crescent-shaped overlap.

Start up slabs to pass the crescent-shaped overlap at the right end and continue up slabs leftwards to belay left of a long grass ledge, below and left of the pink streak (20 m). Go up to the overlap, cross it left of the pink streak and traverse right along the lip under a minor overlap to gain and climb the streak past a hole. Continue straight up the slabs above to a small overlap (45 m, 4c). Go over this and up a slab to the left-hand of two short overhanging cracks in the next bigger overlap (the left arm of the inverted-V overlap). Climb the crack, then continue up right and up slabs to easier ground (40 m, 4c).

189   Pink Dwarf   95 m   Very Severe   (1981)

Climb the widest pink streak towards the right end of the slabs. It leads directly to the small overlap near Tickled Pink (55 m, 4a). Move right and up a slab to the top of the inverted-V overlap. Pull out right from a short corner at the very apex of the V. Go left and right up easy slabs (40 m, 4b).

On the east side of Carn a' Mhaim, the sections of slab overlooking Glen Luibeg are of little interest other than for making sporting lines to the summit from Derry Lodge. Various routes up to Very Difficult have been made from 1940 onwards, including a line from bottom right to top left and a direct route.

The best route to the summit in winter from this direction lies up the little tapering gully in the recess between the slabs, Silver Chimney, 100 m, I. The slabs on the left of Silver Chimney have also been climbed in winter.

THE GREAT AMPHITHEATRE OF BRAERIACH AND CAIRNTOUL

Cairntoul, shapeliest of the greater Cairngorm summits, shares with Braeriach a giant arena of five corries drained by the headwaters of the River Dee. Stretching 3 km across from summit to summit with a rim edging the plateau for nearly 6 km, this cirque is the most alpine of our mountain areas in point of snow accumulation and the prolonged period of its cover (near permanent below Garbh Choire Mor). All but two of the corries lie under the great plateau of Braeriach in the lee of the prevailing winds; and the plateau, itself a vast collecting area, is further backed by a gently sloping tableland extending west to An Moine Mhor (The Great Moss) above Glen Feshie. From this desert of snow, drift is carried by the wind for many km and finally driven into the corries where it piles to great depths. The result is the longest, unbroken cornice found on our mountains; at peak season it reaches awesome proportions over many sections on its 6 km circuit.

Snow in such quantity and permanence gives the area an added attraction in late spring and early summer. Then the buttresses, bare of snow and separated by corniced gullies, rise from unbroken snow-fields and the whole scene creates an atmosphere which is truly alpine. Such a mountaineering attitude is necessary to appreciate these corries. Those seeking technical rock will be disappointed; those who seek the remote mountain setting can only be inspired.

This idyllic summer picture is shattered in winter. The routes, though short, match most for quality but the challenge is the long approach into this snowy wilderness, negotiation of giant cornices and difficult descents from the most hostile of our winter plateaux.

Accommodation
(1) Garbh Coire bothy (NN 959986)

Centrally placed between the corries, it is an ideal base. It sits on the left bank (facing upstream) of the Allt a' Gharbh Choire about 1½ km from the Lairig Ghru and merges well with its background. Solidly built and watertight, though poky, it holds four (or six uncomfortably).

(2) Corrour bothy (NN 981958)

In the Lairig Ghru on the west bank of the Dee, 5 km south of the Garbh Coire bothy. At the point where the path from Derry Lodge into the Lairig Ghru joins the path up the Dee from the white bridge (signpost here), a small path cuts diagonally down to the river and a solid bridge 300 m south-east of the bothy. The bothy holds 10 in comfort, sometimes unpleasantly crowded at peak times (e.g. Easter, July and August weekends).

(3) Sinclair Memorial hut (NH 958037)

Situated on an exposed platform some 50 m above and 50 m west of the Lairig Ghru path, 6 km north of the Garbh Coire bothy. It can be awkward to find in the dark. A good indication is the very steep, heavily eroded path leading up to it from the Lairig Ghru (try not to worsen the erosion).

(4) Camping, bivouac

There are various sites between Corrour and Garbh Coire bothies, and upstream from here. There is a delectable site in Garbh Choire Dhaidh, bordering the Dee where it opens out into small pools just above the lip of the corrie.

Immediately to the north-west of the pools is the Dey-Smith bivouac, a built-up cave under a large boulder (cairn on top)—holds two.

Access

Access is very long from either the north (Aviemore) or the south (Braemar); evening approaches often stop at the Sinclair hut or Corrour bothy respectively.

(1) The north approach is shorter but tricky in the dark. Leave the Cairngorm ski road at the first hairpin bend (NH 985075)—car park on the inside of the bend. From the topside of the bend, follow a path leading down to a bridge. Continue on the path, at first along a ridge, to the Chalamain Gap (NH 965052). After leaving the ridge, the way to the Gap is not obvious—it is best to confirm the correct path by compass bearing. Go through the rocky gap (in soft snow contour the hillside above the gap on the NW side) and descend diagonally into the Lairig Ghru. The Lairig Ghru path is reached close to the Sinclair hut. Follow the Lairig Ghru over its summit, leaving the path to traverse the shoulder of Braeriach to the Garbh Coire bothy. (12 km.)

(2) For a day visit to Coire Bhrochain or Garbh Choire Dhaidh in good weather, one can approach via the summit of Braeriach, climbing Sron na Lairig from the Sinclair hut.

(3) In good weather in summer, a very pleasant approach is to take the Cairngorm chairlift to its top, climb over Cairngorm and the top of

Coire an t-Sneachda and contour the slopes of Cairn Lochan to reach
the broad col between Cairn Lochan and Ben Macdhui. Descend the
left bank (facing downstream) of the March Burn (very steep at the
top) to the Lairig Ghru. The same approach is possible in winter, but
only after careful consideration of weather and snow conditions. The
March Burn descent can be very icy (crampons required) and is very
prone to avalanche (after snowfall and at any time when an easterly
wind has been blowing snow). There have been several accidents
here in the past. (8 km.)

(4) The south approach: starting from the Derry gates, pass Derry
Lodge (see Coire Sputan Dearg) and the Luibeg burn and turn
northwards into Glen Dee. Follow the River Dee until the west branch
leading to the Garbh Coire bothy is taken. A tiny path follows the right
bank (facing upstream) from the fork until approx. 400 m from the
bothy, when it crosses and fades. This approach follows the main
Lairig Ghru path until the last mile—easy walking but 17 km.

COIRE AN LOCHAIN UAINE

The symmetrical hanging corrie between the peaks of Cairntoul and
Sgor an Lochain Uaine (Angel's Peak). Harbouring short mouldering
aretes and uninteresting slabs only, it is of little importance to the
climber in summer. In winter the stream which flows steeply from
Lochan Uaine into the young River Dee near the Garbh Coire bothy
forms great sheets of low angled ice which offer good ice practice or
an interesting approach, II, to the following route.

ANGEL'S PEAK

190 North-East Ridge   300 m   I
The ridge leads from the edge of the corrie to the summit of Angel's
Peak. The most aesthetic approach to Angel's Peak and Cairntoul
from the north end of the Lairig Ghru. More of a scramble than a climb
but the ridge narrows at the top and can be interesting. A fine, easy
scramble in summer.

191 Angel's Delight   400 m   III/IV   (1983)
Climbs a west-facing corner system directly up the large broken face
between the Angel's Peak, North-East Ridge and the Corrie of the
Chokestone Gully. Start about 150 m before the face turns round into

the Corrie of the Chokestone Gully. Gain the corner from the right via a steep little groove (crux, due to thin ice), then follow the corner to a big snow slope (150 m). Cross the snow and continue for another two pitches in corner on upper tier. Scrambling (120 m) leads directly to the summit.

CORRIE OF THE CHOKESTONE GULLY

For some distance west of its North-East Ridge the flanking rocks of Sgor an Lochain Uaine are ill-defined though continuous low down (and contain Angel's Delight, described above). Near the entrance to Garbh Choire Mor they recede upwards to form the headwall of a high corrie or bay. Although arguably part of Garbh Choire Mor, these are traditionally held as distinct and named after an unmistakeable feature—a dark twisting gash cleaving the steepest rocks—the Chokestone Gully. With the exception of the first two pitches of Bugaboo Rib, the rock varies from bad to atrocious.

Winter
Apart from the routes close to the Chokestone Gully, the lines are not well-defined and lack major features. The routes are open to variation, the line frequently depending on the size of a generally large cornice. However, as the cliff faces north, good conditions in most years persist well into April. In late season, the recommended time for a visit, the cliff often has a Nordwand character with mixed ice and rock at a high angle.

Winter Descents
This section of the amphitheatre often has a continuous cornice and finding a descent in misty weather can be difficult (the rope should be kept on until the descent is made). The nearest descent is via the easy-angled spur and shelf which cuts down under the right side of the cliff. The shelf is gained from a small promontory about 300 m west of the top of Chokestone Gully (NN 947976). There is rarely a cornice at this point, though it may be hard to tell from above. Col Gully, on the right of this descent (facing uphill) is more often corniced. The Angel's Peak, North-East Ridge is a longer alternative (no cornice).

192 South-East Couloir 200 m II/III (1970)
This is the shallow rocky couloir in the south-east corner of the corrie. The start is about 50 m left of the Shroud. The first ascent provided six

ice pitches but sometimes it is a snow basin. Finish by a steep prow on the left of a normally huge cornice.

In late season, this whole section of face may be very icy and climbable almost anywhere at the same standard. At least two other lines have been taken between the original and the Shroud.

193   The Shroud   160m   III   (1964)
The route follows the narrow gully parallel and just left of the Chokestone Gully. The foot of the gully proper, which contained three ice pitches on the first ascent, was reached over ice-covered rocks. A good route.

194   Chokestone Gully   150m   III   (1937)
For 60m the gully is straightforward, then it curves, narrows and steepens. Beyond this and above a snow amphitheatre is the great chokestone. Normally this provides a vertical ice pitch, its height depending on the build-up. If ice is lacking it is possible to escape from the gully on the right below the chokestone. The cornice is usually easier on the right.

195   Bugaboo Rib   150m   Very Severe   (1958)
The buttress bounding the right flank of the Chokestone Gully and tapering to a vague ridge above its lower steep section. The first two pitches of this route provide the only good rock in the corrie (4b).

Start between the centre line and the gully and climb easy slabby rocks to a grass platform. A slanting crack on the steep wall ahead leads up right to a prominent block. Climb the crack for 6m, traverse round the block and under an overhang then continue straight up to a large platform (30m). Climb another crack leading right up to a landing place under an overhang (10m), then move round the exposed corner on the right and continue along a tapering shelf to a belay. Above this the ridge falls back and it is an easy scramble to the top.

Winter   V   (1970)

The summer route was followed throughout. Fine technical climbing on snowed-up rock for the first two pitches with a relaxing finish thereafter. The first pitch was considerably banked up but a nut was needed to gain the block. A steep snow–ice ramp led to the second pitch which presented great difficulty (4PA).

The Chimney Start IV

On the right side of Bugaboo Rib is a chimney system leading to the large platform. This is left of a larger depression which could provide a direct start to Sasquatch. The chimney has been climbed (1PA) to finish up the easier upper section of Bugaboo Rib.

196 Sasquatch 120m III (1974)
Right of Chokestone Gully the cliff descends lower into the corrie. Start beyond these lowest rocks at a horizontal ledge traversing left on to the face approx. 50m right of Bugaboo Rib. Use the ledge to gain and climb a shallow icy depression. Either continue direct to the top or trend up leftwards across another depression to finish at the top of Bugaboo Rib. This is often the only reasonable break in a huge cornice.

197 The Wanderer 100m III (1975)
Right of Sasquatch are several left-trending lines which peter out into the easier-angled upper part of the cliff. The most obvious of these is a corner immediately before a compact series of small ribs which terminate the cliff. The Wanderer takes the fault between the first two ribs, starting up a prominent gully with a steep right wall and a narrow rib on the left. With sufficient ice the gully could be climbed direct but on both ascents to date, a deviation left has been made (crux). Continue without difficulty to the cornice.

AN GARBH CHOIRE OF BRAERIACH

The great hollow forming the innermost recesses of the Braeriach Amphitheatre—perhaps the most intriguing corrie in the massif on account of size, remoteness, wildness allied to beauty, and above all climate. Here are found the snowfields of midsummer—our nearest approach in this country to the névé of higher mountains.

A large headland thrusting out from the plateau divides the corrie into two subsidiaries, each of great interest and character. These are Garbh Choire Mor and Garbh Choire Dhaidh; their cliffs are the least known in the massif.

GARBH CHOIRE MOR
The left-hand and larger subsidiary. It has two sections; a lower corrie leading to an upper recessed pocket of buttresses tucked high under the plateau.

Winter Descents

Huge cornices make this descent potentially the most dangerous in the Cairngorms. In very stormy weather it may be impossible to find a break in the cornice and a retreat back down the route of ascent may be the safest alternative (two abseils will be sufficient for many routes). The cornice edge is generally invisible in misty weather and with an overhang of up to 10 m, it is easy to find oneself treading air (it is worthwhile keeping the rope on). At least one person has involuntarily descended the cliff inside a falling cornice (uninjured!)

The spur and shelf just beyond Col Gully and immediately right of the Corrie of the Chokestone Gully is one choice (NN 947976, see page 141). The alternative is the headland between Garbh Choire Mor and Garbh Choire Dhaidh. At peak conditions both alternatives can be corniced but, dependent on previous wind directions etc., at least one of them should be feasible. In an emergency, an easy descent can be made southwards away from the cliffs to the head of Glen Geusachan, but this will be very arduous indeed. In any case, a descent plan should be made before embarking on a route and certainly before emerging on to the plateau where any shelter will be lost.

THE LOWER CORRIE

The rocks here are somewhat indefinite. There are three named features: Col Gully, the prominent scree rake going up to the Cairntoul—Braeriach Col (c. 1125 m); West Buttress on the immediate right of the gully; and West Gully, a long chute separating West Buttress from the buttresses of the upper corrie.

In winter much is wiped out but the gullies give fair grade I climbs, though usually well corniced. Col Gully, is short and open. West Gully, longer, steeper and often heavily corniced, is the better climb. West Buttress gives a pleasant scramble at grade I/II.

THE UPPER CORRIE

An obscure recessed corrie, yet enjoying a considerable reputation largely due to its unique snow formations. The cliff has the classic buttress–gully formation; the buttresses are mainly narrow and compact. It bears a patina of lichen which apparently thrives on granite covered for long periods by snow and is responsible for the greenish hue of the buttresses which is most pronounced when seen in contrast with the snowfield and gullies. Although the rock is sound, extensive shattering occurs in places near the plateau.

Due primarily to its location, the upper corrie is unique in Britain for its annual accumulation of snow and as the site of our most permanent snow beds; in this century these have only disappeared in 1933, 1955, 1959 and 1969. At peak conditions narrow gullies are transformed into open snow slopes and many rock features are wiped out. The main buttresses, due to the build-up at their bases (up to 30 m in a heavy year) are greatly diminished in height. For these reasons, identification will be difficult in thick weather.

The cornice, often without a flaw, reaches giant proportions (over 10 m in height on one long section) and provides otherwise easy climbs with problematic finishes. Climbers should be aware of possible failure at the cornice and choose their route appropriately. The cornice may still be unbroken in June. Another interesting feature is the formation (particularly on the north wall of the corrie) of ice grottoes and tunnels below the plateau after a cornice has fallen. These have provided the key to at least two of the first ascents!

198 Crown Buttress   120 m   III

The large mass separating the lower from the upper corrie is Crown Buttress. Its left flank is broken by a broad scree–grass terrace above and below which are steep walls. On its right flank (in the upper corrie proper) it forms a continuous arete from which vertical walls dip into Great Gully. The Crown—a flake of rock—can be seen against the sky at the top of the arete. Near the top of the buttress, a second arete appears just to the left and the great V-groove between the aretes is the line of the climb.

Climb the edge overlooking Great Gully to a large block. Continue up steps to the base of the great V-groove. The groove is an icy chimney which provides an excellent steep pitch (35 m, crux). Very Difficult in summer.

On the right of Crown Buttress is Great Gully, Easy, I. It is the most defined gully in the corrie. In winter it is straightforward but steep and heavily corniced.

She-Devil's Buttress is the broad buttress forming the right wall of Great Gully. On its front face are twin corners; the left one is taken by the winter line of She-Devil's Buttress and the longer right one is Vulcan. On its right side, right of Vulcan, is an impressive face with a line of overhangs just above mid-height. Tiara follows grooves on the right edge of the buttress and cuts in leftwards immediately above the overhangs into a steep crack (Diagram p. 146.)

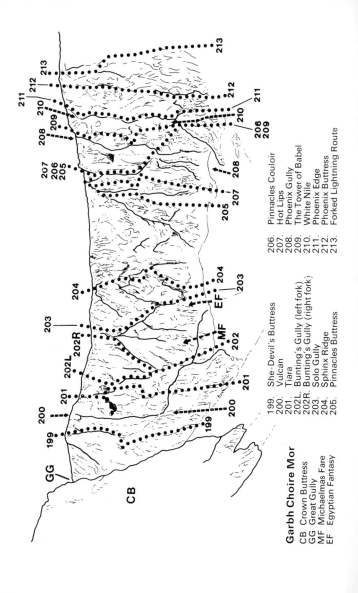

Garbh Choire Mor

CB Crown Buttress
GG Great Gully
MF Michaelmas Fare
EF Egyptian Fantasy

199. She-Devil's Buttress
200. Vulcan
201. Tiara
202L. Bunting's Gully (left fork)
202R. Bunting's Gully (right fork)
203. Solo Gully
204. Sphinx Ridge
205. Pinnacles Buttress

206. Pinnacles Couloir
207. Hot Lips
208. Phoenix Gully
209. The Tower of Babel
210. White Nile
211. Phoenix Edge
212. Phoenix Buttress
213. Forked Lightning Route

199 She-Devil's Buttress 120 m IV (1969)

A good climb. Sixty metres of iced grooves and snow aretes on the edge overlooking Great Gully led to a right traverse over a flake to enter awkwardly the leftmost of the twin corners. This gave 60 m of steep sustained ice climbing to a snow prow breaching the cornice on the left at the top of the buttress. Very difficult in summer, by a line on the Great Gully side of the buttress. (Diagram p. 146.)

200 Vulcan 90 m Very Severe (1968)

The route takes the line of a very prominent V-corner, the rightmost of the twin corners on the front face of She-Devil's Buttress. Start in the bay right of the lowest rocks of She-Devil's Buttress below the groove. Scramble up to a grassy recess and gain the bottom of the groove. Follow the groove all the way (three pitches, 4c). A little dirty in places. (Diagram p. 146.)

Winter IV (1975)

The prominent V-groove forms a series of ice pitches, the lower section being the crux. A first-rate route.

201 Tiara 80 m V (1984)

A sustained climb in icy grooves and cracks. Very hard on the only ascent to date due to thin ice and deep unconsolidated snow. Just left of the crest beside Bunting's Gully is a long groove with an overhang at mid height.

Start up this groove and traverse 5 m right about 6 m below the overhang. Go up and slightly left to gain a smaller groove which starts at the right end of the overhang. Follow this over a steepening to the crest. If protection cannot be found below the steepening, then one can go out right by a short groove and take a belay on the crest, returning to the steepening as an extra short pitch. Above the steepening, go up 5 m to a vertical wall and belay. Descend 3 m to the left and step delicately on to the upper slab in a very exposed position above the main overhangs. Climb a crack near the arete, then a groove a little left. Follow this to the crest, often a very sharp snow arete forming a break in the cornice (Vulcan-winter also finishes here).

Very Severe in summer; unrepeated after 25 years but perhaps a good climb. (Diagram p. 146.)

202   Bunting's Gully: Left Branch (Bunting's Gully Wall)
100m   III   (1964)

Right Branch (Snow Bunting)

100m   II   (1966)

The first shallow gully to the right of Great Gully. On its right are vague twin ridges separated low down by a system of shallow recessed corners but meeting some 30m below the plateau at a col common to both.

The lower gully is easy up to a fork at less than mid-height. The left fork runs up to an overhang. Go on to the right gully wall about 15m below the overhang, work up and rightwards till near the crest on the right, then traverse left to reach an upper corner which leads to the cornice. The right branch runs up to the col of the twin ridges and a finish common to these. A shallow gully leads up to a giant cornice. On the first ascent a huge flake of snow had split off from the cornice proper and the resulting chimney was used to gain the plateau.

The cornice above the Bunting's Gully area is at its largest and usually impossible. Both branches are Moderate with poor rock in summer. (Diagram p. 146.)

The twin ridges to the right of Bunting's Gully are Michelmas Fare on the left and the better defined Egyptian Fantasy on the right. Both are Very Difficult. The recess between the ridges is Gaunt Gully, II/III. At peak snow conditions this section of cliff largely banks out and the routes lose their identity. Michelmas Fare is III, directly following the crest overlooking Gaunt Gully. Egyptian Fantasy has also been climbed at a similar standard although on this occasion, retreat was made from an impossible cornice. (Diagram p. 146.)

203   Solo Gully   100m   I

This gully, narrow at the bottom, is defined low down by Egyptian Fantasy on its left. For much of the winter the route is ludicrous, a straightforward snow slope leading to a massive impassable cornice. It does, however, provide a convenient descent for parties failing at nearby cornices. The first ascent was early in the season, probably the best time for the route. It is easy to traverse under the cornice on to Sphinx Ridge. (Diagram p. 146.)

204   Sphinx Ridge   100m   Very Difficult

Situated at the innermost point of the corrie above the snowfield, Sphinx Ridge rises rather shapely between Solo Gully on its left and, according to the time of visit, either a wide section of slab or a great rock-fringed snow recess on its right. A classic route, but vegetated above the first pitch and melting snow may leave the rock grimy in early summer.

The frontal face is a nearly vertical triangle, on its left side is a slab which is defined on its left by a corner with overlaps. Start just right of the corner and climb the slab rightwards to gain the crest. Go either up left or right on the wall above the gully to a stance below the Sphinx (35 m). Climb the corner on the left of the Sphinx and continue over a narrow ridge and col (25 m). Climb a short wall to reach a recessed corner, go up its right side till above the overlap and traverse left to a platform (crux). Go up the ridge above to the top of the pinnacle (30 m). Descend to the col and scramble to the top (15 m). A direct start up the fine initial wall is Severe. (Diagram p. 146.)

Winter II/III (1966)

A very scenic route, forming a sinuous snow crest in winter. Once the crest of the ridge has been gained, either direct or by a small gully leading off Solo Gully, the crest is followed with one detour to the left. A superb double-corniced arete leads to the main cornice.

To the right of Sphinx Ridge is a broad recess of indeterminate slabs and grass between it and Pinnacles Buttress. On each side of the recess are shallow gullies; the one under Sphinx Ridge is Sphinx Gully, II, the one next to Pinnacles Buttress is Pinnacle Gully, I. Both have been climbed in summer, as has a line between them, starting near Pinnacle Gully.

To the right of the recess is a close-set trio of steep buttresses separated by chimneys. The leftmost is Pinnacles Buttress, formed almost entirely of two pinnacles, the higher and smaller of which rises above a narrow col and stands out against the sky even when viewed from a distance. The lower pinnacle is very prominent from close below and has a crack-seamed north face with a line of overhangs.

205 Pinnacles Buttress 110m III (1968)
Start just left of centre of the buttress via a cracked slab left of the steep north face (may partially bank out) to blocks overlooking and near Pinnacle Gully. Climb a crack in a narrower slab above and up over further blocks. At their top (easy into gully here) climb a short wall on the right to a broad ledge and follow this rightwards to its end at the top of the north face, from where the summit of the lower

pinnacle is soon reached. From here a fine double corniced snow crest led to the col and the plateau was gained from the second pinnacle by a steep snow arete. Difficult in summer. (Diagram p. 146.)

206 Pinnacles Couloir 120 m III (1971)
This is the obvious couloir leading to the col on Pinnacles Buttress. A leftward rising traverse from below the Tower of Babel led across Phoenix Gully to the foot of the couloir. (Diagram p. 146.)

207 Hot Lips 130 m Very Severe (1973)
On the north (right, Phoenix Gully) side of Pinnacles Buttress is an intriguing crack-seamed face containing a band of roofs below which a ramp leads left to top right to finish in Pinnacles Couloir. Climb the ramp to large ledges near its end (40 m). Traverse down and left, then up cracks to an overhang 3 m right of an open groove. Traverse left into the bottom of the groove, climb it and go left to a good ledge on the left arete (airy moves). Go right up a slab to belay near a large, loose block (35 m, 5a). Move left up slabs to belay at the top of the Pinnacle (25 m). Continue to the plateau via the second pinnacle (loose, 30 m). (Diagram p. 146.)

208 Phoenix Gully 100 m IV (1967)
A classic climb amidst fine surroundings. This is the steep icy gully between Pinnacles Buttress and the Tower of Babel. The cornice may be problematic, as described after the first ascent, "The huge cornice, 40 ft up, 20 ft out, dominated the route . . . to the base of the cornice. Here a crescent shaped slit led into a beautiful 15 ft high ice cavern inside the cornice. From this an exposed traverse led out left to a gap behind a detached snow flake and so to the top." Very Difficult in summer. (Diagram p. 146.)

209 The Tower of Babel 120 m Hard Very Severe (1969)
This is the central compact buttress of the Pinnacles trio. It consists of a small overhanging south-west face overlooking Phoenix Gully on the left and a large south-east face containing the route, which is perhaps the best in the corrie and low in its grade.

Start just right of the lowest rocks and at the bottom of a shallow gully descending diagonally from the top of the first pitch in Phoenix Gully. (This is Pinnacles Couloir in winter). Climb easy rocks, then pull up rightwards on to a steep wall. After 5 m, climb a crack on the left and traverse left to a good belay on the edge of the buttress

(20 m). Climb a good crack, move over an overlap using footholds on the left edge of the buttress, follow a fine slab a short way, then work rightwards to a crack. Up this and a steep corner to a stance below a short overhanging crack (30 m, 5a). Climb this crack, then easier up a natural line of cracks. After 15 m the buttress becomes more broken on the right but is still continuous on the left. Follow a diagonal crack left to a perch on the crest below the final short rise of the buttress (25 m). After 5 m take a ledge on the left and so to the top; or, a little below this ledge traverse right and pull on to a slab which gives a few thin moves. (Diagram p. 146.)

210 White Nile 120 m IV (1977)

A continuous run of very steep ice between the Tower of Babel and the rightmost buttress, Phoenix Buttress. The route taken is obvious apart from a slight detour at two-thirds height, where one of the many ice walls encountered can be avoided by a groove running diagonally left to an overlap, above which an iced slab allowed a traverse back right. Possibly the best ice climb on the cliff. (Diagram p. 146.)

211 Phoenix Edge 120 m Very Severe (1979)

Phoenix Buttress is the right-hand of the Pinnacles trio. It has a narrow, leaning left wall overlooking White Nile. The route follows the defined crest between this leaning wall and easier ground on the right. Reasonable climbing but a little artificial.

Start about 30 m up from the lowest rock where the true crest starts. The normal buttress route (Very Difficult, not described) also starts here. Climb a corner and continue up slabs and grooves close to the edge to reach a large platform (45 m, 4b). Climb a slabby wall immediately left of a perched block. Continue up leftwards until a short groove leads to a belay above piled blocks (20 m, 4b). Climb a corner and slabs to easy ground. (Diagram p. 146.)

212 Phoenix Buttress 150 m III (1971)

In summer the buttress is a good line but vegetated, Very Difficult; hence it gives an excellent winter buttress route. Starting at the base of the defined crest of the buttress, work up and rightwards via vegetated grooves for 50 m to a steep nose. Traverse left round this and climb the groove above on to piled blocks beneath a steep wall. Step right and up a short steep corner on to a large slab. Move up right into a groove which is followed to the plateau. (Diagram p. 146.)

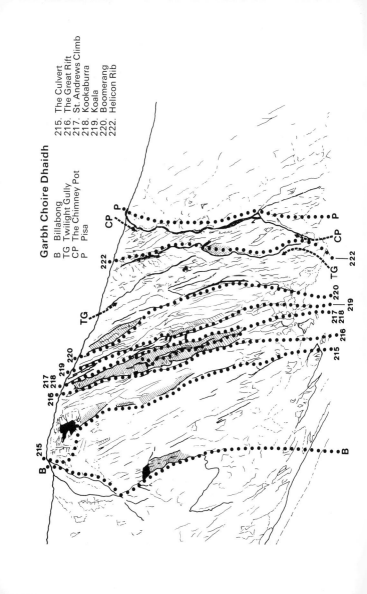

Garbh Choire Dhaidh

B   Billabong
TG   Twilight Gully
CP   The Chimney Pot
P   Pisa

215. The Culvert
216. The Great Rift
217. St. Andrews Climb
218. Kookaburra
219. Koala
220. Boomerang
222. Helicon Rib

213   Forked Lightning Route   100 m   III   (1974)

On the right side of Phoenix Buttress, at the head of a large snow bay, are two ice lines linked by a horizontal traverse along snow. These form a forked lightning shape seen from the hut. (Diagram p. 146.)

GARBH CHOIRE DHAIDH

Garbh Choire Dhaidh (pronounced Yay rhyming with "say") is the right-hand subsidiary of An Garbh Choire. Its cliffs are higher than those of Garbh Choire Mor but it is more slabby in nature. What it lacks in the steep formation of buttress and gully, however, is more than offset by the clean rock and picturesque situation. It is open-walled, south-east facing and sun-catching; and from the plateau rim the young River Dee falls 200 m from its source to the corrie floor where after running a subterranean course among huge boulders it reappears flowing over a charming turf meadow on which it widens into attractive pools.

To the left of the Dee Cascade the corrie wall is continuously steep but vegetated and the rocks lack mass and character. In winter this is often transformed into an open snow slope topped by a huge unbroken cornice.

214   Dee Waterfall   (1810)

This early scramble was probably made up the right side of the cascade over grassy slopes and rock outcrops. In winter it gives a pleasant route to the plateau when ice is present (grade II).

The Main Face

The left side of the face is a high-angled wall of polished, exfoliated slabs which angle into an impressive corner-chimney in the centre—The Great Rift. The Great Rift is not prominent from the normal approach by the right side of the corrie but it is well seen from further left. Unfortunately these slabs are usually streaming with water and the rock should be treated with suspicion as the only two routes here have suffered major rockfall.

The right side between The Rift and The Chimney Pot, a deep gully sunk in an angle formed by a detached buttress on the extreme right (Pisa), is divided into ribs and grooves and gives three fine routes, which offer perhaps the best rock climbing on Braeriach.

In winter the cliff is rarely visited, as its south-facing aspect makes conditions unreliable. Early in the season, the twin icefalls of the Culvert and Great Rift give fine climbs. Later on, the sun plays havoc with the ice and the face may be totally bare after mid-February. The easier routes, however, may still be in condition but cloudy weather is recommended.

Winter Descent
Easier than Garbh Choire Mor. The slope between this corrie and Coire Bhrochain is of moderate angle and rarely has a cornice. Care must be taken to bypass the cornice, which extends well to the right of the cliff.

On the extreme left of the main face is a recent rockfall scar, previously the crux dièdre of Billabong, Hard Severe, III. The route has not been climbed since and looks dangerous. In winter it forms a good, short icefall.

215   The Culvert   125 m   Severe   (1955)
Follows a stepped ramp system left of the Rift. Usually streaming with water but looks good for dry weather. A rockfall in 1957 swept away one of the original features and as the route does not seem to have been climbed since, a cautious approach is advisable.

Start 8 m to the left of the Rift and follow slabs for 10 m to a small platform. Go up the ensuing groove followed by a grassy crack and a short wall to belay (20 m). Climb a groove for 3 m, then traverse right to a ledge, thence up a delicate mantleshelf followed by walls to a ledge (20 m). Move right (past rockfall debris?), then trend slightly left to a waterworn slab (20 m). Go up the slab on small holds and climb a shallow chimney (30 m). Above this go up the wall directly under a large overhang and up the slab going left. Moderate rock leads to the top (35 m). (Diagram p. 152.)

Winter   IV   (1981)

It forms a fine parallel icefall with the Great Rift, probably coming into condition before the Rift at the start of winter. It gives four pitches on steep water ice reminiscent of the best on Hell's Lum Crag.

216   The Great Rift   140 m   Very Difficult   (1954)
The striking corner-chimney in the centre of the face. When reasonably dry it gives one of the best chimney climbs in the massif. The initial smooth pitch is avoided by a start on the right of the waterslide.

Climb two consecutive clean ribs (45 m) to a prominent inset corner which leads leftwards into the Rift itself below a cave. Leave the cave directly or by the slab on the left and enter another and bigger cave with a great overhanging roof. Climb the slabs on the left then return right and overcome the roof by a short steep wall (crux). The Rift now opens and becomes easier, but with short interesting pitches. (Diagram p. 152.)

Winter   IV   (1965)

Sustained and very icy. An excellent climb, recommended early in the season while the sun is still weak.

217 St. Andrews Climb   125 m   (1957)

The first of three very fine, quick-drying climbs on the ridge bounding the Great Rift on the right. It follows a corner system on the wall immediately right of the Rift.

Scramble up the green lower rocks to below a spindle-shaped rock mass. Climb the corner on the right of this feature and at its top step right and go up to a stance (30 m). Climb the right-hand corner until the main corner can be regained and followed to a fine platform (30 m). Above is a corner with an overhang; climb the wall just on its right (5 m, crux). Go up the edge (25 m). Above is a steep, slabby wall which tops this section of cliff. Finish up its left edge, then scramble to the top (35 m). (Diagram p. 152.)

218 Kookaburra   130 m   Hard Severe   (1963)

Follows the prominent arete on the immediate right of St. Andrews Climb. It includes a superb, improbable pitch up the very crest overlooking St. Andrews Climb and the Rift.

Climb awkward slabby rocks to reach the base of the arete. When these are wet, start up St. Andrews Climb and traverse right to gain the arete. Follow the arete as closely as possible (exposed) to reach a ledge system. Finish up the left edge of the slabby walls above, as for St. Andrews Climb. (Diagram p. 152.)

219 Koala   130 m   Very Severe   (1967)

Ten metres to the right of the arete of Kookaburra is a corner system ending in overhangs. Climb to the base of the corner and follow it in two excellent pitches to break right through a nest of overhangs (4c) on to more broken ground. Above this, finish up the centre of the steep, slabby wall above. (Diagram p. 152.)

To the right of Koala is a prominent V-chimney/groove, the line of Kangaroo, Severe, vegetated.

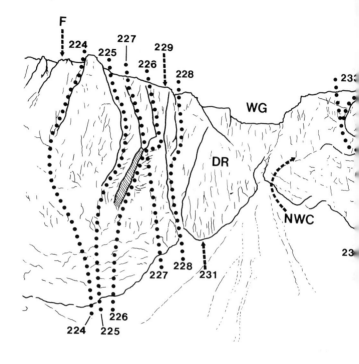

Coire Bhrochain

F	The Fang
DR	Domed Ridge
WG	West Gully
NWC	North-West Chimney
BP	Black Pinnacle
Br. P	Braeriach Pinnacle
ST	Slab Terrace
EG	East Gully
NEB	Near-East Buttress
BR	Babylon Rib
L	The Lion
TC	Tigris Chimney
P	Pyramus

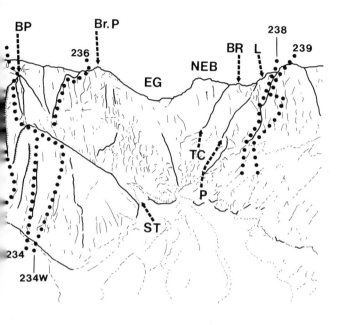

220   Boomerang   150m   III/IV   (1962)
A prominent rib low down bounds Chimney Pot on the left. This is
Helicon Rib. On the left of the open gully (Twilight Gully) which parts
Helicon Rib from the main cliff is a small arete. Boomerang starts in
the groove behind this, curves left and sometimes contains ice. Details
of the exact winter line are scant but it gave three long ice pitches.
Very Difficult and vegetated in summer. (Diagram p. 152.)

221   Twilight Gully   150m   II   (1971)
The open, bow-shaped gully just left of Helicon Rib. Frequently a
snow chute capped by a huge cornice but on this occasion a long
runnel of snow and water ice.

222   Helicon Rib   130m   Difficult   (1949)
The prominent rib forming the left wall of the Chimney Pot. The lower
section forms a narrow crest of good rock. Above this and beyond a
sneck the rock deteriorates and becomes very shattered. (Diagram p.
152.)

Winter   III   (1964)

Follow the summer route.

223   The Chimney Pot   140m   II   (1959)
This chimney-gully should not be mistaken for the Great Rift. It is hidden from most viewpoints by the rocks of Pisa. There is usually one ice
pitch at a great chokestone. Difficult in summer, mostly scree, but has
a very wet through route under the great chokestone. (Diagram p. 152.)

The long buttress on the right of the Chimney Pot is Pisa, Difficult,
II. It is scrappy in both seasons but provides an entertaining summer
descent route from the good climbs around the Rift. Descend Pisa to a
prominent block just above the level of the sneck of Helicon Rib
(cairn). Traverse unlikely ledges into the Chimney Pot and descend
the crest of Helicon Rib (Difficult).

COIRE BHROCHAIN

Coire Bhrochain, on whose cliff edge the summit cairn of Braeriach
stands, is one of the finest in the Cairngorms for cliff height, scenery
and pure corrie form. The cliffs face south providing pleasurable
routes on rough and clean granite. The corrie is, however, very remote

and not in the modern idiom; the routes are natural mountaineering lines in the lower grades and neglected nowadays, even the magnificent West Wall Route (Mild Severe).

In winter the features of the Black and Braeriach Pinnacles lend beauty and grandeur to the corrie but the cliff lacks the classic ice lines and again is rarely visited. In thick weather in winter, the best descent is the slope between this corrie and Garbh Choire Dhaidh (very rarely corniced).

The cliff is divided by two pronounced breaks into three broad masses called West, Central and East Buttresses. On the left is West Buttress separated from Central by West Gully, a broad scree shoot fanning out widely at its base. Central Buttress is cut off from East Buttress by East Gully, narrow for most of its height but funnelling out at the plateau.

WEST BUTTRESS

The main mass above its easy lower rocks is built up of parallel ribs with intervening slabby corners opening out into funnels of poor quality rock. The most striking feature is a great square summit tower at the top left of the face and to the right of an open chimney. There are two smaller buttresses high up and further left. Two obvious ramps slope up rightwards in the lower half of the buttress. These provide the starts to Direct Route and Vanishing Shelf. On the right of the main mass and separated from it by the Great Couloir is Domed Ridge which flanks Lower West Gully. Branching from West Gully and striking up behind Domed Ridge to the plateau is Campion Gully. Between Campion and upper West Gully is Azalea Rib, a smaller subsidiary of Domed Ridge.

224 Pioneers' Recess Route   200m   II/III   (1969)

A route going up the open chimney and recess on the left of the main mass between the square tower and a detached buttress next left which tapers to a spectacular hooked fang, The Fang, Very Difficult. Iced slabs and steep open snow slopes lead to the foot of the chimney which contains ice. Exit steeply on the left from the recess above. Moderate in summer. (Diagram p. 156.)

225 Direct Route   200m   III/IV   (1968)

A fine route, following the most prominent of the grooves on the main mass somewhat right of centre. Start up the left-hand of the two obvious ramps, the right-hand being Vanishing Shelf. Follow the ramp up rightwards to a short chimney. Much variation is possible in the middle and upper sections. The climb was finished by the rightmost of twin chimneys on the right flank of the Tower and then by the rib on its right. The summer route approximates to this line (Severe). (Diagram p. 156.)

226 Vanishing Shelf   200m   III   (1959)
The next prominent shelf and a counterpart to Direct Route. The shelf ends at a high balcony overlooking the pitch in the Great Couloir. Follow the shelf to the balcony at its far end. Go out left on a ledge and make a long upwards traverse to the left to reach a scoop which leads to a huge cornice. Difficult in summer. (Diagram p. 156.)

227 Western Couloir   200m   III   (1970)
The shallow couloir between the upper couloir of Vanishing Shelf and Direct Route. Climb the lower slabs directly, crossing Vanishing Shelf, and follow the couloir to a possibly gigantic cornice. (Diagram p. 156.)

228 The Great Couloir   200m   II/III   (1957)
The long defined gully separating the main mass from Domed Ridge. Above mid-height it bends rightwards round a subsidiary rib on the main mass. Straight ahead in the angle between the rib and the left wall is a prominent deep chimney forming a left branch (Ebony Chimney).

The Great Couloir is named for its character in winter when it forms a most beautiful chute, steep in its upper part and heavily corniced, but generally without pitches in mid-season. Before this the big chokestone may not be built over and may present a hard ice pitch. Very Difficult in summer. (Diagram p. 156.)

229 Ebony Chimney   80m   Severe   (1967)
An entertaining climb in dry weather, well worth groping through the initial 5 m of overhanging slime. Surmount the first big chokestone and continue up the fine chimney above until way is blocked by another enormous chokestone, passed by traversing out right. Above, enter a magnificent through route, emerging higher up beneath great roofs. Go rightwards along a ledge and climb a wall and corner to a stance and belay on the rib on the right. Make a move up the crest, then go right into a steep groove overlooking the Great Couloir and follow this groove to easier ground. (Diagram p. 156.)

Winter V (1982)

One of the best short climbs in the Cairngorms. Very steep and sustained, yet full of variety. Follow the summer route throughout; the through route does not fill up although a little excavation may be required to gain the entrance. The chimney is normally very icy and may be poorly protected.

230 Ivory Tower 65 m Hard Very Severe (1984)
The rib between Ebony Chimney and The Great Couloir. Its base is guarded by a girdling overhang which has thwarted a direct ascent. From a belay on the right of The Great Couloir climb rocks on the right to gain the top of a large chokestone (as for the Couloir). Traverse left on to the wall to a point below a prominent bulging crack. Climb this and another crack which leads up to ledges on the crest (30 m, 5b). Move round right and traverse horizontally right to gain and climb a corner to pale rocks. Continue until possible to move back left across the wall and up to gain the crest once more (20 m, 4c). Ebony Chimney crosses the rib at this point. Climb directly up the wall on the crest to a platform (15 m, 5a). Easy rocks to top.

231 Domed Ridge 200 m II/III (1955)
The broad ridge between The Great Couloir and West Gully.
    A tower at mid height is the crux (easier on the right). After a crest, avoid the final dome on the right. Moderate in summer. (Diagram p. 156.)

    Striking up behind Domed Ridge to the plateau and a left branch of West Gully is Campion Gully, Difficult, II. The ridge between it and the main West Gully is Azalea Rib, Difficult.

232 West Gully 150 m I
Forms a wide snow corridor, steeper at the top and ringed by a big cornice usually complete. A good descent route if the cornice can be passed. Moderate in summer, steep earth and rubble at the top.

CENTRAL BUTTRESS
It has a much more diversified structure than West Buttress, having several distinctive features. Centrally placed and cut off from the mountain on all sides is the Black Pinnacle, a well-known feature, being so visible from the plateau. On the left of Black Pinnacle and almost extending to West Gully is a great recessed area of slabby

ground—the Bhrochain Slabs. On the right of Black Pinnacle and extending to East Gully is the Braeriach Pinnacle, in reality a big individualistic buttress whose top is almost level with the plateau. The Slab Terrace, containing a large, low-angled slab leading to an easy grassy gangway, leads from the foot of the Braeriach Pinnacle up leftwards to the start of the routes on the Black Pinnacle and to Central Buttress Gully. The latter is a broad hidden chute striking up the left side of Braeriach Pinnacle.

233   Bhrochain Slabs   200 m   Very Difficult   (1944)
Pleasant climbing, a little scrappy. On the left of the Black Pinnacle and from the rocks directly below it a continuous sheer wall drops to Bhrochain Slabs forming a vast corner, the line of the climb. The route is open to variation at the same standard; the description should not be taken literally if clean rock is obvious nearby. The climb starts about 50 m up and to the left of the lowest rocks of Central Buttress. This is about 20 m left of the original start, which is a shallow groove.

Go straight up for about 20 m, then trend right over small rock ledges, cracks and walls to a steep slab near the main corner split by several cracks (40 m). Climb the rightmost crack, which slopes to the right, to reach a small platform (25 m). Climb a smooth, easy-angled slab to a large grass platform up on the left. Climb another slab using the right-hand of twin cracks set close together to reach another platform (at this point North-West Chimney crosses. It runs up to the saddle of the Black Pinnacle—Moderate.) Go up the rocks ahead until forced to make a short descent and traverse left along an exposed slab. A rib on the slab partially blocks the way. Climb this to an excellent pulpit stance. Continue along the slab till it ends, and turn a corner into the upper section of the climb. Either follow a shallow groove then the rocks on its right (easy) or (direct finish) climb straight up the huge slab on the left of the shallow groove to a small curving corner near the groove. Climb round the edge of this and go straight up to the plateau. (Diagram p. 156.)

Winter   II/III   (1960)

The route tends to bank out, particularly in late season, but follows a good line.

234   Braeriach Direct   250 m   Severe   (1956)
A direct course from the lowest rocks to the Black Pinnacle and the plateau, which is reached a short distance east of Braeriach summit. A

mountaineering route offering good situations, not quality climbing. The line is open to variation; keep to clean rock. From a frontal view the vertical left wall of the Black Pinnacle stands out from the cliff like the gnomon of a gigantic sundial—the dial plate being a great 80 m slab isolated by sheer walls plunging to Bhrochain Slabs. The route approximates to this crest above Bhrochain Slabs.

Start just left of the lowest rocks and climb easy pink slabs to a long grass ledge. Go to its left end (30 m). From here climb steeper, slabby ground between a recessed groove (often wet) and the crest on the left. Some small overhangs are turned on the right leading to a block-platform on the crest overlooking Bhrochain Slabs (30 m). The way above is smooth so move down and round a little crest on the right. Climb the awkward wall immediately above (crux), then continue up slabs and blocks to the Slab Terrace (30 m). From the Slab Terrace immediately below the sharp edge of the Black Pinnacle, traverse easily left on to the Sundial Slab. Start in the corner, then move on to the left edge until a short thrutch leads to the platform behind the Pinnacle. Climb the summit from here and return back to the Pinnacle neck. Continue to the plateau by the smooth slab ahead using a fault leading right. (Diagram p. 156.)

From the neck, one can scramble down Central Buttress Gully on the right to the start of West Wall Route.

Winter   III   (1983)

The scenery is even better in winter. The lower tier up to the Slab Terrace was climbed by a fine icefall (90 m) about 25 m right of the summer line. The slab corner (as for summer) was spectacular but straightforward in good conditions. (Diagram p. 156.)

235   The Black Pinnacle   150 m   Moderate   II
The ordinary route to the Pinnacle is recommended as an expedition, going by the Slab Terrace which slopes up left below the rocks of Braeriach Pinnacle. It ends in scree below the easy first pitch of Central Buttress Gully which stands between Black Pinnacle on the left and Braeriach Pinnacle on the right. This pitch leads to an amphitheatre where the gully forks. The true gully runs up behind Braeriach Pinnacle. The more open left branch leads to the neck of the Black Pinnacle. A short easy chimney leads to the serrated crest and the outer tooth of the Pinnacle. (Diagram p. 156.)

In winter the ordinary route via Central Buttress Gully Left Branch can be followed to the neck or (as on the first ascent) the slabs on the left of the gully followed by a leftward traverse to a point between the hillward prongs of the Pinnacle. The pinnacle summit from the neck and back is grade II. Snow leads to the cornice, often large. This slope lies on a foundation of slab and is prone to avalanche.

There are two alternative summer routes from the Slab Terrace to the Pinnacle summit, Slab Route (Moderate, the line of the first winter ascent of the Pinnacle) and Direct Route, Difficult, which follows a corner just right of roof tile overhangs and cuts back left to the crest (the best rock of the three possibilities).

The true (right) branch of Central Buttress Gully gives an interesting winter climb through grand scenery, I. In summer it is Moderate but the better summer line (neither is good) is Central Chimney, Moderate, which cleaves the amphitheatre wall between the left and true branches.

Braeriach Pinnacle

The biggest feature of Central Buttress, lying between Central Buttress Gully and East Gully and above the Slab Terrace. Its time-honoured name is rather misleading, for, only from the plateau does it show any trace of pinnacle form. In reality it is a broad-based buttress whose rocks slope up from right to left ending in a ridge formed by an undercut wall overhanging upper Central Buttress Gully. This ridge is the superb West Wall Route.

Variations can and have been made at random on the frontal face and all have tended to be of similar character. The old established routes are Original Route on the left (Difficult; The Lampie, IV, is a direct winter version), South Face, Difficult, III, in the centre and Eastern Route, Moderate, II, on the edge of East Gully.

236   West Wall Route   100 m   Mild Severe (1942)

One of the best routes at its grade in the Cairngorms. Excellent rock, steep and exposed. Start just above the pitch in Central Buttress Gully and traverse to the right to a small platform on the edge of the Pinnacle. Climb on the right of the edge to gain a second platform, smaller and 15 m above the first. Continue directly up the arete or the steep wall just to the right (20 m). Follow a quartz vein straight up the exposed edge overlooking the Gully until it is possible to traverse right into a groove which leads back to the crest at a broad platform. The angle now eases and it is a pleasant scramble along an airy ridge to the top of the Pinnacle. (Diagram p. 156.)

237   East Gully   150 m   I   (1901)
A straight-cut chute, narrow with no pitches. The wide upper funnel is usually well corniced but with an easy exit on the right. A possible descent route in good conditions. Moderate in summer.

EAST BUTTRESS
This is composed of four small, more individualistic buttresses set side by side and divided by three gullies. The rock is rough but in many places very loose and none of the routes is recommended in summer.

Bordering East Gully is Near East Buttress, Moderate, II, and on its right Tigris Chimney, II, a chimney which opens out into a shallow snow scoop. To the right of Tigris Chimney is Babylon Rib, Moderate, II, a ridge in two parts, a narrow wedge-shaped lower section and above a large platform, a narrow arete to the plateau. The next gully is Pyramus, Moderate, I; a pointed rib at the foot furnishes the gully with two branches which join 60 m up. On its right is The Lion, Difficult, II, an attractive ridge with steep walls falling into Thisbe on the right.

238   Thisbe   110 m   III   (1955)
Though short, a fine gully climb, well-defined by high walls and with four varied ice pitches early in the season. Later on, some of the pitches may bank out. Good in summer also as a gully climb, Difficult. (Diagram p. 156.)

The steep buttress on the extreme right of the corrie, forming the right wall of Thisbe, is Ninus, Difficult. Two routes, meeting at less than mid height, have been made. The winter Ninus started on the left at the foot of Thisbe.

239   Ninus   150 m   III   (1970)
A good buttress climb. Start at the foot of Thisbe and climb up right to gain an obvious snow ramp. Continue right into a depression and follow this to a snow basin. Traverse left and climb the rib in two pitches to the plateau. (Diagram p. 156.)

BRAERIACH: COIRE AN LOCHAIN (NH 9400)

This is the rightmost of the triune of corries which gives Braeriach its fine character as seen from Speyside. It is the most interesting scenically of the three and the only one having rock for climbing. The loch from which it derives its name is the finest specimen of mountain tarn in the Cairngorms and the largest sheet of water at such an elevation (998 m) in the country. The loch is girt by slabs but the only defined climb is on the right side where a pinnacled ridge rises on the right of a narrow gully. This is Derelict Ridge, Difficult, III, keeping to the steep, acute edge overlooking the gully. The gully itself is Grade I, short but well-defined.

Coire Ruadh, the central of the three corries, gives fair snow climbing and the narrow ridges bounding it on either side are interesting winter routes to the plateau, that on the left forming the boundary with Coire Beanaidh and leading direct to the summit of Braeriach being the best.

GLEANN EINICH: The Buttresses of Sgoran Dubh Mor and Sgor Gaoith

On the western slopes of Gleann Einich, the peaks Sgoran Dubh Mor and Sgor Gaoith throw down five great buttresses along a 3 km stretch of the glen and shore of Loch Einich. Each buttress is roughly triangular and cut by complex gullies and chimneys into a series of discontinuous aretes which merge near the top into low-angled ridges leading towards the summits above. Distinctive, funnel-shaped hanging corries separate the buttresses.

Access being comparatively easy from the railway, this climbing ground was the first to be opened up by the pioneers in the Cairngorms proper. A substantial initial exploration was carried out on an Easter meet of the SMC in 1902 and their routes were popular for many years, better climbing areas in the Cairngorms suffering neglect as a result. Since the early fifties their popularity has declined; discontinuous rock, abundant vegetation and the Cairngorm ski road being largely responsible. The routes are detailed in the Climber's guide to the Cairngorms Area (Volume 1), by Malcolm Smith, published by the SMC in 1961. Since then, only one rock route has been recorded, offering pleasant climbing on the slabs to the right of The Slash (No. 5 Buttress). This is Resurrection, Very Severe, 4c.

The two routes most praised in the 1961 guide, Robert's Ridge and Rose Ridge, are both loose and probably dangerously so. A rockfall in Spring 1984 has destroyed a pitch in the lower section of Robert's Ridge; bypassing the rockfall is Severe and unpleasant. This is unfortunate because the route has an unusual finish over a flat-topped pedestal called The Anvil. There has also been a winter ascent independent of the summer line, III.

The buttresses are largely unexplored in winter. Although they may be improved under snow, the discontinuity of line would detract interest from many routes. The corries between the buttresses carry steep snow and give entertaining approaches (grade I at most) to the overlooking peaks. Good conditions are rare as the cliff base extends down to 650 metres. If the snow level is low, the glen is ideal for an approach by ski.

Number 5 buttress (Pinnacle Ridge) offers the best winter climbing to date. The crest, including a striking Pinnacle (named A'Chailleach) above mid-height, gives a fine mountaineering route (350 m, II). The deep gully cleaving the right wall of the buttress is No. 5 Buttress Gully, II. The prominent gash in the lower slabs of the buttress, well to the left of No. 5 Buttress Gully, is The Slash (Very Severe in semi-winter conditions).

CORRIES OF BEINN A'BHUIRD   1196 m

Beinn a'Bhuird is the highest summit of the Eastern Cairngorms, and one of the finest mountains in the country for snow and corrie scenery. It is a remote mountain of vast proportions whose approaches are reckoned to be the most beautiful in the area. Great corries walling an extensive plateau form its eastern front and provide, especially in winter, a scene of great beauty to travellers using the road through the Dee Valley.

Only two corries, Coire na Ciche with its characteristic top, A'Chioch, and the expansive Coire nan Clach, are seen from the Braemar approach. The grander Coire an Dubh Lochain, hidden by A'Chioch and remote Garbh Choire at the head of the Slochd Mor reserve their charms for the climber and walker.

Accommodation

There are no recognised huts or bothies close to Beinn a'Bhuird; but there is a small howff at the foot of the Dividing Buttress. This is the Smith–Winram Bivouac (NO 907996), a built-up recess under the second largest boulder immediately below a short belt of pink glaciated slab. The accommodation is rough (capacity 2/3) but ideal as a base close to the crag. Many excellent camp-sites are to be found on the approaches especially in the Fairy Glen below the ruined Slugain Lodge.

Approaches

(1) From Braemar–Aberdeen road A93. This is the recommended approach. (a) Leave the main road 100 m east of the gates to Invercauld House and follow the upper road by-passing the house (locked gate just beyond house). Continue past Alltdourie cottage and enter Glen Slugain through conifer plantation. (b) The River Dee may be forded at several points along a $\frac{1}{2}$ km stretch down stream from Braemar Castle. Once safely across follow the right bank of the Slugain burn through woods to join the Slugain track at the end of the plantation. This is a considerable saving to the pedestrian approaching from Braemar but the hazards of wading the Dee should not be taken lightly. A good stalkers path goes through Glen Slugain, passes Slugain Lodge, and in to upper Glen Quoich. For Coire na Ciche, ford the Quoich at the confluence of the stream issuing from the corrie. For Coire an Dubh Lochain and Coire nan Clach keep to the path leading

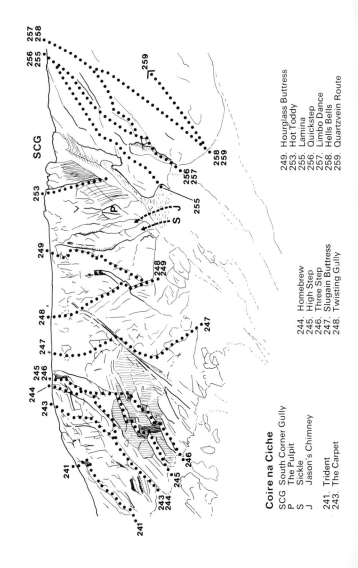

Coire na Ciche

SCG South Corner Gully
P   The Pulpit
S   Sickle
J   Jason's Chimney

241. Trident
243. The Carpet

244. Homebrew
245. High Step
246. Three Step
247. Slugain Buttress
248. Twisting Gully

249. Hourglass Buttress
253. Hot Toddy
255. Lamina
256. Quickstep
257. Limbo Dance
258. Hells Bells
259. Quartzvein Route

to a huge boulder called Clach a Chleirich, breaking off before the final rise to the stone. For the Garbh Choire follow the stream past the stone to the sneck between Ben Avon and Cnap a Chleirich then contour left avoiding rock-ribs by descending. Distances from Invercauld gates:

11 km to Coire na Ciche.
13 km to Coire an Dubh Lochain and Coire nan Clach.
15 km to Garbh Choire.

(2) The plateau of Beinn a'Bhuird may be attained relatively easily, if not aesthetically by following the private landrover track from the Linn of Quoich. This track follows the river Quoich to its confluence with the Dubh Ghleann stream then strikes up the prominent shoulder of An Doillaid to reach the plateau close to the edge of Coire an Dubh Lochain. All the corries may be reached by easy descent on their north side. (11 km from Linn of Quoich to Coire an Dubh Lochain.)

This track may also be reached from Derry Lodge by following the Derry road south for 3 km then crossing through the pass called Clais Fhearnaig.

COIRE NA CICHE (NO 1098)

The symmetrical cup-shaped corrie so well seen from the public road at Invercauld. The north wall is dominated by A'Chioch the great tor rising above the plateau. It is possible to scramble at will on this part of the corrie as the rock, although quite good, lacks continuity. However, most of the climbing is concentrated on the partially hidden south wall which appears as a broad buttress when viewed from the Invercauld approach.

The extreme left of this visible section is a narrow slabby rib. Trident is on the immediate right of this. Passing rightwards there is a large area of slab to the right of a huge alcove set in a vertical blank wall. The Carpet goes up this slab—the Great Slab. The apparent crest on the right skyline is followed by Slugain Buttress. As one nears the entrance to the corrie the whole of the South Wall comes into view. Twisting Gully, which has a right branch ending in a cul-de-sac, separates the triangular-based Slugain Buttress from the much steeper Hourglass Buttress. South Corner Gully, an open scree shoot terminating the main face lies at the back of the corrie. Midway up South Corner Gully beyond a steep left branch is the Grey Tower.

The back wall of the corrie, immediately right of South Corner Gully, comprises a huge area of glaciated slabs known as Slab Buttress.

The rock in the corrie is generally sound, rough and dries relatively quickly. There is a little vegetation which tends to be mossy in nature and should be treated with caution.

Winter

Beinn a'Bhuird is an inhospitable place in winter and climbers are rarely seen. The relative accessibility and sunnier aspect of Coire na Ciche maintains a less hostile atmosphere than the other corries and ensures a steady trickle of visitors. It is a good choice after a late start, in arduous walking conditions and after a visit to the more committing Garbh Choire the previous day. Most of the climbs are short, steep and technical, there being only two major gullies, both easy. A large build-up of snow on the steep South Wall is unusual but Slab Buttress soon disappears and often carries a considerable depth of snow. Big avalanches occur here after heavy snowfall or during a thaw.

Descent in Winter

Gentle slopes well to the left of the corrie lead back to upper Glen Quoich. To return to the base of the cliff, it is better to descend the ridge below A'Chioch. In good conditions, South Corner Gully is faster.

240 The Grinder 90 m E1 (1982)

A slabby rib terminates the cliff at its southern end. Start immediately to the right of this by scrambling up a vegetated groove (start of Trident) to belay below the lower of two steep corners which breach the left wall. Climb this lower corner up round a bulge and follow a crack to a small stance above the higher corner. Continue up the crack until it fades into slabs. Move left and climb a grassy corner to easy ground (40 m, 5b). Easy climbing leads to the plateau.

241 Trident 110 m Severe (1953)

Ascends a line of weakness immediately to the right of the slabby rib containing the Grinder. Somewhat vegetated, but it has had several ascents.

Climb a vegetated groove until very steep rock forces a move right to a sloping platform. Surmount the 4 m wall ahead (crux), then follow a slab for 6 m and traverse left to a flake belay. Continue up the slab straight ahead or climb the obvious layback-crack a few feet to the right. Avoid a vertical wall in front by a traverse right then by an easy slab to piled blocks. Scramble to the plateau. (Diagram p. 170.)

In winter the only ascent to date was grade IV with 2PA in good conditions.

242 Neptune's Groove 100 m IV (1982)
To the right of Trident is a prominent 20 m V-chimney with an overhung top; a natural winter line. Climb the chimney and swing strenuously out left at the top on to a strip of grass/ice in the slab above. Climb this and the easy corner above, then move left into a larger corner (junction with Trident) followed to the plateau.

243 The Carpet 110 m Very Severe (1955)
A good route with a fine pitch on the Great Slab. Start from the right-hand corner of a grassy recess below and to the right of a huge alcove with a blank, vertical left wall.

Climb a slabby depression up rightwards to grass ledges below the Great Slab (30 m). Above the ledges a thin crack leads slightly right up the slab. Climb the crack for about 10 m until it is possible to move left. Continue up via a rock band to easy grass shelves below a short overhanging corner (30 m, 4b). Thread belay. Climb the overhanging corner (4c). The overall grade is reduced to Hard Severe if a shoulder is used here. A short chimney and a traverse to the right lead to a stance in a crevasse. Move left to a slab and climb a line of dimples on the right of a corner. (Diagram p. 170.)

Winter IV/V (1970)

A serious climb involving thin slab climbing, but with adequate belays. The Great Slab faces south-east and catches the sun, so thawing conditions are often present. The Great Slab occasionally ices up and the lower grade will apply; but the route is equally fine under powder. Above the Great Slab the natural winter line is an iced groove on the left. When this is not in condition, follow the summer route starting with the overhanging corner (combined tactics).

244 Homebrew 140 m Very Severe (1973)
A good slab climb. It takes the right-hand of two prominent cracks in the large area of slab right of the Carpet.

Climb the first pitch of the Carpet and traverse right for 20 m to the foot of the crack. Climb the crack to a small stance at its end (5a).

Traverse right into Three Step, up this for 20 m, then go leftwards up slabs, a 5 m crack and a chimney in the centre of an overhung bay. (Diagram p. 170.)

245   High Step   155 m   E1   (1976)
Below and to the right of the Great Slab is an area of slabs and overhangs resembling steps of a giant staircase. Two rightward trending lines of corners break through the overhangs. This is the upper line, which has two great steps. Unrepeated; the grade is uncertain.

Cross a large slab diagonally to belay below the first wall (30 m). Climb a break in the wall, trending leftwards until stopped by loose blocks (possibly dangerous). Gain the second slab and cross this to belay below the second wall (20 m, 5b). Climb a corner-crack and traverse a grass ramp (45 m), junction with Three Step. Move left on to the Great Slab and climb directly to a stance at 35 m (4c). Move right to the edge of the slab, thence by a layback-crack and exposed overhang on the skyline to reach the final slab and so to the plateau (25 m, 4b). (Diagram p. 170.)

246   Three Step   135 m   E1   (1964)
A fine well-protected climb, following three giant steps below and right of High Step.

Start on the lowest slab and climb to belay below an overhanging corner (10 m). Ascend the corner and traverse diagonally right across the slab above to belay below a short wall (25 m, 5b). Climb the wall (5c) and move right round the corner. Go straight up a fault and short wet corner on the right to a grass terrace (40 m), junction with High Step. Move left on to the Great Slab and climb directly to a stance at 35 m (4c). Move right to the edge of the slab, thence by a layback-crack and exposed overhang on the skyline to reach the final slab and so to the plateau (25 m, 4b). (Diagram p. 170.)

247   Slugain Buttress   130 m   III   (1957)
A popular winter climb. The buttress is defined by a slanting groove on the left which forms an apex halfway up the buttress. Start on the right of the buttress (or a chimney on the right). Below the apex, traverse left and climb a steep pitch to a huge, semi-detached block (the apex). Easy climbing in the upper recess to the top. Difficult and grassy in summer. (Diagram p. 170.)

248 Twisting Gully 130 m II (1948)

The best of the lower grade winter routes. The gully twists to the left below a small buttress and ends in easy ground above Slugain Buttress. The lower 60 m often contains ice but with a large build-up the pitches can bank out and the gully become Grade I. Moderate in summer. (Diagram p. 170.)

The right branch of the gully is a cul-de-sac. The small buttress left of this is the Watchtower, Very Severe, 4c.

249 Hourglass Buttress 110 m Very Severe (1953)

A good steep route which dries quickly after rain. Above the neck of the Hourglass the climbing is exposed and on excellent rock.

Start at the foot of Twisting Gully. Climb a long fault to the neck, or climb the lower buttress directly (Severe). From the neck climb easy rock to a large block belay below a steep wall (55 m from start). Go up the wall on good flake holds, traverse right and climb a deep crack to a rock ledge overlooking the chimney of Sickle. A thin crack leads out left to a large platform (35 m, 4b). Climb the difficult wall above the platform at a left slanting crack (4c) and move left to a perched block. Either climb straight up or continue left to finish up a short chimney. (Diagram p. 170.)

Winter IV (1970)

Follow the summer line. The 35 m pitch was technically very hard (2PA). The difficult wall was partly banked up with snow.

250 Joker's Crack 50 m E1 (1982)

A prominent corner-crack set into the right side of Hourglass Buttress, between it and Sickle (see below). Climb up the broken ground of Sickle to belay under the crack. Climb the steep crack until it eases after 12 m and find a belay a little higher (20 m, 5b). Finish in the same line to the top (30 m).

To the right of Hourglass Buttress are three chimney lines, the leftmost, Sickle, is the most prominent, the rightmost, Sandy Crack, Very Difficult, IV, does not reach the base of the cliff, ending at the Pulpit which is passed on the right. Sandy Crack joins the central chimney, Jason's Chimney, 20 m from the top. These three chimneys are tucked in the shade and remain in condition longer than other climbs in the corrie.

251 Sickle 110 m IV (1959)
The prominent leftmost chimney, bounding Hourglass Buttress on the right. Sustained, but low in its grade. Very Difficult in summer. (Diagram p. 170.)

252 Jason's Chimney 100 m IV (1974)
The steep central chimney, again sustained and icy in mid to late season. Start just right of Sickle. Severe in summer, or Very Difficult by a variation using the rib on the left. (Diagram p. 170.)

253 Hot Toddy 100 m Very Severe (1977)
Rearing up from South Corner Gully on its south wall, between Sandy Crack and the fault/fork of Little Tower Gully, is a well-defined bulging headland. The route takes a fairly direct line starting on the right-hand side of an overhanging prow.

Climb the shallow vertical fault tucked under the prow past a rock thread and gain a ledge on the right (25 m). Step up and move left across an undercut wall to laybook up an obvious crack. Move up right and straddle over a rock bollard to a good stance below an overlap (25 m, 5a). Cross the slab on the right below the overlap and up a short grass trough to a big ledge on the brow of the buttress (25 m). Climb the slab and groove directly ahead leading to easy ground. (Diagram p. 170.)

254 South Corner Gully 120 m I
A straightforward snow climb usually with a respectable cornice. The sporting exit is up the left-hand corner. (Diagram p. 170.)

The narrow gully breaking the left wall of South Corner Gully is Little Tower Gully, II. The very steep buttress on the left of Little Tower Gully is Hot Toddy (above). The pinnacle on the right of Little Tower Gully is called the Grey Tower (Severe by two routes, one up its left side and the other up its right).

SLAB BUTTRESS
Slab Buttress is the large area of slabs to the right of South Corner Gully. The rock is clean although occasionally gritty on the surface. Five good routes are described; each is open to variation and protection is limited.

In winter, Slab Buttress carries very large accumulations of snow and at peak periods all but the steepest section of Quartzvein Route is buried. For this reason, no winter routes have been described.

On the left side of the slabs is a lush, green gully which peters out into slabs. Lamina is to the left of this gully; Quickstep is immediately on its right.

255 Lamina 180 m Very Severe (1965)
This route lies on the left flank of Slab Buttress, adjacent to South Corner Gully. It gives good climbing on smooth clean slabs, but with minimal protection. Sustained at 4a. Variations are possible.

Start at the lowest rocks left of the gully. Climb easy slabs for 50 m. Trend right across smooth, clean waterwashed slabs, then up to a ledge just above and right of a large scoop (45 m). Climb a very shallow groove left of obvious parallel right-slanting cracks. This leads into a vague crackline slanting right. Belay below an overlap (45 m). Continue up the crackline to the top (40 m). (Diagram p. 170.)

256 Quickstep 130 m Hard Very Severe (1982)
On the right side of the lush green gully is a prominent diamond-shaped block lying against the slab. The route climbs directly upwards from the block, keeping to the cleanest rock.

Start on top of the block, at its right-hand end. Climb directly up slabs, hardest for the first 5 m, to reach the left edge of a large, shallow depression high up on the slabs (5a, 4c). Continue up rippling slabs left of the depression to the top (4b). Very poor protection overall. (Diagram p. 170.)

Starting near the prominent block of Quickstep are two right-slanting shallow cracklines. The lower starts below the block and is the line of Vatican Steps, Very Severe, 4c, which follows the crackline and traverses to join Hell's Bells. The upper crackline is the main feature of the following route, Limbo Dance.

257 Limbo Dance 125 m Hard Very Severe (1983)
Start on top of the block, as for Quickstep. The first 10 m directly up the slab is common to both routes. One is then at the start of the upper, right-slanting crackline, which is followed to its end (45 m, 5a). Climb obliquely rightwards towards the left end of a large obvious overlap, up through the break and so up to a large terrace (45 m). Climb a rightwards sloping ramp to the top (35 m, common with Hell's Bells). (Diagram p. 170.)

258 Hell's Bells 185 m   Very Severe   (1970/1976)
A good but poorly protected direct route up the highest section of
slabs. Hell's Bells is arguably a long direct start to an older, less direct
route, Vatican Steps. There is some gritty rock. Start at the foot of
Quartzvein Route (15 m left and up from the lowest rocks). 4c with no
definite crux.

Climb directly to a prominent, short, left-facing leaning corner,
midway between the diamond-shaped block at the start of Quickstep
and Vatican Steps and the extreme edge of the buttress on the right
(60 m). Climb the corner, then slabs to a grassy ledge below an
overlap (25 m). Surmount the overlap, go up then left to a triangular
niche at another overlap (junction with Vatican Steps). Climb this to a
poor belay (25 m). Climb a bulge, go left then up and through an
obvious overlap break, then trend rightwards, passing the right end of
a long horizontal roof, to a large grass ledge (40 m). Traverse left, then
up a ramp rightwards to the plateau (35 m). (Diagram p. 170.)

259 Quartzvein Route 195 m   Very Difficult   (1953)
A pleasing route on good rock with ample holds. It follows a dyke
containing a vein of quartz which trends slightly rightwards up the
highest section of Slab Buttress. Start about 15 m up from and left of
the lowest rocks.

Climb the vein over easy angled slabs to a small flake belay (45 m).
Continue up the vein in two pitches to belay below a short vertical
wall (60 m). Climb the wall and go up to ledges and a flake belay on
the left below the steep upper nose (15 m). A grass-lined groove leads
up rightwards. Follow the groove and regain the vein which continues
as an exposed rightwards traverse to a spike belay (30 m). Continue
on the traverse then go up left over slabs to the top (45 m). Winter
III/IV. (Diagram p. 170.)

COIRE AN DUBH LOCHAIN (NO 0999)

One of the most attractive corries in the Cairngorms. Tucked in behind
A'Chioch this corrie's bowl with its lochan nestling in the bottom is
neglected by climbers. The best rock is admittedly limited but there is
enough to justify a weekend in beautiful, remote surroundings. The
sweep of clean, pink slabs at the back of the corrie (Glaucous Buttress) receive much sun and provide a contrast with the steep Bloodhound Buttress high up on the left. The two buttresses are separated

by a prominent diagonal shelf—the Main Rake. Slower to dry than Coire na Ciche.

Winter

The corrie bites into the Beinn a'Bhuird plateau and receives a lot of drifting snow in winter. At peak conditions only Bloodhound Buttress and the final 100 m of Glaucous Buttress remain unsubmerged. In general, the corrie is a big disappointment in winter, although early in the season good ice climbing may be found on the slabs of Glaucous Buttress. The large area of broken cliff to the left of Bloodhound Buttress gives straightforward snow climbing up to grade II standard. In the extreme south-west corner of the corrie, right of Glaucous Buttress, a huge snowfield forms known as the Avalanche Slope. This has been ascended on many occasions to give a long easy snow climb.

Descent

The quickest summer descent is by the Main Rake. This is also true in winter but the cornice may be a problem. A longer but easy alternative is the ridge of A'Chioch between Coire an Dubh Lochain and Coire na Ciche—this is the best way back to upper Glen Quoich.

BLOODHOUND BUTTRESS

The south side of the corrie left of Bloodhound Buttress is composed of short slabby buttresses and broken rock. Two shallow gullies run the full height of the face. These are A Gully on the left and B Gully on the right. Both give grade I winter climbs with possible cornice difficulty while the rib between them is Central Rib, II.

In its upper reaches, the right wall of B Gully has a short belt of steep slabs leading across to the overhanging prow of Bloodhound Buttress. From the top of the main rake, the prow bears some resemblance to the head of a bloodhound. Towards the left side of these slabs is a section of slabby ribs and corners, the line of Tail-end Slabs, III. Below the slabs, at the bottom left of the buttress is a band of overhangs above a prominent incut slab (there is a second incut slab, less obvious, just below and to the right). These overhangs have only been breached using aid—Hooker's Route, Hard Very Severe 4c, climbs the incut slab and penetrates the overhangs above by lassoing a hook *in situ*. The following route climbs the buttress passing just to the right of this band of overhangs.

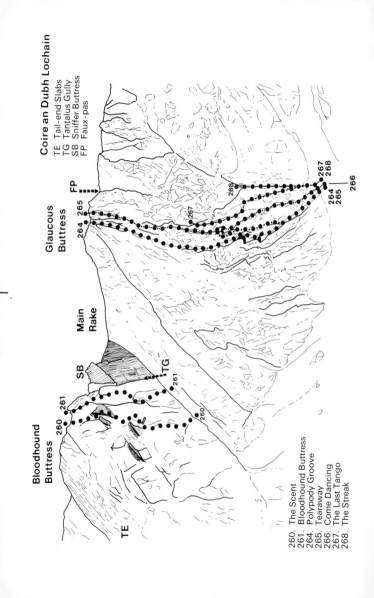

Coire an Dubh Lochain

TE   Tail-end Slabs
TG   Tantalus Gully
SB   Sniffer Buttress
FP   Faux-pas

Bloodhound Buttress

Main Rake

Glaucous Buttress

260. The Scent
261. Bloodhound Buttress
264. Polypody Groove
265. Tearaway
266. Come Dancing
267. The Last Tango
268. The Streak

260 The Scent 125 m Hard Very Severe (1978)
A fine steep route, perhaps the best in the corrie. Very sustained, but with poor protection on the middle pitch. The intention is to gain the large hanging slab directly underneath the nose of the buttress.

From the Main Rake about 50 m below Tantalus Gully, climb up and slightly left, heading for a short left-facing corner which leads up from the left end of a small rectangular roof. Pass a good ledge and belay beside the small roof (50 m). Climb the corner and step right to reach the base of an undercut dièdre (this dièdre has been climbed using 1NA to start— 5b). Instead, traverse right on to slabs until possible to move up and back left to overlook the dièdre. An awkward ramp on the right allows access to the hanging slab (40 m, 4c). Climb the corner at the left side of the slab (the right side is easier, but leads nowhere) and step out on to the rib on the left, finishing by a series of blocks and steep cracks (35 m, 4c). (Diagram p. 180.)

261 Bloodhound Buttress 90 m Very Severe (1964)
This route follows a line just to the right of the overhanging nose of the buttress and is located by a precarious arch of jammed blocks on pitch 1.

Start 20 m below Tantalus Gully, work up leftwards past the arch of jammed blocks and continue to a steep crack. Climb the crack (4c) to a small stance, then move right across a smooth slab to a comfortable platform. Move round to a crack on the right and climb it to easy ground (4c). Finish up the prominent depression, almost a gully, right of the overhangs (loose rock). (Diagram p. 180.)

Winter IV (1975)

The summer line was closely followed. Seven points of aid were used and a freer ascent is awaited.

262 Tantalus Gully 80 m III (1957)
A good short climb and accessible from the plateau (descend Main Rake). It can therefore be combined with a route in Coire na Ciche. This is the first break in the wall of Bloodhound Buttress, about midway up the Main Rake. The lower section forms a steep ice pitch (up to 15 m) which may be fairly hard. Higher up, the gully cuts deep into the cliff but the climbing is straightforward. Severe in summer, with the crux at the start. (Diagram p. 180.)

The small buttress on the right of Tantalus Gully, Sniffer Buttress,

Glaucous Buttress

1. Polypody Groove
1a. Rib variations
2. Tearaway
3. Come Dancing
4. The Last Tango
5. The Streak
6. Faux-pas
7. Crow-step
8. Birthday Route
D. direction of quick descent

has an attractive shape from the corrie floor but the climbing does not match its appearance; Hard Very Severe, 5b, and loose by a line near Tantalus Gully.

263 Main Rake I (1911)
An uncomplicated snow ramp, cornice often easy. A useful means of descent.

GLAUCOUS BUTTRESS
The buttress has two distinct features, a lower apron of clean slabs and grooves, and an upper rampart consisting of a series of small ribs divided vertically by thin converging chimneys. The lower slabs have different aspects on each side of a long central break. On the left side there are a number of easy-angled pillars with their attendant grooves. The right side is an 80 m sweep of smooth clean slab, with a water-course running down its right side—the Waterslide.

Five fine climbs are described on the slabs. The upper buttress is disappointing and only hortophiliacs may wish to continue to the plateau. Descent is possible by traversing right or left above the slabs. The descriptions assume no snow is obscuring the start of the routes.

High up to the right of the main mass there are a number of subsidiary buttresses and chimneys. The broad crescent-shaped rib bounding the Main Rake on the right is May Day Route, Difficult, II.

264 Polypody Groove 200 m Very Difficult (1949)
A good climb, and popular, though marred by vegetatious scrambling in the middle section. Polypody Groove follows the large corner separating the pillared section from the slab section of the lower buttress. A large snow bed lingers late into the summer and much of the good climbing may be obscured until July. After this, the route is still slow to dry although the rib on its left can be followed all the way (a pleasant Very Difficult).

Climb the groove in a long pitch to a bulge. Move out right round the bulge and follow the groove for a further 30 m to a belay. There are now two possibilities. One is to move out on to the rib on the left, climb the rib by a delicate move and continue to a terrace. The second is finer but just Severe in grade. Slant out right and continue up the groove to reach the terrace. Follow a line slightly rightwards to the deepest and most obvious of the chimneys in the upper ramparts. Climb the chimney and exit right across a slab. Easy above to plateau. (Diagrams pp. 180 and 182.)

Winter   III   (1969)

An extremely variable climb, only recommended in early season, when it offers sustained climbing in the iced groove and may be IV. In middle and late season the build-up of snow on the lower slabs is considerable and it is quite normal for the full 100 m of slab to be completely banked out. In fact, a true bergschrund forms at the head of the slabs. Under these conditions, Polypody Groove as such does not exist and it is best to climb the lower rib of May Day Route and traverse in below the upper cliff. On the upper cliff, the deep-set chimney of the summer line is followed. The chimney immediately right of the tapered rib of Tearaway often contains ice and has also been followed.

265 Tearaway   200 m   Very Severe   (1965)
This route follows the shallow corner system right of Polypody Groove on the slabby section of the lower buttress. In the upper section it merges into a tapering rib. The lower slabs provide good climbing on clean rock.
   Climb Polypody Groove for approximately 15 m, move right into the base of the corner system and climb straight up to a small niche and belay (40 m). Continue up the corner to a flake on the rib left of the small first overhang in the corner. Follow cracks in the rib until it is possible to traverse a thin horizontal crack back to the corner immediately above the second larger overhang (4b). Continue up the corner until it meets the tapering rib and follow this to the top. (Diagrams pp. 180 and 182.)

266 Come Dancing   95 m   Very Severe   (1977)
Harder and as good as Tearaway. The route follows the left of two thin cracks on the slabs right of Tearaway. Start at the base of Polypody Groove and go diagonally right up pink slabs to the left end of a long narrow ledge (5 m). From the left end of this ledge, move up to reach the base of the thin crack. A groove on the right of the crack is followed initially, then the crack itself and a slab to reach the first small roof in the Tearaway corner (the roof is avoided on the left by Tearaway), 50 m, 4b. Follow the corner round the roof and a second larger roof and continue up the corner (junction with Tearaway) to grass ledges (40 m, 5a). Either follow the tapering rib of Tearaway to the plateau or traverse left across grass and descend by May Day Route (Diagrams pp. 180 and 182.)

267 The Last Tango   85 m   Very Severe   (1982)

The route follows the right-hand of the thin cracks on the slab. Pleasant, but a little artificial. Gain the ledge at 5 m either by the start of Come Dancing or, if dry, the Streak. From the centre of the ledge, climb straight up the slab to the start of the crack. Follow the crack, or the groove on its right to a belay ledge (40 m, 4b, escape right possible here). Above is a vegetated groove. Traverse left 10 m on to the face and climb shallow grooves about 5 m right of Come Dancing to vegetated ground above the slabs (40 m, 4b). To descend, traverse right off the buttress. (Diagrams pp. 180 and 182.)

268 The Streak   50 m   Hard Severe   (1981)

After a spell of dry weather, the Waterslide dries to a pink streak of delightfully clean rock on the slabs right of Polypody Groove. This catches the sun in the morning and gives a fine solo preamble to one of the harder routes (there are no runners). The first 5 m is the crux; thereafter climb the streak directly on emerging holds. Descend on the right by the lower slabs of Crow-Step Route, Moderate. (Diagrams pp. 180 and 182.)

269 Faux-pas   200 m   III   (1972)

This is the short, right facing corner gully in the upper buttress directly above the Waterslide. It has a pronounced square tower formation on its left (the square tower is just right of the upper rib of Tearaway) and the upper buttress of Crow-Step Route (not described) on its right.

Follow the line of the Waterslide, ice or banked out, directly up to the gully. The initial 30 m corner of the gully is the crux. (Diagrams pp. 180 and 182.)

The upper buttress right of Faux-pas contains two routes. One is Crow-Step Route, Very Difficult, III, which starts up stepped slabs right of the Waterslide, crosses grass and climbs the upper buttress right of Faux-pas. The other is the short Birthday Route, Severe, which is the third chimney right of the upper buttress of Crow-Step, immediately left of a pointed buttress which breaks the skyline.

THE DIVIDING BUTTRESS (NO 096996)

When approaching from the Upper Quoich Water via the Dubh Lochan Burn, the view is dominated by a bold triangular headland. This is the Dividing Buttress, separating Coire an Dubh Lochain on the left and the more extensive Coire nan Clach on the right. The left skyline of this huge buttress is the ridge of Slab and Arete, Moderate, II under powder, which gives a pleasant romp amid grand scenery in either season.

The right skyline is Sentinel Route. Between these routes there is an expanse of slabs containing a large right-facing corner, Jewell-Kammer Route. The Fringe, Very Severe, 4b, climbs cracks in the slabs left of the big corner. Streaker's Root follows the groove line some 10 m right of the big corner. Parkie's route, Hard Very Severe, 5a, is a further 10 m right, climbing slabs, then a corner, then right over a rib into a niche and back left.

270   Jewell-Kammer Route   80 m   Very Severe   (1974)
Takes the right-facing corner mentioned above. The line described is slightly different from the first ascent. The first part of the corner is bypassed on the right by a slab and wall (4c) leading up to the right-hand end of a big roof. Follow the corner which curves right thereafter.

271   Streaker's Root   110 m   Hard Very Severe   (1982)
A lovely route, sustained climbing on excellent rock. It takes a series of left-facing corners some 10 m right of the big corner of the Jewell-Kammer Route. A grassy rake runs up the left side of the lower slabs passing below the start of the Jewell-Kammer Route. Start in this, at the foot of the lowest tongue of slab.

Climb the tongue, and the first steepening by a corner. Step out left at the top of the corner and climb slabs to enter a shallow corner which is climbed to a ledge, below the main groove (35 m, 4b). Climb a slab to reach the groove, then follow it over a bulge to a tiny ledge beneath a steep wall (30 m, 5a). From the left end of the wall, climb the direct continuation corner (20 m, 5a). Scramble up right, then away left (25 m).

Moving into Coire nan Clach from the Smith-Winram Bivouac it will be seen that the Dividing Buttress ends abruptly with a short very steep wall dropping into and overhanging a slanting corner gully— The Ramp, II. A rib, broad at its base and tapering towards a grassy glacis at mid-height separates The Ramp from Sentinel Gully, II/III on the left. Sentinel Route, Difficult, III, ascends the rocks to the immediate left of Sentinel Gully.

COIRE NAN CLACH (NO 0900)

Though containing limited rock of interest to the climber, Coire nan Clach with its extensive floor and chaos of boulders, may attract a visit through its beauty and air of seclusion. At the back of the corrie a rock promontory contains two short easy climbs. In winter the corrie is ringed by a continuous cornice and gives good straightforward climbing, especially on the wall running west from the Dividing Buttress. Four gullies of 150–200 m are found here running up through the small upper buttresses. Of these, the rightmost, which is called Crocus Gully, is the better and more defined. All are Grade I climbs.

There is a small south-west facing outcrop situated below the plateau rim approximately 400 m ESE of North Top (NO 097004). This is called Black Crag and it has the following climb.

272 Twister 30 m E1 (1984)
It starts at a small recess below a large rectangular overhang at the top of the crag and climbs the slabby wall left of a fierce diagonal crackline.

From two large flakes go up left following shallow cracks until a thin move right gives access to a line of flakes leading up into a big bay below the final overhangs. Finish up left of capping chokestone (30 m, 5b).

GARBH CHOIRE (NJ 1001)

For those who seek remote seclusion in which to climb there can be few finer places in this country than the lonely Garbh Choire of Beinn a'Bhuird. Hidden on the northern slopes of this complex mountain at the head of the Slochd Mor, the corrie reveals its secrets only to the determined few. In recent years, the quality of its climbing is becoming recognised, thanks partly to the inclusion of Squareface and Cumming–Crofton Route in "Classic Rock". One can no longer expect to be alone in the corrie in summer.

The main area of crag, averaging 200 m in height, extends north-westwards from the Sneck for about 400 m. Two superb buttresses are situated at each end of this main face. These are Squareface and the Mitre Ridge. Between them a stretch of cliff of lesser character contains many gullies. One of these, the Flume, encloses a large stream—a good pointer in thick weather. To the right of the main face

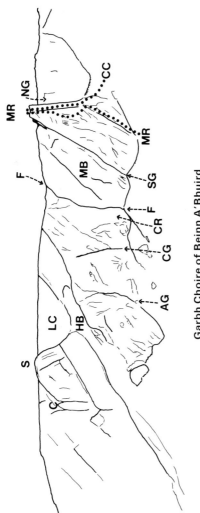

Garbh Choire of Beinn A'Bhuird

C	The Crucible
S	Squareface Buttress
LC	Laminated Crag
HB	High Bay
AG	Approach Gully
CG	Consolation Gully
CR	Comala's Ridge
F	The Flume
MB	Mandarin Buttress
SG	South-East Gully
MR	Mitre Ridge
CC	Cumming—Crofton Route
NG	North-West Gully

the continuity of the cliff is interrupted by a wide, gravelly depression beyond which a series of miniature aretes run up to the backbone of Stob an t-Sluichd.

The best rock climbing is to be found on the clean, rough granite of Squareface and the Mitre Ridge. The west face of Mitre Ridge has recently been opened up to give several fine Hard Very Severe climbs on perfect steep rock.

Winter

A combination of its magnificent isolation and the shortness of a winter's day will ensure the continued obscurity of the Garbh Choire. Nevertheless, it is one of the finest winter corries in the Cairngorms. The seriousness of climbing in such a remote place cannot be over-emphasised but with a bit of luck, those who are prepared to make the effort will be justly rewarded. In common with the other corries on Beinn a'Bhuird good snow and ice conditions could occur any time from November to April. The most reliable time would be fairly late in the season (February–March) when the days are longer, the build-up is at its maximum, and there is less chance of deep powder on the walk-in. A continuous cornice usually forms for the full length of the main face well round the extreme north-west corner. The safest approach from the south will always be via the Sneck.

Descent in Winter: The quickest route off the plateau in wild weather is to follow the corrie edge back to the Sneck. Keep well up the slope from the cliff edge and take care to avoid a small slab outcrop on the east-facing slope of Cnap a'Chleirich about 400 m south of the Sneck. In better weather, and especially when there is powder in the valleys, it is easier to go to the summit of Cnap a'Chleirich and follow the blunt ridge back to Clach a'Chleirich (the edge of Coire nan Clach on the right is usually corniced).

SQUAREFACE BUTTRESS

A fascinating buttress with two sharply contrasting faces, the slabby west face high up which contains one of the best Very Difficult routes in the Cairngorms, and the formidable North Face.

From the Sneck westwards, a series of ill-defined ribs and buttresses lead up to the North Face, which has a short lower tier separated from the huge wall above by a prominent terrace. On the left of this face the rock is appalling, crumbling and vegetated. Here is the Crucible, a large basin high up. As one moves rightwards the rock steepens to a smooth clean face, capped by a blank gritty band of rock which has ended all attempts to date. The magnificent flake-crack slanting right into the centre of the face has been climbed to its top, about 10 m from the plateau, Hard Very Severe, but a free finish is "impossible". Further right, beyond a loose overhanging fault, the cliff is split by a ledge which leads leftwards from the west face and passes under two intriguing cracks. These are overhanging and the rock has a crumbly surface.

The name Squareface is derived from the 100 m rectangular west face which overlooks a large grassy amphitheatre, the High Bay. Squareface route is on this slabby west face (hidden from below).

273 Alchemist's Route 230 m III (1980)
This route lies towards the left end of the North Face. The main feature is a zig-zag ramp which bypasses an obvious chimney halfway up the face.

Start at the foot of an obvious ice gully (taken by Crucible Route) but slant up left to gain a snow slope. Climb this until an obvious branch leads rightwards across the bounding rocks and then up to the chimney. Follow a ramp on the left wall, then climb up to reach the top of the chimney. Climb the shallow gully above, which gives out on to steepish snow slopes. The cornice on this face is notorious, both for its height and its continuity leftwards almost to the Sneck. To pass it, traverse right into the Crucible and exit up right.

274 Gold Coast 190 m V (1982)
High up on the face, just left of the very steep part of the upper buttress, is a snow basin (the Crucible) usually capped by an enormous cornice. Below the basin a rock snout splits the drainage into twin icefalls, the left-hand usually containing more ice. This fine route climbs steeply into the Crucible by the left-hand icefall. Poor protection.

Climb a short ice gully below the Crucible, then go up to steep ground. The left icefall flows down a very steep wall on to a slab. Climb up to and follow rightwards a shallow corner which is formed by the junction of slab and wall, crossing the icefall to gain a large block, almost a pinnacle (belay). Go diagonally leftwards heading for the icefall above its steepest section. The line ended on a grass ledge 2 m right of the icefall. A poor, low peg was used to reach grass beside the icefall. Follow the icefall and the left side of the snout to reach the cornice, avoided on the right. A truly direct ascent of the icefall would be very worthwhile but the required amount of ice does not form readily.

275 Crucible Route 210m IV (1978)

An alternative line into the Crucible, based on the right-hand icefall but climbed in conditions of deep, partially consolidated snow with little ice.

Climb the short ice gully as before but move right until under the line of the right-hand icefall. Go slightly left then right across the "icefall" by a ramp. Climb steeply up and back into the line of the icefall. Gain a pedestal on the snout to the left, then traverse left (tension used) to gain the left-hand icefall near its top. Enter the Crucible and exit on the right.

A similar line has been climbed in summer. All the unpleasant features of this face were encountered (Rocky Mountain Horror Show, Hard Severe).

276 Squareface 100m Very Difficult (1953)

This excellent route ascends the steep slab face of the west wall of Squareface Buttress. It combines continuously exposed climbing with impressive situations and is remarkable in its low technical standard. The face dries quickly after rain. Access from either plateau or corrie floor is via a wide easy rake which slants rightwards from the lowest rocks into the High Bay and continues to the plateau.

The left side of this face is a stepped arete bordering the North Face. Start just round the crest of the arete, near the foot of Back Bay Gully, and climb 30m to a large platform. Go 10m up the arete to belay below an overhang. Launch out on to the wall by a 10m traverse, past the first obvious vertical crack, then climb straight up and return left to a platform on the edge (30m). Return to the face and follow cracks up to the right for 10m to a short horizontal crack. Two metres on the right a deep fissure cleaves the final section. Either climb the fissure, Severe, or layback a flake on the right for 4m, then leave it for a shelf on the right, thence gain the top by an awkward traverse.

Variation

Angel's Edgeway—a direct variation to the second pitch. From the belay below the overhang, move out on to the face and climb directly up the edge, Very Severe, 4b.

Squareface has had one ascent in winter, IV, in unusually banked up conditions. The route will always be hard, due to its slabby nature and absence of vegetation.

277 Rhombus 60 m Severe (1981)
Start in gully bed at a point directly below the "deep fissure" in the top pitch of Squareface. Climb up and slightly left to join the second pitch of Squareface at the end of "the 10 m traverse". Follow Squareface up to a small ledge in the middle of the face (30 m). Climb diagonally right step round a rib into a shallow groove and follow this up and right to a small stance below the obvious finishing crack (15 m). Climb the crack to the top (the lower section may be varied by an airy excursion on to the right edge via the obvious horizontal crack) (15 m).

Back Bay Gully, Difficult, II, is the narrow gully ascending to the plateau from the High Bay close under the west wall of Squareface. The left branch is steeper but the cornice will provide less of a problem. The squat crag right of Back Bay Gully gives Laminated Crag, Very Difficult. Both the gully and the crag appear dangerously loose in summer.

Between the rake leading to the High Bay and the Flume is a big area of scrappy cliff. A steep lower section is crowned by a belt of vegetation. Above this a margin of broken rock forms a frieze under the plateau. The lower section is split by two defined gullies, the left-hand being Approach Gully, II, which leads into the High Bay and the right-hand being Consolation Gully, II. A rightward slanting ramp starting at the bottom of Consolation Gully is Nomads Gully, I/II, and the broad rib between Nomad's Gully and the Flume is Comala's Ridge, I/II.

278 The Flume 200 m II (1954)
               Direct IV (1974)
The Flume is the channel gouged in the cliff by the Allt an t-Sluichd, already a lusty stream on the plateau before it drops over the edge. The gully ends under the plateau in a huge waterfall which freezes in winter and provides the Direct Route. The easier version, also very icy, threads its way between the Direct icefall and another big ice pitch which forms to the left. There is often a massive cornice, usually avoidable on the left. Both variations are recommended. Salamander, II/III, starts up the Flume, then exits right and climbs left of Mandarin Buttress crest. (Diagram p. 188.)

279 Mandarin Buttress 200m III (1959)
The large buttress between the Flume and South-East Gully of Mitre
Ridge. The steep lower section may be quite difficult if the build-up is
poor. Thereafter the upper ridge gives fine exposed climbing. The
buttress is not a safe alternative in avalanche conditions as a cornice
forms at the top and can sweep the buttress. Difficult in summer.

On the lower section of Mandarin Buttress, there is an area of
surprisingly good rock. There are two obvious large slabs, one on each
side of the buttress. The left-hand slab is climbed by Surgeon's Slab,
Severe. A second route, of good quality, climbs a triangular section of
rock between Surgeon's Slab and the slab further right. This is Witch
Doctor, Very Severe, 4b, which follows an obvious crackline, avoiding
the bulge at the apex of the triangle on the right.

MITRE RIDGE
One of the finest pieces of rock architecture in the Cairngorms. It
thrusts out boldly between its gullies, 200m from scree to plateau in
two walls meeting at an acute angle and topped by three towers. The
West Wall is nearly vertical, while the East is less steep but slabby and
somewhat vegetated. The West Wall has seen several fine additions in
the last ten years and now sports the best rock climbing on Beinn
a'Bhuird.

280 South-East Gully 200m IV (1959)
The shallow gully bounding the Mitre Ridge on the left. A superb
climb in good conditions, but often has unconsolidated snow and
becomes very serious, as rock protection is minimal. The crux is a
steep narrows just above half height. The cornice is seldom trouble-
some. Severe and dangerous in summer. (Diagram p. 188.)

281 East Wall Direct 220m IV (1974)
A fine climb with well-sustained difficulties from start to finish. Start
about 20m left of the lowest point of the slab apron on the East Wall
of the Mitre Ridge. After 30m of climbing a short, thin ice traverse left
gave access to a long chimney system. Above mid-height, a set of
stepped ramps lead underneath an imposing vertical wall to reach an
ice couloir. Climb the ice couloir to its top, then exit left of overhangs
ringing the top and follow an easy gully leading to the final col of the
Mitre Ridge. It is possible (the original route) to reach the ice couloir

West Wall of Mitre Ridge

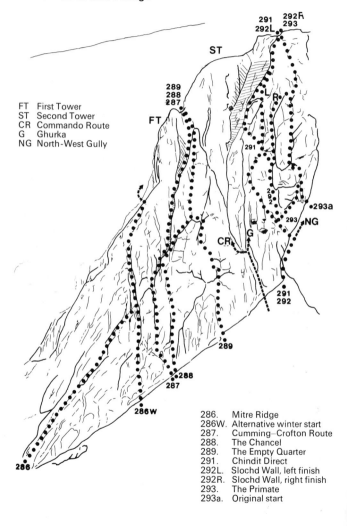

FT First Tower
ST Second Tower
CR Commando Route
G   Ghurka
NG North-West Gully

286.   Mitre Ridge
286W.   Alternative winter start
287.   Cumming–Crofton Route
288.   The Chancel
289.   The Empty Quarter
291.   Chindit Direct
292L.   Slochd Wall, left finish
292R.   Slochd Wall, right finish
293.   The Primate
293a.   Original start

West Wall of Mitre Ridge

FT First Tower
ST Second Tower
C   Commando Route
G   Ghurka

3. The Chancel
4. The Empty Quarter
5. Chindit
6. Slochd Wall

6l. Left finish
6r. Right finish
7. The Primate
7a. Original start

1. Helter Skelter
2. Cumming–Crofton Route
2a. variation

from just below the depression of South-East Gully. The route is Severe and rather vegetated in summer.

282   The Grail   250 m   V   (1984)

A direct and natural winter line up the centre of the East Wall. Low in its grade. Start just left of the lowest rocks and about 15 m right of East Wall Direct. Climb very directly up a vegetated fault in three pitches to the terrace left of The Shoulder. Go up to the steep wall above and traverse left over a small rib to gain the base of a ramp overlooking "the couloir" of East Wall Direct. Climb the ramp to reach the col between First and Second Towers (two pitches, crux).

283   The Bishop   200 m   Hard Very Severe

A direct line to the right of East Wall Direct and to the left of and parallel to Mitre Ridge Direct. Good climbing in the lower part, although more vegetated than the West Wall routes.

Start at the lowest point of the apron of slabs, about 15 m left of the big groove of Mitre Ridge. Climb crack to bulge. Move left then continue more easily to belay at the foot of a grass tongue (5a). Move up right into a corner and climb slabs and grooves up rightwards to belay on a turf ledge below and left of a pink rock scar (35 m, 4b). Go up left and climb the left-hand of three cracks. Continue rightwards on to a steeper wall (30 m, 4b). Climb the wall to exit beside a loose block. Scramble across broken ground to belay below an impending wall (level with the shoulder on Mitre Ridge) — (4c). From a flake on the left climb a groove to gain a thin crack which leads out to a ledge on the left edge. Go up right through a slot to belay on a large ledge (20 m, 5b). Follow a deep fissure and continue straight up the edge overlooking the East Wall meadows. Scramble up the crest to the col below the second tower of Mitre Ridge.

284   The Actress   250 m   V   (1984)

A hard winter route starting near Mitre Ridge Direct and finishing by The Bishop. Start 2 m left of the big groove of Mitre Ridge. Climb straight up a shallow corner/fault line for 70 m. From here an inviting ramp (Helter Skelter) slopes up right but is a winter cul-de-sac. Traverse left and slightly down for 10 m to gain a small ramp leading up and back right to the base of a steep right-facing corner. Climb this (1 PA) and a chimney above to reach the terrace left of The Shoulder. The steep wall above is cleft by twin narrow chimneys. Climb the left one (with a desperate start) to the slab above. Traverse easily left and follow the edge overlooking the ramp of The Grail (this edge is The Bishop in summer) to reach the col between First and Second Towers.

285 Mitre Ridge Direct 200 m Hard Very Severe (1975)

A mountaineering route taking a classic line, including a spectacular crux pitch up the crest of the First Tower. The pitch grades are unknown, probably 4c or less (except for the crux), with vegetation on easier ground. Start 6 m left of the big groove of the normal route. Move left on to a rib and climb cracks and grooves for 45 m to belay below twin breaks in an overlap (poor stance). Climb the overlap and continue up to belay below an obvious notch in a steep wall (45 m). Traverse slightly rightwards, climb a steep corner, go up cracks on the edge of the buttress to an obvious poised flake, then continue to the shoulder of the ridge (45 m). Traverse right, then go up to a steep wall (30 m, pitch common to normal route). Traverse right across a slab to make an awkward mantleshelf on to a sloping shelf below an over-hanging wall. Make a delicate traverse back left to gain the leftmost of twin cracks. Climb the crack up a gently overhanging wall to reach easier ground (10 m, 5b). Continue to the top of the tower and scramble along an arete (friable rock) to the foot of the second tower. Finish by Bell's Variation on the right.

286 Mitre Ridge 220 m Hard Severe (1933)

One of the great classic ridges of the Cairngorms. There is some vegetation and a little loose rock. Nevertheless it is a fine natural line with rewarding situations. The first pitch is Hard Severe; subsequent pitches are not more than Very Difficult.

The first pitch ascends the big groove set midway between the lowest rocks and the right corner of the ridge. Start up slabs and follow the corner directly to a short bulging wall. Climb the wall in the corner to a small stance (35 m, crux). Follow the general line of a rising shelf round to below a deep-cut chimney on the west face. Climb the chimney and enter a shallow gully which leads to a shoulder on the ridge. A short wall blocks progress. Make a delicate traverse right, then go straight up to the steep wall below the first tower (30 m). Above and to the left is a large grass platform which may be gained directly by a short, inset right-angled corner or, slightly easier, by moving leftwards across a slab and climbing a splintered chimney. Climb the wall above the platform and ascend rightwards to the col between the first and second towers. There are now three variations to climb the second tower. By far the best (Bell's Variation) is to follow a shelf to the right corner and climb a very exposed crack on the west face. Step back left from the crack and finish straight up. The other alternatives are to climb the tower by a steep crack from the col or to turn the tower on the left. From the top of the second tower, finish along a narrow horizontal arete over the final tower. (Diagram p. 194.)

Winter V (1953)

One of the finest winter expeditions in the area. In good conditions the initial groove makes a superb start. Otherwise it is avoided by a line of weakness at the right corner of the ridge which joins the route above the groove. The short wall after the shoulder will probably require a point of aid in powder conditions. Above this the splintered chimney is used to gain the platform. The second tower is turned on the left (Bell's Variation has not been climbed in winter). The final arete is an impressive finish.

THE WEST WALL
Very steep and impressive, but has more holds than would appear. Two obvious corner gullies run up either side of a 100 m subsidiary cuneiform buttress which stands out from the wall of the ridge above the first tower. Cumming–Crofton Route follows the left corner to the arete between the first and second towers; Commando Route the right corner to a point where it forks—the left fork joining the top of Cumming–Crofton, the right fork running up to the final col on the ridge.

287 Cumming–Crofton Route 160 m Severe (1933)
The most outstanding pre-war route in the Cairngorms. Steep and sustained. Start directly below the corner and go straight up to a small platform. Climb the prominent chimney, which has a hanging flake forming a constriction at mid-height, to a stance in a cleft at the top (30 m). Traverse rightwards for 10 m by way of a short, smooth groove. When stopped by a vertical wall return left by an airy traverse across a wall and over a bulge into the main corner (15 m). The variation leaves here. The general line is now up the corner. For the first 5 m, climb the wall just to the right of the corner. Step left into the corner-crack and climb to a broad platform (25 m). Climb a crack in the left wall then traverse right and follow a sloping ledge to a short wall. Pursuing the same line, follow a loose gully for 25 m to reach the ridge between the first and second towers. Climb the second tower by Bell's Variation on the right. (Diagram p. 194.)

Variation

A link pitch, Very Severe, joins Cumming–Crofton Route to the Mitre Ridge routes and allows a fine, hard finish, leaving the normal route after 45 m. Continue in the corner for 3 m then traverse left to a protruding block. Follow the obvious cracks straight up to the crest of the ridge (18 m, 4c). From here it is possible to traverse left 5 m to join Mitre Ridge Original Route but it is recommended to go straight up the edge to the foot of the first tower (10 m). Climb the first tower by Mitre Ridge Direct (5b), starting with the awkward mantleshelf.

Winter   V   (1977)

A superb, sustained and technically hard winter route, the scene of several epic attempts before its successful ascent. Follow the summer line (two ascents to date).

288   The Chancel   120 m   Hard Very Severe   (1978)

This good route climbs the left edge of the cuneiform buttress right of Cumming–Crofton Route. Start 6 m right of that route at a large block. Climb a prominent cracked groove to a niche, belay ledge on right (20 m, 4c). From the niche move up left and climb a shallow corner to a bulge (crux). Pull out on to the left wall then go left and up to belay on the second pitch of Cumming–Crofton Route (20 m, 5b). Continue up an obvious ramp leading rightwards away from Cumming–Crofton to a grass terrace girdling the face of the buttress (25 m, 4b). At the mid point of the terrace climb the wall above, going leftwards to a ledge (4c). Go straight up to easy ground below the second tower. (Diagram p. 194.)

289   The Empty Quarter   40 m   E3   (1983)

Climbs the wall right of The Chancel, using an obvious shallow vertical corner towards the right side of the wall. An excellent, well-protected pitch.

Scramble up to a ledge, then move out right onto the wall and up to the corner. Climb it and exit left at the top. Follow a good crack leftwards until possible to move up on to a little foot ledge under an overlap. Step up, go left under the bulge then pull over and up the wall at diagonal cracks to reach easier rock. A direct finish from here would be best but on the first ascent rope drag necessitated a left traverse and finish up an obvious fault (40 m, 5c). One is now on the terrace. The crest of Mitre Ridge can be reached by finishing up The Chancel (50 m, 4c). (Diagram p. 194.)

290   Commando Route   140 m   IV   (1969)

An excellent winter route. It follows the corner gully forming the right side of the cuneiform buttress. The difficulty is to get started on the corner which does not begin until 20 m up. It is reached by a tension move from a minor gully on the right. Once gained, follow the corner gully by its right fork in three steep sustained pitches. Probably worth Very Severe in summer, being dangerously loose. (Diagram p. 194.)

THE SLOCHD WALL

On the right of Commando Route is a very steep wall with a prominent roof system at 30 m. This wall provides three very fine, technically interesting routes on steep rock with surprising holds.

291   Chindit   100 m   Original: Very Severe   (1979)
                              Direct: E1   (1982)

Follows the left edge of the wall. The direct version, finer but harder, stays on the wall. The original route makes a short detour into the fault on the left. This fault is Gurkha, Very Severe, 4c, 1 PA, which starts as the minor gully of Commando Route.

Start at the foot of North-West Gully and climb the gully to the first depression. Traverse left on to the wall via a grass shelf and belay at an obvious stance (15 m). Climb diagonally left to the edge, then follow a crack for about 10 m to a steepening. For the direct route, step right and up to the overlap, make a difficult mantleshelf into an obvious small corner and traverse from the corner up left to join cracks on the original route (5b). The original route traverses left under the steepening into the fault on the left and regains the edge 2 m above via a sloping foothold on the arete. Move up, then make an exposed rising traverse rightwards (4c, rejoining the direct route) until it is possible to move back left to the edge. Follow the edge, then traverse left across the top of the fault to belay (20 m). Climb an obvious crack past a knob of rock at a steepening and continue straight up the exposed right edge to the final tower. Here one can go left to the plateau but a good finish is to traverse right on to the front wall and finish straight up as for Slochd Wall. (Diagram p. 194.)

292   Slochd Wall   110 m   Hard Very Severe   (1969/1982)

A superb route, ascending a large vertical corner which leads up from the left end of the roof system. Higher up, the corner diverges into two corners, providing the left and right (original) finishes. The left finish, which makes a more sustained route, is described, although both finishes are good. The original finish shares its top pitch with The Primate.

Start at the foot of North-West Gully and climb the gully to the first depression. Traverse left onto the wall via a grass shelf and belay at an obvious stance (15 m, common with Chindit). Follow a crack right and climb the steep slab trending slightly leftwards alongside a small corner (old bolt runner) to a big overhang. Swing right under the overhang into a shallow corner and climb this (crux) to belay in the main corner (30 m, 5a). The original route continues in the main corner (which trends right), starting on the right wall for 3 m and joining The Primate at the grass terrace (5a). For the left finish, traverse left to enter and follow another corner until possible to step right on to a large ledge (the last few metres are common to Helter Skelter—described below) (15 m, 4c). Climb the rib at the left end of the ledge for a short way, then swing left to regain the corner. Go straight up, turn the overhang on the left, then move diagonally left to gain the arete of Chindit. Belay a little higher (20 m, 5a). Continue up the edge and finish by the final crack of The Primate (30 m). (Diagram p. 194.)

293   The Primate   95 m   Hard Very Severe
This is the wide crack splitting the roof system right of Slochd Wall. Another fine route; the roof gives a fascinating sequence of moves. Start from the first stance of Slochd Wall. Climb the obvious crack going out right to reach cracks which lead to a ledge below and right of the roof crack (25 m, 4c). If the initial crack is wet, one can start at two large jammed blocks in North-West Gully. Traverse left and follow the crack through the roof. Continue up the crack to a grass terrace below the final wall (25 m, 5b). Continue by short walls to gain a left-slanting groove in the final headwall. Climb the groove almost to the left edge and finish by the crack above (45 m). (Diagram p. 194.)

A route has been climbed, starting at the jammed blocks in North-West Gully and taking steep cracks going initially rightwards (Hard Very Severe, 5b). The route deteriorates towards the top.

294   Helter Skelter   270 m   Very Severe
A rising girdle of Mitre Ridge with a spectacular finish on the Slochd Wall. It crosses some improbable pieces of rock for its grade.

Start by two large blocks on a ledge near the foot of South-East Gully. Move right into a crack, climb this for 10 m then traverse right and belay above an isolated overlap on East Wall Direct (25 m). Move down right into a grassy crack, traverse right, then climb up to overlap and traverse right beneath it (4c) to gain a central crackline. Move up and right to a steepening, cross The Bishop, belay just left of the orange scar beneath an overhang (35 m). Climb the groove left of the overhang, cross Mitre Direct and climb diagonally right up a ramp to a fine balcony overlooking Mitre Ridge normal route (35 m). Climb a slot-chimney in the left corner of the balcony, then spiral round crest on superb holds to emerge above the chimney on Mitre Ridge normal route. Move right into Cumming–Crofton, climb the ramp of the Chancel and belay on the large ledge. Follow the ledge into Commando Route, then go up and right to belay on a bay below an overhanging slot (35 m). Descend slightly and gain a sloping foothold on the arete (as for Chindit). Move up then make an exposed rising traverse (4c, crux) to a corner on Slochd Wall (left finish). Climb the corner for 3 m then move right to the large ledge (20 m). Move right beneath a corner on Slochd Wall (right finish) and climb the left edge of the wall above. Finish up the headwall as for The Primate. (Diagram p. 195.)

295   North-West Gully   150 m   III   (1956)
The corner gully tucked hard against the west wall of Mitre Ridge. A very good winter gully which varies greatly in difficulty. After a period of freezing and thawing, a superb 30 m ice pitch may form. Early in the season, under powder, it is much harder. The approach from the corrie floor is by a graceful arete of snow which swings up round the base of the Ridge. (Diagram p. 194.)

There is another shallower gully in the slabby buttress right of North-West Gully. This is North-West Couloir, III. The buttress to its left has been climbed, Moderate, as has the one to its right in winter (North-West Groove, II/III).

STOB AN t-SLUICHD

This isolated top of Beinn a'Bhuird sports an array of miniature aretes and buttresses which face across to the Mitre Ridge. The best defined arete is at the left end (Pinnacle Ridge—Difficult, III). The broader buttress on the extreme right beyond a wide scree chute is M and B Buttress, Moderate. Between these two are four more or less defined aretes. These have all been climbed in summer and on the first one left of M and B Buttress is Token Groove, II/III, a shallow, left-trending groove system left of the main crest.

COIRE SPUTAN DEARG OF BEN MACDHUI (NO 0099)

Coire Sputan Dearg lies at the head of Glen Luibeg, high on the south-eastern flank of Ben Macdhui. In spring and early summer its dark buttresses stand out boldly against the old snow and are often clearly visible from as far away as the Braemar–Linn of Dee road. "Sputan" is a unique corrie with a charm all of its own. The south-facing crag is a rarity in the Cairngorms and the granite is rough, clean, sound and very quick to dry. The corrie's open, sunny situation lends an unusually friendly atmosphere and although the routes are short (30–150 m) descents are quick and easy, making it possible to accomplish many routes in one visit. Few climbers could fail to enjoy a day climbing in Sputan Dearg. Sputan is not a place for the hard man, since its slabby nature and good jugs preclude the modern, technical route. For the lower grades, however, there is no better place in the Cairngorms.

Winter:

With a cliff base at 1100 m, Sputan is one of the highest corries in the area. A considerable build-up of snow may accumulate during the season and many of the rock features may be buried. The climbing is of a less exacting nature than on Creagan a'Choire Etchachan but it serves as a useful alternative to that cliff when the freezing level is above the 1000 m mark or during periods of hard frost and sunny weather, when the snow in Coire Sputan Dearg consolidates quicker. In late season the buttresses are quickly stripped of snow by the sun but can give good climbing after a fresh fall of powder any time between October and May.

Approaches
1. From Braemar via Derry Lodge and Glen Luibeg
   From Braemar by public road to the Linn of Dee and back towards Braemar on the north side of the Dee for 700 m to the Derry Gates (locked). From the Gates to Derry Lodge, 5 km, then follow the Lairig Ghru track for 3 km and fork right up a steep rising path some 150 m short of the Luibeg burn. Follow the path up the burn; it gradually peters out 8 km from Derry Lodge.

2. From the Hutchison Memorial Hut (See Creagan a'Choire Etchachan).

Follow the stream coming down the wide grassy basin to the left of the cliffs of Creagan a'Choire Etchachan and go over the col between that top and Derry Cairngorm. 2 km.

Accommodation

The Hutchison Memorial Hut (see Creagan a' Choire Etchachan) is the closest reliable shelter for Coire Sputan Dearg; but there are one or two draughty "howffs" amongst the boulders in the corrie suitable for dry summer weather.

Luibeg Bothy (NO 036933). For many years the keeper at Luibeg Cottage, beside Derry Lodge, kept a small bothy open for climbers. Although Luibeg Cottage is now unoccupied, the bothy is still open. Traditionally one of the best bothies in the area and a great favourite with local climbers, its existence is entirely due to the good relationship between the estate and the climbers. Future availability requires the relationship to be maintained.

Camping: Good camping sites exist at the Robber's Copse—a stand of old Caledonian pines at the ford over the Luibeg, 3 km from Derry Lodge and also further up Glen Luibeg on the raised green shelves at the confluence of the Allt Carn a'Mhaim on the left bank. There is excellent camping just beyond Derry Lodge itself.

Descents

Descent presents no problem. Glissade Gully (scree) is the easiest and centrally situated.

THE RED SLABS

These are the gently inclined glaciated slabs approx. 200 m left of the leftmost buttress (Pinnacle Buttress). The slabs are affected by melt water well into the summer and it is doubtful whether they are ever completely dry. However, the granite is very rough and may be climbed at almost any point, even when wet. They freeze up readily and provide good ice practice at the start of the winter before banking out quickly.

The large prominent corner on the upper left-hand section of the slabs is Rainmate, Severe, III. Umbrella, Very Severe, takes a fairly direct line up the slabs, starting at an undercut crack just right of the lowest rocks. The best rock climbing, however, is described below.

296 Sundance 120 m   Very Severe   (1970)

The route is a rising traverse across the slabs below the big overlap (it crosses Umbrella). Start 15 m up from the lowest slabs on the left at an obvious corner.

Climb the corner, go right across glacis, surmount the overlap and continue to a ledge below the vegetated corner-crack (30 m). Traverse horizontally right and climb a slab to ledge. Go up to the main overlap. Traverse right below an overhanging block studded with quartz crystals and work up right to the edge of the upper slab. Step across a corner and continue to a ledge. Climb a vertical crack to the roof. Move right under the roof and go up to a belay below the final corner. Climb the corner to easy ground. Probably 4b.

A winter ascent has been made at grade III but the route is more usually banked out.

THE BUTTRESSES

They start high on the left of the corrie, adjacent to the Red Slabs and extend north in a descending line, merging gradually into broken rock near the low col leading to Loch Etchachan. They are intersected at three points by wide scree gullies (the Red Spouts) which provide easy means of descent.

297 Pinnacle Buttress 110 m   Moderate   (1948)

The first buttress from the left. It is easily recognised by a ledge of easy ground coming in from the right, halfway up. In winter, this looks like a notch.

Start up an obvious line of weakness at the foot of the buttress to reach a long groove forming an angle between the true crest on the right and a 30 m cracked slab on the left. Start in the groove but leave it soon to slant up the slab to reach its top left corner. Scramble to plateau.

Variation: Direct Route, Severe

Follow the true crest of the buttress overlooking the cracked slab. Pleasant airy climbing. A variation start, Severe, has also been made to the right of the crest up a smooth slab bounding the Red Gully.

Winter II   (1950)

An enjoyable winter route. The lower rocks are easy but the long groove may contain ice (crux).

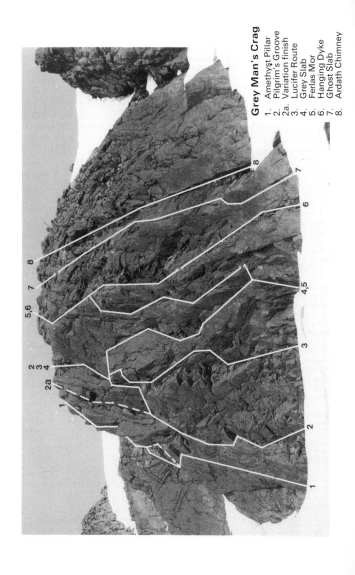

Grey Man's Crag

1. Amethyst Pillar
2. Pilgrim's Groove
2a. Variation finish
3. Lucifer Route
4. Grey Slab
5. Ferlas Mor
6. Hanging Dyke
7. Ghost Slab
8. Ardath Chimney

298 The Red Gully 120m I

A straightforward snow climb.

299 Crystal Ridge 90m Difficult (1948)

A grand little climb, very popular. As closely as possible, follow the crest of a great slab, angling into and bolstering up the upper left flank of Grey Man's Crag. The ridge has a steep left wall bordering the Red Gully.

Winter III (1949)

An attractive snow arete provides the finish to the route.

300 Slab Chimney: Right Branch 120m II/III (1949)
Left Branch I (1949)

The best winter gully in the corrie. It cuts deeply into the flank of Grey Man's Crag, showing up as a perfect Y from the Luibeg approach. Easy snow leads to the junction. The right branch contains two chokestones which give awkward ice pitches but the difficulty eases with an increased build-up of snow. The left branch gives a good introduction to snow climbing, a scenic position. Unpleasant and Difficult in summer.

GREY MAN'S CRAG

This is the name given to the largest buttress in the corrie. It is defined by Slab Chimney on the left and Anchor Gully on the right. The longest and some of the best routes in the corrie are on this crag. The frontal face is scored by numerous grooves and narrow slabs which tend to lean leftwards towards the very steep wall above Slab Chimney. High on the left overlooking Slab Chimney a remarkable crack can be seen cleaving the steep face, The Plumbline, Hard Severe. A girdle traverse of Grey Man's Crag has been made, Hard Severe, starting in Anchor Gully and finishing up The Plumbline.

301 Amethyst Pillar 100m Hard Very Severe (1964/1979)

Amethyst Wall, Hard Very Severe, follows a meandering route on the steep wall between Slab Chimney and Pilgrim's Groove. This direct line to its right (originally called Topaz) gives an excellent steep climb, probably the best at Sputan.

Start at the foot of a prominent slanting chimney-fault. Move out right on to the steep slabs, starting about 5m below a curious round niche. Alternatively, climb up into the niche and exit right. Climb up

the wall above (Pilgrim's Groove crux is now 3 m to the right). Go left
and pull over a bulge into an obvious hanging corner. Step left at a
small roof, then down left and traverse along a flake-ledge to belay at
its end (40 m, 4c). The flakes of Amethyst Wall can now be seen to the
left. Above is a shallow cracked groove with a bulge. Climb the groove
and exit right on to a ramp which ascends from the depression of
Pilgrim's Groove. Alternatively, climb diagonally rightwards across
the steep wall above the flake-ledge to gain the same ramp lower
down. Follow the ramp up left to its top (25 m, 4c). Go up right to an
obvious vertical crack above a rock pedestal. Use a loose jammed flake
to overcome the initial bulge and continue directly up the crack to
slabs which lead to the top (35 m, 5a). (Diagram p. 206.)

302 Pilgrim's Groove   120 m   Hard Severe   (1949)

Situated just left of centre on the buttress and to the left of the lowest
rocks. It follows a defined groove developing into a prominent
chimney. Somewhat vegetated and the chimney is usually wet. A fault
right of and parallel to Pilgrim's Groove, blocked by a large overhang,
is the line of Lucifer route, Severe, which joins Pilgrim's Groove near
the top.

   Start in the groove and climb moderate rock to a stance about 10 m
below a triangular overhang. Continue up the groove to the overhang,
turn it on the left wall and climb steep rock to a large grassy
depression. The next pitch is the continuation chimney which rises for
20 m in four steps, each progressively more difficult. The remainder of
the chimney is easy. (Diagram p. 206.)

Variation Finish: Very Severe, 4b: better than the original.

Starting from the grassy depression, a groove and chimney line on the
left, finishing by a swing out left under an overhang.

Winter   V   (1981)

A natural winter line with a very technical but well protected crux. The
upper chimney is often a fine icefall. Follow the summer route to the
grassy depression. On the first (and only) ascent, in lean conditions,
the ice in the chimney was very thin and it was preferred to use the
Variation Finish, using tension below the overhang to regain the
summer line.

303 Lucifer Route   120 m   Severe   (1956)

Follows a fault parallel and to the right of Pilgrim's Groove. The fault is blocked by a large overhang. A vegetated route, although the crux is clean.

Climb the fault to belay under the overhang. Go up the vertical right wall on good flake holds (crux), then continue up the fault to belay beside the large depression of Pilgrim's Groove. Climb to the right over a huge detached block onto the Grey Slab and up to a belay on a ledge near its top. Move left and step down into the chimney of Pilgrim's Groove, which is followed to the top. (Diagram p. 206.)

Winter   V   (1983)

One winter ascent by the summer line, using 1 PA on the summer crux. The route is interchangeable with Pilgrim's Groove at the large depression.

304 Grey Slab   120 m   Hard Severe   (1963)
This excellent route follows a conspicuous corner trending left up the centre of the buttress. Near the top it climbs the right side of a large slab—the Grey Slab. Scramble up broken rocks to a good platform 10 m below the corner.

Start up a shallow depression and move awkwardly right to a good stance below the corner (10 m). Climb the corner to a grass platform (20 m, crux). Continue up the corner to an overhang. Turn this on the left and go up to a ledge (possible belay). Climb by the corner at the right-hand edge of the Grey Slab, until forced to move left at its top (40 m). Step down and enter the chimney of Pilgrim's Groove on the left (as for Lucifer Route). Better but Very Severe, is to climb a short slab and enter Pilgrim's Groove higher up. Finish by Pilgrim's Groove. (Diagram p. 206.)

Winter   V   (1984)

A sustained and very hard climb by the summer route; 1 PA on pitch 2 on the only ascent to date. Not a traditional type of winter climb, as the first two pitches have little vegetation and do not hold any ice.

305 Ferlas Mor   120 m   Hard Severe   (1971)
A direct line between Grey Slab and Hanging Dyke. The climbing is as good as Grey Slab and the standard similar, although it lacks such a prominent line.

Climb the first pitch of Grey Slab to the stance at the foot of the corner (10 m). For an independent first pitch, climb the layback corner right of the normal start (5a, not led). Swing up right and climb grooves and ribs on the edge overlooking the Grey Slab to a basalt fault. Climb the fault to a ledge and belay below the crux of Hanging Dyke (30 m). Move left and continue up grooves, exiting on to the crest on the right, level with the top of the Grey Slab (40 m). Continue on the skyline, via a short easy chimney and an arete to the top. (Diagram p. 206.)

306   Hanging Dyke   120 m   Very Difficult   (1949)

A deservedly popular route. The climb follows the backbone of this buttress by the line of a geological dyke. The crux is delicate and exposed.

Start to the right of the lowest rocks at the foot of a broad slab. The dyke goes up the centre of this slab. Follow the dyke to a small ledge, then climb a grass-filled crack to a good stance. Climb a wide slab inclining left by a series of parallel cracks to a sloping corner. The dyke steepens, forming a rib to the left of a groove. Climb the rib for 20 m on small holds (crux) until the dyke falls back into a chimney. Follow the continuation of the dyke up left on the crest for a further 30 m. (Diagram p. 206.)

Winter   IV   (1971)

A sustained climb. The crux is the steep rib, as in summer. On the first (only) ascent, the rib was abandoned after 5 m and a shelf high on the right gained with a peg. This was followed for 10 m, then a step left led back onto the rib and into the chimney.

307   Ghost Crack   90 m   Very Severe   (1972)

This is the shallow crack slightly left of the crest between Hanging Dyke and Ardath Chimney. Technically interesting climbing but a little artificial.

Climb the crack to a ledge and go slightly rightwards by a short, deeper crack to another ledge below obvious stepped overlaps (40 m, 4b). Surmount the overlaps and climb the thin crack above until a smooth wall forces a traverse up right to a slab overlooking Ardath Chimney. An easier alternative is to step round the arete on the left and follow cracks, initially overlooking Hanging Dyke, to reach the slab. Climb a crack in the slab, then easier rock to a belay (45 m, 4c). Five metres of rock leads to scrambling. In dry weather it is possible to descend Ardath Chimney, Difficult.

308 Ardath Chimney 120 m III (1955)
A good winter climb, best climbed early in the season or after a thaw when the chimney holds plenty of ice. A short ice slab about 30 m above the chimney may prove to be the crux. In summer, Difficult for the 45 m of the chimney, then scrambling. (Diagram p. 206.)

309 Anchor Gully 120 m I
The gully between Grey Man's Crag and Anchor Route. So named from the formation of snow at its foot (in spring). There may be a pitch early in the season. Later the gully becomes quite straightforward except for the cornice which can usually be outflanked on the right. Moderate in summer.

310 Anchor Route 120 m III (1955)
The route lies on the double tiered buttress bordering Anchor Gully on the right. In winter the rocks of the lower tier tend to bank out and it is best to start in Anchor Gully. On the upper tier, start and finish right of the crest but there is an excursion onto the steeper gully wall in the middle.
  In summer, the route is pleasant but a little scrappy, Difficult.

Glissade Gully
Set near the centre of the cliff this is the natural highway summer and winter between plateau and corrie floor. In summer it is scree filled, in winter a snow slope. There may be a cornice which is avoidable on the left.
  The small broken buttress on the left of Glissade Gully is Glissade Buttress, II.
  On the right of Glissade Gully are twin ridges: the left ridge, split into two sections by a deep chimney low down, is Janus and the right ridge is Snake Ridge.

311 Hackingbush's Horror 130 m Very Severe (1956)
The route starts by the steep rib on the left of the chimney (the left leg of Janus) and above the chimney takes the upper buttress which has a notched terminating ridge. A good first pitch, just Very Severe, strenuous. After this the climbing is Difficult in standard, scrappy but interesting.
  Climb the groove from the foot of the rib to a ledge then move right to the crest. Step awkwardly left and up to a platform. Climb the shallow depression above to the foot of a vertical crack with an

overhung top. Use a good layback and traverse right to the crest (4b). Follow the ridge to easy ground below the upper buttress. Climb the upper buttress on the left side above Glissade Gully by going round a ledge to the left past an initial groove. When the ledge peters out bear sharp right up a second groove to the crest.

Janus, starting by the right-hand rib, is Difficult and in winter, III with 2PA in the second groove. The chimney which splits the two ribs in the lower section is Janus Chimney, Very Difficult.

312   Snake Gully   130 m   II   (1963)
This is the dividing fault between Janus and Snake Ridge. It gives a good, natural winter climb. The gully starts as steep snow and curves up leftwards to an ice pitch. This will vary in length according to the build-up. Easier climbing leads to the level of the upper buttress of Janus. Go up the right side of the upper buttress via a short arete and an ice groove. Thereafter, snow slopes lead to the plateau.

313   Snake Ridge   130 m   Severe   (1949)
An excellent climb, one of the original classics of the corrie. Snake Ridge is the second of the long ridges to the right of Glissade Gully, so named from its fancied resemblance, as seen from the top, to a snake head down. For easier recognition its lower rocks fan out into three ridges giving a fair impression of inverted Prince of Wales feathers. The left side of the ridge is low and angles easily into a grassy gully running alongside.

Start on the left "feather" and follow the crest directly for two pitches to a platform and belay below a step on the ridge (60 m). Climb this on the left to a stance and spike belay on the right (15 m). The crux pitch follows. Go up to a short wall and use good holds to pull up into a groove. Continue rightwards up the groove to the crest, or (easier) leave the groove and climb to a good hold on the left. Further climbing for 30 m leads to the broken upper buttress.

Immediately to the right of Snake Ridge is a slender gully, The Ladders, II. To the right again is the well-defined gully, Narrow Gully, I.

The compact buttresses forming a close-set trio to the right of Narrow Gully are named from left to right: Cherub's Buttress, The Black Tower and Flake Buttress. They are separated from each other by wet slabby depressions which become icefalls in winter.

Cherub's Buttress is Difficult, III, by a line close to the crest on the left (overlooking Narrow Gully). An alternative winter line is a flying ridge which forms a separate leg on the right in the lower section, II.

314 Left-Hand Icefall 90 m IV (1977)
A short, steep icefall in the depression between Cherub's Buttress and the Black Tower. Difficulties are concentrated in the steep ice-filled groove hard against the left wall of the Black Tower. After this an easy snow gully leads to the col behind the Black Tower summit. An attractive snow arete leads to the plateau.

315 The Black Tower 110 m Severe (1952)
The climb, though short, is excellent and has great character. Unfortunately, it also has a very unpleasant approach pitch. From the corrie floor the buttress is squat and compact; its finer and truer form is best seen from Cherub's Buttress from where it appears as a tapering, twisted spire having a curious, square summit block reminiscent of the greater Aiguilles.

Start to the left of the buttress by climbing into an unpleasant slabby basin oozing with wet vegetation (the Left-Hand Icefall in winter). From the right side of the basin, about 20 m above the lowest rocks, follow a groove developing into a narrow chimney (25 m). Climb broken slabs on the left for 10 m to a platform at the foot of a steep 6 m groove on the edge of the tower. Enter the groove on the right and climb it to a platform and block (crux). Move round a corner on the left and climb a crack to a short arete. Thence, by a delicate traverse across a slab on the right it is possible to regain the crest and summit of the tower by a short steep crack. The tower is linked to the plateau by a broken arete.

Winter IV (1979)

Climb the first pitch as for summer, then gain the summit by a line well to the right of the summer crux section.

316 Right-Hand Icefall 80 m II (1967)
A prominent cataract of ice between the Black Tower and Flake Buttress. The angle is not excessive.

317 Flake Buttress 110 m Moderate (1949)
An interesting variety of pitches. More difficult variations have been made in the lower section.

Start just right of the lowest rocks and follow a grassy depression rightwards to a stance on the broken crest (20 m). Continue the same line until a flake-crack leads back left to a short right-angled corner. Swing up left on good holds. Go up a chimney on the right and then by easy ledges to a stance and belay below an overhang on the crest. Behind a huge flake on the left climb a vertical crack on grand holds and continue up slabby blocks to a gap. Ignore the easy ground on the right and take the arete straight ahead to the plateau.

Winter   120 m   III   (1950)

The buttress gives a fine winter climb which should be possible in almost any conditions.

SPIDER BUTTRESS
This is the slabby buttress between Flake Buttress and The Main Spout. It has two overhangs on its left flank, the right one containing a prominent crack and the smaller left one being cigar-shaped. Right of the overhangs is a steep, cracked wall containing The Fly.

318   The Skater   45 m   E4   (1984)
Takes the left edge of the buttress, overlooking a big low-angled corner. Good climbing, but short and a little artificial. Start at the base of the big corner.
   Climb a shallow corner just right of the right arete of the big corner. Exit right at the top to join the Chebec for a move. Go diagonally left across the slab to a jug on the arete and a poor peg runner. A good hold above is tantalisingly out of reach and the slab on the right climbed to the obvious corner at the left end of the cigar-shaped overhang (an easier solution may be possible, especially for the very tall). Belay at the top of the corner (30 m, 6a). Continue up and a little left over easy blocks to finish by a short overhanging crack (15 m, 4b).

319   The Chebec   60 m   Very Severe   (1975)
The route takes a line between the overhangs on the left flank of the buttress. From the left end of the buttress, scramble up right for 10 m to a belay below the cigar-shaped overhang. Move left and climb a groove to the right end of the overhang, pull out right and climb a crack, then a slab to a ledge and belay (35 m, 4c). Go left and climb a rightward overhung corner to a horizontal crack, traverse right, then up more easily to finish.

320   The Fly   45 m   Hard Severe   (1971)
A technical pitch on fine rock, high in its grade but well protected. The object is to reach a prominent S-shaped crack high on the steep cracked wall. Start at base of wall. Climb a crack up leftwards, then move right to gain a horizontal crack. Traverse this across the wall and climb easily up left to the deep S-shaped crack. Climb the crack, then the slab above or the deep flake-crack on its right.

A poor route, The Web, Severe, has been climbed on the wall to the right of The Fly.

THE MAIN SPOUT: TERMINAL BUTTRESS
The right flank of the Main Spout sports numerous short ribs and walls which diminish in size towards the plateau. Terminal Buttress and Terminal Wall lie on the largest piece of rock at the foot of the Spout. A grassy shelf slants down from the final crest of Terminal Buttress into the Main Spout. This offers a useful means of descent for all the routes on this section of cliff. A route has been climbed on the right side of the wall above the shelf, April Wall, Severe. It can be used as a continuation to the "Terminal" routes. Above the descent shelf is a steep wall overlooking the Spout and including The Chute and The Swing. Though short, all the routes described are recommended.

321   The Chute   45 m   Hard Very Severe   (1970)
Left of the descent shelf is a steep wall containing several grooves. The leftmost of these grooves forms an open corner capped by a curious jammed block.
    Climb the corner, going behind the jammed block. Step left and follow an obvious left-trending crack to a shallow groove left of a prominent overhanging prow. Climb the groove to a good platform and scramble to the top (5a).

From the top of the block, Wee Heavy, Very Severe, 4b, goes steeply up rightwards to follow a shallow gully to the top.

322   The Swing   35 m   Severe   (1960)
Follows the steep rib, 15 m left of The Chute. Climb the rib crest directly, then up an obvious hanging V-corner above. The corner on the right of the rib has also been climbed, Very Severe, 4b, finishing by the V-corner.

323   Terminal Buttress   70 m   Very Difficult   (1949)
On the lower section of cliff. The route follows a prominent, crescent-shaped groove.

Start in a short gully at the foot of the lower wall. Climb a fault on wrinkled and puckered rock for a steep, initial 10 m; a little higher traverse left round a rib and move up over a projecting spur to a deep V-groove and a belay on the edge. Follow the groove for 10 m, passing an overhang on the left, until forced out horizontally left round a corner to a large ledge. Ten metres of climbing straight ahead end at the broad shelf. Climb a shattered rib on the right to finish.

Winter   IV   (1961)

A short, technical problem. Late in the season, the first pitch usually banks out.

324   Terminal Wall   70 m   Hard Severe   (1963)
This fine exposed route ascends a series of cracks and grooves on the left edge of the big wall right of Terminal Buttress.

Start 3 m right of the Terminal Buttress fault. Climb straight up over an overhang on an unusual formation of huge jugs, then left to the edge and belay. Move right, climb cracks above, then a fault to a sloping ledge leading right. From the end of this ledge go straight up and make an awkward move left round a corner. Finish by cracks and blocks.

325   The Hin'most   80 m   Very Severe   (1976)
On the slab wall right of Terminal Wall. Climb the first pitch of Terminal Wall to belay ledge. Make a long rightwards rising traverse following obvious parallel folds. Where the folds almost meet the flanking gully go up left to the foot of a prominent crack in the centre of the wall. Climb the crack, starting on the wall to its right (4c).

CREAGAN A'CHOIRE ETCHACHAN (NO 016997)

This fine crag is situated high on the east-facing slopes of Choire Etchachan just a few hundred metres left of the tourist path to Ben Macdhui. It presents a very bold straight face of granite averaging 120 m in height.

The large buttress at the left-hand end of the crag is called The Bastion. It is defined by the hidden Forked Gully on its left and the prominent slabby trench of The Corridor on its right. Between The Corridor and a much shallower slabby gully, Square Cut Gully, lies Juniper Buttress. Pioneer Buttress is the triangular mass of rock right of Square Cut Gully. A prominent line of overhangs rises diagonally rightwards from the foot of Pioneer Buttress across the face above two large grass depressions—the Meadows. Finally, the dark vertical fault of The Red Chimney separates this Meadow Face from the great sweep of Crimson Slabs on the extreme right. As a general guide, the areas of the Corridor Recess and the Crimson Slabs have the soundest and cleanest rock and consequently the best climbing.

As a great winter cliff the Etchachan face only lacks length. The vegetated buttresses, wet slabby gullies and smooth slabs become liberally plated in snow and ice and offer some of the finest sport in the area. An east-facing aspect and a moderate altitude (base of cliff approx. 850 m) account for more variable conditions than higher cliffs but this, along with the persistence of the drainage lines on the face, frequently results in very icy conditions. The Bastion is the safest place to climb when the condition of the snow is doubtful.

Approaches

1. From Braemar via Derry Lodge (see Coire Sputan Dearg)

Two hundred metres beyond Derry Lodge, turn right at the public telephone, cross a bridge and follow a path through the forest up into Glen Derry. Under powder it is better to follow the bulldozed road on the right side of Glen Derry. Instead of crossing the bridge, follow the right side of the shallow valley bottom for about 200 m until the road starts just up on the hillside. A path branches left from Glen Derry to the Hutchison hut. In thick weather in winter (in the dark), both the hut and the correct point to branch left are difficult to find. Eight kilometres from Derry Lodge.

2. From Glenmore via Shelter Stone and Loch Etchachan

Quickest way is to ascend Coire Cas to the plateau, or take chair lift and walk over Cairngorm. In either case descend Coire Raibert and follow the path round the head of Loch A'an to the Shelter Stone (many good howffs) 5 km from Cairngorm Car Park. Considerable ascent and descent. Take track over Beinn Mheadhoin—Cairn Etchachan col to the outflow of Loch Etchachan and descend to hut. ($3\frac{1}{2}$ km.)

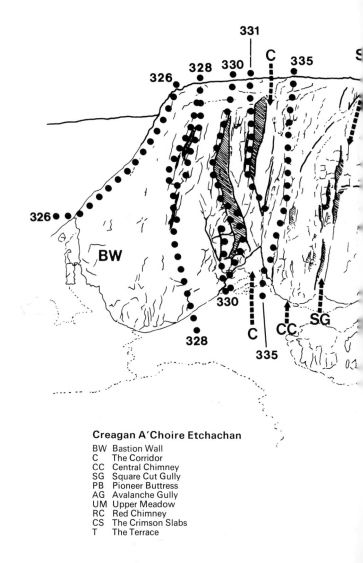

Creagan A'Choire Etchachan

BW Bastion Wall
C   The Corridor
CC Central Chimney
SG Square Cut Gully
PB Pioneer Buttress
AG Avalanche Gully
UM Upper Meadow
RC Red Chimney
CS The Crimson Slabs
T   The Terrace

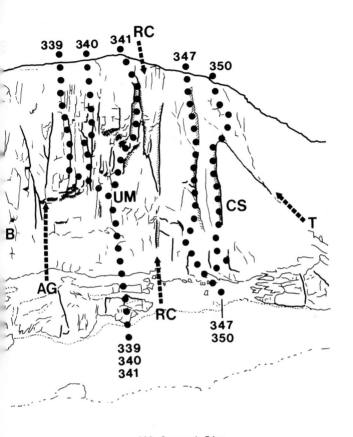

326. Quartzvein Edge
328. Original Route Direct
330. Talisman
331. Henchman
335. Pikestaff
339. Bodkin
340. Carmine Groove
341. Umslopogaas
347. Djibangi
350. The Dagger

Accommodation
The Hutchison Memorial Hut (NO 024998): this open shelter built in 1954 in Choire Etchachan is an ideally situated base amidst wonderful scenery. It has an earth floor—take polythene. Being rather cold and bleak in winter, some may prefer to stay at Luibeg bothy (see Coire Sputan Dearg).

Descents
Descent can be made at either end of the cliff. At the left (Bastion) end, Forked Gully, I, is a sporting descent. In summer Forked Gully is unsatisfactory due to loose rock and vegetation and it is better to descend the steep grass and scree further left. At the right (Crimson Slabs) side, a line of small crags beyond the Slabs must be skirted before a descent can be made.

THE BASTION

This is the largest buttress on the left of the crag. It has two major features: the easy-angled left-hand crest, Quartzvein Edge, alongside Forked Gully and a very impressive gable wall overlooking The Corridor recess. The lower half of this wall is a huge slab taken by Talisman, one of the best routes on the crag. Higher up The Corridor two great corners break the continuity of the wall. The central area of the Bastion is rather featureless consisting mainly of slabby ribs and grooves. Here climbing is possible almost anywhere at Difficult to Severe standard. The routes are much better in winter, as the grooves are vegetated. A number of climbs have been made in this section, including Bastion Wall, Difficult, III/IV, towards the left, Original Route, Severe, IV, just right of centre and Red Scar Route, Severe, IV, close to the right edge of the Bastion. A direct version, however, of Original Route gives fair rock climbing, although a little contrived (described below).

326 Quartzvein Edge 120m Moderate (1952)
A popular climb on reasonable rock following the left edge of the Bastion overlooking Forked Gully.

Start at the foot of Forked Gully beyond a detached block by climbing a 3m wall with a piece of quartz inset. Follow the edge at first, then find a way up slabs which develop into a shelf leading round a false tower on the left. A scree funnel leads to the top. A better but harder variation is to climb the false tower on its right side. (Diagram p. 218.)

Winter   III   (1956)

A good choice when snow or weather conditions are doubtful as it should be possible in most conditions. The false tower at the top is usually the crux. No cornice.

327   Bastion Wall   150 m   III/IV   (1963)
The route takes a line on the left side of the Bastion and is open to variation. The main features on the first ascent were long iced grooves and a 30 m chimney just below the plateau. Difficult and not unpleasant in summer. (Diagram p. 218.)

328   Original Route Direct   130 m   Severe   (1972)
The route follows a line of grooves just right of centre of the Bastion. Start to the right of the lowest rocks on the right of the buttress and scramble left up an easy depression ending at a deep V-groove, almost a chimney (this groove is the best means of locating the route, though it is most prominent from the base of the buttress, left of the start of this route). Climb the groove, then the rocks on its left (it becomes grassy) to gain the right side of a prominent red slab in a depression. Traverse the slab to belay on its left wall (40 m). Return to the right side, climb up 3 m and swing out right on a prominent jug. Go up, then left to follow a large V-groove to easy ground (45 m). (Diagram p. 218.)

Variation: Very good, but harder, Very Severe, 5a.

From the left side of the red slab, step left low down and follow the arete overlooking the red slab, then overlooking the large V-groove to easy ground (40 m).

329   Original Route, Winter   140 m   IV   (1969)
A good winter line, though not as direct as the best summer line. Relatively steep and sustained in the middle section. Start left of the Direct (whose line will still be visible under snow) and go up for 45 m to a steep wall left of the first V-groove of the Direct. Avoid the wall on the left and work rightwards underneath the Red Slab, crossing the Direct to reach a large platform. Gain a left-slanting ramp above and follow it to the large V-groove of the Direct, which leads to the top. Mild Severe in summer.

330   The Talisman   100 m   Hard Severe   (1956)
An excellent route following the defined right edge of the Bastion on

the brink of The Corridor. Steep and clean with continuous difficulty. Dries quickly after rain.

Start from a platform beside a huge block set against the wall 10 m up The Corridor. Climb the crack behind the block to a ledge. Move right and climb straight up until it is possible to traverse left across the huge slab to a belay on the crest (35 m). Detour left round an overhang and climb a corner to regain the crest. Move left to a groove and up to a short overhanging corner. Climb the corner to a good stance and block belay (20 m, crux). Follow the crest directly, starting on the face overlooking The Corridor (45 m). Scrambling to plateau. (Diagram p. 218.)

Direct Start   40 m   E1   (1981)

Though not in keeping with the standard of the normal route, this start is worthwhile in its own right. Sustained and well protected. The line follows the obvious corner system just left of the arete below Talisman.

Starting at the lowest rocks, climb the corner to an overlap (peg runner in place), then take the continuation corner on the left (25 m, 5b). Traverse back right immediately across a steep wall on good holds to reach the arete which is followed to the stance on Talisman (after the traverse).

Winter   IV/V   (1965)

A very sustained ascent on snow-covered rock. The hardest pitch was the 15 m traverse to reach the crest. The overhanging corner was climbed with 1PA and the final crest passed on the left by an iced groove.

331 Henchman   50 m   E3   (1983)

The route follows the clean, right-hand of the corners on the steep wall between Talisman and The Corridor. A fine line; regrettably short. Scramble up The Corridor to belay below a flake on the right-hand side of the corner line. Step left round the flake and climb the chimney formed by it to near its top. Step left into a groove and climb it round two small bulges to a V-notch. Belay on top of the roof above the notch (30 m, 5c). Climb the jam crack above and move right on to the wall under a block. Climb round this and finish steeply by a crack in the right wall (20 m, 5b). (Diagram p. 218.)

332 The Corridor 120 m III/IV (1954)
A first-rate winter route, popular and variable in standard. There are usually two major ice pitches; one leading over jammed blocks into a cave and one immediately above. This pitch above the cave will generally constitute the crux and may be very steep. There is often a large cornice which is best taken on the left. Severe in summer. (Diagram p. 218.)

333 Architrave 120 m III/IV (1969)
This is the prominent groove in the slabs close to the right wall of The Corridor recess. In winter the groove forms an impressive ribbon of ice, a more sustained climb than The Corridor but less steep. Climb the groove directly on ice to a point below a chimney. Either go straight up or move left across an obvious ramp and finish as for The Corridor.

In summer the groove gives a good climb when dry (which is rare). Start up the rib left of the groove for 45 m; thereafter follow the groove and continuation chimney, Severe.

JUNIPER BUTTRESS
Between The Corridor and Square Cut Gully, the buttress is split by the Central Chimney into two ribs. That on the left is Pikestaff; the right is Juniper Rib.

334 The Hex 80 m Hard Severe (1971)
A short, steep route on the Corridor flank of Juniper Buttress. Good, clean rough rock, sustained. Start 6 m above the rock pocket of Pikestaff (arrow). Climb a vague fault to the left of a system of grass cracks to belay at the top of these cracks beneath a small bulge (40 m). Step left and follow the continuation crack on the smooth Corridor Wall until it becomes grass choked. Traverse right to the crest and finish by Pikestaff.

335 Pikestaff 120 m Very Difficult (1954)
Follows the left-hand rib. A pleasant climb, a little vegetated but with good views of Talisman. Start just inside The Corridor at a curious little pocket in the rock. Slant up The Corridor wall to reach the crest and follow the rib as closely as possible, keeping to good rock. In winter the route is grade IV and sustained but very artificial. (Diagram p. 218.)

336 Central Chimney 120 m II/III (1955)
A good winter climb, following the chimney separating the two ribs.

Start at a fault leading leftwards from the base of Square Cut Gully into the chimney proper. A more sporting start is an obvious V-cleft splitting the lowest rocks. The chimney itself gives 60 m of climbing over small ice pitches to the foot of a right-slanting snow ramp, which provides a beautiful finish. Difficult and unpleasant in summer. (Diagram p. 218.)

The rib on the right of Central Chimney is Juniper Rib, III, a good choice in powder snow but not in avalanche conditions, as there is a snow slope at the top (Winter Route is safer).

337   Square Cut Gully   150 m   IV   (1966)
The gully is dominated by a magnificent ice pillar (or an icicle) at a big overhang. The initial 80 m will normally give straightforward climbing on snow and ice. The ice pillar is climbed direct. A second difficult pitch may be the final slab covered in unconsolidated snow. Severe in summer. (Diagram p. 218.)

338   Winter Route   150 m   II/III   (1949)
A fair winter climb taking the easiest and most natural line on this section of the cliff.
Start up Square Cut Gully and take an obvious line of weakness leading up on to Pioneer Buttress. Mixed climbing leads to an ice pitch on the left near the top.

PIONEER BUTTRESS
This is the large triangular buttress, between Square Cut Gully and Avalanche Gully. Cambridge Route, Severe, III, was the first recorded route on the cliff in 1949 and follows an obscure line up the easier left edge of the buttress. A direct line has been made up a broad rib on the frontal face of the buttress, Pioneer Buttress Direct, Very Severe, 5a. Avalanche Gully itself is blocked at 45 m by large overhangs but has been climbed by avoiding the overhangs on the left. The gully is loose, dangerous and Very Severe.

THE MEADOW FACE
A barrier of overhangs rises diagonally rightwards from the foot of Pioneer Buttress to the upper reaches of the Red Chimney. Two prominent grass scoops, the Meadows, are situated below the largest section of overhangs, just left of Red Chimney. The routes follow a

number of steep grooves which cut through this upper section of the face.

339 Bodkin 140 m Severe (1954)

This route makes for the upper meadow, traverses out above the lower overhangs, then up a groove and rib to finish beside a curious horizontal flake well seen in profile from the right-hand side of the crag. The route is more popular than is justified by the quality of the climbing.

Start directly below a recent rock scar in the lower overhangs and scramble up rightwards to the upper meadow (60 m). From its left edge go left past a clean groove (Carmine Groove) and up to a stance. To the left again there is a smooth slab poised over space and angling into a large groove. Move down into the groove, ascend across the slab at its lower end and climb the rib at the far side to a stance. Move up left and climb a groove until it steepens at 10 m. Step round left and climb cracks to gain the crest of a rib. Follow this to the top. The rib finish is a finer alternative to the original line up the grassy groove on the right. (Diagram p. 218.)

Winter IV

The original summer line was followed using two aid points on the poised slab. Much better in winter than summer.

340 Carmine Groove 80 m Very Severe (1971)

This is the prominent red groove on the upper cliff left of the big overhangs. Unfortunately the groove is often wet but when dry it gives two excellent pitches on steep clean rock.

Use the first section of Bodkin to gain the upper meadow. From its left edge start up the groove then move right to a flake. Climb straight up, re-enter the groove and continue to a belay below an overhang (20 m, 4b). Step left on to a steep red slab and climb the corner directly to a roof. Exit right to a small ledge and climb a thin crack in the slab to ledges (25 m, 4b). Move right and climb a narrow grey rib to easy ground. (Diagram p. 218.)

Winter IV (1974)

An excellent, short winter line; quite often in condition. The groove was followed throughout on ice except for a move on to the rib on the right at the top.

Crimson Slabs

RC Red Chimney

1. Cutlass
2. Scalpel
3. Djibangi
4. King Crimson
5. Sgian Dubh
6. Stiletto
7. The Dagger
8. Crimson Cringe
9. Scabbard
10. Sheath
11. Scythe
12. Sabre

341 Umslopogaas 100 m Hard Very Severe (1974)
Takes the big slab corner, the left and more prominent of two such corners high up on the face left of Red Chimney.

Gain the upper meadow (60 m). Five metres above its upper left extremity a thin rib separates a clean-cut V-groove on the left from an open corner on the right. The rib and V-groove is the start of another route, The Serpent, Very Severe, 5a, which crosses Umslopogaas and finishes up the right-hand of the two slab corners, entering Red Chimney near its top.

For Umslopogaas, climb directly up the pink rock right of the open corner. Move right below overhangs to a moss ledge below the corner (35 m, 4c, often wet). Zig-zag up the slab for 10 m to a nook on the right edge and straight up cracks to the top (25 m, 5a). Go left round a rib and up pleasant rocks to the top. (Diagram p. 218.)

342 Flanking Ribs 150 m III/IV (1967)
The climbing is undistinguished but the upper rib provides an escape below the top section of Red Chimney.

Climb the rib on the left of Red Chimney and cross the chimney at its easy middle section, pulling out awkwardly on to the rib on the right. Follow this to the top. Very Difficult and grassy in summer.

343 The Red Chimney 150 m IV (1959/1967)
A very fine ice climb. The Red Chimney is a natural ice trap and may be relied on to give good conditions in all but the leanest winters. The lower section is usually filled with a cascade of clear ice overflowing the Crimson Slabs on the right. The upper chimney becomes choked by a series of very steep ice bosses. These are hard for the grade and the discrete may climb the final pitches of Flanking Ribs.

Under normal conditions the start is made up the twin corners on the right and the chimney gained higher up by iced slabs. In lean conditions the ice may be thin and tension has been used. Above this the chimney is climbed directly to the base of the upper amphitheatre. Here a way must be found up leftwards through the ice bulges into the final corner which itself may be initially awkward.

The lower section has been climbed in summer and is Severe on sound but wet rock.

THE CRIMSON SLABS
These are the finest single feature of the crag—a spectacular sweep of slabs approx. 100 m in breadth and up to 150 m in height rising to the

right of Red Chimney. They provide some of the best rock climbing in the area. Continuity of the slabs is broken by two great corners, The Dagger on the right and Djibangi on the left. Away to the right a steep raking terrace ascends to a platform near the top of The Dagger and provides a useful means of descent for those who wish to avoid the inferior upper tier of slabs.

The corners of Djibangi and The Dagger are slow to dry, as they collect drainage water from above. Both have been climbed when wet; Djibangi is perhaps less gripping. The ribs on the right of each, however, dry very quickly and provide equally good routes. All the routes on the Crimson Slabs are recommended.

344   Cutlass   140 m   Hard Very Severe   (1969)
Between the Red Chimney and Djibangi there is a large bow-shaped overlap. This route follows the edge of the overlap then goes straight up parallel to Red Chimney. The crux pitch is poorly protected and serious for the grade.

Start 3 m right of Red Chimney and climb either of twin corners to the left end of the large platform on Djibangi. Belay below overlap (35 m). Step onto the edge of the overlap, climb straight up over a small bulge, then step right to a small belay ledge (10 m). Regain the edge and follow it delicately to a point 2 m right of Red Chimney where an upward move can be made over a small overlap to gain a grassy corner and belay (20 m, 5a). Continue up a rib to join Flanking Ribs (chossy) or bear right easily to the upper pitches of Djibangi and descend the Terrace. (Diagram p. 226.)

345   Scalpel   120 m   Hard Very Severe   (1977)
Takes the very shallow tilted groove between Cutlass and Djibangi. A better climb than Cutlass.

Climb the arete overlooking the initial grooves of Cutlass to the belay ledge (30 m, 4b). Climb Cutlass for 10 m to the small stance. Continue straight up the shallow groove for some 20 m to exit left onto a small belay ledge (30 m, 5a). Above is a curving corner. Move left into another corner and climb this to join the curving corner higher up. Go up this and trend right to join Djibangi (40 m, 4c). Scramble to the Terrace. (Diagram p. 226.)

346   King Crimson   125 m   E3   (1984)
An eliminate with a fine crux pitch on perfect pink rock between the

corners of Scalpel and Djibangi; sustained with limited protection. Start at the alcove as for Djibangi.

Climb a flake-crack between Djibangi and its direct start (Sgian Dubh) then go left round a bulge and up to join Djibangi, following its small corner to the ledge at the foot of the main corner (35 m, 4c). At the left end of the ledge a prominent streak of grey unwashed rock sweeps down from the apex of the slabs left of Djibangi. Climb straight up pink rock to fix runners under a shallow curving overlap. Go up left onto grey rock and continue to below an obvious notch in the main overlap. Move right, then go up through the overlap just right of a small corner forming the notch. Continue straight up, then pull left into a small groove which is followed to belay on broken ground below an area of clean cracked slabs (45 m, 5c). Climb straight up the slabs by cracks, going through a break in the overlap and passing right of a large block. Scramble to the top (45 m, 5a). (Diagram p. 226.)

347 Djibangi 140 m Very Severe (1956)
Djibangi is the left-hand of the two great corners. The easiest route on the Crimson Slabs and the most popular.

Start at a grassy alcove (containing a recessed right-facing corner, often wet) beneath the main corner and follow a diagonal line up leftwards to a large platform overlooking the first pitch of Red Chimney (20 m). Trend right and climb a small corner set in the middle of the slab. Easier climbing now leads to a good stance in the main corner (25 m). The crux pitch follows. Climb the corner directly passing an overlap. Exit by pulling out right to a stance on the rib (35 m, 4b). Step back left into the corner and climb it for a short way Work up left to gain an obvious groove and follow this in two pitches to a huge block (60 m). Climb round the block and continue up a rib to easy ground. (Diagrams pp. 218 and 226.)

After the crux pitch it is possible to follow grassy grooves rightwards to join Dagger and descend by the Terrace.

Winter IV

An outstanding winter climb, but not often in condition. To reach the foot of the main corner, either follow the summer line or, if conditions allow, climb direct up iced slabs. The corner is climbed throughout and may prove straightforward on good snow–ice. Above the corner a snow ramp leads rightwards to join Dagger but is better and probably easier to work up left and up grooves as for the summer line.

348   Sgian Dubh   110 m   Hard Very Severe   (1978)
Climbs the arete right of the Djibangi corner. It dries quickly after rain.
The first pitch can be used as a direct start to Djibangi. Start at the
grassy alcove (as for Djibangi).

From its left side, follow a series of shallow left-facing corners,
really a lower continuation of the main Djibangi corner, to belay below
the main corner of Djibangi (35 m, 4c). Climb the arete overlooking
the Djibangi corner, moving away from the arete in the middle
section—a fine exposed pitch (35 m, 5a). Follow grassy grooves
rightwards to the Terrace. (Diagram p. 226.)

Direct Route: E2

Start just left of Stiletto at twin cracks. Climb these, then the
continuation crack to reach the traverse line of Crimson Cringe.
Traverse left to the stance of the normal route below Djibangi main
corner (15 m, 5b). Climb the arete direct (the normal route takes a
deviation on the right)—35 m, 5b.

349   Stiletto   110 m   E1   (1966)
Midway between the corners of Djibangi and The Dagger, an impressive thin vertical crack splits the slab. This is the line of Stiletto which
gives technically hard but very well-protected climbing.

Climb the lower continuation of the crack or the first pitch of The
Dagger and belay under the crack (25 m, 4b). Climb the crack past
two hard sections (40 m, 5c). Traverse right into The Dagger and
follow it easily to the Terrace. (Diagram p. 226.)

350   The Dagger   130 m   Very Severe   (1955)
The right-hand corner. The Dagger was the original Crimson Slabs
route which, at the time of its first ascent, represented a breakthrough
in Cairngorm climbing. It is now a classic.

Start in the grassy alcove (as for Djibangi). Traverse right and a little
up for 5 m (nearly to the arete of Crimson Cringe, i.e. above the start of
Scabbard). Move back left into a short corner, then slightly left again
to reach easier ground leading up and right to the base of the main
corner (25 m, 4b). It is easier to reach this point by a vegetated line
coming in from the right (original and winter route). Climb the corner
to a hanging stance with a huge spike belay below an overhang
(35 m, 4c). Avoid the overhang by moving left below the bulge.
Regain the grass groove above the bulge and scramble to a large
platform below the last slab (the Terrace descends from here). Climb

the slab by a crack slanting right, then continue straight up to the top. (Diagrams pp. 218 and 226.)

Winter   IV

The original summer line was followed throughout. The dièdre was straightforward on snow–ice but in leaner conditions could be very hard. In good conditions the final slab will be the crux. Superb climbing.

351   Crimson Cringe   100 m   E2   (1984)
A traverse line with minimal protection for the hard sections.

Climb the clean rib which overlooks the initial corner of Scabbard/ Sheath, bypassing an overhang by moving left and back right. Belay at the foot of Dagger corner (20 m, 5a). Go up Dagger corner for about 10 m, taking the second traverse line out left to meet Stiletto at a small niche. Continue traversing slightly down then up to the belay at the base of Djibangi main corner (25 m, 5b). Climb Djibangi corner till below the lower small overlap. Traverse more or less horizontally to the small belay ledge of Scalpel (15 m, 5b). Finish up Scalpel (or Cutlass). (Diagram p. 226.)

352   Scabbard   105 m   Very Severe   (1966)
A fine exposed climb following the rib to the right of The Dagger. It dries very quickly and is always the first route to come into condition.

Start by a clean-cut, right-facing corner directly below the right-bounding rib of the Dagger corner. Move a little left to a stance level with the start of the Dagger corner (20 m, 4c). Climb an obvious finger-crack, then further cracks to a small overlap. Continue up the edge and belay using the huge spike at the top of the Dagger corner (35 m, 4c). Move right, descend a short way and pull out right onto an edge. Climb a series of cracks and blocks to reach the Terrace at its highest point (50 m, 4b). (Diagram p. 226.)

To the right of Scabbard are three right-facing corner systems; the left is Sheath (pitch 2), the middle one, which starts higher up and leads to a roof is Scythe and the right one, which starts higher still and has a cracked arete on its right is Sabre.

353   Sheath   105 m   Hard Very Severe   (1961)
The route starts at the clean cut corner common with Scabbard and

goes up to a conspicuous red slab usually streaked with water. The crux is poorly protected.

Climb the corner (4c), move right, then go up to belay on top of a huge detached block at the foot of the red slab. Climb a good layback-crack on the left of the slab and continue until forced to make a delicate horizontal traverse across the slab to a grass niche. Go up a vertical crack for 6 m, move right below a bulge and climb a smooth corner groove to an overlap. Break out left and belay (5a). Move leftwards to join Scabbard and climb cracks and blocks to reach the Terrace (4b). (Diagram p. 226.)

354 Scythe 50 m E2 (1983)
A good, sustained pitch but very poorly protected, following the middle corner system. Climb the slab about 3 m to the right of the initial corner to a prominent roof. Step right and pull over a bulge into a smaller corner. Follow this to easier slabs which lead to the Terrace (5b). A peg runner under the prominent roof would probably be justified (pegs not carried on the one ascent to date). (Diagram p. 226.)

355 Sabre 45 m Very Severe (1982)
A good pitch, useful as a filler-in at the end of a day. The climb follows the rightmost corner, starting up an awkward pale-coloured slab and surmounting an overlap at 25 m. A cracked slab leads to the Terrace (4b). (Diagram p. 226.)

Above the top of the Terrace and descending rightwards is an area of largely vegetated slabs containing the finish to The Dagger and lower down, the shallow stepped corners of the Gangway, Severe. These slabs are bounded on the right by a clean, cracked arete about 20 m down from the top of the Terrace (described below). The corner immediately right of the arete is perhaps Enigma, Very Severe, precise line unknown. Next right is a grassy fault and beyond it the corner system of Stanley, Hard Severe.

356 Delicatessen 40 m Very Severe (1983)
This is the clean cracked arete mentioned above, climbed directly, keeping near the crest (4c). It provides the best continuation for routes leading to the Terrace (Scythe and Sabre).

LESSER CRAGS OF STOB COIRE ETCHACHAN
Stob Coire Etchachan (NJ 0200) is the shapely, pointed summit of

Beinn Mheadhoin overlooking Coire Etchachan. It displays a high, wedge-shaped face very prominent from Glen Derry. Unfortunately, the face consists of easy-angled, broken ribs and buttresses separated by scree-filled gullies and offers very little to the rock climber, although many of the buttresses have been climbed (up to 40 m). In winter, however, the ribs and open gullies make for sporting, direct routes to the top of Beinn Mheadhoin.

The biggest mass of rock on the face, situated almost opposite the door of the Hutchison Hut, is Bellflower Buttress (100 m, a loose Difficult, III). Low down on the extreme left of the face, just above the Macdhui path, the rocks become more continuous and the buttresses form a frieze to the skyline. Routes are 50 m long. The attractive, steep rib forming the lowest rocks at the head of the corrie and skylined as seen from the hut, is Stag Buttress, Very Difficult. The obvious corner-crack at the bottom left of Stag Buttress, Hard Severe, is a good start and makes the route worthwhile for an evening. On the rocks higher and to the right of Stag Buttress, and beyond a slanting gully, is the prominent Amphitheatre Edge, Very Difficult.

The forlorn little buttress lying high up under the 1163 m top of Beinn Mheadhoin is The Slug, Difficult. The highest point of Beinn Mheadhoin itself is on top of a tor, the Great Barn of Beinn Mheadhoin, requiring a short scramble by its easiest way.

CRAGS ABOVE LOCH ETCHACHAN

The crags of Loch Etchachan are indefinite and provide poor rock climbing. The small, isolated buttress on the south side of the loch provides short problems up to 25 m. The only recorded climb is Lochside Chimney, Difficult, I, in the centre of the east-facing crag of Cairn Etchachan (NJ 003009). The short, deep gully right of this crag has been climbed many times in winter and is grade I.

THE LOCH A'AN (AVON) BASIN

Loch A'an lies at 730 m in the heart of the Northern Cairngorms entrenched between Cairngorm, Ben Macdhui and Beinn Mheadhoin. At its head a superb arc of cliffs cluster round its main feeder streams, the Garbh Uisge, Feith Buidhe and Allt a Coire Domhain. Dominating this scene is the spectacular square topped Shelter Stone Crag and on its left the sharp and pointed Cairn Etchachan. At 270 m these are the highest cliffs in this area.

The horseshoe extends from the Beinn Mheadhoin—Cairn Etchachan col to Coire Raibert. The main easings in this line of cliffs are where the Garbh Uisge and Feith Buidhe cascade from the plateau over a series of glaciated slabs and steps, alongside the Allt a Coire Domhain and by the Allt a Coire Raibert. These breaks give the normal access routes into the basin.

From its southern toe Cairn Etchachan neighbours the Shelter Stone Crag after which is the smaller broken Garbh Uisge Crag. At the western and head end of the horseshoe is an area of water-washed and glaciated slabs down which the Garbh Uisge and Feith Buidhe make their way. East of the latter is the flat faced Hell's Lum Crag which runs round to Coire Domhain. Between these and the Allt a Coire Raibert, Stag Rocks form the horseshoe's right leg. Still on the north side of the loch but lying below Cairngorm is a line of glaciated slabs just beneath Stac an Fharaidh. After these the plateau swings round above the Saddle and into Strath Nethy. On the south side Beinn Mheadhoin has its own cliff at Stacan Dubha just east of the col by Loch Etchachan. These look promising from a distance but are less satisfactory on closer acquaintance.

At the foot of the Shelter Stone Crag is the Clach Dhian or Shelter Stone which provides a climbing base in the many huge boulders that have sloughed off the cliff some time in the distant past. Also amongst these boulders are several other howffs which, although smaller, may provide more savoury accommodation than the Shelter Stone itself. At the head of the loch and along the banks of the inlet streams are several good camp-sites.

Approaches
There are many ways to approach the Shelter Stone and the cliffs of the Loch A'an basin.

From the north:

The plateau can be gained in a variety of ways from the Coire Cas car park. From the top of the chair-lift then over or round Cairngorm: via Coire Cas or the Fiacaill a'Choire Chais, the Fiacaill Coire an t-Sneachda or the Goat Track in Coire an t-Sneachda. From there, the main descents are down the shoulder overlooking the Saddle at the east end, Coire Raibert in the centre and Coire Domhain in the west. Diagonal Gully which cuts Stag Rocks gives quick access for competent parties.

From the south:

From Loch Etchachan a good path leads down by the Allt nan Stacan Dubha which runs north into the head of the loch. A scrambling descent exists on the east bank of the Garbh Uisge and interesting ways up and down can be found on the slabs at the west end of the loch. The south end of the loch can be reached from Glen Derry via the Lairig an Laoigh.

Access and Accommodation

The most convenient centre for access and accommodation in this area is Aviemore which lies on the main railway and road, the A9, between Perth and Inverness. Public transport to Aviemore is regular and convenient. From the village a further bus service runs up to the Coire Cas car park, the most convenient access point for most of the area. Above that the two stage chair-lift on Cairngorm can be worthwhile for the time and effort it saves on certain approaches. The top stage is particularly handy but there can be queues during the ski season and it does not operate in high winds.

Aviemore and the Spey Valley provide a wide range of accommodation from hotels and chalets to caravans but last minute bookings may be difficult at the height of the tourist and ski seasons. There are Youth Hostels at Aviemore and at Glenmore, $9\frac{1}{2}$ km up the Coire Cas ski road. Camping is not permitted in Rothiemurchus or Glen More forests but there is an official (but paying) camp-site at Glen More near Loch Morlich. Camping in the mountains is unrestricted at most times of the year but not recommended in winter when the weather can be Arctic. There are several bothies in the area some of which can be used constructively.

Ryvoan (NG 006114)

Situated on the track between Glen More and Nethy Bridge about

3 km from Glen More. A well built stone cottage which is generally well maintained but a bit out of the way.

Nethy Bothy (NJ 020105)

Situated at the mouth of Strath Nethy at the end of the track from Glen More. A rather unsavoury corrugated iron shed well away from the climbing area.

Fords of A'an Refuge (NJ 032042)

Situated on the north bank of the River A'an where the Lairig an Laoigh track fords it. A small refuge of wood and stone. Not very useful as a climbing base.

Sinclair Hut (NH 958036)

This is a solid two roomed building situated on the knoll on the right of the Allt Druidh, just above a point where the Lairig track is ascended and crosses from right to left. Of limited use as a climbing base except for routes on Lurcher's Crag.

Jean's Hut (NH 981033)

A wooden structure in a poor state of repair situated in Coire an Lochain. Only really of use for climbing in that coire and at present very unsavoury. Subject to final confirmation, due for removal in summer 1986.

Shelter Stone (NJ 001016)

Situated below the Shelter Stone Crag there is a cave under a large boulder (cairn on top) which provides shelter. There are many other boulder howffs in the jumble of large boulders below the cliff, many of which are less used and more pleasant than the Shelter Stone itself. In winter they may however fill up with snow. There are several good camp-sites on the valley floor.

STACAN DUBHA OF BEINN MHEADHOIN (NJ 0101)

The crags to the left (east) of the Beinn Mheadhoin–Cairn Etchachan col. They look quite good from a distance but are disappointing on closer acquaintance. They are broken, consisting of many short ribs and buttresses and the rock is poor in places. Several winter lines are obvious but usually lacking in continuity. There are three summer routes.

Zig-Zag   140 m   Very Difficult
The slab on the extreme left. It is climbed first leftwards then up a rib.

Ribbon Ridge   120 m   Moderate
At the eastern end of the cliff above a chute of red scree. The rib lies between deep gullies.

The Shuttle   100 m   Very Difficult
The highest and most prominent buttress. It starts with a detached section of cracked slabs then a chimney on the right of a terrace. Above climb the buttress with deviations on the right.

CAIRN ETCHACHAN (NJ 003012)

This great pointed crag has two distinct faces: the Main Face which looks north over the head of Loch A'an and the Gully Face which drops into Castlegates Gully.

The Main Face is cut at about mid-height by the Great Terrace which can be reached and followed from the Beinn Mheadhoin col until it vanishes near the junction of the faces. Above and below the terrace the cliff has differing aspects. The Upper Cliff, which holds most of the routes is a complex area of steep towers, ribs, chimneys and cracks. These rise to 100 m in height and give the best rock climbing on the crag. The Lower Cliff is more open and slabby and scored by several left-leaning ramps the largest of which near the right-hand end is the Diagonal Shelf. This is a grassy slope or a snow field depending on the season. Some routes in this area climb the full height of the cliff.

THE UPPER CLIFF, MAIN FACE

A complicated face which gives some good routes and some excellent pitches. The rock is fairly quick drying in spite of its northerly aspect but climbs towards its right-hand side are fairly vegetated.

Passing along the Great Terrace from the Beinn Mheadhoin col and Loch Etchachan the first main buttress houses Crevasse Route; a large diagonal ramp marks its left side. Next comes the obvious gully fault of Equinox with a steep square cut tower on its right. To the right of this tower is an upper amphitheatre whose left wall holds the prominent final crack of Boa. Next is the square pink spur of Python and where it meets the face on the right is the corner-crack of Nom-de-Plume. Right of this is the long slanting chimney of Pagan Slit then a more broken spur of pinkish rock. The Great Terrace merges into the face about this area but ledges trend upwards to the large V-groove of The

Cairn Etchachan: The Gully Face

365. Route Major
366. Red Guard
367. Scorpion
368. False Scorpion

369. Siberia
370. Sideslip
371. Castle Gully

Diagonal Shelf   Sentinel   Breach Gully

Battlements. This climb, once located, provides a convenient means of descent to the routes. Its top is situated close to a rock window near the highest part of the crag. By scrambling right from the end of the Great Terrace the cliff may be traversed as far as Scorpion.

357   Crevasse Route   75 m   Mild Severe   (1955)
The first buttress from the left on the Great Terrace. It has a prominent window high up, well seen from the Beinn Mheadhoin col. A charming, exhilarating route giving a varied series of pitches. Start at the lowest rocks.

Climb steep rock just right of the midline to a rock crevasse (20 m). Continue up for 20 m and move into a corner on the right and climb a large, leaning block. The overhanging curving crack above is lay-backed (crux) then step left and climb huge flakes to a crevasse. A queer, contorted chimney exits through a hole to a fine eyrie. Climb the first crack above for 24 m veering right at the top up a nose to the true finish of the buttress. This climb is Grade IV in winter.

Variation   Severe   (1967)

Instead of climbing the large leaning block continue left up a wide sloping shelf then the left edge of the buttress.

358   Poison Dwarf   75 m   Hard Very Severe   (1978)
A good climb which reaches the window on the buttress from the right-hand side. Start about 6 m up the Equinox gully.

Climb the overhung ramp sloping left until a ledge on the left can be gained and the corner above climbed to a ledge (36 m, 5a). Climb the wide crack above (crux) to the rock window (15 m, 5b). Go up the wide groove above to a recess, use the large flake to gain the arete on the right and follow it to the top (24 m, 4c).

359   Time Traveller   75 m   Hard Very Severe   (1978)
Follows the thin crack system high on the right wall of the buttress. A fine route but slow to dry. Start at the foot of the gully.

Climb the gully to a large block (30 m). Step left and go up the groove and crack to a ledge (12 m, 5a). Continue up the crack system (24 m, 5a). Finish via the short corner above (9 m).

360   Equinox   75 m   V   (1981)
A good route in the steep vegetated recess between the spurs of Crevasse Route and Python.

Climb the corner/gully formed by the recess and the smooth wall of Time Traveller for two pitches; the second is the crux. Move right and climb two short, overhanging steps to a platform below a constricted chimney. Climb this and another on the left to finish.

In summer this is Very Severe and often greasy.

361 Pythagoras 90 m Very Severe (1978)
Lies on the left wall of the upper amphitheatre right of Equinox gully. Poor lower pitches lead to an excellent upper section. Start left of the pink spur of Python and Boa.

Follow a grassy groove leading left to where it splits (30 m). Continue up right-facing corners and pass right of a huge flake to a large platform below the final wall (30 m). Climb the fine crack till it ends and traverse left to an exposed stance on the buttress edge (21 m, 4c). Go up the left slanting groove until possible to move right and so to the top (9 m).

362 Boa 60 m Severe (1954)
The main feature of this route is the superb crack in the left wall of the shallow amphitheatre. Start below the amphitheatre left of the pink spur of Python.

Zig-zag easily to the foot of the wide chimney on the immediate left of Python spur. Slant left by ledges and corners to easier ground in the upper amphitheatre. Move left then climb the wide crack passing a hanging chokestone about 20 m up. A fine and exposed pitch.

This climb is V in winter conditions.

363 The Guillotine 75 m Mild Severe (1955)
An interesting chimney route with the crux right at the top. Start as for Boa.

Zig-zag to the foot of the wide chimney and climb it direct. Continue into the upper amphitheatre. Take the second chimney on the right which cuts deeply into the spur and pass below a huge blade of rock. Exit by a tunnel roofed by blocks to a platform on the spur. Climb the chimney above with an overhang at its top (crux).

In winter this route gives a good IV climb, the last pitch constituting the crux.

The next feature reached when moving right is an obvious pink spur. Python, Hard Severe, V, climb this first on the right by the obvious crack and large flake before moving left to a chimney in the rib's left flank to finish as for The Guillotine. Then comes Nom-de-Plume, Very Severe, V, which takes the chimney-crack in the right corner of the spur. Right again is the obvious rightward slanting chimney of Pagan Slit, Hard Severe, IV. These routes are mossy and often damp in summer but in winter give better quality climbs although they have little build-up of ice.

The next feature right is a more broken rib of pink rock. This gives The Hairpin Loop, IV, which starts up a right to left fault, then loops rightwards to penetrate the walls above and finishes up the left rib of The Battlements.

364 The Battlements 120m Moderate (1954)

Once located this route provides a handy descent to gain access to climb on the Upper Cliff.

Near the end of the Great Terrace the cliff becomes more broken. From near the end of the terrace ledges trend naturally upwards to a large V-groove climbed on its right wall. Above easier climbing leads left then right to finish near the top of Cairn Etchachan by a rock window.

THE LOWER CLIFF, MAIN FACE

The face below the Great Terrace is open and characterised by several leftward slanting ramp lines, the largest of which by far is the Diagonal Shelf. Right of this in a huge bay is the big chimney of Red Guard which marks the junction of the two faces. Near the left margin of the face is Eastern Approach Route, 110m, Difficult and III. It takes the right-slanting weakness and provides a means of access to the Great Terrace.

365 Route Major 285m IV (1957)

The longest winter climb in the area; with its continually complex route finding, fine climbing and good situations it is a Cairngorm winter classic. Starting at the Diagonal Shelf it uses the Battlements in the upper section to finish near the summit.

Start right of the lowest rocks and climb the largest left-leading ramp, the Diagonal Shelf, for two pitches until it is possible to move up and right on a ramp to reach a snow basin. (This point can be reached by more interesting climbing by following much narrower ramp lines from the foot of Red Guard to the bottom right corner of the snow basin). Exit from the basin by the obvious tapered chimney moving left when it becomes too constricted. Another ramp now leads to more broken ground. Go diagonally rightwards for two pitches until the deep V-groove of The Battlements is gained (difficult to see from below). Follow this groove, steep at first, to a bend and continue up leftwards more easily. Then take a chimney leading up right to finish near the top. (Diagram p. 238.)

Between Route Major and Red Guard is the line of Bastille, Very Severe, IV/V. It first follows the narrow ramp above the Diagonal Shelf (winter) or the rib between this and Red Guard (summer) to a two-tiered corner leading to the ledge system cutting the face. It then continues up the face to meet the top end of the Red Guard ramp above which (summer) it goes over the collar-shaped overhang, then up cracks to finish. In both seasons the crux is the two-tiered corner which is technical but well protected (1 NA winter).

THE GULLY FACE

This face starts right of the Diagonal Shelf where the cliff bends round to overlook Castlegates Gully. The Great Terrace fades out just as the Gully Face is reached. Near the bottom of this face is the deep chokestone filled chimney of Red Guard, then comes a prominent vertical triangular wall about 15 m high. This is the Sentinel which marks the start of the gully proper. Going up Castlegates from there is first the wider broken fault of False Scorpion then the large buttress distinguished by a great pink ramp formed by a huge rock-fall scar. On its right is the fault of Castle Gully after which the cliff diminishes in height.

The rock on this face is inferior to that on the Main Face. Much is vegetated and some is loose. However, in winter this face comes into its own with a fine selection of long and interesting snow and ice routes. These are often in condition and of good quality.

366   Red Guard   250 m   Severe   (1977)
The best of the rock climbs on the Gully Face. It follows a natural line the full height of the cliff. Start below the obvious block-filled chimney just above the Diagonal Shelf.

Enter the gully and climb cracked slabs on the left to below a steep blank wall. On the left margin of the wall the obvious chimney gives excellent climbing including two through routes to land in a grassy bay. The continuation groove looks dirty so move down and right into a groove. Follow this exposed groove which becomes more broken to a ledge system traversing the cliff. Ahead is a steep cracked wall forming the left flank of a clean, wide, pink, cracked shelf. Scramble rightwards along the ledge until access to the shelf is gained. Climb this as far as a short corner on the right-hand side leading up to a balcony stance atop the prominent square cut overhang. Easier progress now as the cliff tilts back to meet the plateau. (Diagram p. 238.)

Winter   V   (1978)

An excellent and interesting route with a hard crux. Above the deep chimney either the summer route (tension and 3PA) or the dirty continuation groove may be climbed. The climb then continues to the short corner leading off the pink cracked shelf. Here the natural winter line is a snow-covered ramp round the profile then directly up steep mixed ground to the cornice.

367   Scorpion   240 m   V   (1952)
A fine and aptly named route. It takes a line near the boundary of the Main and Gully Faces before finishing up the huge square-shaped fault. It starts about 15 m below the Sentinel, midway between it and the initial chimney of Red Guard.

Climb a steep corner left of a V-groove, at 18 m continue left for 9 m below a steep wall cut by a slanting crack. Enter the crack after 3 m; the route is now subterranean. Above the exit climb an overhung wall on the immediate right on good holds then go round a corner to the right and go up on a leftward line to cross left over a slab by a crack in its lower margin. The route is obvious for the next 45 m to easy ground below the upper fault. A long chimney below a leaning wall leads back right into the main fault which is climbed to the top. It may contain several ice pitches and be heavily corniced. (Diagram p. 238.)

In summer this route is Very Difficult with a fair variety of pitches.

Between Scorpion and False Scorpion is The Sword, V. It takes the open groove on the left of the Sentinel then its continuation to reach Scorpion which it crosses to finish up the top portion of Red Guard.

368   False Scorpion   240 m   V   (1970)
This route follows the main fault which starts just inside Castlegates Gully. It usually has more ice but less interest than Scorpion. Start just above the Sentinel.

Climb the main fault keeping to the left until the main upper gully is reached above a narrower and steeper section. Finish as for Scorpion.

In summer it is Very Difficult, loose and unpleasant. (Diagram p. 238.)

369   Siberia   210 m   IV   (1979)

The main feature of this climb is the hanging gully right of the Scorpion Fault. It is reached by following the bottom edge of the pink scarred buttress. Start below this buttress.

Follow ramps easily up and left for two pitches to below the first steepening. Go right and climb ramps which lead left and overlook the main gully to reach a cul-de-sac level with two large blocks on the right skyline. Move onto the rib on the right and descend to gain a groove which leads to the hanging gully. This funnel-shaped fault leads to the plateau. (Diagram p. 238.)

370   Sideslip   150 m   III   (1975)

Takes the pink rock-fall ramp and the hanging gully on the left of the buttress.

Climb the ramp to its top and traverse left to the foot of the gully. Climb this to the plateau (as for Siberia). (Diagram p. 238.)

371   Castle Gully   150 m   III   (1964)

This is the gully on the right of the pink scarred buttress. The lower section is open and slabby but it becomes more defined towards its top. An alternative start lies further right and comes in along an obvious snow ledge.

In summer the route is Very Difficult but keeps more to the crest on the left in the top section. (Diagram p. 238.)

372   Attic Rib   100 m   III   (1977)

Lies to the right of Castle Gully. Start leftwards up a ramp then move right and up a short step to gain the left side of an arete. Follow this to the top.

SHELTER STONE CRAG (NJ 001013)

This 270 m flat-topped cliff (sometimes known as the Sticil) is one of the most impressive in the Cairngorms. It thrusts out boldly between Castlegates Gully on the left and Pinnacle Gully on the right. They are loose and unpleasant scree filled scrambles in summer and Grade I in winter. These, however, give the crag its main north face and the two lesser triangular faces which overlook the gullies.

Although at first sight the crag appears as a great unbroken tower of granite, there are several well-defined and distinct features. Starting in Castlegates Gully is the rib of Castle Wall which is separated from the tapered tower of Raeburn's Buttress by the curved fault of Breach Gully. Right of Raeburn's Buttress and left of the chimney line of The Citadel are the Central Slabs. Right of these impressive boiler-plate slabs the cliff is at its steepest and most continuous and gives some superb long climbs. This part of the crag fades out in the region of Clach Dhian Chimney after which the face soon takes a turn to overlook Pinnacle Gully and diminishes in height and quality.

373 Castle Wall   210m   III   (1970)
This is the initially well-defined arete which starts near the foot of Castlegates Gully. The ridge is followed throughout, the lower 90m being the most difficult. Above the ridge merges into the upper rocks and gives interesting climbing with fine situations.

In summer it is Difficult with much scrambling.

374 Breach Gully   240m   IV   (1977)
The prominent gully between Castle Wall and Raeburn's Buttress. The very steep blank section about 18m above the initial snow-bay is passed on the right and the gully regained above. A through-route followed by a traverse right leads to the upper couloir which leads more easily to the plateau. (Diagram p. 238.)

375 Raeburn's Buttress   240m   IV   (1971)
A fine winter climb which takes the left side of the tower-like buttress. Start in the bay on the left.

Follow a line of rightward trending grooves until a move right leads to a stance. Traverse left up a series of ledges then left to a line of weakness splitting the buttress. Climb this to below a steep chimney then up the chimney and exit right onto the arete and continue up. Above the angle eases and a line leads up leftwards.

In summer the route is Severe, vegetated and dangerous.

376 Consolation Groove   260m   Hard Very Severe   (1969)
A worthwhile route which takes the groove line on the crest of Raeburn's Buttress. Start at the right side of the buttress.

Climb a steep groove and break left to a grass ledge (18m). Step right onto a slab and up to an overhang, move up and traverse right to a corner and climb this to a grass ledge below a steep groove slanting up left (30m). Climb the groove to a ledge (24m). Continue up the groove breaking left at 18m to the left edge and climb it to a grassy ledge (36m). Go straight up the groove to a large ledge and scramble up to the foot of the wall above with a long overhang (27 m). Climb up and traverse right, then go up a crack through a break at the right end of the overhang to a ledge (24 m). Step left and go up to a large terrace (10 m). Scramble to a higher buttress (30 m). Climb up the prominent arete to an overhang, surmount this and continue (45 m). Scramble to the top (15 m). (Diagram p. 252.)

The right-hand side of Raeburn's Buttress is climbed by Threadbare, Extremely Severe, which follows a line of cracks and grooves. Some aid is used in its central section.

THE CENTRAL SLABS
These are the magnificent and unmistakable high angle slabs set in the centre of the cliff. They are defined on the left by the open vegetated corner of Sticil Face, and on the right by the lower chimney of The Citadel. They lie between the Low and High Ledges and route lengths given are between those two ledge systems. The Low Ledge is most easily approached from the left.

The main feature and reference point in the middle of the slabs is the diagonal dièdre of Thor. It faces right and its lower end finishes in an overlap which runs leftwards. The lower corner of the dièdre is reached via a left facing corner system which marks the start of several routes.

377 Sticil Face 240 m V (1957)
An excellent route which climbs the shallow angle between Raeburn's Buttress and the Central Slabs. Start below Raeburn's Buttress.

Climb up and right to gain, then traverse the Low Ledge for about 20 m (30 m). Climb the shallow depression trending slightly left to the big ledge below a steep wall (50 m). Climb steep iced corner on right (crux) then continue more easily to below a narrow chimney (24 m). Climb this awkward chimney to easy ledges (18 m). It is now possible to go up easily to the right across the High Ledge to eventually gain a deep 30 m chimney (100 m). Either climb the chimney or traverse right from beneath an overhang and then use combined tactics on the ensuing 4 m wall to gain the snow arete leading to the top.

The original route climbed on the left of the ice pitches to join the route described below the narrow chimney. It finished via the snow arete.

In summer the route is Hard Severe, wet and vegetated, The summer crux is the steep 12 m edge overlooking the winter crux, a wet slabby holdless gully. (Diagram p. 252.)

378   The Harp   110 m   E3   (1983)
This fine route starts at the left edge of the slabs and runs diagonally
rightwards. Starts from the left-hand end of Low Ledge.

Climb grassy corners as for Sticil Face (20 m). Move up right to a
ledge on the slab and up a thin crack to the overhang, pull over this
and up 5 m to a ledge and belay (15 m, 6a). Follow the thin crack in
the slab for 30 m to an old peg, step right across Snipers to a ledge, go
up the crack rightwards to a small ledge and peg belay junction with
Run of the Arrow (40 m, 5c). Follow the obvious rightward slanting
line to a junction with Cupid's Bow just below its final flake-crack and
finish up this. (As for Run of the Arrow) (25 m, 5b).

379   Snipers   105 m   E2 (2PA)   (1969)
A good route which follows the thin crack on the left of the slabs. The
overlap constitutes the crux and above the climbing is quite bold. Start
on Low Ledge at the left facing corner system which leads to the foot
of the main Thor dièdre.

Climb the corner to an overhang, move left then up to below the
overlap to belay above the loose flake (36 m, 5a). Cross the overlap
above (2PA) and climb the thin crack to a niche (24 m, 5b). Continue
up the crack to High Ledge (45 m, 5a). (Diagram p. 252.)

380   The Missing Link   123 m   E4   (1981)
This takes a line diagonally rightwards across the slabs. Sustained and
quite serious on pitch 3. The start is for Thor and Snipers.

Climb the left facing corner to an overhang, move left then up to
below the overlap to belay above the loose flake (36 m, 5a). Continue
up the Thor dièdre to a hanging belay below a ledge (24 m, 5b).
Traverse right to follow the long narrow overlap (poor peg runners) to
reach a hollow sounding flake. Traverse this to its end and pull into
Pin, move up to belay (42 m, 5c). It is also possible to move down Pin
to belay. Finish up The Pin.

381   The Run of the Arrow   100 m   E5   (1982)
A modern desperate. It takes the faint crackline in the slab between
Snipers and Cupid's Bow. Start from Low Ledge at the foot of the
initial corner of Snipers and Thor.

Go easily up rightwards for 10 m, move left round the rib and follow
a crack up into the base of the Thor dièdre. Climb this for 6 m to belay
on pegs (42 m, 5a). Swing left onto the rib and move up left to a thin
crack line. Follow this and the slab above to reach two poor *in situ*
wires. Make delicate moves up and left to gain a small ledge in a

scoop. Step left and up a crack to belay on sloping ledges on the left (34 m, 6b). Follow the obvious rightward slanting line to a junction with Cupid's Bow, just below its final flake-crack. Finish up this (24 m, 5a).

382   Cupid's Bow   84 m   E4   (1978)

A fine, difficult route which takes the bow-shaped corner above the upper part of the Thor dièdre.

From the Low Ledge below the initial Thor corner, climb up right for 6 m to belay in a small niche. Gain grassy bay above and climb out of this via cracks on the left. Move right into a shallow corner which is climbed to pull out left onto the rib. Go up and left to a hanging belay below a ledge in the Thor dièdre (39 m, 5a). Climb the dièdre to the ledge and continue up until a swing out left enables a ledge at the foot of the "bow" to be gained. Climb the corner with difficulty past a peg runner until possible to gain the left arete. Go up this to climb an awkward bulging section at the top of the corner then follow the continuation of the bow to where it curves right. Step left and climb the steep slabby wall to traverse right to below the final headwall. Finish out left by an obvious flake-crack (45 m, 6b). (Diagram p. 252.)

383   The Pin   75 m   E2   (1968)

This route takes the striking crackline near the right margin of the slabs and gives very fine and sustained climbing. Start high up on the right of Low Ledge below the crack.

Climb the crack directly up the steep slab to a stance (18 m, 5b). Continue up the crack crossing an awkward bulge, trend right then back to the crack and a good thread belay (22 m, 5b). Go up and climb the overhanging wall to a poor stance at 10 m. Continue up the continually interesting crackline to High Ledge (35 m, 5a). (Diagram p. 252.)

There is a further route on the slabs, Thor, Extremely Severe and A2. This takes the slanting dièdre all the way and finishes as for "The Pin". Aid and a tension are used on the third pitch.

From the upper right end of High Ledge an obvious chimney with huge chokestones cut the left side of the Main Bastion. This is the line of Blockbuster (E2, 5b) which provides a suitable finish to some of the routes on the Central Slabs. The chimney is gained from the left and the fault followed to the top of the cliff. It can also be reached via the lower section of The Citadel.

THE MAIN BASTION

This forms the centre piece of the cliff. A magnificent sweep of rock nearly 300 m high which steepens from slabs at its foot to vertical rock at the top. The left side is defined by the chimney of The Citadel and its continuation fault, the right side with its two distinct steps high up is the edge overlooking Pinnacle Gully. These lines bound a narrowing and steepening wedge of good continuous rock although the right side, cut by Clach Dhian Chimney, is more broken. The main features low down are the right facing corners of Steeple starting near the toe of the buttress. High up are two large and impressive right-facing corners, the left one fails to reach the top of the cliff and is taken by Steeple, the right-hand one rises to a distinctive notch on the skyline and is taken by The Needle. Although there are few large horizontal features there are several lines of ledges that partially cross the bastion. These and the tapering nature of this section of cliff means that some of the routes share stances particularly in the upper reaches.

384 The Citadel   270 m   Very Severe   (1958)

A traditional Cairngorm classic with all that that implies. The lower section takes the conspicuous chimney bounding the right side of the Central Slabs; the upper is on the steep nose on the left of the great upper bastion. Start below the chimney line.

Grassy cracks lead in two pitches to the Low Ledge. Above a further three pitches lie up the chimney until overhangs force an exit to ledges on the left. The next pitch is the lower crux. Go up and left on slabs then make a right traverse to a corner with a crack on the right wall. Move up this then right again to gain the slab above then a grassy fault which leads to a belay (4c). Traverse right into an obvious corner. Climb this and the corner into which it develops to gain a ridge. Follow this then go left to a stance by a huge flake. Next is the upper crux. Hand traverse left then climb the crack and chimney system above to a good stance (4c). Now work up and right following the rim of the overhanging wall then up to a ledge. Climb the ensuing fault until the left of two short chimneys leads to the plateau. (Diagram p. 252.)

Winter   VI   (1980)

An extremely hard route with the major difficulties in the upper section. The summer route is followed throughout; one peg is used at the lower crux. The Winter Variation, V, climbs the summer route to above the lower crux where one or more aid points may be required. It then escapes up left to join Sticil Face on the High Ledge.

385 Haystack 280 m E2 (1971)

This route climbs the nose of the buttress. It is strenuous, exposed and excellent. Start at the very toe of the buttress.

Climb the right-facing corner to belay below a short corner (30 m, 4c). (This is very often wet and can be avoided by going 6 m up the grassy gully as for Steeple.) Climb the short corner and exit left onto slabs. Continue up and left to a good grass ledge below a shallow corner (30 m, 4b). Climb the corner, moving right and cross the overlap above via a prominent crack. Move left then up a rightwards-sloping corner to belay on the terraces (42 m, 4c). Follow short walls and grass ledges leftwards (approximately as for Steeple) to belay under a steep wall (42 m). The "ramp" pitch of Steeple goes right-wards from here. Climb the steep line of weakness (as for Steeple) and continue straight through the slight break then rightwards up a ramp (above the Steeple ramp) to belay in a slight recess (42 m, 5c). Make delicate moves left onto a ledge and climb pleasant cracks leftwards to a break on the arete. Follow a crack, steep initially, to a ledge below an overhanging wall (42 m, 5a). Climb a spectacular overhanging crack on the right past a prominent flake at the start of the difficulties (30 m, 5b). Move right and climb a short vertical crack in the wall above (common with Steeple) then move more easily to the top (24 m, 5a). (Diagram p. 252.)

386 The Spire 280 m E3 (1982)

Another fine, difficult and spectacular climb. The first three pitches are as for Steeple to belay on the grass terrace mid-way between the crux pitches of Steeple and Needle.

Climb the groove, pull right over the bulge at the top and continue up to the Steeple/Needle belay (45 m, 5b). Climb directly above to belay by a large pointed block (10 m). The corner on the right is Steeple: above is an obvious ramp. Gain this ramp and follow it and cracks above to belay to the left of the large blocks sitting at the foot of the Steeple corner (45 m, 6a). Climb the short crack above to the belay of Haystack (10 m, 5a). Climb up rightwards across the wall via grooves to the arete overlooking the Steeple corner and up to ledges (40 m, 5a). Finish as for Steeple.

387 Steeple 247 m E2 (1968)

A superb route, in many ways the finest on the crag. It takes a fine line connecting the obvious lower and upper corner systems. Not technically high in its grade, it is however long and sustained. Start at the right-facing corner, just left of a grassy gully and about 6 m up the grassy gully.

Climb the corner crossing two small overlaps and belay beyond the second (30 m, 4c). Continue up the second corner and exit left (24 m, 5a). Climb by short walls and grass ledges to below a steep line of weakness which leads to a rightward-slanting ramp (45 m). Climb this slabby fault to below an overhang, move right with difficulty to gain the ramp then climb this (36 m, 5b). Go up the obvious line of layback-cracks up and right to the foot of the obvious and impressive corner (45 m, 4c). Climb this corner using a hidden crack to a niche (possible belay, 16 m) then continue to its top (40 m, 5b). Above is a thin and surprisingly difficult crack which leads to easier cracks and ledges which in turn lead to the top (27 m, 5a). (Diagram p. 252.)

388 Postern Direct 250 m Very Severe (1957)
Generally uninspired climbing in the lower section leads to a better and airier finish. Start at the grassy gully right of the lowest rocks.

Climb the grassy gully (unpleasant) and move left to below a smooth right-facing corner, right of and parallel to, the Steeple corner (45 m). Climb this fine corner then broken ground to a terrace (30 m, 4c). Go up and right to the next terrace (35 m). Above lies the Slanting Crack running rightwards. Climb this fault easily to where it develops into a deep chimney (60 m). From a short way up this chimney move left into a deep groove (the right hand of two). Climb the groove past some bulges and a wide crack and move left at its top (35 m, 4c). Climb the steep slab above to the Second Step (15 m, 4b). (The original route gained this point via a left traverse from the top of the deep chimney then a rightward slant; then finish up Clach Dhian Chimney.) Above is a huge brown rectangular recess with a jutting block at its top. Climb wide cracks in the left wall of the recess till moves left round the edge in a dramatic position allow blocks and cracks to be climbed to the top (35 m, 4b). (Diagram p. 252.)

Winter VI (1980)

The ordinary route is followed except for the second pitch, the smooth corner. The second pitch of Steeple was climbed instead. This route is long, difficult and serious.

Shelter Stone Crag

376. Consolation Groove
377. Sticil Face
379. Snipers
382. Cupid's Bow
383. The Pin

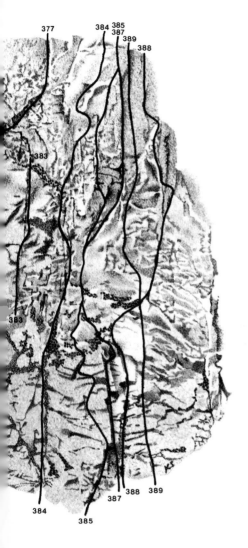

384. The Citadel
385. Haystack
387. Steeple
388. Postern Direct
389. The Needle

389   The Needle   264 m   E1   (1962)

A classic climb, long and extremely good but not too high in its grade. It takes a fairly direct line up the crag, the main feature being the imposing top corner. Start below the corner about 30 m right of Steeple.

Climb straight up the slab with a step left on to a nose at 20 m to a ledge and block belay (30 m, 4b). Above are twin zig-zag cracks. Gain these from the right and follow them to a short steep wall at 40 m. (Possible belay on right side of ledge below this wall.) Climb the steep rib on the right to a stance below a grassy terrace (45 m, 5a). Cross the terrace and climb a slab till a flake leads left to a huge block (24 m). Go up left for 6 m then move right into a flake-crack. Climb this until a narrow ledge leads left to a bulging crack. Follow the crack to a stance (30 m, 5b). Go up from the left end of the ledge to gain a slabby ramp and climb this diagonally right to ledges. Move right to belay (21 m). Climb the left facing corner via "the crack for thin fingers" and break out rightwards, then up and left by blocks and ledges (36 m, 5a). Go up grooves to the foot of the chimney-crack (21 m). Climb this, the Needle Crack, to a ledge (33 m, 5a). Continue by the line of the chimney to thread a pile of chokestones to emerge on the plateau (24 m). (Diagram p. 252.)

390   Clach Dhian Chimney   220 m   Very Difficult   (1947)

A mountaineering route, some loose rock and fine situations. It follows the big chimney starting just left of Pinnacle Gully.

Climb the wide chimney. The first chokestone pitch is climbed by a crack on the left which leads to a groove then easier ground. Two more pitches up the chimney, here virtually a gully, lead to where it ends below a steep wall. Exit left then zig-zag up for 60 m to meet an easy but sensational horizontal shelf which leads left into the Slanting Crack. Climb this fault to the lower step on the skyline. Continue up to below the final wall and finish up and right by the fan-shaped slab staircase overlooking Pinnacle Gully. (A variation finish, 50 m, Severe, takes the prominent V-groove.)

Winter   III/IV   (1972)

The summer route is followed but further traversing right is employed on the top pitch.

391   Western Grooves   220 m   III/IV   (1978)

Basically a variation to the lower part of Clach Dhian Chimney but more often in condition. Start mid-way between Clach Dhian Chimney and the edge of the face.

Climb wide shallow grooves into a short, deep, red chimney. Climb this, awkward exit and continue in a groove until a ramp leads left into the slanting fault of Clach Dhian Chimney. Follow this to the top.

Right of Clach Dhian Chimney the cliff soon swings round into Pinnacle Gully where it tapers off in size and quality. West Ridge Route, 240 m, Difficult, follows the rib on the edge for 120 m, moves down right, then climbs the right edge of the buttress above to finish as for Clach Dhian Chimney. Unknown Gully, III, takes the obvious left slanting gully starting from the first big bay to reach the first step then finishes as for Clach Dhian Chimney.

At the top of Pinnacle Gully is the aptly named Forefinger Pinnacle, a curious rock formation, unique for Cairngorm granite which bears a striking resemblance to a hand with the index finger pointing heavenward and breaks the skyline at the head of Pinnacle Gully.

It has been climbed from all sides, the routes varying from 10 m on its upper side to 30 m on its lower and from Moderate to Hard Severe.

GARBH UISGE CRAG

This is the smaller more broken cliff on the right of the Shelter Stone Crag and Pinnacle Gully. It is not a summer cliff but does give some pleasant winter routes, which because of their northerly aspect, can be in condition when other routes in the area are not.

392 Blunderbuss 135 m III (1978)
This route follows the buttress on the left of Garbh Gully. Start at the foot of the buttress on the immediate left of the gully and climb a steep chimney (45 m). Continue by grooves and short walls to finish by an open snow slope.

393 Garbh Gully 150 m III (1972)
This is the obvious Y-shaped gully in the centre of the crag. Climb the gully and the right branch, the crux being the tapered ice corner after the fork.

394 Quartz Gully 90 m II/III (1972)
This is the slabby open gully on the right of the crag. The gully is climbed direct. The top section may give a long but easy angled ice-pitch.

HELL'S LUM CRAG (NH 9901)

The smooth clean crag lying between the Allt Coire Domhain and the Feith Buidhe. It looks south-east across the trough of Loch A'an and has a very fine selection of routes in the middle grades on excellent rock.

The Crag's name is taken from the huge gully on the left-hand side. This cannot readily be seen from below as it cuts back diagonally into the cliff. Deep Cut Chimney, however, is more conspicuous, a thin black fault cutting the upper cliff. It has a curious diagonal introduction which runs across the centre of the cliff. The two features divide the crag into three main sections;

    (i) the rocks left of Hell's Lum;

    (ii) the grey buttress between Hell's Lum and Deep Cut Chimney;

    (iii) the frontal face.

In winter, this crag, with its south-east aspect, seeps and springs can give excellent climbing especially in cold weather, when ice in quantity can build up. Vast quantities of snow can also accumulate, banking out the lower slabs and shortening many routes.

Bergschrunds may even form creating a barrier to summer rocks. During sunny or thaw conditions, however, the face is liable to avalanche and icefall danger, particularly on the smooth frontal face.

THE LEFT SECTOR

This is the slabby area left of Hell's Lum. It is split by three obvious faults. The slabs on their left are climbed by Raw Mince, 75 m, Very Difficult, III. The left-most fault is Sic, 75 m, Very Difficult, III; the right-most is Puke, 75 m, Very Difficult, III. The Gullet is the central fault. Boke, 105 m, IV takes a line between Puke and the steeper rocks taken by The Chancer.

395   The Gullet   135 m   III   (1969)

The central and best defined of the three faults. Start about 20 m left of Hell's Lum and climb the fault which is slabby and shallow at first, to reach the deeper central section. Continue up the fault with occasional diversions on the left. The cornice can be large and awkward.

396   Styx   105 m   Very Severe   (1969)

Lies on the clean rocks immediately left of Hell's Lum. A good route but often wet.

Start 15 m up the gully on the left wall. Climb an obvious slanting groove to an easing, then move right to an ochre slab. Climb this to a corner (36 m, 4b). Climb the corner then a short slab to below the overlap. Surmount this via the left-hand break and then trend right to turn the next lap. Trend back left and belay in a niche in the next overlap (33 m, 4c). Leave the niche on the left then gain the crack in the wall above. Follow this to an easing in angle (36 m, 4b). Scramble to the top.

397 Chancer 90 m IV/V (1970)
A short but difficult ice climb on the left wall of Hell's Lum. Start at the top of the main ice pitch in the Lum and climb ice into a cave below a large overhang. Climb the icicle (crux) onto easier angled ice then the summit snowfields.

398 Hell's Lum 150 m II/III (1956)
A classic route up the major fault which splits the crag. It gives interesting climbing through superb scenery, but with a noticeable lack of good protection. It can vary from high angle snow to having up to four ice pitches. The cornice, which can be huge, can normally be turned on the right.

In summer this is a drainage line with some steep pitches separated by scree slopes. The first "summer" ascent used old snow patches to reduce the difficulties. The main pitch is now climbed by cracks, first the right crack is climbed on the inside then move left to the outside of the crack. It is Severe and normally a waterfall.

THE GREY BUTTRESS
This is defined by Hell's Lum on the left, and Deep Cut Chimney on the right. It has an impressive left wall leaning over the Lum. It is very quick drying in summer because of its detached nature. Deep Cut Chimney cuts behind the buttress to appear near the top of Hell's Lum where it gives The Pothole, a 45 m Very Difficult (access from above). There is little ice build-up here in winter.

The climbs on the frontal face all have excellent pitches low down, but higher up they are much easier and the lines less well-defined.

399 Drop Out 110 m E1 (1969)
Follows the rake on the wall overlooking Hell's Lum. Start at broken green rocks just right of the Lum. Climb easy broken ground to a ledge below the overhang on the edge of the buttress (36 m). Traverse left

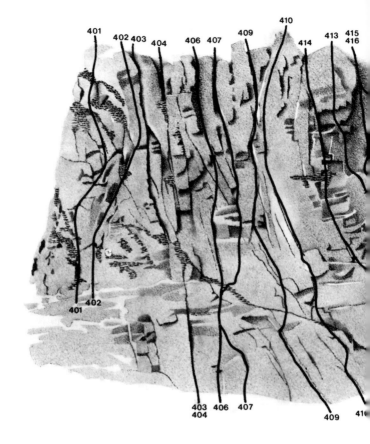

Hell's Lum Crag

401. The Exorcist
402. Hell's Lump
403. Deep-Cut Chimney
404. Nobody's Fault
406. Brimstone Groove
407. Salamander
409. Hellfire Corner

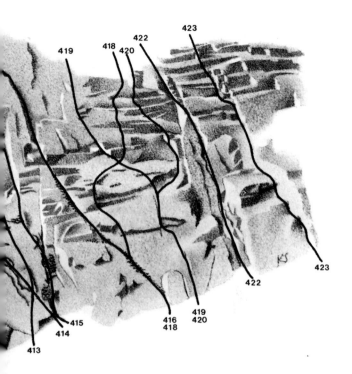

410. The Clean Sweep
413. Prince of Darkness
414. Devil's Delight
415. The Wee Devil
416. Kiwi Gully
418. Big De'il
419. Devil Dancer
420. Auld Nick
422. Escalator
423. Sneer

under the overhang and round onto the ramp line. Climb this rake (loose in places) to a ledge at 18 m. Continue up the ramp to a stance (30 m, 5a). Climb the crack continuation to where it curves left and follow it left to the edge. Go up into corners above (24 m, 5b). Continue by the same line to the top.

400   Good Intentions   120 m   Very Severe   (1969)
The main feature of this climb is the isolated groove on the left edge of the buttress. The difficulties are short and well protected.

Climb broken ground and a short wall to gain the ledge below and right of the groove (18 m). Go up diagonally left to gain the groove. Climb this and the wall above to a ledge (36 m, 5a). Go diagonally left to a ledge below the wall with a prominent groove (36 m). Climb this and exit over blocks. Climb the final short wall direct (30 m).

401   The Exorcist   102 m   Hard Very Severe   (1975)
This route is based on the left-facing corner high in the centre of the face.

Start at the foot of the buttress and climb the right-facing corner to grassy ledges (22 m). Climb the wide crack in the recess above, then go diagonally right and gain the corner via a shallow groove. Up the corner to the roof and break right to a stance on the rib (34 m, 5a). Climb the rib above to easy ground (45 m). (Diagram p. 258.)

402   Hell's Lump   100 m   Severe   (1961)
A good little route. Start at the pink and green slab about 45 m right of Hell's Lum.

Climb the quartz band up the slab to a large flake (15 m). Continue by the groove and crack above for 12 m, move up rightwards and turn the obvious square roof by the crack on the right and gain a grassy bay, then up to the recess above (30 m). Follow this then by cracks and corners trend slightly right. Gain the rib adjoining Deep Cut Chimney (24 m). Climb this to the top. (Diagram p. 258.)

403   Deep-Cut Chimney   150 m   Very Difficult   (1950)
An impressive slit, vegetated in its lower part, but with walls close enough for using back and feet to avoid the greenery. A pleasant climb with a spectacular and unexpected finish.

Start either directly below or by the easy terraced fault cleaving the smooth, lower slabs. Once in the chimney there are a number of pitches to overcome, mostly fern and grass-grown, hence climb them back and foot leaving the herbage untouched. About 45 m from the top, the scenery becomes quite remarkable; the chimney cuts far into the cliff and chokestones are jammed well out between the walls forming a tunnel. Back and foot outwards below the final overhang to reach a craggy pile of boulders wedged in the outer jaws. The finish comes with startling suddenness. (Diagram p. 258.)

Winter   III/IV   (1958)

An excellent route. The upper fault can be approached in a variety of ways depending on build-up. Once gained, the route is obvious, but it does have its surprises.

THE FRONTAL FACE

This is the largest and most important part of the crag reaching 200 m in height in its central section. It gradually steepens from bottom to top and the rock is clean and sound. There are few really large features, but Hellfire Corner, the left-facing corner system in the centre of the face, is a useful landmark. Further right is the fault of Kiwi Gully whose shape is roughly similar to Deep Cut Chimney with a diagonal lower section. Right again is the broken fault of The Escalator and between the two is an area of fine pink slabs cut by overlaps. To the right of The Escalator the cliff is cut by a broken terrace and soon merges into the hillside.

404 Nobody's Fault   150 m   IV   (1979)
This is the obvious fault parallel to and right of Deep Cut Chimney. It gives a superb winter climb.
　　Start as for Deep Cut Chimney then follow the corner/chimney to the top. The initial bulge and the hanging chimney on pitch 2 are of considerable technical interest. (Diagram p. 258.)

405 Towering Inferno   180 m   Mild Severe   (1978)
Right of Deep Cut Chimney is the similar but shallower Nobody's Fault. This route lies on the pillar just right of this and is characterised by two large, rectangular roofs.
　　Start directly below the pillar and right of a straight fault. Climb cracked green slabs to the easy terraced fault of Deep Cut Chimney (60 m). Go up to the pink rock above and move left to a red vein. Follow this to the corner leading to the lower roof, swing right on to the rib and go up to a shallow chimney level with the roof (42 m). Climb the corner to below the next overlap and move left on to the

nose. Regain the fault and follow it to a grassy recess (33 m). Continue up cracks and blocky walls to the top (45 m).

406   Brimstone Groove   150 m   Severe   (1958)
Takes the huge upper fault between the enormous beaks of rock. Start as for Towering Inferno.

Climb cracked slabs to the diagonal fault (60 m). Work rightwards into a steep left-facing corner, make a few moves up this (P.R.) then pull on to the right rib (crux). Continue up the line of corners to a belay (40 m). Climb up into the huge fault of blocky fine grained rock and follow this to the top (50 m). (Diagram p. 258.)

Winter   IV   (1970)

In winter a fine sheet of ice forms on the rocks left of Hellfire Corner. The route follows the left edge of this ice and breaks through the steep upper rocks by the largest and widest fault on the left. A good ice climb.

407   Salamander   156 m   Hard Very Severe   (1971)
A direct line on good rock parallel to and left of Hellfire Corner. It gives fine climbing but is often wet. Start below an obvious right-facing corner about 30 m left of Clean Sweep's green whaleback.

Climb up into corner and follow this to a ledge. Continue in the same line to go through a steeper section by a bulging slab to reach a platform (42 m, 4b). Follow easy rocks to the diagonal terrace (20 m).

Climb twin cracks up steep slabs left of an obvious corner to a platform (20 m, 5a). Go through the overlap by the short black corner then follow the crack to obvious recess (20 m, 4b). Continue up to shallow groove and follow this to break through upper overhangs by a striking chimney slit (30 m, 4b). Continue up open funnel to easy ground (24 m). (Diagram p. 258.)

Winter   IV   (1973)

Climb the centre of the ice-sheet left of Hellfire Corner breaching the steep upper rocks by the steep chimney slot. Above easier ground leads to the top.

Midway between Hellfire Corner and Salamander is a cluster of cracks which run up into a left-leaning corner. This is The Vacuum, 60 m, Severe, which can be an alternative start to Salamander or a short route.

408 Damien 180 m Hard Very Severe (1984)
An eliminate between Hellfire Corner and The Clean Sweep. Start at a
thin crack just left of Hellfire Corner.

Climb the thin crack and its continuation to belay in the left-facing
corner (40 m, 5a). Go easily rightward crossing the diagonal fault to
the huge block belay of The Clean Sweep (42 m). Climb the grassy
cracks to belay at the foot of the obvious corner (24 m, 4b). Climb the
corner to a junction with The Clean Sweep. Continue up this to belay
at the foot of a large bay (42 m, 5a). Move back right on to front face
and climb to top (30 m, 4b).

409 Hellfire Corner 185 m Very Severe (1958)
An excellent route though usually wet at the crux but graded for damp
conditions. It follows the main left-facing system of corners in the
middle of the face. Start at a crack (arrowed) about 30 m left of the
easy terraced fault leading to Deep Cut Chimney.

Climb the crack which runs into a left-facing corner and up this to
the diagonal terraced fault (60 m, 4b). Climb the short deep left-facing
corner which leads into a corner system which is then climbed to
below a large overhang (45 m, 4a). Go up the depression and the
continuation corner until an awkward move leads to a platform where
this merges with the main corner (20 m, 4b). Climb the steepening
corner then through the overlap by airy chimneying moves then move
right to easier ground (20 m, 4b). Up the big obvious fault to the top
(40 m). A better finish is up the right-facing corner left of the big fault.
(Diagram p. 258.)

410 The Clean Sweep 180 m Very Severe (1961)
An extremely good route which takes the pink leaning corner overlooking the much larger Hellfire Corner. Start at a green whale-back
buttress left of the diagonal fault of Deep Cut Chimney.

Go up the corner on the left of the buttress a short way to gain a
groove. Either go up the groove to cracks or go right to cracks. These
lead to the top of the buttress (30 m, 4c).

Step over the fault and climb slabs and corners to a huge block
below the pink corner (45 m, 4a). Climb the corners and the continuation fault, a superb pitch (45 m, 4c). Continue by cracks, corners and
bulges up the round grey edge above to the top (60 m, 4a). (Diagram p. 258.)

In winter this route is grade V.

411   The Omen   174 m   Hard Very Severe   (1976)
This route lies to the right of Clean Sweep. Start at the base of introductory fault of Deep Cut Chimney.

Gain the slab above the short vertical wall and follow this in a left-rising traverse (30 m, 5a). Go left then back right on the ledge above and climb the thin crack in the slab to below the obvious left-facing corner (just left of a huge block in a triangular niche) (18 m, 4c). Climb the corner to reach the huge block on Clean Sweep (18 m, 5a). Climb the crack 6 m right of that route (30 m, 4b). Move up and right over a bulge then a quartzy crack to reach the Haven, a series of grassy ledges (18 m). Climb to the top of a huge block then climb cracks in the pink rock then easy rocks to finish (60 m, 4c).

412   Second Sight   171 m   Hard Very Severe   (1982)
This climb lies between Devil's Delight and The Omen and gives good climbing but is often wet. It follows crack lines which run to the left side of the huge triangular niche. Start about 10 m up the diagonal fault of Deep Cut Chimney.

Cross the steep wall and gain the right-hand of two cracks above. Climb this then a short shallow corner to a huge triangular block (42 m, 5a). Climb the block to exit from the recess then work left and into the crack (often wet) which leads to the bottom left of the huge triangular niche (30 m, 5a). Follow the same fault line via corners to reach the grass ledges of the Haven (24 m, 4b). Go left and climb the crack line left of the pink crack (taken by The Omen). Trend up and left via bulges and cracks to some jammed blocks (34 m, 4c). Climb directly up the fine grey pillar above then easy rocks to the top (42 m).

413   Prince of Darkness   150 m   Hard Very Severe   (1984)
Takes a line left of the corner of Wee Devil. Start by the foot of the diagonal fault.

Climb the thin crack in the green slab and follow cracks and corners to below the prominent red slab (70 m, 4b). Climb cracks in this big red slab to a good ledge (30 m, 4b). Work up into the right-facing corner with overlaps and climb this to a ledge on the left, a good pitch (20 m, 5a). Return rightwards into the continuation corner and crack which lead to the top (30 m, 4c). (Diagram p. 258.)

414   Devil's Delight   165 m.   Hard Severe   (1957)
A pleasant route with only a short crux section. It lies on the slabs

left of Wee Devil and is characterised by a large wet triangular niche. Start at the vegetated fault leading into the left-facing corner.

Climb cracks and shallow corners up leftwards to reach a big recess in the glacis (60 m). From atop a 3 m block climb the crack into the triangular niche. Leave this via a crack to reach the Haven, prominent grassy ledges below the steeper upper walls. On the right is a wide shallow chimney fault. Follow the cracks in this fault passing some awkward bulges to a chimney behind a huge block. Finish straight up. (Diagram p. 258.)

Winter IV/V (1973)

A superb ice route when in condition. A cascade of ice leads into the triangular niche then on to the Haven. Above, narrow ice runnels in grooves and corners follow the summer line and constitute the crux.

415 The Wee Devil 150 m IV (1971)
The route follows the prominent left-facing corner system half-way up the face. There is an obvious red slab on its left.

Climb the discontinuous gully into the corner, up this then exit left below the overhang. Above go up and right via a large flake until a right-facing corner line right of a steep tower can be followed to easier ground and the top. (Diagram p. 258.)

In summer this route is Hard Severe.

The Underworld 180 m, Very Severe, starts up Prince of Darkness then goes right to the open corner below and right of the main corner of Wee Devil. It then follows the rib above then goes left to finish up the corner on the left of the steep upper tower.

416 Kiwi Gully 150 m III/IV (1972)
The obvious gully, it slants left in its lower section and is deepest at about two-thirds height. The gully is climbed direct and where it fades out trend left to finish up the top right-facing corner of The Wee Devil. (Diagram p. 258.)

417 Kiwi Slabs 150 m III/IV (1959)
Climb Kiwi Gully to its deepest section and break up and right on easier angled ice smears. These lead to a slanting left-facing corner which is normally ice-filled. This leads to the snow apron and hence the top.

In summer this is Very Difficult. The original start, Hard Severe, climbs the green buttress directly below the chimney.

418 Big De'il 145 m Very Severe (1971)
Climbs the left of the slabs initially then goes diagonally right into the centre. Start at the foot of Kiwi Gully.

Scramble up Kiwi Gully then climb a vertical crack to below the overlap (45 m). Gain continuation crack above and go left into obvious two-tiered right-facing corner (20 m, 4a). Climb the corners then go right into circular depression (20 m, 4b). Go diagonally right then work up by a corner system which leads to the break on the right of the long low roof. Climb this and belay above (40 m, 4b). Work diagonally right across grey walls above (20 m, 4a). (Diagram p. 258.)

419 Devil Dancer 145 m Very Severe (1977)
Climbs the centre of the slabs then goes diagonally left. Start about 10 m right of Kiwi Gully at an obvious crack.

Climb the crack and the corner continuation to below the first overlap (45 m). Go up the obvious right-facing corner in the overlap and the continuation crack to the next bulge and follow the crack through it to the glacis. Go diagonally left and belay below the deep left-facing corner (45 m, 4b). Climb this and continue to belay in the recess at the left end of the long low roof (25 m, 4b). Gain a horizontal flake and from its left end go up the pink streak to a diagonal crack (hidden protection). Climb this crack to a ledge. Go left and up an easy corner (30 m, 5a). Scramble to the top. (Diagram p. 258.)

420 Auld Nick 155 m Severe (1965)
A very pleasant route on the right of the slabs. Start about 10 m right of Kiwi Gully. The first 60 m are common with Devil Dancer.

Climb the crack system to below the overlap (45 m). Climb the right-facing corner and the crack in the slab to the next bulge. Go right on the horizontal crack then diagonally right to belay (45 m). Climb the left-facing corner by a series of steps to a belay below a rightward tapering roof (20 m). Go past the roof on the right and continue leftwards passing a big block to reach a big ledge. Climb the wall above by a thin crack then finish on either side of the big grey block (45 m). Scramble to finish. All pitches can be split. (Diagram p. 258.)

Winter III (1971)

A very variable route which can give excellent climbing. The lower slab to the second overlap often blanks out and the route follows short ice walls and snow-fields by the corner. Finish either side of the steeper grey block then the upper snow-fields.

421 The Devil's Alternative 180 m Hard Very Severe (1981)
A direct line on the right of the slabs. Interesting climbing on excellent rock. Start at a greenish buttress just left of The Escalator.

Climb shallow cracks in the greenish rock to a huge terrace (45 m). Twin cracks rise above the overlap. Gain these from a scoop on their right and follow them to the next overlap (Auld Nick is crossed here). Work left through the overlap on to a glacis (45 m, 5a). Above is a stepped wall. Zig-zag up this to a short left-facing corner above which moves up and right lead to the next glacis (45 m, 5a). Climb into a niche in the grey wall above, go left to a horizontal crack, above which easier ground is reached. An easier rib leads to the top (45 m, 5a).

422 The Escalator 150 m Moderate (1955)
The watercourse fault on the right of the cliff, the route is obvious up pink water-worn rocks.

Easy scrambling up the initial gully leads to a large platform below the steeper section where an easy shelf runs off to the right. Pleasant climbing follows finishing just left of the watercourse. (Diagram p. 258.)

Winter II/III (1960)

A good route following the summer line. The initial gully is usually straightforward snow but ice in quantity can form in the upper fault.

423 Sneer 120 m Very Difficult (1963)
A varied route on the clean rocks right of Escalator. Start 30 m right of Escalator.

Climb the obvious open corner which leads to easier rocks and a terrace. Climb the right-hand crack through the overlapping slabs.

In winter the lower rocks normally blank out but the upper slabs are often thick in ice which gives good individual pitches. (Diagram p. 258.)

Between Escalator and Sneer is Squirk, 120 m, Very Difficult. It first climbs the buttress by a crack then a groove and finishes up the left-hand crack in the upper slab.

The cliff also has a Girdle, Severe, which starts up The Escalator and finishes up Hell's Lump crossing at about the level of The Haven.

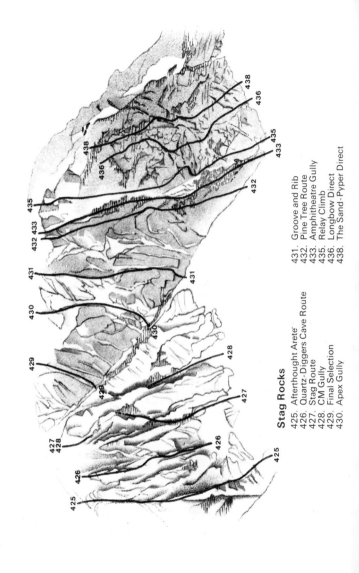

Stag Rocks

425. Afterthought Arête
426. Quartz-Diggers Cave Route
427. Stag Route
428. CM Gully
429. Final Selection
430. Apex Gully

431. Groove and Rib
432. Pine Tree Route
433. Amphitheatre Gully
435. Relay Climb
436. Longbow Direct
438. The Sand-Pyper Direct

THE STAG ROCKS (NJ 0002)

The collective name for the cliffs lying on the south side of Cairngorm between Coire Raibert and Coire Domhain. They look out over the head of Loch A'an and are easily approached from the loch by either of the descents into the horseshoe. The rock is rough and quick drying but less likely to give good winter conditions except in the main fault lines.

   The rocks consist of two main sections separated by Diagonal Gully, a long open chute whose screes almost reach the loch. This provides a descent route for competent parties in summer and winter, but care must be taken with the steep broken ground near the top.

THE LEFT SECTION
The bulk of this lies between an open unnamed gully on the left and Diagonal Gully on the right. It consists of several well-defined ribs separated by grassy faults. The three main ribs are Afterthought Arete, Triple Towers and Serrated Rib which forms the left wall of Diagonal Gully. All are Moderate summer climbs and Grade II in winter.

424   Cascade   45 m   IV   (1977)
This is the obvious steep icefall which forms on the largest outcrop mid-way between Coire Domhain and the Left Section proper. The ice-sheet is climbed direct, usually steep and serious.

425   Afterthought Arete   150 m   Moderate   (1956)
The best route of its grade in the area, it follows the left-hand and most regularly shaped arete bounding the right side of a wide, scree gully. The first pitch from the lowest rocks is surprisingly difficult, but can be avoided. After this the rocks develop into an excellent, steep knife-edge and maintain their interest to the top. (Diagram p. 268.)

Winter   II   (1969)

The arete is gained from the right and the summer route followed. Difficulties are usually at the knife-edge and a chimney leading to the plateau.

426   Quartz-Diggers Cave Route   78 m   Very Difficult
                                                              (1957)
On the buttress to the immediate right of Afterthought Arete is an

artificial cave hollowed out by the gemstone seekers of the past. The climb starts on the rib to the left of the cave and 5 m beneath the entrance.

Follow the rib till forced left into an open groove climbed on its right wall. Trend up and left to a stance (33 m). Climb the wall above into a large open groove. At its top move left and climb the clean rib to the top (45 m). (Diagram p. 268.)

427 Stag Route 135 m II (1969)
This route follows the shallow gully left of Triple Towers, the central of the three ribs, and enters a narrow snow runnel below the final tower. The lower gully contains several ice pitches the largest of which is avoided on the right. If all pitches are climbed direct the climb is grade III. (Diagram p. 268.)

428 C.M. Gully 135 m II/III (1970)
The gully which separates Triple Towers and Serrated Rib. It curves round leftwards below the impressive left wall of Serrated Rib and finishes up a narrow snow runnel (common with Stag Route). (Diagram p. 268.)

THE RIGHT SECTION
The rocks here are more massive and are divided into two by Amphitheatre Gully. On its left is the inverted triangular-shaped Pine Tree Buttress with its grooved face forming the right wall of Diagonal Gully. To the right of Amphitheatre Gully is the larger flat-faced Longbow Crag. This cliff does not extend all the way to the plateau, but is topped by about 60 m of broken scrambling.

429 Final Selection 60 m Difficult (1956)
An excellent little climb on the last defined arete near the top of Diagonal Gully. The right side is steep and the left side is a cracked slab angling into a huge groove.

Start up the huge groove then break right on to the arete. Continue up the edge and cracks on the left of the edge to a platform on the right, just below the level of the obvious overhang. A corner on the right then leads to the top. (Diagram p. 268.)

In winter this gives a short grade II. The slab on its left can be climbed at Very Severe. Right of Final Selection are two more routes. Purge, 90 m, Very Difficult, takes the groove below the previous route for a pitch then climbs the slab above. Alb, 80 m, Very Difficult, starts right of Purge at a slab corner. It climbs slabs to a steepening then works right and up.

430   Apex Gully   144 m   III   (1971)

The obvious icefall and fault starting about halfway up Diagonal Gully.

Climb an ice-boss then a series of corner grooves up the obvious line of weakness to a snow-field. Go up this to a chimney-crack and climb this direct. Easier ground leads to the top. (Diagram p. 268.)

431   Groove and Rib   135 m   Severe   (1962)

Starts in Diagonal Gully at about the level of the lowest rocks on the left and below the leftmost and cleanest of three large open grooves.

Climb a 5 m left-facing corner and move delicately right (crux) to join the main groove just above the level of the big roof. Climb the main groove to a stance (27 m). Then up the groove which becomes grassy then right on to the rib (36 m). Climb the crest then finish by steeper cracks and flakes (72 m). (Diagram p. 268.)

The lower of the twin grooves below Groove and Rib gives Deception Inlet, 150 m, Severe and IV. It takes the right-hand groove into an amphitheatre then the continuation depression.

432   Pine Tree Route   III   (1970)

Follows the broad rib overlooking Amphitheatre Gully. It starts up broken rocks often covered with ice from the gully which the route comes close to at about mid-height. The upper section is steeper, rockier and open to variation. (Diagram p. 268.)

In summer the route is Difficult but of more interest to a botanist than rock climber. A choice of routes is available.

433   Amphitheatre Gully   225 m   IV   (1971)

This obvious gully which splits the Right Section gives a good winter climb.

The gully is followed into the upper amphitheatre and gives at least one long ice pitch. The final two pitches lie up the left corner of the large wedge-shaped wall which backs the amphitheatre. The lower of these is usually the crux but this depends on build-up. The route finishes through the rock window. (Diagram p. 268.)

434　Amphitheatre Wall　60 m　Hard Severe　(1977)

A pleasant route which makes a reasonable finish to routes which end lower down. It can also be reached by scrambling from the plateau. It lies up the wedge-shaped wall at the top of Amphitheatre Gully.

Climb the corner-crack on the left of the wall to a grassy bay. Move up and right to a blocky ledge (36 m). From the blocks step left and climb the crack into the tapered chimney and so to the top (24 m).

LONGBOW CRAG

This lies right of Amphitheatre Gully and takes its name from the large roof about half-way up the crag on its left side. It is of good slabby rock and very quick to dry. The routes generally end on broken ground well below the plateau.

435　Relay Climb　200 m　Hard Severe

Follows the left edge overlooking Amphitheatre Gully. Start at the gully edge.

Work up the edge to below the bulge at mid-height (60 m). From the extreme left edge go up to gain a ledge below a large overhang. Go right on this to gain a groove (crux) which is then climbed. Continue the line of the edge to the plateau. (Diagram p. 268.)

Winter　IV/V

Follow an iced groove system right of the summer line, climb the summer crux then take the line of least resistance.

Shotgun, 135 m, Very Severe starts 15 m left of Longbow Direct and follows the rib then cracks close to the left end of the Longbow roof.

436　Longbow Direct　135 m　Very Severe　(1962)

Takes a line leading up to the Longbow roof, the largest overhang on the left side of the front face. Start at the pink water-worn fault left of centre.

Climb the right side of the fault to below a steep wall (30 m). Traverse across the wall for 2 m then up and left to below the obvious steep red wall (24 m). Climb an improbable line of jugs and blocks up the red wall. Make a short traverse left across a slab and follow a thin crack to a stance (18 m, 5a). (An easier alternative is to climb the left margin of the red wall.) Hand traverse right and up a short corner to a ledge, go up to below the Longbow roof, traverse right again and swing round an arete to a good stance (18 m, 4c). Climb the layback-crack above or follow the fine cracks on the slab to its left to reach easier ground. There is now a choice of routes, but the square chimney above is an appropriate finish (45 m). (Diagram p. 268.)

An Alternative Start, Very Severe, runs up the right side of the water-worn fault (arrow) to join the route above the level of the Longbow roof.

437 Windchill   159 m   Very Severe   (1977)
Follows the vague rounded rib just right of the pink water-washed fault and gives some pleasant, if devious climbing. Start 5 m right of chipped arrow.

Climb slab to a diagonal overlap, cross this on the right and continue to stance below shallow corner in the next overlap (36 m). Traverse 4 m left to a left-facing corner, climb this a short way then traverse back right to a flake below a roof. Continue slightly right to a stance below a long diagonal roof (common with The Sand-Pyper). Climb the roof on the left then move down and left until a fault and crack lead up and right to a grassy ledge (24 m) (common with The Sand-Pyper). Move left for 6 m to a smooth recess by a small natural arch. Climb the recess into a scoop and go up this till a ledge leads right. Go up the steep slab, then a groove into a juniper filled bay (30 m, 5a). Traverse right past blocks to gain a groove with wide crack. Climb this and a fine crack to a good ledge (39 m). A chimney and scrambling lead to the finish.

438 The Sand-Pyper Direct   150 m   Very Severe   (1962)
A pleasant route which increases in interest and difficulty with each pitch. Start near the centre of the frontal face about 30 m right of Longbow Direct.

Go left over slab shelves and climb the rounded rib to below a long, low, diagonal overlap (24 m, 4a). Go between overlaps, traverse left then up to a small right-facing groove. Up this, then trend left to a ledge below a large cracked overlap (30 m, 4b). Traverse right and up on slabs for 12 m, then cross the overlap near its right end. Go back diagonally left to grass ledge (27 m, 4c). Follow the diagonal fault right over the block (the normal finish follows this diagonal fault for a further two pitches). Step left over the lap and follow the groove left to a grass ledge (24 m, 4c). Climb the short corner above to the roof, swing right into the next corner and return left as soon as possible (crux). Follow this corner and finish by a pleasant crack and easier ground (45 m, 4c). (Diagram p. 268.)

In the centre of the cliff between The Sand-Pyper and Wigwag is a series of grassy depressions. In winter Central Route, V, climbs these to the obvious diagonal break of The Sand-Pyper ordinary route. The climb then goes rightwards along this break to gain easy ground after short hard corner. Just left of the vegetation is Addenda, Very Severe, which runs up leftwards to join The Sand-Pyper at the top of pitch 3 then finishes up Windchill.

439 Wigwag   150 m   Severe   (1962)

An interesting route on the clean rock between the meadows in the centre of the face and the grassy gully on the right margin. Start below and left of the obvious wide corner-crack (arrow).

Climb the right edge of the slab to Juniper Ledge then go left to behind a flake (30 m). Continue up to overhangs which are avoided on the left, traverse rightwards along a shelf then up to belay on the left of the prominent triangular overhang (30 m). Climb good rock above (30 m). Go rightward for 9 m then up and left to gain the top of a large flake. Continue to the left end of the flake and along a narrow shelf to gain a large vegetated groove and then the grassy amphitheatre (27 m). Climb a series of short walls on the left (33 m). A further 75 m of easy rock leads to the plateau.

In winter a line approximating to this route is V.

440 The Tenements   156 m   Very Difficult   (1955)

On the right the main rocks merge into a grassy gully which leads to a grassier amphitheatre. The climb lies on the rock right of this vegetation.

Start at the left edge and climb cracked slabs and blocks to a ledge (18 m). Go left into a recess, exit right awkwardly and work up leftward to fine bubbly rock to easier ground (36 m). Climb the big open groove above (36 m). Turn the steep overlap above on the right and go back diagonally left (30 m). Continue diagonally left to the top.

Grade IV in winter.

The slab on the left flank left of the obvious roofs gives a two pitch Very Severe which finishes up a groove overlooking the grassy amphitheatre.

STAC AN FHARAIDH (NJ 0103)

These cliffs lie on the south flank of Cairngorm, overlooking Loch A'an near the Saddle at the head of Strath Nethy. It is an area of glaciated slabs which give climbs up to 140 m in length on rough and generally sound granite. The slabs themselves are divided into an east and west flank by a shallow grassy gully, Rectangular Gully, I/II.

Approaches

From the north side of Loch A'an walk uphill to the slabs.

From the Spey Valley, go to the top station of the chairlift, contour the east side of Cairngorm (or go over the top) and descend to the top of the cliff. The best descent to the foot of the cliff is either by the easy slopes overlooking the Saddle, or down the west side of the stream which drains south-west into Loch A'an. (Scrambling.)

WEST FLANK

This section of the cliff is characterised by a diagonal wall cutting the slabs at about mid-height and increasing in size leftwards finally to merge into a steeper slabby pillar on the extreme left. A useful reference point here is a long block lying some way up the initial very easy angled slabs.

Just left of the main slab is a regular, low-walled rib with a red gully on its left. This gives the line of Rectangular Rib, 120 m, Very Difficult, II/III.

441 Mack's Dilemma 132 m Very Severe (1969)

Follows the left edge of the West Flank. Start at the left edge of the slabs.

Climb cracked slabs to belay 6 m below a right-facing corner (30 m). Climb this and continue up the rib with a short excursion to the left before reaching a block platform (22 m). Continue over an awkward bulge and up the rib to a ledge (22 m, 4c). Go a short way up the right side of the arete, move left on to the edge and continue up to a large ledge (27 m, 4b). Climb easier ground in the same line to the top. (Diagram p. 276.)

442 Speakeasy 120 m Very Severe (1978)

A pleasant climb which takes a line parallel to, and right of the left edge of the slabs.

Start at the left end of the long block. Climb the slab over two small

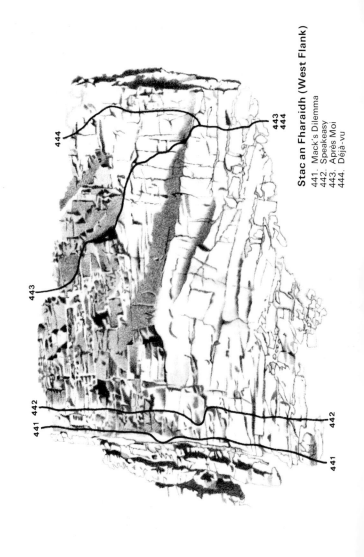

Stac an Fharaidh (West Flank)

441. Mack's Dilemma
442. Speakeasy
443. Après Moi
444. Déjà-vu

overlaps to a belay in the corner in the large overlap. Exit left from the corner on to the ledge and traverse on the shelf above this to a small corner. Climb the corner, move right then back left with an awkward mantleshelf (4c) then straight up to a grassy ledge. Follow the fault above into a short deep chimney. Climb this and the crack above. A short easy pitch then leads to the top. (Diagram p. 276.)

The fault line right of this, parallel cracks going to a prominent chimney, is the line of Sermon, 120 m. Very Severe and often wet.

Right of Sermon the central wall angles down to the right, on its left is an obvious corner. Right of this is an arrow-head like formation. Cherry, Extremely Severe, climbs the lower slab, through the central wall via this feature and up the slabs above. Right again is a shallow chimney cutting the steep wall. This is taken by The Deluge, Extremely Severe, which goes up slab corners to this, through this fault (1PA) and then on up the slabs above.

443 Après Moi 150 m Very Severe (1969)
A rather wandering line which makes the best use of the right-hand side of these slabs.

Start at cracks near the right edge of the slab, climb these to below the steep central wall and move left to a small recess (30 m). Go up the recess, break left at the top and move left to a shallow corner. Climb this till it ends, move left then up cracks to a belay (40 m, 4c). Go diagonally left over easy slabs to a large right-facing corner (25 m). Climb this and continue leftwards (45 m, 4b). Continue this leftward line to the top. (Diagram p. 276.)

Winter III (1980)
Climb ice smears and falls approximating the summer line.

444 Déjà-vu 120 m Severe (1971)
Follows the cracks on the right edge of the slab. Start just left of the Gully, as for Après Moi.

Climb cracks to steep wall (27 m). Follow the continuation crack to a grass ledge (39 m). Trend up and left via cracks and slabs (36 m). Climb the easy left-sloping corner to the top (18 m). (Diagram p. 276.)

A winter climb, Hoite-y-Toity, 166 m, IV starts as for Après Moi and follows a rising right to left line above the diagonal central wall to gain and follow the central icefalls via a short exposed traverse on the lip of the overhang.

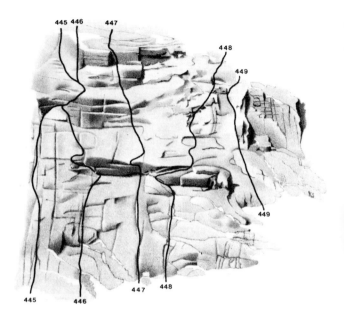

Stac an Fharaidh (East Flank)

445. Whispers
446. Bellows
447. Pushover
448. Pippet Slab
449. Linden

EAST FLANK

This right-hand section of cliff gives good slab climbing on rough granite. However, belays can be difficult to arrange and 45 m of rope is necessary on these climbs. A large boulder at the foot, near the centre of the slab, is an obvious feature.

445 Whispers 135 m   Very Severe   (1969)

A pleasant and popular route following cracks on the left edge of the slab.

Start at the second crack system from the left. Climb the crack, vegetated at first, to an easing in the angle (45 m, 4a). Continue up the same crack system, very close to the left edge at one point, to a huge flake below a steep grey wall (45 m, 4b). From the top of the flake traverse right for about 6 m then move diagonally right through the bulge onto the slab above (4c). Go diagonally left then straight up to finish (45 m). (Diagram p. 278.)

446 Bellows 141 m   Hard Very Severe   (1970)

Another good route up cracks parallel to and about 12 m right of Whispers.

Start 6 m left of the large boulder and climb an easy, vegetated crack to below a bulge (15 m). Climb the corner-crack through the bulge and continue up the slab to an enormous scoop below the large overlap (45 m, 4a). Climb a series of slabs diagonally leftwards to a crack where the final bulge is crossed (5a) and continue up the crack to a huge flake. Alternatively go right on pockets after the bulge to a small corner, after which trend up and left to the same huge flake. Go up the crack then diagonally right through the bulge (as for the crux of Whispers). Continue to the top first straight then trending left. (Diagram p. 278.)

Throwover, Very Severe, starts left of and finishes right of Bellows. It crosses Bellows below the lap and goes over this via a wide crack (1NA). Above a thin rib and crack (1PA) leads to the top slab.

Nosey Parker, Hard Very Severe, is an eliminate line between Bellows and Pushover. Start up Pushover, move left then up to the overlap which is crossed rightwards. Above, go straight up.

447 Pushover 138 m   Hard Very Severe   (1969)

The most substantial route here taking a line up the centre of the slab.

Start at the crack on the left of the large boulder at the cliff bottom.

Climb the cracks (sustained) to below the crescent-shaped overlap (45 m, 4c). Pull onto the overlap and move left until the upper slab can be gained and move up to a ledge and peg belay (12 m, 5a). Trend up and leftwards to a steeper wall which is climbed by a series of cracks to below mossy blocks (42 m, 4c). Climb over the blocks and up slabs to a chimney to finish up the wall above (42 m, 4b). (Diagram p. 278.)

Alternative finish

From the top of the second pitch climb up and right to surmount a nose of rock by a seam and continue up the slab (45 m). Continue up a corner then move up and go left to the chimney and so to the top.

448   Pippet Slab   135 m   Mild Severe   (1970)
A good route but sparsely protected in places. Start at the crack on the right of the large boulder.

Climb the crack system to below a steep wall (45 m). Go diagonally left until move can be made right onto the slab above the wall. Regain the line of the crack and bear slightly left to below an overlap (30 m). Go up the shallow stepped right-facing corner system to a niche in a steeper section (42 m). Continue in the same line to the top (18 m). (Diagram p. 278.)

The wide crack in the overlap above pitch 1 gives a Hard Severe variation.

449   Linden   60 m   Very Difficult   (1970)
Lies on the right of the slab and high up takes the fine obvious sloping ramp. Start in the large grass bay on the right where a narrow grass ledge runs to a right-facing corner-crack.

Climb a short crack 5 m right of this corner and follow thin flakes up the blunt arete. A short steep crack then leads to a sloping stance (30 m). Climb the ramp by the layback-crack then the steep continuation corner to the top (30 m). (Diagram p. 278.)

Sheilden, 75 m Very Difficult, takes a line left of Linden starting up the left-hand chimney from the grassy bay and following cracks above. Jillden, 40 m Difficult, lies right of Linden. It climbs a rib into an easy angled corner and finishes up the obvious chimney.

COIRE AN t-SNEACHDA (NH 9903)

Coire an t-Sneachda is the central of the three north-facing corries of Cairngorm. It is separated from Coire Cas ski area, by Fiacaill a'Choire Chais and from Coire an Lochain by Fiacaill Coire an t-Sneachda (un-named on 1 : 50 000 map). The latter is a hump-backed ridge which steepens after a shallow col to form a narrower rocky ridge leading to the plateau near Cairn Lochain, the Westerly top of Cairngorm. This is a pleasant scramble in summer and known as the Fiacaill Ridge.

The corrie itself is deceptive in size as it has a recess which extends Westwards. This cannot be seen from the Glenmore area and it contains a large mass of rock buttressing the Fiacaill Ridge.

There are four main rock masses in the corrie. High on the left is a rectangular buttress, the Mess of Pottage, which is bounded on the right by Jacob's Ladder, an obvious straight gully.

Aladdin Buttress lies in the centre of the corrie. It has as its lower section a steep dome-shaped rock mass. Above and to the right is more broken but shows three prominent ribs jutting up to the skyline. This buttress is bounded on the left by the large dog-leg of Aladdin's Couloir. It is separated from the Mess of Pottage by a wide area of broken ground. Right of Aladdin Buttress is the more complex Fluted Buttress. This is cut by many gullies particularly on its left, where Central Gully, the left-most of the Trident Gullies, forms the boundary between these two buttresses. On the right Fluted Buttress fades out near the lowest point of the skyline, where the Goat-track, a con-venient if steep ascent route leads onto the plateau at the head of Coire Domhain.

The Fiacaill Buttress lies at the head of the Westerly recess below the summit of the Fiacaill Ridge.

Because of the broken and vegetated nature of the rock in this corrie the summer climbing is generally poor. However, in winter these cliffs give a large number of easier but interesting routes. Some areas of the cliff, such as around the Trident Gullies, are climbable virtually anywhere and a large number of variations are possible on most of the easier climbs. Due to its wealth of lower grade winter climbs and its ease of access, this is a very popular winter corrie.

Approaches

To Coire an t-Sneachda from Aviemore:

(a) Follow the ski road to the car park in Coire Cas and contour the Fiacaill a'Choire Chais into the corrie. Then follow the vague

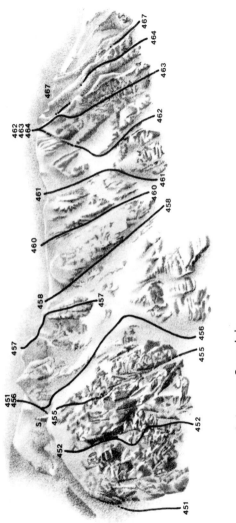

Coire an t-Sneachda

451. Aladdin's Couloir
452. Doctors' Choice
455. Original Route
456. Aladdin's Mirror
457. Pygmy Ridge
458. Central Gully

460. The Runnel
461. Crotched Gully
462. Spiral Gully
463. Fluted Buttress Direct
464. Broken Gully
467. Red Gully

path (on the east of the stream) south-westwards to the back of Coire an t-Sneachda.

(b) An alternative from the car park is to go to the White Lady Shieling. Then follow the Fiacaill Ski Tow to the crest of the Fiacaill a'Choire Chais. An easy descending traverse then leads to an obvious moraine which in turn leads to the corrie floor.

The Mess of Pottage
This small slabby buttress high up on the left of the corrie gives several winter lines which are fairly obvious and vary in standard from grade I to grade III. They are in the region of 75 m long.

450   Jacob's Ladder   105 m   I   (1939)
The gully bounding the right side of the buttress is generally very straightforward. There may be steeper sections when there is a poor build-up. The cornice can be large.

Between Jacob's Ladder and Aladdin's Couloir is an area of broken ground with a steeper rock band just below the plateau edge. Many lines of grade I to grade II can be worked out here, the best of them being Forty Thieves, I, the rib and wide slot overlooking Aladdin's Couloir.

451   Aladdin's Couloir   180 m   I   (1935)
The obvious dog-leg gully; an easy ice pitch may form at the narrows before the bend. Above, the gully widens and leads to the col above Aladdin's Seat. The gully is then wide to the top and the cornice fairly easily out-flanked. It has been skied down. (Diagram p. 282.)

ALADDIN BUTTRESS
This is the obvious buttress in the centre of the corrie right of Aladdin's Couloir. Its lower section is a steep dome-shaped mass of rock at the top left of which is a 10 m pinnacle, Aladdin's Seat. Above and right of the lower buttress and separated from it by a diagonal break of easier ground that leads to Aladdin's Seat are several triangular rock buttresses. The right-hand and best defined is Pygmy Ridge. The ground below Pygmy Ridge is easy angled and normally blanks out in winter.

The lower dome-shaped buttress gives some of the best rock climbing in the corrie. Its left edge is taken by Original Route, 150 m, Very Difficult, which takes the initial rib, big groove and then follows the left-hand triangular rock mass on the upper buttress. This is III in winter. The Lamp Direct, Severe, is a variation on its right after 65 m. Right of the corner of Doctor's Choice are four other left-facing corners which are Severe to Very Severe, and are approached by The Magic Crack or Damnation. Right of Original Route (the winter one) is Goodgame, 150 m, Hard Severe, which follows the left edge of the right-most slabs.

452   Doctor's Choice   105 m   III/IV   (1972)
Takes the obvious large left-facing corner in the centre of the buttress. Start below the corner and climb up to a cave below an overhang. Turn this on the left to gain the main corner above and follow this to reach Aladdin's Seat. Finish as for Aladdin's Couloir. (Diagram p. 282.)

453   The Magic Crack   100 m   Hard Very Severe   (1981)
A good route with an unique finger crack. Start at a deep left-facing corner by a huge beak of rock.

Climb the corner and the broad blunt rib above to a platform and large spike belay (35 m, 4b). Climb the rib a few feet then the thin clean crack on the right. This leads into corners which are climbed to below the prominent corner (20 m, 4c). Move right and climb the superb finger crack in the shallow corner then climb the cracked wall above to easy ground (45 m, 5a). To descend, traverse right and go down the line of Aladdin's Mirror.

454   Damnation   90 m   Hard Very Severe   (1969)
The right most corner of the four. Start a short way up from the lowest rocks.

Climb easy cracked slabs and corners to a huge spike by a pale coloured corner (45 m). Climb this corner then the main one to its top. Finish up the cracked wall on the left (45 m, 5a). Descend via Aladdin's Mirror.

455   Original Route (Winter)   120 m   IV   (1959)
This lies on the lower tier only and follows the obvious large chimney on its right flank. There are two main pitches, both of which give steep sections where they narrow. At the top this climb joins Aladdin's Mirror which can be ascended or descended. Alternatively Pygmy Ridge or one of the steeper gullies in the top rocks can provide a more interesting way to the plateau. (Diagram p. 282.)

456   Aladdin's Mirror   180 m   I   (1946)
A snow climb taking the easier ground right of the lower section of the buttress.

Climb the diagonal snow shelf on the right-hand side to reach open slopes. Trend back left under the upper rocks to Aladdin's Seat. Finish up Aladdin's Couloir. (Diagram p. 282.)

Direct Start   24 m   III

Climb the ice pitch on the right of Aladdin's Buttress up from the start of Aladdin's Mirror. An easy chimney then leads to the main route.

457 Pygmy Ridge   90 m   Moderate   (1904)
The right-hand triangular rock mass on the upper section of Aladdin's Buttress gives an excellent little route.

Climb from the lowest rocks and follow the well-defined rib at one section crossing a horizontal arete. (Diagram p. 282.)

Winter   III   (NR)

The summer route is followed giving an enjoyable buttress climb. The start can be reached from above or below.

FLUTED BUTTRESS
The cliff west of Aladdin's buttress to the lowest point of the corrie rim is Fluted Buttress. A recessed section on its left is split by the Trident Gullies: Central Gully, the boundary between the two buttresses, The Runnel and Crotched Gully. These all spring from the same prominent snow bay which extends high up the cliff. Right of Crotched Gully the cliff becomes steeper and its top is cut by the left to right fault which is the top of Spiral Gully. Right again are more gullies. First Broken Gully separated from Red Gully by a slabby tapering rib culminating in several obvious pinnacles, Finger's Ridge. The area of the Trident Gullies is fairly low angled and the ribs between the gullies give routes only slightly harder than the gullies themselves. Further right at the highest part of the cliff the buttress has a slabby lower section which usually blanks out. If this is not the case Spiral Gully and Fluted Buttress Direct may have an extra easy pitch to start.

458 Central Gully   135 m   I   (1940)
The left-most of the Trident Gullies, it slants leftwards separating Aladdin and Fluted Buttress. Straightforward with no pitches and easily outflanked cornices. (Diagram p. 282.)

459 Central Left-hand   135 m   I   (NR)
Goes up the rib overlooking the gully then the funnel on the right of Pygmy Ridge.

460   The Runnel   135 m   II   (1946)
The central and best defined of the three gullies rising from the top of the snow bay. Straightforward climbing to near the top where a fine icy chimney leads to the upper slopes. (Diagram p. 282.)

461   Crotched Gully   135 m   I/II   (1946)
Start up the right-hand branch from the initial snow bay which steepens near its head. From its top go right to gain the larger gully leading to the top. Alternatively, traverse right from the snow bay onto the rib, then go straight up to the larger gully. This has no pitches but may have a large cornice which can be difficult. (Diagram p. 282.)

462   Spiral Gully   150 m   II   (1959)
The upper section takes the diagonal fault which runs rightward to finish near the highest point of the buttress.
    From the rib just right of Crotched Gully to twin gullies below the foot of the upper fault a variety of starts can be found. The twin gullies are probably the best. The upper fault ends at a small col below the plateau. The cornice is fairly easily avoided. (Diagram p. 282.)
    The grooves above the diagonal fault give a variety of short climbs.

463   Fluted Buttress Direct   135 m   III/IV   (1978)
One of the best routes in the corrie. It follows the narrow but defined chimney system on the left of the most continuous section of slabby rocks.
    Climb the chimney for a pitch to where it splits and increases in size. Continue up the right fork to reach the crest of the buttress. Follow the ridge to the col between Spiral and Broken Gullies. (Diagram p. 282.)

    Cruising, 200 m, IV, follows a crack and groove system on the right side of the buttress overlooking Broken Gully and finishing up Fluted Buttress Direct.
    Broken Pillar, 110 m, Difficult, takes a fairly direct line up the ill-defined pillar just left of the gully.

464   Broken Gully   135 m   III   (1967)
The fault between the highest part of the buttress and Fingers' Ridge. The gully is more obvious in its upper sections.
    Start in the first large bay right of the lowest rocks. Climb the steepening gully up rightwards till a traverse left can be made over the

top of the slabby pillar into the main gully. Follow this with no further difficulty to finish at the top of Spiral Gully or Fingers Ridge. (Diagram p. 282.)

An alternative and harder start takes the smaller gully on the left of the ordinary start and leads directly in to the upper fault.

465 Fingers Ridge 135 m Difficult (1954)
The slabby rib which culminates in several obvious pinnacles. Start at the foot of Red Gully.

Go up and left over slabs and ledges to near the left edge of the buttress. Climb up a slight rib to an open groove on the left of some slabs. Go up this groove to a narrow ridge and follow this over the Fingers and another short ridge to the top.

Winter III/IV (1969)

Climb the summer route

466 Fingers Ridge Direct 110 m Very Severe (1984)
Pleasant though escapable climbing. Start in the middle of the ridge.

Climb directly up pink slabs, cross an awkward bulge and belay in the open groove (35 m, 4b). Work up and right by cracks to a stance by Red Gully (20 m, 4b). Climb the diagonal crack in the fine slab to ledges (30 m, 4c). Go up the next diagonal crack to join the normal route (25 m).

467 Red Gully 120 m II/III (NR)
A good climb, one of the best at its grade in the corrie. It follows the fault right of Fingers Ridge. The lower narrow chimney often contains ice in quantity and leads into the easier funnel-shaped upper gully. (Diagram p. 282.)

Between Red Gully and Goat Track Gully is Western Rib, 120 m, Moderate, II. The rib proper is gained above the toadstool pinnacle and followed throughout. A sling for aid may be required in winter on the top tower.

468 Goat Track Gully 120 m II (NR)
The gully on the extreme right of the buttress starting just right of Red Gully. It cuts up deeply rightwards and has one short pitch. Above the line is more open and less defined.

FIACAILL BUTTRESS

This is the fine mass of rock high up in the western sector of the corrie buttressing the Fiacaill Coire an t-Sneachda. It is split by the large diagonal gully of Fiacaill Couloir but this is hidden from most angles. Left of the couloir the rock is scored by slabby ramps; above and to the right the rock is slightly more broken and gives good winter climbing.

The broken face of the buttress is taken by Fiacaill Buttress Direct, 120 m, Extremely Severe (2PA), which takes the wide crack in the centre of the buttress then goes diagonally right to the edge. The right edge overlooking Fiacaill Couloir is taken by Fiacaill Buttress, 120 m, Difficult, III. The steep top wall can be turned on the left.

469   Fiacaill Couloir   150 m   II   (1958)

The diagonal gully which cuts deeply through the buttress and ends at a col near the left-hand edge.

Start at the highest snow bay in the centre of the buttress and follow it up and left. Near the top a chokestone may prove awkward if the build-up is poor. From the col at the gully top go diagonally left to finish.

Rampant, 75 m, IV, goes up steep ramps leading left from the start of Belhaven then takes a deep groove on their right.

470   Belhaven   75 m   IV (1979)

Follows the large left-facing corner immediately above the start of Fiacaill Couloir.

Climb Fiacaill Couloir for a pitch to below the corner which is gained direct or by a traverse in from higher on the left. The main corner is then followed to the Fiacaill Ridge.

471   Invernookie   120 m   III   (1969)

A good route which takes the line of ramps on the wall above and right of Fiacaill Couloir.

From the foot of the Couloir move up and right onto the ramps which are followed to below an overhanging wall. Turn this via the right corner and go up into the chimney-cave. From high up this traverse right to gain a short groove leading to the ridge.

472   Fiacaill Ridge

A simple scramble in summer. In winter of some interest if the crest is followed (grade I). Moving right decreases the difficulties.

COIRE AN LOCHAIN (NH 9802)

This corrie lying below Cairn Lochain, the most westerly top of Cairngorm, is compact and well defined. It consists of four main buttresses separated by obvious gullies. These form an arc overlooking the corrie's most outstanding feature, the Great Slab. This is a huge, easy-angled slab of pink granite which is visible from a considerable distance. It is also a notoriously avalanche-prone slope especially in thaw conditions. This is particularly so in the spring when huge full-depth avalanches can occur. Large quantities of easy-angled ice can also make this slope treacherous when slab avalanche conditions exist. It is usually advisable to approach winter climbs up the flanks of the Great Slab.

The four buttresses are numbered from left to right. The Vent separates No. 1 and No. 2 Buttress while the obvious diagonal fault of The Couloir in the centre of the corrie lies between No. 2 and No. 3. Between No. 3 and No. 4 is a large recess tucked in the corner of the corrie and housing the two branches of Y gully.

Approaches
To Coire an Lochain from Aviemore:
   (a) From Coire Cas car park contour round the base of the Fiacaill a'Choire Chais and follow the path across the Allt Coire an t-Sneachda. After 500 m the path forks and the left branch leads to Jean's Hut and the corrie.
   (b) From the Sugar Bowl, the parking area just above the forest boundary on the Ski Road, the path by the Allt Creag an Lethchoin leads into the corrie.

NO. 1 BUTTRESS
On the extreme left of the corrie. It has a steep gully wall which turns into a frontal face before easing into more broken ground on its left flank. In winter Iron Butterfly, 170 m, III, takes this margin starting about 30 m left of The Vent and working up and left to finish up a gully at the top.

473 Auricle 110 m   Severe   (1969)
A steep climb on the front face of the buttress. Start below a broken, rather easy-looking crack.

Climb the crack and easy walls above, bearing left to a good rock ledge beneath the obvious crack. Climb the crack and continue to a

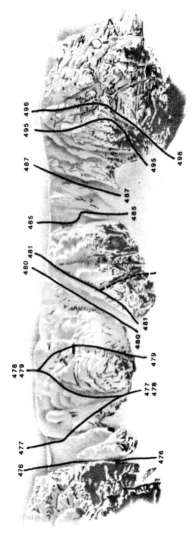

Coire an Lochain

476. The Vent
477. The Milky Way
478. Andromeda
479. Central Crack Route
480. The Couloir
481. Ewen Buttress
485. Left Branch Y Gully
487. Right Branch Y Gully
495. Sidewinder
496. Western Route

large fin-like flake. From the top of the flake climb an overhanging recess to the top of the buttress which is separated by a crevasse from the main face. Step across and up to the plateau.

474   Ventricle   93 m   Hard Very Severe   (1968)
Take the cracks and grooves on the left wall of The Vent. Start near the bend in the face.

Climb an overhanging crack (crux), move right along a ledge and up a wall near the right edge to a small mossy recess (15 m). Climb directly above the belay and up the face heading for an obvious groove and make an awkward move onto a ledge (15 m). Take the right-hand of two shallow grooves to reach the steep groove and climb this till a traverse can be made to the top of a groove and block belay (18 m). Climb the wide crack in the groove and the steep wall above to ledges and a block belay (45 m).

475   Daddy Longlegs   70 m   Hard Very Severe   (1968)
A route with two good pitches but escape is possible at half height. Start up the steep groove on the left wall of The Vent about 15 m below the chokestone.

Climb the groove, step right into a second groove and follow this past an overhang to ledges (35 m, 5a). Scramble up left (10 m). Climb two consecutive vertical cracks in the wall right of the wide corner-crack of Ventricle (25 m, 4c).

476   The Vent   115 m   II/III   (1935)
A pleasant but short-lived route up the obvious gully between No. 1 and No. 2 Buttress. It is narrow and defined at the bottom opening out into an easy angled funnel above. The difficulties depend on the build-up and amount of ice on the lower chokestone section. (Diagram p. 290.)

In summer it is a very wet and mossy Severe.

NO. 2 BUTTRESS
This, the widest buttress, lies between The Vent and The Couloir. Its left-hand side consists of several vertical ribs which do not extend all the way to the plateau. The central and right-hand sections are characterised by steep walls and horizontal breaks and is topped by a conspicuous square-cut wall. It is noted for its winter routes rather than its rock climbs.

The attractive rib bounding the right side of The Vent is taken by Vent Rib and Traverse, 115 m, Difficult, which climbs the rib to the smooth section at 45 m and turns this by a long rightward deviation. In winter the easiest line approximating to this is II and also known as Ventilator.

477   The Milky Way   100 m   II/III   (1959)
This pleasant winter route follows the diagonal line on the left of the more massive section of No. 2 Buttress. Start on the snow bay about 30 m right of The Vent.

Go up the bay to below a steep ice chute then traverse right onto the spur. Alternatively, from the foot of the snow bay climb the ramp line slanting up leftwards. Continue up and left to finish in the amphitheatre near the top of The Vent. (Diagram p. 290.)

The steep ice gully leading up from the top of the snow bay is Chute Route, IV.

478   Andromeda   130 m   III/IV   (1971)
This climb lies on the left of the buttress. Start just right of the initial snow bay of The Milky Way.

Go up and rightwards in the steep open corner fault for about 60 m until the buttress crest can be gained. Continue steeply upwards to finish left of the great square wall in the same area as the top of Central Crack Route. (Diagram p. 290.)

479   Central Crack Route   150 m   III   (1958)
A fine climb. It takes the fault right of the centre of the buttress. Start just right of the lowest rocks.

Climb the right-facing corner-crack and continuation fault for about 75 m. Then zig-zag up to below the great square wall and exit on its left. The cornice can be large and necessitate a long traverse. (Diagram p. 290.)

In summer the route is an unpleasant Moderate.

Crows Nest Crack, 100 m, Difficult takes the chimney and corner line further right. In winter this is III but much can bank out.

480   The Couloir   150 m   I   (1935)
Loose and unpleasant in summer, this obvious wide slanting gully is usually straightforward under snow. The cornice can be large but a way through is normally found above the small col. (Diagram p. 290.)

EWEN BUTTRESS   (NO. 3 BUTTRESS)
A well defined buttress lying between the diagonal of The Couloir and
the upright Left Branch of Y Gully. Its left flank forms an easier angled
rib overlooking The Couloir but it steepens rightwards into an impressive frontal face.

481   Ewen Buttress   90 m   III   (1959)
Follows the left edge of the buttress overlooking The Couloir. Start at
the foot of The Couloir.
    Climb steep broken ground to a saddle. The face above is cut by an
open gully which may be difficult to gain but above it straightforward
climbing leads to the top at the same point as The Couloir. (Diagram
p. 290.)

Alternative Start   45 m   IV

The obvious fault right of the toe of No. 3 Buttress leads steeply up
and left to join the normal route above the first pitch.

    Left of the centre of the buttress is a large recess bounding the left
side of a very steep section of cliff. The Vagrant, 85 m, Very Severe,
takes the prominent rib on the left of this recess. Nocando Crack, 70 m,
Hard Very Severe, starts up The Vicar then climbs the corner and huge
flakes on the right wall of the recess.

482   The Vicar   70 m   E1   (1968)
A magnificent top pitch but the start can be slimy. It takes the shallow
corner and arete on the right of the recess.
    Climb a vile overhanging groove then go up left towards the back of
the recess. Under a second overhanging groove, traverse right and
mantleshelf onto a ledge with large blocks. Climb a steep crack to a
second ledge directly above the first (35 m, 5a). Climb the shallow
corner directly above the belay sometimes on the wall just to its left.
Move out to the arete after about 20 m and follow this to the top
(35 m, 5a).

483   The Demon   60 m   E2   (1983)
An excellent route, strenuous and intimidating, which climbs the
steep section in the middle of the buttress. It starts under the arete of
The Vicar and goes diagonally right to join a crackline which comes up
from the undercut base of the wall.
    Start just right of the toe of the arete, go up for 3 m then step left into

a shallow groove and follow it to a roof. Traverse right under the roof then go up and slightly right into a thin crack, at the top of which is a cramped stance (30 m, 5b). Go up and right on steep layback flakes to enter the main crack system which is followed to easy ground (30 m, 5a).

484 The Overseer 70 m IV (1983)
A steep interesting line up the extreme right edge of the buttress. Start at the foot of the Left branch Y Gully.

Traverse left along a ledge (may bank out) and climb two consecutive steep corners to reach slabs. Climb these diagonally right to a perch overlooking the gully. Follow the chimney system above but before the last bulge, exit left onto a pinnacle and up the corner-crack above.

Very Difficult in summer.

485 Left Branch Y Gully 100 m III (1952)
The gully between the steep pillar and No. 3 Buttress. Start at the top left of a large recess.

Climb up to a belay right of the icicle. Surmount this (crux) then follow easier ground to the top. May not be possible unless the icicle is fairly well formed. (Diagram p. 290.)

A steep narrow pillar is the main feature of the recess which bites back into the plateau between No. 3 and No. 4 Buttresses. This rises between two gullies, the Branches of Y Gully. The groove line on the left side of the pillar is taken by Grumbling Grooves, 80 m, Severe, V.

486 Never Mind 60 m Hard Very Severe (1 PA) (1969)
An interesting route up the front of the steep pillar which separates the forks of Y Gully. Start at the lowest rocks.

Scramble up to stance below a groove (10 m). Move up and left to climb the left side of the pillar by a crack in the pink wrinkled wall which is on the right side of a large groove (Grumbling Grooves) until delicate moves lead right into the wide crack. Follow this up and left to a stance on the edge (30 m, 5a). Go up the wide crack above and the continuation corner until a tension traverse allows a foothold on the lip of the roof on the right to be gained. Move right then up to the top (20 m, 5a).

487 Right Branch Y Gully 100 m II (1934)
On the extreme left of No. 4 buttress. A wide high angle gully generally without pitches though the cornice may be large and difficult. (Diagram p. 290.)

NO. 4 BUTTRESS
The largest and most important buttress. From its left side starting by the Right Branch of Y Gully it shows a fine, steep blocky wall cut by several compelling vertical lines of which the large central corner of Savage Slit is unmistakeable. On the right side this wall swings round to form a longer but less steep face looking north. This degenerates into easier ground on its right flank where several short Grade II routes can be found in winter. Right of the main buttress are several small buttresses and gullies just below the plateau rim.

488 Oesophagus 75 m II/III (1970)
About 10 m right of the Right-hand branch of Y Gully is a groove which often holds ice in quantity.
   Climb the groove into the upper snow amphitheatre which is followed to the top. This climb appears to be the same as the route Day Dream.
   In summer this climb is Severe. It starts up the initial groove and finishes up a rotten gully.

   Puffer, 80 m, Severe climbs a pinkish slab 25 m left of Savage Slit, then finishes up an open corner above and to the right.

489 Glottal Stop 90 m III (1975)
Start 15 m left of Savage Slit below a prominent groove topped by a square-cut overhang. Climb up to the roof, turn it on the right and climb to a belay (45 m). Climb narrow chimney splitting the small buttress above to the top (45 m).

490 Gaffer's Groove 80 m Severe (1963)
Takes the line of disconnected grooves to the left of Savage Slit. Interesting climbing but some loose rock. Start just left of Savage Slit.
   Move up and traverse left into an easy large groove. Up this to stance and belay (20 m). Traverse left into a groove and climb this to a bulge. A good move left leads into the main groove (15 m). Climb the groove to the top finishing by the more pleasant right wall (25 m). Scramble to the top.

Winter   IV   (1975)

Gain the main ice-filled groove from below or by a traverse from the right above the rectangular roof. Climb the groove and finish up the wide chimney left of the summer route.

491   Savage Slit   90 m   Very Difficult   (1945)
A very fine climb up an impeccable line. It takes the wide crack in the big right-angled corner in the centre of the buttress. Start below the corner.

Moderate rock leads to below the corner (10 m). Climb the wide crack between the blocky walls of the corner to its top, several belays possible (35 m). Continue in the same crack-line or the wall on its right to the top (45 m).

Winter   IV   (1957)

Follows the summer route. It seldom holds ice in quantity because of the impressive depth of the slit. A technical route.

The aretes on either side of the corner provide climbs. Bulgy, 60 m, Very Severe, climbs the arete then the wide corner-crack past two roofs on the left. Prore, 90 m, Very Severe takes the obvious curving arete on the right of Savage Slit.

492   Fall-out Corner   70 m   Very Severe   (1964)
An excellent climb up the impressive corner right of Savage Slit. Start below the corner.

Go up to below the roof blocking the foot of the corner (10 m). Cross the roof and climb the corner till it ends (30 m, 4c). Continue in the same line then scramble to the plateau (30 m).

493   War and Peace   60 m   Hard Very Severe   (1968)
Lies on the steep blocky wall right of Fall-out Corner. Start at the leftmost of three corners 10 m right of the previous route.

Climb the left corner to its top then swing left to a belay (20 m, 4c). Go left below a roof then up to above it. Up the narrow bulging chimney above, then up a groove until one can go left under jutting blocks to belay above Fall-out Corner (30 m, 5a). Finish up the right slanting crack just on the right (10 m, 5a). A pitch of scrambling leads to the top.

494 Procrastination 90 m Severe (1968)
Pleasantly steep, it starts up the central and thinnest of three corners; the right-hand one is vegetated.

Climb to the start of the corner (10 m). Up this turning a small roof on the right to a belay (40 m). Move back left and climb the continuation of the groove to a large ledge (20 m). Climb the wall above then scramble to above Savage Slit then to the top (20 m).

495 Sidewinder 100 m III (1983)
A devious line. Right of the three corners (the higher two being War and Peace and Procrastination) an easy ramp leads on to the buttress crest.

Climb this ramp under the right corner, then up blocks for 5 m until a traverse leads back left to the top of the corner. Climb a short strenuous wall above to a large platform then go straight up to steep ground. Climb a chimney on the left (the opposite side of Savage Slit) and squeeze through a gap to gain and finish up the top easy part of Savage Slit. (Diagram p. 290.)

Sidewinder Direct, IV, gives finer climbing. It climbs the lower corner (entry from the ramp) then up the original route to the steep ground where it goes straight up a shallow corner-crack.

496 Western Route 120 m Severe (1949)
Lies up the edge of the front face. Start near the left corner of the buttress.

Go up a crack and ledge slanting right to a platform then up to a grassy recess. Climb the corner (crux, originally combined tactics). Follow the chimney with smooth V walls to easier climbing up the prominent final gully.

Winter IV (1959)

An excellent sustained climb following the summer route. (Diagram p. 290.)

No. 4 Buttress is girdled by Transformer, 90 m, Very Severe, which starts up Gaffer's Groove and follows the obvious horizontal break rightwards to finish up Western Route.

NORTHERN LAIRIG GHRU

CREAG AN LETH-CHOIN (LURCHER'S CRAG) (NH 9603)

This lies on the flank of the Lairig Ghru below the summit of the same name. It is basically a broken, rambling cliff divided into three sections—North, Central and South by North and South Gullies, scrambles in summer. The Central Section lies directly below the summit of Creag an Leth-choin but is best defined in the Southern Section.

In summer the ribs give climbing of about Moderate standard and scrambling on reasonably sound rock. In winter various routes can be worked out depending on conditions. Because of the cliff's westerly aspect conditions here can be different from other crags in the area and can occasionally give the best climbing around.

There are three main climbs.

497   North Gully   240 m   III   (1965)
The big sprawling gully at the highest section of the most northern section of cliff. It usually has two big but not too difficult ice pitches.

498   Central Gully   300 m.   III   (1970)
The most obvious gully in the middle of the cliff. Several ice pitches are found in the bottom half and the left branch is followed at the top.

499   Window Gully   220 m   III   (1972)
Midway between North and South Gullies is a large icefall halfway up the face.

Climb quite steeply for 75 m to an overhanging wall from which the ice falls in a screen. Go left between the ice and the rock, cut a window and follow steep ice to easier ground. Continue up the gully to the top.

SRON NA LAIRIG (NH 964006)

The crags on this peak overlook the Lairig Ghru. At the north end of this very broken and indistinct section of steeper ground are several ribs which give generally undistinguished climbing in summer. In winter the most obvious and best-defined gully gives Gormless, II/III.

Further south at the summit end of the crag is Lairig Ridge, 135 m, Difficult. This is approached by the right edge of its lower wall after which scrambling leads to the ridge proper. This is followed throughout and gives a sporting way to the top.

GLEN FESHIE: COIRE GARBHLACH (NN 879945)

This corrie has been long regarded as obscure and of scenic interest only. It lies well away from climbers' trade routes, being situated on the western border of An Moine Mhor, the vast, gently sloping tableland above Glen Feshie. Access is by public road to Achlean, on the East bank of the River Feshie. The best accommodation is the excellent bothy, Ruigh-aiteachain (NN 847297).

It is a narrow, trenched valley rather than a cirque, with steep walls composed in the main of grass rakes with vegetated, fragmentary buttresses. The corrie rises in two great steps, the lower bending and narrowing before opening out into the upper, which is more bowl-shaped. The upper corrie drains into the lower via a waterfall. High up on the left of the waterfall lies Hermit's Ridge, Very Difficult, III; to its right a steep recess rises to a prominent cave. The Waterfall Gully itself gives a climb, III/IV; climb directly on the left of the waterfall, then a rock gully with a steep ice pitch to reach an isolated rib of rock on the right which leads to the lip of the upper corrie.

UPPER GLEN FESHIE

Upper Glen Feshie is framed between two crags. On the right (south-west) is Creag na Caillich (NN 853903); facing it on the left is Creag na Gaibhre. At the right end of Creag na Caillich is a prominent buttress with a large crack at mid-height and flanked on the right by a gully. The gully and buttress give Coylum Crack, III/IV. The rocks of Creag na Gaibhre are high up and divided by a waterfall/icefall (Cascade Cave, IV). On the hillside to the right of Creag na Gaibhre are two chasms. The more prominent one has been climbed at Grade II.

The faces of Coire Mharconaich (NN 910933) and Creag Mhigea-chaid (NN 867024) are apparently devoid of climbing interest.

BYNACK MORE (NJ 042064)

In Coire Dearg (032067) on the West flank overlooking Strath Nethy are some short indefinite buttresses and easy snow climbs, the best being the centrally placed Y-shaped gully.

The top on the east side of Bynack More are known as the Barns of Bynack. These reach over 20 m and are massive and coarse grained. The climbs here tend to be easy or very hard.

Lesser Rocks

There are short routes to be found on the north-east side of the Chalamain Gap (965053). These are generally of moderate difficulty on good rock on a series of well-defined little buttresses.

Much more accessible but of poorer quality and shorter are the climbs on Cranberry Rocks (001069), the small outcrop at the outlet of Coire na Ciste just above the Ciste car park.

ADDENDA

LOCHNAGAR

5a   *Slime Lords,* V   G. Livingston, E. Clark   4 Dec. 1984.
     A steep route between Shadow Rib and Original Route, Direct
     Start, starting up the former and diverging right.

7a   A left to right route on the minor buttress below the Spiral
     Terrace, starting by the left-hand of two corner lines (with
     two caves) and moving right. IV, very short. C. MacLean,
     A. Nisbet, 7 Feb. 1985.

31   *Tough-guy,* V   C. MacLean, A. Nisbet   18 Dec. 1984.
     Loosely based on the summer line. Also an alternative start
     by the first pitch of Mort and a long traverse right (B. Davison,
     A. Nisbet, 26 Dec. 1984).

40   *Katsalana,* VI   D. Hawthorn, G. Livingston   26 Dec. 1984.
     By the summer line to the fault of Winter Face, then diagonally
     left by a corner to join Grovel Wall.

54a Twin Chimneys Route does not take the big, obvious cor-
     ner line. Instead, the second chimney goes right on to
     the bounding rib. The big corner is *The Ice Ox,* IV/V,
     G. Livingston, A. Mathieson, 24 Dec. 1984. The rib has also
     been climbed from the bottom at grade IV—G. Livingston,
     G. Strange, 25 Nov. 1984.

54b The steep wall left of The Ice Ox is climbed by *Solstice,* V, G.
     Livingston, G. Strange, 22 Dec. 1984. It starts by a vegetated
     corner slanting left from the start of Twin Chimneys Route,
     then continues by a steep crackline. Short but high quality.

55a The short icy corner just right of Pinnacle Gully 2, III/IV,
     C. MacLean, A. Nisbet, 6 Feb. 1985.

CREAG AN DUBH LOCH

145a An icefall which formed on the left side of North-West Gully
     Buttress, IV, C. Jamieson, G. Livingston, C. Ord, G. Strange,
     E. Todd, 13 Jan. 1985.

BRAERIACH: COIRE BHROCHAIN

236   *West Wall Route,* IV   G. Livingston, D. Lawrence, A. Nisbet
16 Dec. 1984.
By the summer route.

BEINN A' BHUIRD: GARBH CHOIRE

291a   *Ghurka,* V   C. MacLean, A. Nisbet   22 Dec. 1984.
By the summer line, except that the exit from the cul-de-sac
was by the left-hand slot (no aid).

CREAGAN A'CHOIRE ETCHACHAN

338a   *Avalanche Gully,* IV/V   D. Hawthorn, D. Dinwoodie,
17 Feb. 1985.
The icicle was climbed direct, then the icy groove above,
finishing leftwards by snowy grooves on to the upper part of
Pioneer Buttress.

352   *Scabbard,* V   C. MacLean, A. Nisbet   10 Feb. 1985.
By the summer line.

SHELTER STONE CRAG

389   *The Needle (winter variations),* VI   C. MacLean,
A. Nisbet   13–14 Feb. 1985.
The route started up a big left-facing corner just left of Clach
Dhian Chimney, then took a ramp slanting left to the terrace
(the Gallery). The Needle was followed for three pitches (one
rest on summer crux), then the "layback cracks" pitch of
Steeple (one rest) to a bivouac at the base of Steeple Corner.
The Needle was then rejoined (easily). 1PA was required to
start the Needle Crack pitch and the crack itself was quit halfway up for a ledge on the left. The arete above was climbed
and The Needle rejoined for its last pitch.

HELLS LUM CRAG

409   *Hellfire Corner,* IV   M. Slater, J. Grosset   13 Feb. 1985.
By the summer route.

STAG ROCKS

431 *Groove and Rib,* IV   M. Hamilton, R. Anderson   Jan. 1985.
By the summer route, except that the main groove was gained
from the right.

COIRE AN t-SNEACHDA

452a The next corner left of Damnation, by R. Clothier,
D. Hawthorn, Dec. 1984. Grade V in thin conditions.

463a *Wavelength,* III/IV   A. Fyffe, D. Bowen   13 Feb. 1985.
Climbs the left branch of the fault taken by Fluted Buttress
Direct; the fault was gained from the initial twin gullies of
Spiral Gully.

COIRE AN LOCHAIN

473 *Auricle,* IV   C. MacLean, A. Nisbet   29 Nov. 1984.
By the summer line.

474 *Ventricle,* VI   C. MacLean, A. Nisbet   27 Dec. 1984.
A line close to the summer route, but only the initial crack and
pitch three coincided. Two fierce overhanging grooves left of
summer pitch two were the crux. 1 PA, one axe rest overall.

494 *Procrastination,* IV   M. Fowler, A. Henderson   28 Dec. 1979.
By the summer route.

FIRST ASCENTS

The list of first ascents is comprehensive. When a route has not been fully described in the text, the list includes a reference to the most recent source of further information. The following abbreviations for references have been used.

Vol. 1, Vol. 2 *Climbers Guide to the Cairngorms Area*, Volumes One and Two, by Malcolm Smith, SMC, 1961

Vol. I *Climbers Guide to the Cairngorms Area*, Volume One, by W. March, SMC, 1973

Vol. II *Climbers Guide to the Cairngorms Area*, Volume Two, by G. S. Strange, SMC, 1973

Vol. V *Climbers Guide to the Cairngorms Area*, Volume Five, by A. F. Fyffe, SMC, 1971

Vol. IV/V *Climbers Guide to the Cairngorms Area*, Volume IV/V, by G. S. Strange, D. S. Dinwoodie, SMC, 1978

Number *Scottish Mountaineering Club Journal*, issue number, e.g., 175 is the issue number of the 1984 journal

CCJ Number *Cairngorm Club Journal*, issue number

NE Outcrops *North-East Outcrops of Scotland*, by D. S. Dinwoodie (ed.), SMC, 1984

NR not recorded

Aid: The aid used on the first ascent has been listed. The routes now go free except where noted in the text, which describes the freest version to date. In some cases the free line is slightly different from the original. Ice pegs used to assist stepcutting have not been recorded, nor have first free ascents in winter.

FFA first free ascent

PA peg for aid or tension

NA nut for aid or tension

LOCHNAGAR

1893	12 March	Black Spout, Left Hand Branch (W)	J. H. Gibson W. Douglas	
1895	16 Aug	Tough–Brown Traverse	W. Tough W. Brown	
1898	12 Nov	Raeburn's Gully Popular, till the main cave pitch collapsed in 1940	H. Raeburn J. Rennie H. Lawson	Vol. IV/V
1902	19 Oct	West Gully	H. Raeburn A. M. Mackay F. S. Goggs	Vol. IV/V

1908	17 April	Black Spout Buttress	T. E. Goodeve	
			W. N. Ling	
			H. Raeburn	
1913	21 Dec	Crumbling Cranny (W)	Miss Inglis Clark	
			Mrs. Hunter	
			H. Alexander	
1926	1 Aug	Black Spout, Left	G. R. Symmers	
		Hand Branch	F. King	
		First appearance of Symmers, who		
		with Ewen, climbed many of		
		Lochnagar's natural lines, often on		
		appalling rock and vegetation		
1926	1 Aug	Crumbling Cranny	G. R. Symmers	
			F. King	
1927	21 Aug	Pinnacle Gully 1	G. R. Symmers	Vol. IV/V
			J. Silver	
1928	26 Aug	Central Buttress	Miss N. Bruce	
			G. R. Symmers	
1930	10 Aug	Giant's Head Chimney	G. R. Symmers	Vol. IV/V
			W. A. Ewen	
1930	17 Aug	Parallel Gully A	G. R. Symmers	Vol. IV/V
			W. A. Ewen	
1932	3 July	Pinnacle Gully 2	W. J. Middleton	Vol. IV/V
			R. Lees	
			W. A. Ewen	
1932	July	Shallow Gully	Miss N. Bruce	Vol. IV/V
			H. A. Macrae	
1932	18 Sept	Shadow Buttress A, Original Route	G. R. Symmers	
			W. A. Ewen	
1932	27 Dec	Raeburn's Gully (W)	G. R. Symmers	
			A. W. Clark	
			W. A. Ewen	
1932	28 Dec	Pinnacle Gully 2 (W)	A. W. Clark	
			W. A. Ewen	
1933	6 Aug	Gargoyle Chimney	G. R. Symmers	Vol. IV/V
			W. A. Ewen	
1933	12 Sept	Douglas–Gibson Gully	C. Ludwig	Vol. IV/V
		An extraordinary solo ascent, after		
		30 years of attempts on the route.		
		Right branch by A. Nisbet, D.		
		Wright, Sept 1979		
1933	16 Sept	Polyphemus Gully	G. R. Symmers	Vol. IV/V
			W. A. Ewen	
1936	7 June	Eagle Buttress	J. H. B. Bell	Vol. IV/V
			W. G. McClymont	
			D. Myles	

1939	28 May	Parallel Buttress 2PA FFA: J. Bruce, W. Stewart, May 1953 Direct start: W. D. Brooker, D. A. Sutherland, J. W. Morgan, 1949 Variation start: D. Reid, D. Pyper, May 1961	J. H. B. Bell W. H. Murray	
1939	28 May	Backdoor Route (in descent)	J. H. B. Bell W. H. Murray	Vol. IV/V
1940	Aug	Eagle Ridge (Dundee Route) The main section of the ridge was avoided	W. S. Scroggie J. G. Ferguson	Vol. 2
1941	July	Eagle Ridge 1PA The most significant of Bell's routes, and the one most to inspire the next generation. Perhaps FFA was second ascent by S. Thomson, Mrs. Thomson, June 1944. Third ascent was free by W. D. Brooker, D. Sutherland, 1949	J. H. B. Bell Miss N. Forsyth	
1941	July	Shadow Buttress A, Bell's Route	J. H. B. Bell Miss N. Forsyth	Vol. IV/V
1941	July	Shadow Buttress B, Bell's Route 1PA FFA: unknown	J. H. B. Bell Miss N. Forsyth	
1941	July	Slab Gully	J. H. B. Bell Miss N. Forsyth	Vol. IV/V
1941	July	Tough–Brown Ridge Direct 2PA FFA: G. S. Strange, A. McIvor, 8 Aug 1976	J. H. B. Bell Miss N. Forsyth	
1945	June	Gully Route, Sinister Buttress	G. Scott W. T. Hendry	Vol. IV/V
1946	19 May*	Gargoyle Direct	D. H. Haworth G. J. Ritchie	Vol. IV/V
1947	5 Oct	Lemming's Exit, Raeburn's Gully	I. F. Roberts G. A. Roberts	CCJ 86
1948	Jan	Central Buttress (W) The start of eight years intensive winter development, when Lochnagar reigned supreme	S. R. Tewnion J. Tewnion	
1948	28 March	Parallel Gully A (W)	G. W. Ross R. Still	
1949	9 Jan	Black Spout Buttress (W)	J. Tewnion C. Hutcheon D. A. Sutherland K. Winram	

1949	1 May	West Rib	W. D. Brooker D. A. Sutherland K. Winram	Vol. IV/V
1949	29 May	Sunset Buttress Combined tactics used FFA: unknown	W. D. Brooker D. A. Sutherland	Vol. IV/V
1949	11 June	Jacob's Slabs	K. Winram R. Porter	Vol. IV/V
1949	13 Aug	Route 1 1 PA FFA: unknown	D. A. Sutherland W. D. Brooker	Vol. IV/V
1949	27 Aug	Giant's Head Chimney Direct	W. D. Brooker D. A. Sutherland	Vol. IV/V
1949	27 Aug	Multiple Chimneys	W. D. Brooker D. A. Sutherland	Vol. IV/V
1949	27 Dec	Shadow Buttress A, Original Route (W)	W. D. Brooker J. W. Morgan	
1950	29 Jan	Giant's Head Chimney (W)	W. D. Brooker J. W. Morgan	
1950	11 March	Forsaken Gully (W)	Miss E. Lawrence R. L. Mitchell	Vol. IV/V
1950	28 Dec	Douglas–Gibson Gully (W) Perhaps the most significant ascent of all; Tom Patey bursts on the scene	T. W. Patey G. B. Leslie	
1951	27 Jan	Pinnacle Gully 1 (W)	T. W. Patey C. Morrison	
1951	10 June	Causeway Rib	J. C. Stewart W. D. Brooker	Vol. IV/V
1951	30 Aug	Shadow Chimney	T. W. Patey M. D. Coutts	Vol. IV/V
1951	15 Dec	Scarface	T. W. Patey G. B. Leslie J. M. Taylor	Vol. IV/V
1952	20 Jan	Gargoyle Chimney (W)	J. M. Taylor W. D. Brooker	
1952	20 Jan	Tough–Brown Traverse (W)	T. W. Patey D. A. Aitken	
1952	8 June	Parallel Gully B Top half previously by I. M. Brooker, A. D. Lyall, 26 May 1952 Direct start by D. Stuart, B. S. Findlay, June 1970 (1 PA) FFA: G. S. Strange, W. McKerrow, July 1976	T. W. Patey J. M. Taylor W. D. Brooker C. M. Dixon D. A. Aitken M. C. S. Philip C. Morrison J. Henderson	
1952	13 Aug	Central Buttress Direct	T. W. Patey C. Morrison	Vol. IV/V
1952	31 Aug	Shadow Rib	T. W. Patey J. M. Taylor	Vol. IV/V
1952	31 Aug	Twin Chimneys Route	T. W. Patey J. M. Taylor	Vol. IV/V

Year	Date	Route	First Ascent Party	Vol.
1952	7 Oct	The Stack Combined tactics used FFA: unknown	T. W. Patey J. M. Taylor W. D. Brooker	
1952	22 Nov	Shadow Chimney (W)	F. R. Malcolm D. J. Ritchie	Vol. IV/V
1952	29 Nov	The Stack (W) Combined tactics, 1 PA	J. M. Taylor G. B. Leslie T. L. Fallowfield	
1953	24 Jan	Polyphemus Gully (W)	K. A. Grassick H. S. M. Bates	
1953	25 Jan	Eagle Ridge (W) Combined tactics used on Tower and summer crux. Hardest route of this generation and still respected today. The time of $4\frac{1}{2}$ hours showed how advanced winter buttress climbing had become	T. W. Patey J. M. Taylor W. D. Brooker	
1953	25 Jan	Gelder Gully (W)	M. C. S. Philip J. Henderson A. Grattidge	Vol. IV/V
1953	28 Feb	Route 2	T. W. Patey J. M. Taylor	
1953	Dec	Shadow Buttress A, Bell's Route (W)	W. D. Brooker J. W. Morgan J. M. Taylor	Vol. IV/V
1954	27 Feb	Western Slant	T. W. Patey J. W. Morgan J. M. Taylor L. S. Lovat	Vol. IV/V
1954	20 March	Backdoor Route (W)	T. W. Patey A. O'F. Will G. McLeod A. Thom	
1954	25 Sept	The Gutter (Raeburn's Gully)	W. D. Brooker H. S. M. Bates J. Y. L. Hay	Vol. IV/V
1954	27 Sept	The Clam	T. W. Patey J. M. Taylor F. R. Malcolm A. Thom M. Smith	
1954	5 Dec	Gargoyle Direct (W) 1 PA	R. H. Sellers G. Annand	Vol. IV/V
1955	23 Jan	The Gutter (Raeburn's Gully) (W)	T. W. Patey A. O'F. Will	
1955	23 Jan	Shadow Buttress B, Bell's Route (W)	T. W. Patey A. O'F. Will	Vol. IV/V
1955	May	Girdle Traverse	T. W. Patey A. G. Nicol A. O'F. Will	Vol. IV/V
1955	21 Aug	Direct Route, Sinister Buttress	T. W. Patey W. D. Brooker	Vol. IV/V

1955	4 Sept	Pinnacle Face	J. Smith	
		Same day as The Dagger, and a similar breakthrough	J. Dennis	
1956	4 March	Parallel Buttress (W)	T. W. Patey	
		4PA	J. Smith	
			W. D. Brooker	
		Direct and Variation Start (W), Jan 1972		
1956	11 March	Route 1 (W)	J. Smith	
		1PA	W. D. Brooker	
1956	31 March	Eagle Buttress (W)	W. D. Brooker	
			J. M. Taylor	
1956	1 April	Transept Route	R. H. Sellers	Vol. IV/V
			J. White	
			D. J. Ritchie	
1956	16 June	The Link	K. A. Grassick	
		Direct start and finish by G. P. Muhlemann, G. S. Strange, 29 June 1974	W. D. Brooker	
1957	10 March	Amphitheatre Route (W)	T. W. Patey	Vol. IV/V
			G. H. Leslie	
			S. Long	
1957	6 April	Shylock's Chimney	T. W. Patey	Vol. IV/V
			J. R. Marshall	
1957	20 April	Grovel Wall	T. W. Patey	Vol. IV/V
			W. D. Brooker	
1958	22 Feb	Parallel Gully B (W)	J. R. Marshall	
			G. Tiso	
1958	March	Parallel Gully A, Right Fork (W)	A. G. Nicol	
			T. Weir	
			N. Tennant	
1959	8 Feb	Shallow Gully (W)	D. L. Macrae	
			F. G. Henderson	
1961	April	Twin Chimneys Route (W)	T. W. Patey	
			W. D. Brooker	
			C. M. Dixon	
1966	16 Jan	Pinnacle Face (W)	K. A. Grassick	
		Combined tactics, 3PA	J. Light	
		First ascent to plateau by D. Dinwoodie, A. McIvor, 1974. Last (and hardest) major ascent by the tricouni tricksters. A modern testpiece	A. G. Nicol	
1966	4 April	West Gully (W)	A. F. Fyffe	
		Upper gully only by P. McIntyre, A. Nash, 21 March 1948	M. D. Y. Mowat	
1967	15 Jan	Slab Gully (W)	M. Forbes	Vol. IV/V
			M. Rennie	

1967	11 June	Mort 10PA FFA: D. Dinwoodie, R. A. Smith, Aug 1976. A leap ahead for Lochnagar, and the first route to show the modern potential	M. Forbes M. Rennie	
1967	16 Sept	Crypt 3PA FFA: D. Dinwoodie, R. A. Smith, 1975	M. Rennie M. Forbes	
1969	23 Dec	Tough–Brown Ridge Direct (W) 4PA	M. Rennie N. D. Keir	
1970	2 Jan	Shadow Rib (W)	J. Bower B. S. Findlay G. S. Strange	
1970	March	Forsaken Rib (W)	J. Bower G. R. Simpson	Vol. IV/V
1970	Aug	Post Mortem An aid route (A3) A. Nisbet, D. Wallace, 1978 (3PA) FFA: A. Nisbet, S. Kennedy, 2 Aug 1981	M. Forbes M. Rennie	
1972	12 Feb	Scarface (W)	D. Stuart G. S. Strange	
1972	12 Feb	Giant's Head Chimney Direct (W)	D. Dinwoodie N. D. Keir	
1972	5 March	Shadow Buttress B, Original Route (W)	A. J. Bolton C. Butterworth	
1972	18 March	Penumbra (W)	C. Butterworth P. Arnold	
1972	Summer	Psyche 1 tension peg FFA: D. Dinwoodie, R. A. Smith, 1974	M. Freeman B. T. Lawrie	
1973	25 Feb	Douglas–Gibson Gully, Right Fork (W)	D. Dinwoodie Miss C. Heap M. Ross D. Innes	
1974	2 Feb	The White Spout (W)	M. Freeman N. D. Keir	Vol. IV/V
1974	3 Feb	Centrist (W) 1PA	M. Freeman N. D. Keir	
1974	17 Feb	Winter Face (W)	N. W. Quinn D. F. Lang	Vol. IV/V
1974	20 Feb	Tower Variation, Polyphemus Gully (W) 1PA	A. J. Bolton C. Butterworth	Vol. IV/V
1974	Summer	Nymph	D. Dinwoodie R. A. Smith	
1974	14 Sept	The Straight-jacket 4PA	D. Dinwoodie N. D. Keir	Vol. IV/V

1975	18 Jan	Causeway Rib (W)	R. J. Archbold	Vol. IV/V
			G. S. Strange	
1975	18 Jan	West Rib (W)	R. A. Smith	Vol. IV/V
			G. Stephen	
1975	23 March	Central Buttress Direct (W)	M. Geddes	Vol. IV/V
		3PA	N. D. Keir	
1975	31 March	Terrorist (W)	N. D. Keir	Vol. IV/V
		Some aid used	D. Mardon	
1975	May	Dirge	D. Dinwoodie	Vol. IV/V
		1 tension peg	A. McIvor	
		FFA: D. Dinwoodie, A. McIvor,		
		1976		
1975	29 June	Pinnacle Grooves	R. J. Archbold	
			G. S. Strange	
1976	13 June	Mantichore	G. P. Muhlemann	
		2PA	G. S. Strange	
		FFA: B. T. Lawrie, P. Tipton, 1978		
1976	8 Aug	Parallel Buttress, Left Edge	A. McIvor	Vol. IV/V
			G. S. Strange	
1976	8 and 10	Black Spout Wall	D. Dinwoodie	
	Aug	2PA	R. A. Smith	
		FFA: B. T. Lawrie, N. Morrison,		
		Sept 1983. An impressive ascent of		
		a magnificent route		
1976	10 Aug	Fool's Rib	D. Dinwoodie	
			R. A. Smith	
1976	10 Aug	Hood Route	D. Dinwoodie	
			R. A. Smith	
1976	Aug	Nihilist	B. Lawrie	
		Variation start by G. P. Muhlemann,	D. Innes	
		G. S. Strange, 28 Aug 1983		
1977	5 Feb	Grovel Wall (W)	M. Freeman	
		Lower half previously by G. Cohen	A. Nisbet	
		and party, 1975		
		Upper half previously by J. Bower,		
		A. Corbett, G. R. Simpson, G. S.		
		Strange, 1968		
1977	5 March	West End (W)	G. P. Muhlemann	
			G. S. Strange	
			A. Nisbet	
1977	12 March	Lemming's Exit, Raeburn's Gully (W)	A. Robertson	
1977	13 March	The Clam (W)	R. A. Smith	
			D. Wright	
1977	10 July	Epitome	R. J. Archbold	
		Variation by R. J. Archbold. H.	M. Freeman	
		Towler, Aug 1981	G. P. Muhlemann	
1977	12 Dec	Right Chimney, The Cathedral (W)	M. Freemen	169
			G. S. Strange	
1978	5 April	Sciolist	A. McIvor	170
			G. S. Strange	
1978	12 July	Sylph	D. Dinwoodie	
			R. Renshaw	

1978	16 July	Pantheist	D. Dinwoodie	
			R. A. Smith	
1978	16 Dec	Parallel Gully A, 1930's Route (W)	A. Nisbet	170
			N. McCallum	
1979	27 Jan	The Link (W)	J. Anderson	
		A significant ascent by Anderson, first route in the Cairngorms graded above V	A. Nisbet	
1979	4 Feb	Crypt (W)	B. Sprunt	
		1 tension peg	A. Nisbet	
1979	Feb	Girdle Traverse (W)	N. Keir	170
			H. Towler (day 1)	
			G. P. Muhlemann (day 2)	
			A. Nisbet (day 2)	
1979	Feb	The French Connection (W)	B. Sprunt	NR
			J.-M. Boivin	
1980	Feb	Far Left Fork, Douglas–Gibson Gully (W)	A. Nisbet	171
			N. Spinks	
			J. Unwin	
1980	8 March	Epitome (W)	J. Fijalkowski	
		This desperate route was the first on which axes were used to rest. Conditions were excellent this month. Second ascent next day by a slightly different line (1NA, no rests)	R. A. Smith	
1980	8 March	Multiple Chimneys (W)	A. Nisbet	171
			M. Hutchinson	
1980	9 March	Left Edge, Parallel Buttress (inc Variation Start) (W)	R. Anderson	172
			M. Hamilton	
1980	17 March	Pinnacle Grooves (W)	A. Nisbet	
		1NA	S. Kennedy	
			M. McLeod	
1980	21 March	The Straight-jacket (W)	A. Nisbet	
			N. Spinks	
1980	17 May	Tough-guy	R. J. Archbold	
			G. P. Muhlemann	
1981	29 July	Dod's Diversion	G. S. Strange	173
			G. Thompson	
			R. A. Smith	
1981	7 Sept	The Outlands	W. Todd	
			B. T. Lawrie	
			D. Dinwoodie	
1981	Dec	Unnamed Corner Left of Pinnacle Gully One	A. Paul	NR
			G. Reilly	
1982	23 July	Crazy Sorrow	D. Dinwoodie	
			C. MacLean	
1982	31 July	Katsalana	B. S. Findlay	
			G. S. Strange	

1982	4 Aug	The Vault	D. Dinwoodie	
			C. MacLean	
1982	4 Aug	Drainpipe Crack	D. Dinwoodie	
			C. MacLean	
1982	5 Aug	Rolling Thunder	R. D. Barton	
			A. F. Fyffe	
1982	Dec	Sunset Gully (W)	I. Dalley	175
			G. S. Strange	
1982	Dec	Steep Wall, Sinister Buttress (W)	M. Hamilton	175
			G. S. Strange	
1983	Jan	Transept Groove (W)	R. J. Archbold	175
			G. S. Strange	
1983	Aug	Tough–Brown Integrale	R. J. Archbold	
			G. S. Strange	
1984	6 Jan	Psyche (W)	A. Paul	
			D. Dinwoodie	
1984	3 March	Central Fork, Douglas–Gibson Gully (W)	A. Paul	
			D. Dinwoodie	
			C. MacLean	
1984	17 March	The Link Direct (W) 1PA	C. Dale	
			E. Todd	
1984	19 March	Nymph (W) 3 rests on axes	C. MacLean	
			A. Nisbet	
			A. Clifford	
1984	21 March	Direct Route (W), Shadow Buttress A	C. MacLean	
			A. Nisbet	
1984	4 April	Pantheist (W) 2 rests on axes	D. Dinwoodie	
			A. Nisbet	

LOCHNAGAR: COIRE NA SAOBHAIDHE

| 1975 | March | The Watercourse (W) | D. King | Vol. IV/V |
| | | | G. S. Strange | |

LOCHNAGAR: CNAPAN NATHRAICHEAN

1969	Dec	Shortcake (W)	N. D. Keir	Vol. IV/V
1976	June	All Rock Routes on the Sleac Ghorm Some climbing was done in the fifties	D. Dinwoodie A. McIvor	Vol. IV/V
1977	Feb	The Plaid (W)	G. S. Strange	Vol. IV/V
1979	28 Jan	Four Winter Routes on the Sleac Ghorm	S. Evans A. Robertson R. A. Smith	170

EAGLE'S ROCKS

| 1967 | 14 June | Lethargy The start of a rapid development at the same time as Creag an Dubh Loch, although F. R. Malcolm and others are believed to have climbed here in the fifties | J. McArtney D. Duncan | |

1967	14 June	Indolence	J. McArtney	
			D. Duncan	
1967	16 June	Nomad's Crack	J. McArtney	
			D. Duncan	
1967	17 June	Abstention	A. Fyffe	Vol. IV/V
			J. Glennie	
1968	22 June	Nameless	D. Pyper	
			S. Wilkinson	
1968	25 Aug	A Likely Story	G. N. Hunter	
		5PA	D. F. Lang	
		FFA: A. Fyffe, J. Grieve, Oct 1970		
		The best route on Eagle's Rocks		
1968	28 Aug	Green Slab	G. N. Hunter	
			D. F. Lang	
1968	Aug	Bumble	M. Main	Vol. IV/V
			B. T. Lawrie	
1969	9 June	Gibber	A. F. Fyffe	
			J. Grieve	
1969	17 Aug	The Waterfall	G. R. Simpson	Vol. IV/V
			G. S. Strange	
1970	3 Jan	Lethargy (W)	J. Bower	
		The winter possibilities were slow	G. R. Simpson	
		to be recognised		
1970	13 June	Whisper	A. F. Fyffe	Vol. IV/V
			R. Zorab	
1970	28 Aug	Nimrod	G. N. Hunter	Vol. IV/V
		1 PA	D. F. Lang	
		FFA: unknown		
1971	8 May	Spectrum	G. S. Strange	
			D. Stuart	
			D. Dinwoodie	
1971	1 Dec	Spectrum (W)	D. Dinwoodie	
			J. Mothersele	
1974	2 Jan	Bumble (W)	N. D. Keir	Vol. IV/V
		2 separate lines, each solo	J. Taylor	
1974	2 Jan	The Waterfall (W)	N. D. Keir	
			J. Taylor	
1974	2 June	Flanker's Route	R. J. Archbold	
			G. S. Strange	
1974	22 June	Stratus	R. J. Archbold	Vol. IV/V
			G. S. Strange	
1974	Summer	Left Edge, Likely Story Slab	I. Duckworth	Vol. IV/V
			G. Smith	
1974	15 Dec	Sliver (W)	R. J. Archbold	
			G. S. Strange	
1975	4 May	Flamingo	R. J. Archbold	Vol. IV/V
			G. S. Strange	
1975	4 May	The Stretcher	D. Dinwoodie	
			A. McIvor	
1975	14 June	Taboo	A. Lawson	Vol. IV/V
			G. S. Strange	

1976	31 Jan	Shiver (W)	R. J. Archbold	
			G. S. Strange	
1976	19 July	Jade Pavement	D. Dinwoodie	Vol. IV/V
			A. McIvor	
			J. B. Porteous	
1976	12 Dec	Indolence (W)	A. Nisbet	
		This ascent marked an increase in popularity and the remaining winter lines were soon climbed	A. Robertson	
1976	26 Dec	Nomad's Crack (W)	A. Nisbet	
			A. Robertson	
1976	28 Dec	Abstention (W)	A. Nisbet	Vol. IV/V
			A. Robertson	
1977	2 Feb	Gibber (W)	A. Nisbet	
			N. Spinks	
1977	20 Feb	Whisper (W)	A. Nisbet	Vol. IV/V
			A. Robertson	
1980	Winter	The Drool (W)	D. Dinwoodie	Vol. IV/V
		Had surprisingly survived earlier attempts	A. Williams	
1981	30 Aug	Vanguard	R. J. Archbold	Vol. IV/V
			T. Syme	
1984	16 June	Fraud Squad	A. Ross	
			G. Reilly	
			Miss C. Harper	
		Unknown: Prohibition		

CREAG AN DUBH LOCH

1928	Sept	South-East Gully	G. R. Symmers	Vol. IV/V
			Miss N. Bruce	
1930	May	South-East Buttress	G. R. Symmers	
			Burnett	
1933	Feb	Central Gully (W)	Miss McHardy	
			Miss Stewart	
1940	July	North-West Gully	J. Scott	Vol. IV/V
			K. McLaren	
1941	27 July	Labyrinth Route	J. H. B. Bell	Vol. IV/V
		A formidable route for its time	Miss N. Forsyth	
1944		Central Gully Buttress	Mr. & Mrs. S. Thomson	Vol. IV/V
1946	5 May	North-West Gully Arete	W. T. Hendry	Vol. IV/V
			G. Lumsden	
1947	26 Jan	South-East Gully (W)	W. A. Russell	
			M. Smith	
			W. Stephen	
1948	March	South-East Buttress (W)	F. Patterson	
			A. Alexander	
1948	8 May	Hanging Garden Route	J. H. B. Bell	Vol. IV/V
		Left fork by A. Robertson, Summer 1976	Mrs. Bell	
			W. S. Thomson	
1951	8 Sept	Labyrinth Edge	W. D. Brooker	
			G. B. Leslie	

1952	10 May	False Gully Lassoed flake on left arete of chimney pitch. The move was free on FA of Cayman (1977), but may have been done before	T. W. Patey W. D. Brooker J. M. Taylor	Vol. IV/V
1952	12 Aug	Sabre Edge Combined tactics from top of pinnacle FFA: J. Dennis, J. Smith, 3 Sept 1955	T. W. Patey C. Morrison	Vol. IV/V
1952	29 Dec	North-West Gully (W)	T. W. Patey J. M. Taylor; W. D. Brooker J. W. Morgan	
1954	17 April	Bower Buttress	L. S. Lovat T. W. Patey; W. D. Brooker C. D. Thompson	Vol. IV/V
1954	10 Oct	Vertigo Wall Climbed in rain in tricounis. A very bold venture on to a futuristic line; 4PA With 1PA by J. Smith, J. Dennis, 3 Sept 1955. No known free ascent	T. W. Patey G. McLeod A. O'F. Will	
1955	March	Central Gully Buttress (W)	T. W. Patey	
1956	21 Oct	The Aqueduct	J. Smith T. W. Patey	Vol. IV/V
1956	21 Oct	Minotaur	T. W. Patey J. Smith	Vol. IV/V
1957	13 Jan	Sabre Cut (W) First summer ascent uncertain	T. W. Patey F. R. Malcolm A. Thom	
1958	2 July	Caterpillar Crack 2PA FFA: G. S. Strange, D. Stuart, 1970	R. W. P. Barclay W. D. Brooker	Vol. IV/V
1958	10 July	Theseus Grooves	R. W. P. Barclay W. D. Brooker	Vol. IV/V
1958	26 Aug	Waterkelpie Wall Combined tactics, 1PA FFA: D. Dinwoodie, D. Innes, mid 1970's Lower Section: J. McArtney, D. Mercer, 2 Aug 1964 (1PA) FFA: A. Nisbet, P. Langhorne, Aug 1983 A Breakthrough on the Central Gully Wall	R. W. P. Barclay W. D. Brooker	
1959	10 Feb	Labyrinth Edge (W) Excellent conditions in Feb showed the winter potential	W. D. Brooker D. Duncan	

1959	Feb	Hanging Garden Route, Right Fork (W) Hanging Garden Route is the probable line of this 1959 ascent First definite ascent by D. Dinwoodie, G. S. Strange, 9 Dec 1972	R. H. Sellers G. Annand J. Smith	
1959	Nov	The Mousetrap Hardest route in the Cairngorms at the time; another pointer to the future	J. R. Marshall R. Marshall R. Anderson	
1964	25 July	Dinosaur 1PA FFA: It became normal to go left on to Labyrinth Edge below the aid move, although it has since been freed (D. Dinwoodie, A. McIvor, 1974/5) First route on the Central Slabs. Direct finish: D. Dinwoodie, A. Beyts, 1976	J. W. Stenhouse B. T. Lawrie	Vol. IV/V
1964	19 Dec	False Gully (W) 1PA	K. Grassick W. James J. M. Taylor	
1965	23–24 Oct	The Giant Much aid used (A2) An epic ascent including a forced bivouac FFA: N. Estcourt, P. Braithwaite, Summer 1974	D. Bathgate A. Ewing J. Brumfitt	
1966	9 July	Yakaboo Approx. 10PA Route now obsolete. Known ascents with 1PA, a free ascent unknown	G. N. Hunter G. Milller	Vol. IV/V
1967	March	North-West Gully Arete (W)	D. Pyper S. Wilkinson	
1967	July	Culloden First route on the Broad Terrace Wall, ahead of its time 4PA FFA: J. Lamb, P. Whillance, 1975	A. D. Barley R. R. Barley	
1967	July	The Four Corners Route 1PA on first corner, A1 on fourth corner Ascent with 1PA by D. Dinwoodie, G. S. Strange, June 1977	R. Sharpe K. Spence	Vol. IV/V
1967	16–17 Sept	Blue Max 1 rurp for tension and spike lassoed on crux pitch, A1 on Quartz Corner FFA: J. Fraser and party, May 1975	B. W. Robertson A. F. Fyffe W. T. Wilkins	

1968	9 June	King Rat 5PA FFA: P. Thomas, M. Fowler, June 1977 taking a different line at the first roof	A. F. Fyffe J. Bower	
1968	15–16 June	Cougar Much aid used. Approx. 16PA FFA: D. Cuthbertson, M. Hamilton, June 1977. A bold ascent on an intimidating wall (1968). Also in 1977; an influential ascent, demonstrating the free climbing potential of such walls	M. Rennie P. Williams	
1969	12 Jan	Theseus Grooves (W)	J. T. Campbell B. S. Findlay; G. R. Simpson G. S. Strange	
1969	1 June	False Impression Direct finish: A. F. Fyffe, J. Savory, 7 June 1970	B. S. Findlay G. S. Strange	Vol. IV/V
1969	7 June	Black Mamba A classic route, and the start of a week when the Dubh Loch "came of age". Later Fyffe wrote a new guide (1971)	A. F. Fyffe J. Grieve	
1969	7 June	Falseface 14 points of aid used Free ascent of pitch 2 and a new free pitch 3 by D. Wright, G. S. Strange, 18 July 1976 FFA: R. A. Smith, D. Dinwoodie, July 1977 Variation start: R. Archbold, G. S. Strange, July 1977	G. N. Hunter D. F. Lang	
1969	7 June	Goliath 4PA FFA: I. Nicholson and party, 1970 Direct start: S. Docherty, N. Muir, 22 May 1971 (2PA, 2NA) FFA: B. Davison, A. Nisbet, Aug 1983 The Shelf variation: J. McArtney, B. T. Lawrie, 1967	B. S. Findlay M. Rennie	
1969	9 June	Late Night Final	A. F. Fyffe J. Grieve	
1969	10 June	The Kraken	J. Grieve A. F. Fyffe	Vol. IV/V
1969	12 June	Catwalk	J. Grieve A. F. Fyffe	
1969	14 June	Pink Elephant	J. Grieve A. F. Fyffe	Vol. IV/V

1970	31 Jan	Mammoth	J. Bower	Vol. IV/V
			J. Furnell;	
			N. Blenkinsop	
			I Rae	
1970	14 March	Centaur (W)	A. F. Fyffe	
		Direct finish: D. Wright, N. Keir,	D. Whitcombe	
		Winter 1975		
1970	March	Bower Buttress (W)	J. Bower	
			G. R. Simpson	
1970	17 May	Predator	B. S. Findlay	
		5 aid points	G. S. Strange	
		FFA: D. Dinwoodie, D. Lang, 9 July		
		1972		
		Direct start: D. Dinwoodie, R.		
		Renshaw, Summer 1978		
1970	18 June	Dubh Loch Monster	I. Nicolson	
		1PA	D. Knowles	
		FFA: J. Lamb, P. Whillance, 1975		
1970	20 June	Gulliver	I. Nicolson	
		A bold lead for 1970	D. Knowles	
1970	20 June	The Sword of Damocles	G. N. Hunter	
		A controversial ascent, using 14	D. F. Lang	
		pegs and 3 bolts for aid		
		Variation, which also eliminated		
		some aid by D. Wright, G. S.		
		Strange, 17 July 1976		
		FFA: D. Dinwoodie, R. A. Smith,		
		July 1977		
		Smith trundled the Damoclean flake		
1972	Winter	Eastern Ramp (W)	J. Bower	Vol. IV/V
			and party	
1972	11 March	Labyrinth Direct (W)	A. J. Bolton	
		A very bold and early front-pointing	P. Arnold	
		solution to a last great problem. The		
		crux was climbed without resting,		
		from a psychological belay of ice		
		screws and axes. Unrepeated till		
		1979		
1972	12 March	Mistral (W)	G. S. Strange	Vol. IV/V
			J. Tweddle	
1972	Summer	The Bower–Lang Route	J. Bower	Vol. IV/V
			D. F. Lang	
1972	20 Sept	The Last Oasis	J. Bower	
		2PA	J. Ingram	
		FFA: D. Dinwoodie, R. A. Smith,		
		1976		
1972	4 Oct	Dragon Slayer	D. Dinwoodie	
		1PA, 2NA	B. T. Lawrie	
		FFA: B. Davison, A. Nisbet, Aug		
		1983 (without precleaning or chalk)		
		Alternative finish: B. Davison, C.		
		Ord, Aug 1983		

1972	8 Oct	Vampire 4PA, 1NA FFA: B. T. Lawrie, A. Nisbet, July 1977 Direct corner by B. T. Lawrie, M. Freeman, July 1977 (2PA, 1NA) FFA: D. Dinwoodie, G. Livingstone, Aug 1983	D. Dinwoodie G. S. Strange	
1973	19 May	Cyclops	G. S. Strange M. Freeman	
1973	19 Aug	Falkenhorst 2 slings on spikes, 2PA, 3NA FFA: W. Todd, A. Last, June 1977	L. Brown D. F. Lang G. S. Strange	
1973	Summer	Girdle Traverse, Central Slabs 2PA FFA: route unrepeated?	J. Mothersele D. Riley	Vol. IV/V
1973	Summer	Nemesis	J. Mothersele W. Nicholls	Vol. IV/V
1974	July	The Strumpet	D. Dinwoodie R. A. Smith	
1975	Feb	The Aqueduct (W)	J. Moreland R. A. Smith	
1975	Feb	Yeti (W)	J. Moreland R. A. Smith	
1975	22 March	Caterpillar Crack (W) 4PA	G. Stephen D. Dinwoodie	Vol. IV/V
1975	June	The Sting	L. Brown P. Nunn	
1976	8 May	Rock Island Line	M. Freeman G. Stephen	Vol. IV/V
1976	10 July	Death's Head Route 3PA Dinwoodie starts to fill several gaps before the new guide (1978)	D. Dinwoodie J. Mothersele	
1976	11 July	Mirage Variations by G. Cohen, J. Hutchison, 1982	D. Wright G. S. Strange	Vol. IV/V
1976	17 July	The Crow Flaked lassoed, 2PA FFA: D. Dinwoodie, G. Livingstone, Aug 1983	D. Dinwoodie A. McIvor	
1976	Aug	Sous Les Toits 1 pendulum used	D. Dinwoodie B. T. Lawrie	
1977	6 Jan	Hanging Garden Route, Left Fork (W)	A. Nisbet A. Robertson	
1977	Feb	The Snow Desert	R. A. Smith D. Wright	
1977	June	Vixen 1PA FFA: A. Paul, D. Hawthorn, July 1984	R. J. Archbold G. P. Muhlemann	Vol. IV/V

1977	June	Dogleg	T. Syme	
			N. D. Keir	
1977	July	Cayman	D. Dinwoodie	
		Independent finish by R. Anderson,	G. S. Strange	
		A. Russell, 17 June 1984		
1977	3–4 Dec	Vertigo Wall (W)	A. Nisbet	
		6 pegs, 2 ice screws for aid	A. Robertson	
		A forced ascent, but still a step		
		ahead in mixed climbing		
1978	17 June	The Prowl	D. Dinwoodie	
			R. Renshaw;	
			R. J. Archbold	
			G. S. Strange	
1978	June	Ariadne	D. Dinwoodie	170
			R. Renshaw	
1979	March	Labyrinth Left Hand (W)	D. Dinwoodie	
		1NA	A. Williams	
		Variation by A. Nisbet, G. Harper,		
		24 Feb 1983		
1979	1 April	Trunk Line	N. D. Keir	172
			H. M. Towler	
1979	June	Sans Fer	M. Hamilton	
		First new route for Hamilton on	K. Spence	
		Creag an Dubh Loch, and at E4, 6b,		
		the start of the modern era		
1980	12 Jan	The White Elephant (W)	R. Anderson	
		Lower section previously by N. Keir,	R. Milne	
		D. Wright, Feb 1975		
		Late season alternative: J.		
		Anderson, A. Nisbet, 31 March		
		1979		
		A week with the best conditions		
		since 1972; the advantage was		
		taken with three long hard routes		
1980	16 Jan	Goliath (W)	A. Nisbet	
		1PA	N. Morrison	
1980	19 Jan	The Mousetrap (W)	M. Hamilton	
		1PA, seconds jumared	K. Spence	
			A. Taylor	
1980	30 March	The Last Oasis (W)	A. Nisbet	
		1PA, 1NA	N. Spinks	
1980	25 May	Coon's Yard	R. J. Archbold	172
		1PA after rain started	G. S. Strange	
1981	11 May	Dragonfly	R. J. Archbold	
			G. S. Strange	
1981	23 June	Raptor	D. Dinwoodie	
			J. Wyness	
1982	Feb	Unnamed (South-East Buttress) (W)	C. Jamieson	NR
			A. Paul	

1982	30 May	Slartibartfast The start of a two year blitz of improbable lines by Hamilton and Whillance	M. Hamilton P. Whillance (alts) R. Anderson	
1982	31 May	Bombadillo	P. Whillance M. Hamilton R. Anderson (alts)	
1982	5 June	The Israelite	P. Whillance J. Moore	
1982	24 July	The Ascent of Man	M. Hamilton R. Anderson	
1982	1 Aug	The Naked Ape	P. Whillance P. Botterill R. Anderson M. Hamilton	
1982	4 Sept	The Wicker Man	P. Whillance R. Anderson	
1983	24 Feb	Labyrinth Route (W) A winter version of the top half of Labyrinth Route	A. Nisbet G. Harper	174
1983	22–23 July	Flodden	M. Hamilton K. Spence R. Anderson	
1983	24 July	Friends Essential	M. Hamilton K. Spence R. Anderson	
1983	28 July	Masque	M. Hamilton P. Whillance	
1983	29 July	Alice Springs	M. Hamilton P. Whillance	
1983	29 July	Range War	D. McCallum K. Spence	
1983	12 Aug	Voyage of the Beagle Originally known as the Boysen Line, after an early attempt	M. Hamilton R. Anderson	
1983	18 Aug	Perilous Journey	D. Dinwoodie G. Livingstone	
1984	9 Feb	Black Mamba (W) 1PA	S. Allan A. Nisbet	
1984	9 June	Cannibal	M. Hamilton R. Anderson	
1984	4 Aug	The Snake	D. Dinwoodie G. S. Strange	
1984	11 Aug	Jezebel	G. Livingstone A. Ross	
1984	15 Aug	The Improbability Drive	G. Livingstone D. Dinwoodie	
1984	22 Aug	Iron in the Soul	D. Dinwoodie B. Lawrie	

BROAD CAIRN BLUFFS

Year	Date	Route	Party	Vol.
1948	21 Nov	Rakes Rib	K. Winram E. L. Smith M. Smith	Vol. IV/V
1952	3 May	Coffin Chimney	J. M. Taylor T. W. Patey	Vol. IV/V
1970	March	Coffin Chimney (W)	A. Fyffe R. Zorab	Vol. IV/V
1974	3 March	Funeral Fall (W) Popular nowadays	M. Freeman N. D. Keir	
1975	Jan	Yoo-Hoo Buttress (W)	T. MacLellan A. Nisbet	Vol. IV/V
1975	Jan	Rakes Rib (W)	Mrs. V. Frost D. Boyne Miss L. Brown A. Espie B. Robertson	Vol. IV/V
1983	30 July	Solitaire	G. S. Strange B. S. Findlay	

GLEN CLOVA/GLEN DOLL

For many routes, particularly in the Winter Corrie of Dreish, the first ascentionists are unknown

Year	Date	Route	Party	Vol.
1910	1 Jan	Craig Rennet (W)	H. G. Drummond J. A. Parker	Vol. V
1911	3 Jan	Pinnacle Ridge, Craig Maud	H. G. Drummond H. Alexander J. B. Miller	Vol. V
1915	May	B Gully (W)	H. Raeburn W. Galbraith W. A. Reid	Vol. V
1915	May	B Gully Buttress	H. Raeburn W. Galbraith W. A. Reid	Vol. V
1934	Feb	Diagonal Crack, Juanjorge	R. Scott J. Beedie	Vol. V
1935	Nov	Glen Doll Gully	J. D. B. Wilson D. A. Rait	Vol. V
1939	28 May	The Comb	J. G. Ferguson W. S. Scroggie	Vol. V
1939	4 June	Slanting Gully First winter ascent by F. Old and party, 1950's	G. S. Ritchie J. Brown A. Powley E. Urquhart	Vol. V
1939	15 Oct	Maud Buttress, Cairn Damff	J. H. B. Bell D. Myles	Vol. V
1946	Aug	Romulus and Remus	G. S. Ritchie E. Maxwell P. D. Ritchie L. Ferguson	Vol. V

1948	3 Oct	Gimcrack Gully, Juanjorge	K. Winram	Vol. V
			J. Tewnion	
			W. A. Russell	
1948	14 Nov	Hooker's Joy	E. L. Smith	Vol. V
			A. Alexander	
			M. Smith	
1948	Nov	B Gully Chimney	R. F. Entwhistle	Vol. V
			A. M. Kinnear	
			Miss E. R. Robertson	
			J. B. Hyne	
1950	5 March	The Pyramid	J. Tewnion	Vol. V
			K. Winram	
1953	15 Feb	Look C Gully (W)	C. L. Donaldson	
		The best ice climb in the Clova area. There are rumours of an earlier ascent	J. R. Marshall	
1954	27 Feb	Glen Doll Gully (W)	G. Smith	Vol. V
			E. W. Thomson	
			N. W. Thomson	
1954	Feb	Curving Gully, Craig Maud (W)	G. Smith	Vol. V
			E. W. Thomson	
			J. Sime	
1954	Feb	North Gully, Craig Rennet (W) (in descent)	G. Smith	Vol. V
			E. W. Thomson	
			J. Sime	
1962	29 Dec	B Gully Chimney (W)	D. Crabb	
			D. F. Lang	
1965	March	Slanting Gully, Craig of Gowal (W)	G. N. Hunter	
			S. A. M. Viveash	
1968	10 Aug	The Gowk	G. N. Hunter	
		1 tension traverse	D. F. Lang	
		FFA: G. Reilly, I. Reilly, B. Simpson, M. Webster, 1974		
1970	Winter	Girdle Traverse, Corrie Fee (W)	M. Forbes	Vol. V
			G. Miller	
1972	30 Jan	Wet Knees (W)	N. D. Keir	163
			A. Lawson	
1972	5 Feb	A Gully Buttress (W) 3PA	A. MacDonald	163
			J. MacKenzie	
1973	20 Jan	The Comb (W)	I. Robb	164
			J. Thomson	
1975	Feb	The Skiver (W)	G. Reilly	NR
			W. Taylor	
1975	1 March	Central Route (W)	I. Reilly	166
			A. Paul	
1975	Nov	The Pyramid (W)	A. Paul	NR
			G. Reilly	
			I. Reilly	
			W. Taylor	
1979	Feb	The Gowk (W)	E. Cameron	
			G. N. Hunter	

1979	31 Dec	Hogmanay Gully (W)	A. J. Thomson I. D. Shepherd S. F. Cameron	172
1980	12 Jan	The Wild Places (W)	A. Lawson A. Smith	171
1980	3 Feb	Farchal Gully (W)	A. J. Thomson I. D. Shepherd	172
1980	Winter	Diamond Slab, Winter Corrie (W)	G. R. Simpson and party	
1983	21 June	Roslin Riviera, Juanjorge	M. Hamilton G. S. Strange	NE Outcrops
1983	July	Ladies of the Canyon, Juanjorge	K. Spence M. Hamilton	NE Outcrops

GLEN ISLA: CAENLOCHAN GLEN

1947	1 July	Craig Herrich Buttress	J. Y. Macdonald H. W. Turnbull	Vol. 2
1980	28 Dec	Central Runnel	G. S. Strange	NR
1983	4 Jan	The Ramp	R. J. Archbold W. S. McKerrow	174

GLEN CALLATER: CORRIE KANDER

		Snow routes: first ascents not recorded		Vol. 2
1981	Jan	The curving recess	A. Nisbet C. Brooker E. Clark N. Mollison N. Spinks	172
1981	Dec	Snip-Snip	G. Mackenzie S. Mackenzie G. Peat N. Quinn	174

GLEN CALLATER: CREAG AN FHLEISDEIR

1948	Summer	Central Slabs Cleft	G. Taggart A. McLaren	Vol. 2
1966	24 Dec	Central Slabs Cleft (W)	B. S. Findlay N. D. Keir	159

DEVILS'S POINT

1908	April	South-East Corner	S. H. Cowan E. B. Robertson	Vol. 1
1926	Winter	Geusachan Gully (W)	Unknown	Vol. 1
1929		First visit to Devil's Cave		
1940	March	Corrour Slabs	Dr. Hobson W. L. Walker W. T. Hendry	Vol. 1

1949	March	South-West Arete	A. Parker	Vol. 1
			J. Young	
1966	3 April	Corrour Slabs (W)	G. R. Simpson	NR
			J. Elrick	
			G. S. Strange	
		Other routes not recorded		

DEE FACE, BEINN BHROTAIN

1949	Sept	Green Gully	M. Smith	Vol. 1
			C. Petrie	
1952	April	Green Gully (W)	B. Furmiston	Vol. 1
			D. Hilton;	
			J. Kershaw	
			G. Whitham	
1970's		V. Diff. Slabs	B. T. Lawrie	170
			D. Mercer	
1983	11 July	Brodan's Dyke	B. S. Findlay	
			G. S. Strange	
1984	31 May	Klonedyke	S. Allan	
			A. Nisbet	

COIRE CATH NAN FIONN, BEINN BHROTAIN

1931	29 March	B Gully (W)	P. D. Baird	Vol. 1
			R. N. Traquair	
1950	Sept	A Gully	C. Petrie	Vol. 1
			M. Smith	
1950	Sept	B Gully	C. Petrie	Vol. 1
			M. Smith	
1952	8 June	Tiered Cracks	K. Winram	Vol. 1
			G. C. Greig	
			M. Smith	
1969	20 April	A Gully (W)	G. Boyd	161

THE PALETTE, CARN A' MHAIM

1955	July	Gadd's Route	J. Gadd	
		Combined tactics, 1PA	Mrs. Gadd	
		FFA: D. Dinwoodie, G. S. Strange,		
		22 Aug 1981		
1981	22 Aug	Tickled Pink	D. Dinwoodie	
			G. S. Strange	
1981	22 Aug	Pink Dwarf	C. Miller	
			A. Paul	
1984	30 May	Medium-Rare	A. Nisbet	
			S. Allan	

LUIBEG SLABS, CARN A' MHAIM

1940	July	The Diagonal Route	W. L. Walker	CCJ 85
			W. T. Hendry	

1943	April	The Direct Route	J. D. Auld	CCJ 85
			G. Lumsden	
			W. T. Hendry	
		First ascentionists unknown: Silver Chimney		

CORRIE OF THE CHOKESTONE GULLY, CAIRNTOUL

1911	25 Sept	Chokestone Gully	J. McCoss and party	Vol. 1
1958	July	Bugaboo Rib	R. W. P. Barclay	
			G. Annand	
			M. Smith	
			D. Steele	
1964	9 Feb	The Shroud (W)	J. Knight	
			I. A. MacEacheran	
1970	13 April	Bugaboo Rib (W) 3PA, 2NA Alternative start: D. Hawthorn, D. Lawrence, Dec 1983 (1PA)	B. S. Findlay G. S. Strange	
1970	19 April	South-East Couloir (W)	J. Campbell	
			G. R. Simpson	
1974	31 March	Saskwatch (W)	R. J. Archbold	
			D. King	
			G. R. Simpson	
			G. S. Strange	
1975	1 March	The Wanderer (W) 1PA	R. A. Smith G. S. Strange	
1983	3 April	Angel's Delight (W)	B. S. Findlay	
			G. S. Strange	

GARBH CHOIRE MOR, BRAERIACH

1924	20 July	Pinnacle Gully First winter ascent uncertain	J. A. Parker H. Alexander	Vol. 1
1941	July	Solo Gully	A. Tewnion	Vol. 1
1941	Sept	Pinnacles Buttress	A. Tewnion	Vol. 1
			S. Tewnion	
			A. McArthur	
1950	13 Aug	Crown Buttress	K. Winram	Vol. 1
			C. Petrie	
			M. Smith	
			J. Tewnion	
1952	25 May	Sphinx Ridge	K. Winram	
			G. Dey	
			M. Smith	
			W. Kelly	
1952	22 July	Bunting's Gully, by right fork Left fork: K. Winram, M. Smith, Aug 1953	G. Dey M. Smith K. Winram G. C. Greig	Vol. 1

1953	24 May	She-Devil's Buttress	K. Winram M. Smith	Vol. 1
1953	14 June	Egyptian Fantasy	K. Winram C. Petrie; G. C. Greig M. Smith	Vol. 1
1954	29 Sept	Michaelmas Fare	J. M. Taylor G. B. Leslie	Vol. 1
1954	31 Oct	Sphinx Gully (W)	A. Watson P. D. Baird	Vol. 1
1957	Summer	West Buttress (Lower Corrie)	R. H. Sellers G. Annand M. Smith	Vol. 1
1959	June	Tiara	A. Thom G. Annand R. Wiseman	Vol. 1
1964	8 Jan	Solo Gully (W)	J. J. Light O. J. Ludlow	
1964	9 Jan	Bunting's Gully (W) (by left fork) Right fork (Snowbunting): J. J. Light, J. Vigrow, 15 March 1966	J. J. Light O. J. Ludlow	
1966	14 March	Sphinx Ridge (W)	J. J. Light J. Vigrow	
1966	18 June	Phoenix Gully	J. J. Light	158
1967	26 Jan	Crown Buttress (W) The party were forced to bivouac on the plateau in a blizzard and descended into Glen Geusachan next day	J. Bower P. Kale	
1967	19 March	Phoenix Gully (W)	J. J. Light G. McGregor M. McArthur D. Halliday	
1967	17 Sept	Phoenix Buttress	J. J. Light A. W. Manwell A. G. Nicol R. A. North	160
1968	12 April	Pinnacles Buttress (W)	J. Bower G. R. Simpson G. S. Strange	
1968	4 July	Vulcan 1PA FFA: G. Cohen, G. Macnair, July 1979	J. J. Light J. Vigrow	
1969	19 April	She-Devil's Buttress (W)	G. Boyd B. S. Findlay G. R. Simpson G. S. Strange	
1969	20 April	West Buttress (Lower Corrie) (W)	P. C. D. Kale C. A. MacIntyre	161

1969	6 July	Tower of Babel 2PA FFA: G. Cohen, G. Macnair, July 1979	J. J. Light A. G. McGregor	
1971	10 April	Pinnacles Couloir (W)	J. Bower B. S. Findlay G. S. Strange D. Stuart	
1971	10 April	Gaunt Gully (W)	D. B. Redway	164
1971	21 Dec	Phoenix Buttress (W)	M. G. Geddes J. S. Robinson	
1973	Aug	Hot Lips	G. Cohen G. Hardy	
1974	30 March	Forked Lightning Route (W)	R. J. Archbold D. King G. R. Simpson G. S. Strange	
1975	1 March	Vulcan (W)	J. Bower J. Ingram K. Turnbull	
1977	12 March	White Nile (W)	R. J. Archbold M. Hillman	
1979	7 July	Phoenix Edge	R. J. Archbold G. S. Strange	
1982	5 Dec	Michaelmas Fare (W)	A. Nisbet C. Bruce	174
1984	22 Feb	Tiara (W)	A. Nisbet E. Clark	

GARBH CHOIRE DHAIDH, BRAERIACH

1810	17 July	Dee Waterfall	Dr. George Skene Keith Mr. Warren	
1942	Aug	The Chimney Pot	W. T. Hendry G. Lumsden	Vol. 1
1942	Aug	Monolith Gully	W. T. Hendry G. Lumsden	Vol. 1
1942	Aug	Slab and Groove	W. T. Hendry G. Lumsden	Vol. 1
1949	16 April	Helicon Rib	K. Winram R. Porter J. W. Morgan	
1951	5 Aug	Pisa	J. Tewnion M. Smith	Vol. 1
1954	March	Monolith Gully (W)	M. Scott G. Sievwright	Vol. 1
1954	5 Sept	The Great Rift	F. R. Malcolm A. Thom M. Smith	
1955	12 June	Boomerang	R. H. Sellers G. Annand	Vol. 1

1955	3 July	The Culvert	R. H. Sellers	
			G. Annand	
1957	31 March	St Andrews Climb	L. J. Morris	
		4PA	W. S. Yeaman	
		An early free ascent (perhaps first)		
		by G. R. Simpson, G. S. Strange, 23		
		Sept 1967		
1959	Feb	The Chimney Pot (W)	R. H. Sellers	
			K. A. Grassick	
1962	23 Feb	Boomerang (W)	D. Pyper	
			D. Reid	
1963	June	Kangaroo	J. McArtney	159
			B. T. Lawrie	
1963	June	Kookaburra	J. McArtney	
			B. T. Lawrie	
1964	7 Jan	Slab and Groove (W)	O. J. Ludlow	156
			J. J. Light	
			D. K. Mardon	
1964	March	Helicon Rib (W)	D. W. Duncan	
			A. J. D. Smith	
1964?		Billabong	J. C. Innes	
			M. Higgins	
			A. J. D. Smith	
			D. W. Duncan	
1965	21 Feb	The Great Rift (W)	A. G. Nicol	
			J. J. Light	
1967	April	Pisa (W)	D. W. Duncan	159
			S. P. Hepburn	
1967	23 Sept	Koala	D. W. Duncan	
			A. F. Fyffe	
			J. McArtney	
1969	18 April	Billabong (W)	G. Boyd	161
			B. S. Findlay	
			G. R. Simpson	
			G. S. Strange	
1971	11 April	Twilight Gully (W)	J. Bower	
			B. S. Findlay	
			G. S. Strange	
			D. Stuart	
1981	17 Dec	The Culvert (W)	A. Nisbet	
			P. Barrass	

COIRE BHROCHAIN, BRAERIACH

1898	10 Sept	West Gully	A. Fraser	
		First winter ascent unknown	A. W. Russell	
1901	5 April	East Gully (W)	J. Drummond	
			T. Gibson	
			A. W. Russell	
1908	20 April	Central Buttress Gully (W)	W. N. Ling	Vol. 1
			H. Raeburn	

1911	Oct	Black Pinnacle, Ordinary Route	J. A. Parker	
			H. Alexander	
			J. B. Millar	
			W. A. Reid	
1925	22 Aug	Pioneer's Recess Route	A. Harrison	Vol. 1
			L. StC. Bartholomew	
1931	27 March	Braeriach Pinnacle, Original Route	P. D. Baird	Vol. 1
			R. N. Traquair	
1931	22 June	Braeriach Pinnacle, South Face	J. Sutherland	Vol. 1
			P. D. Ritchie	
1933	July	Eastern Route, Braeriach Pinnacle	C. G. Cowie	Vol. 1
			S. R. Tough	
			G. L. Ritchie	
1938	19 June	Direct Route, Black Pinnacle	J. H. B. Bell	Vol. 1
1940	July	East Gully	W. T. Hendry	Vol. 1
			L. Durno	
			G. Morrison	
			W. L. Walker	
1942	Aug	Campion Gully	W. T. Hendry	Vol. 1
			A. Tewnion	
			G. Lumsden	
1942	Aug	Slab Route, Black Pinnacle	W. T. Hendry	Vol. 1
			A. Tewnion	
			G. Lumsden	
1942	Aug	Central Chimney	W. T. Hendry	Vol. 1
			A. Tewnion	
			G. Lumsden	
1942	Aug	West Wall Route	A. Tewnion	
			W. T. Hendry	
			G. Lumsden	
1942	Aug	Pyramus	W. T. Hendry	Vol. 1
			G. Lumsden	
1942	Aug	Thisbe	W. T. Hendry	Vol. 1
			G. Lumsden	
1944	Aug	Bhrochain Slabs Direct start: D. Pyper, D. Reid, May 1961. Direct finish: B. T. Hill, D. J. Pullin, I. T. W. Sloan, J. Thomson, 8 July 1967	G. W. Ross G. O. Clark	
1948	27 March	Near East Buttress	I. M. Brooker	Vol. 1
			A. D. Lyall	
			D. McConnach	
1948	18 Sept	North-West Chimney	G. W. Ross	Vol. 1
			Miss J. Fleming	
1949	March	Black Pinnacle (W)	A. Parker	
			J. Young	
1949	17 April	The Lion	K. Winram	Vol. 1
			R. Porter	
			J. W. Morgan	
1950	12 April	Pyramus (W)	W. D. Brooker	Vol. 1
			S. McPherson	

1952	29 June	Ninus	G. C. Greig	Vol. 1
			J. Tewnion;	
			K. Winram	
			G. Dey	
			M. Smith	
1953	1 March	Babylon Rib	G. C. Greig	Vol. 1
			M. Smith	
			K. Winram	
1953	28 June	Azalea Rib	K. Winram	Vol. 1
			C. Petrie	
			M. Smith	
1954	5 April	Campion Gully (W)	K. A. Grassick	Vol. 1
			A. G. Nicol	
1955	3 Jan	Thisbe (W)	G. H. Leslie	
			M. Smith	
1955	9 April	Domed Ridge (W)	A. G. Mitchell	
			W. P. L. Thomson	
1955	19 June	Vanishing Shelf	G. H. Leslie	Vol. 1
			M. Smith	
1955	17 July	Direct Route, West Buttress	A. Stevenson	Vol. 1
			J. Y. L. Hay	
1955	7 Sept	The Great Couloir	J. Y. L. Hay	Vol. 1
1956	24 Sept	Braeriach Direct	R. H. Sellers	
			M. Smith	
			R. W. P. Barclay	
1957	28 Dec	The Great Couloir (W)	J. Y. L. Hay	
			Miss H. Ross	
1959	Feb	Vanishing Shelf (W)	R. H. Sellers	
			K. A. Grassick	
1960	Feb	Bhrochain Slabs (W)	W. Gault	
			D. Bruce	
			A. Milne	
1965	4 April	The Lion (W)	W. J. Luke	157
			M. D. Y. Mowat	
			R. Robertson	
1967	10 Sept	Ebony Chimney	P. Macdonald	
			D. K. Stephen	
1968	13 April	Direct Route, West Buttress (W)	J. Bower	
			G. R. Simpson	
			G. S. Strange	
1969	3 Feb	Near East Buttress (W)	P. C. D. Kale	161
			C. A. MacIntyre	
1969	16 Feb	Eastern Route, Braeriach Pinnacle (W)	J. Bower	161
			J. Buchanan	
			A. Sproull	
1969	19 April	Tigris Chimney (W)	P. C. D. Kale	161
			C. A. MacIntyre	
1969	20 April	Pioneers Recess Route (W)	G. R. Simpson	
			G. S. Strange	
1969	17 July	The Fang	B. S. Findlay	161
			G. S. Strange	

1970	12 April	Ninus (W)	B. S. Findlay	
			G. S. Strange	
1970	14 April	Western Couloir (W)	B. S. Findlay	
			G. S. Strange	
1970	18 April	South Face, Braeriach Pinnacle (W)	J. Campbell	162
			G. R. Simpson	
1978	25 March	The Lampie (W)	J. C. Higham	170
			J. H. Moreland	
1981	18 Dec	Babylon Rib (W)	P. Barrass	174
			A. Nisbet	
1982	Feb	Ebony Chimney (W)	A. Nisbet	
			C. McLeod	
1983	30 Jan	Braeriach Direct	E. Clark	
			A. Nisbet	
1984	12 Aug	Ivory Tower	R. J. Archbold	
			G. S. Strange	

BRAERIACH: COIRE AN LOCHAIN

1945	June	Derelict Ridge	R. B. Frere	Vol. 1
			P. A. Densham	
1980	26 Oct	Derelict Ridge (W)	I. Dalley	NR
			R. J. Archbold	
			G. S. Strange	

GLEANN EINICH (selected routes)

1902	Easter	Several Routes by SMC		
1938	24 April	Robert's Ridge	J. H. B. Bell	
			E. E. Roberts	
			D. W. Howe	
1956	2 Jan	No. 5 Buttress Gully (W)	T. W. Patey	Vol. 1
			A. Beanland;	
			L. S. Lovat	
			J. Y. L. Hay	
			Miss E. M. Davidson	
1959	15 Feb	The Slash	T. W. Patey	Vol. 1
			V. N. Stevenson	
1960's early		Pinnacle Ridge (W)	T. W. Patey	NR
		1 PA	(party unknown)	
1979	6 Jan	Robert's Ridge (W)	N. D. Keir	170
			R. A. Smith	
1981	13 Sept	Resurrection	R. J. Archbold	173
			W. McKerrow	
			G. S. Strange	
			H. Towler	

COIRE NA CICHE, BEINN A'BHUIRD

1948	28 Feb	Twisting Gully (W)	K. Milne	
			J. Davidson	
			J. Reid	

1949	20 Aug	Slugain Buttress	W. D. Brooker	Vol. II
			D. A. Sutherland	
1949	21 Aug	Sickle	W. D. Brooker	Vol. II
			D. A. Sutherland	
1953	10 May	Hourglass Buttress	A. Thom	
		1 PA	F. R. Malcolm	
		FFA: unknown		
		Direct start by A. O'F. Will, T. W.		
		Patey in April 1955		
		A very early VS, and a classic		
1953	28 June	Trident	A. Thom	
		Combined tactics used; freed on	Miss E. Gordon	
		second ascent in 1953/4	F. R. Malcolm	
			Miss S. Anderson	
1953	30 June	Quartzvein Route	Q. T. Crichton	
			F. L. Swinton	
1953	18 Oct	Jason's Chimney	A. Thom	Vol. II
			F. R. Malcolm	
			A. O'F. Will	
1953	18 Oct	Grey Tower; Grey Tower Chimney	A. Thom	Vol. II
		Route	F. R. Malcolm	
			A. O'F. Will	
1954	17 Jan	Little Tower Gully (W)	F. R. Malcolm	Vol. II
			A. Thom	
1955	Aug	The Carpet	F. R. Malcolm	
		Combined tactics, several pegs for	A. Thom	
		aid. Pegs soon eliminated	G. Malcolm	
		and the route became a classic	R. W. P. Barclay	
		companion to Hourglass Buttress	G. Adams	
		FFA: unknown		
1955	28 Aug	Sandy Crack	F. R. Malcolm	Vol. II
			A. O'F. Will	
			G. McLeod	
1957	10 Feb	Slugain Buttress (W)	G. Adams	
			D. Macrae	
1959	Jan	Quartzvein Route (W)	W. A. Christie	Vol. II
			J. W. Vigrow	
1959	March	Sickle (W)	A. Thom	
			R. Wiseman	
1964	25 May	Three Step	R. H. Ford	
		A controversial ascent; aid used to	R. A. North	
		solve an outstanding problem		
		FFA: C. MacLean, A. Paul, 1 Aug		
		1982		
1965	28 Aug	Lamina	M. Rennie	
			R. Stirton	
			J. Bower	
1967	15 Jan	Trident (W)	J. Bower	Vol. II
		2 PA	M. C. MacLennan	
1968	2 June	The Watchtower	J. Bower	Vol. II
			A. Fyffe	

1970	19 March	The Carpet (W) Combined tactics, 3PA Very hard for its time. Unrepeated for 13 years	J. Bower G. Boyd	
1970	29 March	Hourglass Buttress (W) 2PA Still unrepeated	J. Bower G. Boyd	
1970	6 Sept	Vatican Steps	G. N. Hunter D. F. Lang	Vol. II
1973	1 March	Sandy Crack (W) 1NA	C. Anderson R. J. Archbold N. D. Keir	165
1973	8 Sept	Homebrew	R. J. Archbold N. D. Keir A. Lawson	
1974	31 March	Jason's Chimney (W)	M. Freeman N. D. Keir	
1976	18 July	Hell's Bells	S. Falconer G. Reilly I. Reilly G. Stephen	
1976	Sept	High Step	J. Moreland D. Wright	
1977	2 July	Hot Toddy	R. J. Archbold N. D. Keir	
1982	Feb	Neptune's Groove (W)	A. Nisbet G. S. Strange	
1982	24 July	The Grinder	G. S. Strange H. Towler	
1982	1 Aug	Joker's Crack	D. Dinwoodie K. Murphy	
1982	Aug	Quickstep An unsuccessful attempt to find the line of Silk Cut, unrecorded in mid seventies	R. F. Allen A. Nisbet	
1983	Aug	Limbo Dance	G. Reilly F. Templeton	

COIRE AN DUBH LOCHAIN, BEINN A'BHUIRD

1911	April	Main Rake (W)	H. Alexander A. A. Longden A. M. Watt	
1949	1 May	May Day Route	J. Tewnion E. L. Smith W. A. Russell M. Smith	Vol. II
1949	21 Aug	Crow-step Route	C. Petrie M. Smith	Vol. II
1949	21 Aug	Polypody Groove	J. Tewnion E. L. Smith	

1950	July	Central Rib	K. Winram	Vol. II
			C. Petrie	
1950	26 Nov	Winter Rib (W)	J. Tewnion	Vol. II
			G. Dey	
			M. Smith	
1952	7 June	Birthday Route	K. A. Grassick	Vol. II
			J. G. Lillie	
			R. Preshaw	
1953	15 March	Tantalus Gully	G. C. Greig	Vol. II
			M. Smith	
			K. Winram	
1957	10 Feb	Tantalus Gully (W)	R. Ellis	
			M. Scott	
1964	July	Bloodhound Buttress (1 PA)	M. Higgins	
		Climbed with toprope on crux pitch,	J. C. Innes	
		T. W. Patey, W. W. Hutchison, Sept		
		1953		
		FFA: D. Dinwoodie, B. T. Lawrie, A.		
		McIvor, mid seventies		
1965	9 Oct	Tearaway	A. F. Fyffe	
			M. D. Y. Mowat	
1967	15 Feb	May Day Route (W)	N. D. Keir	Vol. II
			B. S. Findlay	
1969	Jan	Polypody Groove (W)	D. W. Duncan	
			G. R. Simpson	
1972	30 Jan	Faux-pas (W)	J. Bower	
			B. Clarke	
			A. Morgan	
1975	15 Feb	Bloodhound Buttress (W)	R. A. Smith	
		7 PA	G. Stephen	
1977	April	Crow-step (W)	R. J. Archbold	NR
			G. Cohen	
1977	9 July	Come Dancing	S. Falconer	
			G. Stephen	
1978	24 June	Sniffer Buttress	A. Nisbet	170
			N. Spinks	
1978	25 June	The Scent	A. Nisbet	
			N. Spinks	
1981	10 Aug	The Streak	A. Nisbet	
1981	10 Aug	Hooker's Route	A. Nisbet	173
			N. Spinks	
1982	Feb	Tail-end Slabs	A. Nisbet	174
			G. S. Strange	
1982	Aug	The Last Tango	R. F. Allen	
			A. Nisbet	

THE DIVIDING BUTTRESS, BEINN A'BHUIRD

1948	4 April	Slab and Arete	J. Tewnion	Vol. II
			M. Smith	
1949	28 May	Sentinel Route	K. Winram	Vol. II
			M. Smith	

1967	15 Jan	The Ramp (W)	D. Cameron	Vol. II
			G. S. Strange	
1970	14 Nov	Sentinel Gully (W)	G. S. Strange	Vol. II
			D. Stuart	
1970	14 Nov	Sentinel Route (W)	M. Rennie	Vol. II
			D. Riley	
1974	Summer	Jewell–Kammer Route	J. Jewell	
			P. Kammer	
1982	30 July	Streaker's Root	R. J. Archbold	
			H. Towler	
			D. Wallace	
1983	July	The Fringe	A. Nisbet	175
			M. Ross	
			D. Strickland	
1983	July	Parkie's Route	A. Nisbet	175
			M. Ross	

COIRE NAN CLACH, BEINN A'BHUIRD

1984	8 July	Twister	G. S. Strange	
			R. Ross	

GARBH CHOIRE, BEINN A'BHUIRD

1933	4 July	Mitre Ridge	E. A. M. Wedderburn	
			P. D. Baird	
			E. J. A. Leslie	
1933	4 July	Cumming–Crofton Route	M. S. Cumming	
		Variation by R. J. Archbold, H. Towler, 5 Sept 1981	J. W. Crofton	
		Two very significant routes, the hardest pre-war in the Cairngorms and also of classic quality. Many early routes were on bad rock and vegetation		
1943	June	Commando Route	Sgt.-Major Langlands	Vol. II
			A. D. M. Cox	
1943	June	North-West Gully (in descent)	Sgt.-Major Langlands	Vol. II
		First ascent by M. Smith, J. Tewnion, 19 Sept 1948	A. D. M. Cox	
1943	June	South-East Gully	J. Hunt	Vol. II
			A. Y. Greenhalgh	
1950	30 July	Consolation Gully	J. Tewnion	Vol. II
			K. Winram	
1952	24 Aug	Back Bay Gully	G. C. Greig	Vol. II
			M. Smith	
			K. Winram	
1953	8 March	Laminated Crag	K. Winram	Vol. II
			M. Smith	
1953	2 April	Mitre Ridge (W)	W. D. Brooker	
		A "matter of fact" ascent of a classic hard route	T. W. Patey	

1953	July	Squareface	T. W. Patey	
		Angel's Edgeway variation by W. B.	J. M. Taylor	
		Gault, A. Kane, Aug 1959		
		A little gem		
1954	31 March	Approach Gully (W)	T. W. Patey	Vol. II
			G. B. Leslie	
			A. G. Nicol	
			J. M. Taylor	
1954	31 March	Back Bay Gully (W)	T. W. Patey	Vol. II
			G. B. Leslie	
			A. G. Nicol	
			J. M. Taylor	
1954	31 March	The Flume	J. M. Taylor	
			G. B. Leslie	
1954	29 Aug	Mandarin Buttress	T. W. Patey	Vol. II
			A. Watson	
			K. Winram	
			M. Smith	
1954	29 Aug	East Wall Direct	T. W. Patey	Vol. II
1956	15 April	Consolation Gully (W)	T. W. Patey	Vol. II
			R. H. Sellers	
			R. Harper	
1956	16 Dec	North-West Gully (W)	R. H. Sellers	
			G. Adams	
1959	Feb	South-East Gully (W)	R. H. Sellers	
			G. Annand	
1959	March	Mandarin Buttress (W)	W. A. Christie	
			W. B. Gault	
1966	13 March	Nomad's Gully (W)	M. D. Y. Mowat	Vol. II
			A. McR. Corbett	
1967	Feb	North-West Couloir (W)	M. Rennie	Vol. II
			D. W. Duncan	
1969	9 March	Commando Route (W)	P. F. MacDonald	
		1 tension peg	I. G. Rowe	
1969	31 Aug	Slochd Wall	M. Rennie	
		Mostly aid (A3)	G. S. Strange	
		FFA: B. T. Lawrie, A. Nisbet, 3 July		
		1979		
		Left finish by R. J. Archbold, H.		
		Towler, D. J. Wallace, 31 July 1982		
1970	25 March	Back Bay Gully, Left Branch (W)	N. D. Keir	Vol. II
1971	27 March	Comala's Ridge (W)	G. R. Simpson	Vol. II
			G. Boyd	
1972	Jan	Squareface (W)	C. Butterworth	Vol. II
			R. C. Maguire	
1974	23 Feb	East Wall Direct (W)	N. D. Keir	
		Original Route (W) by T. W. Patey,	J. Mothersele	
		A. G. Nicol, 31 March 1954	R. A. Smith	
1975	28 June	Mitre Ridge Direct	G. Stephen	
		The start of a new wave of	A. McIvor	
		exploration in summer		

1975	28 June	Crucible Route	R. J. Archbold	167
		(Rocky Mountain Horror Show)	G. S. Strange	
1977	26 Feb	Cumming–Crofton Route (W)	R. Renshaw	
		The scene of several previous failures	G. S. Strange	
1977	April	North-West Groove (W)	R. J. Archbold	NR
			G. Cohen	
1977	3 July	Gurkha	R. J. Archbold	169
		1 PA	N. D. Keir	
		Demonstrated that the west face of Mitre Ridge had better holds than previously thought and opened the way for several fine routes		
1978	7 April	Crucible Route (W)	R. J. Archbold	
		1 peg for tension	D. Dinwoodie	
1978	27 May	The Chancel	D. M. Nichols	
			G. S. Strange	
1978	28 May	The Bishop	D. M. Nichols	
			G. S. Strange	
1978	3 June	Helter Skelter	R. J. Archbold	
			W. McKerrow	
1978	4 June	Surgeon's Slab	R. J. Archbold	171
			W. McKerrow	
1978	4 June	Witch Doctor	R. J. Archbold	171
			W. McKerrow	
1979	9 July	The Primate	J. Anderson	
		Pitch 1 by G. S. Strange, R. Ross, 8 July 1984	A. Nisbet	
1979	15 July	Chindit	R. J. Archbold	
		Direct by D. Dinwoodie, C. Jamieson, 31 July 1982	N. D. Keir	
1980	2 March	Alchemist's Route (W)	R. J. Archbold	
			D. M. Nichols	
1981	5 Sept	Rhombus	R. J. Archbold	
			H. Towler	
1982	11 Feb	Gold Coast (W)	A. Nisbet	
		1 PA	C. McLeod	
1982	31 July	Slochd Wall, Right Edge	A. Paul	NR
			G. Reilly	
1983	6 Aug	The Empty Quarter	D. Dinwoodie	
			G. S. Strange	
1984	15 Feb	The Grail (W)	A. Nisbet	
			A. Clifford	
1984	16 Feb	The Actress (W)	A. Nisbet	
		1 PA	A. Clifford	

STOB AN T-SLUICHD, BEINN A'BHUIRD

1948	4 July	Pinnacle Ridge	G. W. Ross	Vol. II
			A. E. Anton	
1949	28 May	M and B Buttress	G. Mathieson	Vol. II
			I. M Brooker	

1977	11 April	Pinnacle Ridge (W)	M. Freeman	169
			G. S. Strange	
1983	30 Jan	Token Groove (W)	B. S. Findlay	175
			G. S. Strange	

COIRE SPUTAN DEARG

1948	2 May	Pinnacle Buttress	S. R. Tewnion	
		Variation start by J. McArtney, D.	J. Tewnion	
		Pyper in Summer 1964	W. A. Russell	
1948	16 May	Anchor Gully	I. M. Brooker	Vol. II
			A. E. Anton	
			G. Mathieson	
1948	1 Sept	Crystal Ridge	R. Still	
		Soon became a classic, and	Miss E. J. Lawrence	
		changed the poor reputation of		
		Sputan		
1949	5 Jan	Crystal Ridge (W)	W. D. Brooker	
			M. Smith	
1949	17 March	Slab Chimney: Right Branch (W)	A. Parker	
		Left branch by same party in same	J. Young	
		month		
1949	29 March	Hanging Dyke	A. Parker	
			J. Young	
1949	22 May	Flake Buttress	J. Tewnion	
			E. L. Smith	
			M. Smith	
			K. Winram	
1949	22 May	Janus	K. Winram	Vol. II
			M. Smith	
			E. L. Smith	
			J. Tewnion	
1949	25 June	Snake Ridge	W. D. Brooker	
			D. A. Sutherland	
			C. Hutcheon	
1949	26 June	Anchor Route	W. D. Brooker	Vol. II
			C. Hutcheon	
			D. A. Sutherland	
1949	3 July	Cherubs Buttress	J. Tewnion	Vol. II
			A. Alexander	
			E. L. Smith	
			M. Smith	
1949	11 Sept	Terminal Buttress	J. Tewnion	
			E. L. Smith	
			M. Smith	
1949	18 Sept	Pilgrims Groove	S. R. Tewnion	
		Variation finish by R. Kerr, M. Main	J. Tewnion	
		(date uncertain, early sixties?)	E. L. Smith	
1950	5 Jan	Pinnacle Buttress (W)	W. D. Brooker	
			J. W. Morgan	
1950	10 April	Flake Buttress (W)	W. D. Brooker	
			S. McPherson	

1950	20 May	Ardath Chimney	J. Tewnion	Vol. II
			M. Smith	
1950	1 July	Janus Chimney	E. L. Smith	Vol. II
			T. Shaw	
			A. Cameron	
1951	Feb	Glissade Buttress	J. Tewnion	Vol. II
			G. Dey	
1952	21 April	The Black Tower	T. W. Patey	
			G. B. Leslie	
			J. M. Taylor	
1952	21 April	April Wall	G. B. Leslie	Vol. II
			T. W. Patey	
			J. M. Taylor	
1954	22 Aug	Slab Chimney	G. H. Leslie	Vol. II
			M. Smith;	
			J. Harper	
			G. Davidson	
1955	2 April	Ardath Chimney	J. Y. L. Hay	
1955	25 Dec	Anchor Route (W)	G. Adams	
			R. W. P. Barclay	
1956	12 April	Hackingbush's Horror	J. Y. L. Hay	
		Approx. 4PA	A. O'F. Will	
		FFA: B. T. Lawrie, J. McArtney,	J. Ross	
		1966	C. Martin	
			G. Adams	
1956	10 June	Amethyst Wall	R. W. P. Barclay	Vol. II
		Combined tactics used. Two known	W. D. Brooker	
		repeat ascents, also using combined		
		tactics		
1956	10 June	The Plumbline	R. W. P. Barclay	Vol. II
			W. D. Brooker	
1956	21 Oct	Lucifer Route	M. Scott	
			D. Macrae	
			R. Ellis	
1960	Sept	The Swing	D. Reid	
			D. Pyper	
1961	4 Feb	Terminal Buttress (W)	D. Reid	
			D. Pyper	
1963	2 March	Snake Gully (W)	J. McArtney	
			T. Mackie	
			B. T. Lawrie	
1963	8 Sept	Terminal Wall	B. T. Lawrie	
			J. McArtney	
1963	14 Sept	Grey Slab	M. Higgins	
			J. C. Innes	
			B. T. Lawrie	
1964	13 July	Girdle Traverse	B. T. Lawrie	Vol. II
			D. Mercer	
1966	4 Jan	Flying Ridge (W)	M. D. Y. Mowat	Vol. II
			A. Fyffe	
1966	15 May	The Web	M. Rennie	Vol. II
			M. C. MacLennan	

1967	3 Jan	Right-hand Icefall	A. Fyffe	
			P. Williams	
			M. McArthur	
			I. McLean	
1970	7 June	Umbrella	B. Lawrie	Vol. II
			J. Bower	
			H. Thain	
1970	13 June	The Chute	J. Ingram	
			B. S. Findlay	
			G. S. Strange	
			D. Stuart	
1970	20 June	Rainmate	B. Lawrie	Vol. II
			R. Kerr	
1970	27 June	Sundance	G. S. Strange	
			D. Stuart	
1970	21 Nov	Cherubs Buttress (W)	G. S. Strange	Vol. II
			D. Stuart	
1971	2 Jan	Hanging Dyke (W)	J. Bower	
		1PA	D. F. Lang	
1971	5 Jan	Janus (W)	J. Bower	Vol. II
		2PA	D. F. Lang	
			G. R. Simpson	
1971	21 Feb	The Ladders	G. R. Simpson	Vol. II
			Miss K. Menmuir	
1971	22 May	Ferlas Mor	J. Mothersele	
			G. S. Strange	
			D. Stuart;	
			B. T. Lawrie	
			D. Dinwoodie	
1971	19 June	The Fly	D. Dinwoodie	
			B. T. Lawrie	
1971	19 June	Wee Heavy	B. T. Lawrie	Vol. II
			D. Dinwoodie	
1972	July	Ghost Crack	B. T. Lawrie	
			R. Kerr	
1975	March	Sundance (W)	J. Fyfe	NR
			G. Reilly	
			W. Taylor	
1975	28 June	The Chebec	G. Skelton	
			I. Vause	
1976	20 June	The Hin'most	R. J. Archbold	
			G. S. Strange	
1977	6 March	Left-hand Icefall (W)	R. J. Archbold	
			D. M. Nichols	
1979	10 June	Amethyst Pillar (Topaz)	R. J. Archbold	
		Final crack (crux) previously	D. M. Nichols	
		climbed by J. McArtney, J.		
		Stenhouse on 13 July 1964		
1979	10 Nov	The Black Tower (W)	R. Smith	
			G. S. Strange	

1981	22 Feb	Pilgrim's Groove (W)	S. Kennedy
			A. Nisbet;
			E. Clark
			N. Morrison
1983	30 Dec	Lucifer Route (W)	G. Livingstone
		1 PA	A. Nisbet
1984	12 Jan	Grey Slab (W)	S. Allan
		1 PA	A. Nisbet
1984	26 July	The Skater	C. MacLean
			A. Nisbet

CREAGAN A'CHOIRE ETCHACHAN

1949	2 Jan	Winter Route (W)	W. D. Brooker	
			J. W. Morgan	
			D. A. Sutherland	
1949	26 March	Cambridge Route	A. Parker	Vol. II
			J. Young	
1950	26 March	Flanking Ribs	W. D. Brooker	Vol. II
			D. A. Sutherland	
1950	1 April	Original Route	D. A. Sutherland	Vol. II
			K. Winram	
1950	6 July	Juniper Rib	I. M. Brooker	Vol. II
			Miss M. Newbigging	
1952	15 June	Quartzvein Edge	K. Winram	
			G. C. Greig	
			M. Smith	
1953	31 May	Bastion Wall	W. Kelly	Vol. II
			P. Leys	
1953	25 Oct	Red Scar Route	T. W. Patey	Vol. II
			W. D. Brooker	
1954	20 March	The Corridor (W)	F. R. Malcolm	
		First of Etchachan's classic ice	A. Thom	
		routes. An achievement in		
		stepcutting		
1954	9 July	Bodkin	T. W. Patey	
		Rib finish by G. Reilly, B. Simpson,	W. W. Hutchison	
		M. D. Webster, 28 Sept 1975	A. Watson	
1954	7 Aug	Pikestaff	T. W. Patey	
			W. D. Brooker	
			J. Y. L. Hay	
1955	27 Feb	Central Chimney (W)	T. W. Patey	
			G. Adams	
			M. Smith	
			A. O'F. Will	
1955	21 July	The Corridor	J. Y. L. Hay	Vol. II
		Direct version by T. W. Patey, A.	A. P. Crichton	
		Duguid on 15 Aug 1955	W. Christie	
1955	July	Avalanche Gully	J. Gadd	Vol. II
		A considerable achievement on a	Mrs. Gadd	
		hard and dangerous route		

1955	July	The Red Chimney (Lower Half)	J. Gadd	Vol. II
		The upper part is unclimbed in summer, being very wet and loose	Mrs. Gadd	
1955	4 Sept	The Dagger	T. W. Patey	
		4PA	J. Y. L. Hay	
		A breakthrough: first route on the Crimson Slabs		
		FFA: unknown, early sixties?		
1956	24 June	The Talisman	W. D. Brooker	
		Another summer classic	K. A. Grassick	
		Direct start by A. Nisbet, S. Kennedy, N. Mollison on 13 July 1981		
1956	22 July	Djibangi	J. Y. L. Hay	
		2PA	R. Wiseman	
		FFA: unknown, early sixties?	A. Cowie	
		Last 2 pitches by M. Main, M. George, E. Brown, 1963		
1956	29 Dec	Quartzvein Edge (W)	J. Y. L. Hay	
			G. Adams	
			A. Thom	
1960	Aug	Architrave	C. A. Sands	Vol. II
			M. Main	
1961	June	Girdle Traverse	T. W. Patey	Vol. II
1961	July	The Serpent	T. W. Patey	Vol. II
			A. O'F. Will	
			F. R. Malcolm	
1961	Aug	The Gangway	M. Main	Vol. II
			A. Milne	
1961	15 Nov	The Sheath	R. Kerr	
			A. Kane	
1962	15 Feb	Pikestaff (W)	D. Pyper	Vol. II
			W. B. Gault	
1963	23 Feb	Bastion Wall (W)	J. McArtney	
			D. Pyper	
1965	31 Jan	Djibangi (W)	J. McArtney	
		A modern-style route. Unrepeated for 18 years	W. J. Barclay	
1965	20 Feb	Juniper Rib (W)	M. D. Y. Mowat	Vol. II
			J. E. Inglis	
1965	14 March	The Talisman (W)	K. A. Grassick	
		1PA	J. Light	
1966	Winter	Cambridge Route (W)	J. McArtney	Vol. II
		(taking left edge of Pioneer Buttress)	D. Halliday	
1966	March	Square-Cut Gully (W)	M. Forbes	
		2 ice screws for aid	M. Low	
1966	17 Aug	Stiletto	M. Forbes	
		3PA	M. Rennie	
		A jump in technical difficulty		
		FFA: D. Dinwoodie, A. McIvor, 1976		

1966	Sept	Scabbard	M. Rennie	
			M. Forbes	
1967	6 Jan	Flanking Ribs (W)	J. McArtney	
			A. Fyffe	
1967	Jan	The Red Chimney (W)	I. A. Paterson	
		Lower section by J. Y. L. Hay, R.	S. P. Hepburn	
		Ibbotson in Feb 1959		
1969	19 Sept	The Cutlass	B. T. Lawrie	
			J. Bower	
1969	Sept	Enigma	M. Rennie	Vol. II
			I. Staples	
1969	23 Dec	Original Route (W)	J. Bower	
			G. Boyd	
1969	29 Dec	Architrave (W)	A. Fyffe	
			J. McArtney	
1970	1 Aug	Square-Cut Gully	D. Stuart	Vol. II
			G. S. Strange	
1971	10 July	The Hex	M. Forbes	
			B. T. Lawrie	
			D. Dinwoodie	
1971	17 July	Carmine Groove	G. S. Strange	
			D. Stuart	
			D. Dinwoodie	
1971	17 July	Pioneer Buttress Direct	D. Dinwoodie	Vol. II
			D. Riley	
1972	Sept	Original Route Direct	N. D. Keir	
		Variation by A. Nisbet, Miss B.	G. S. Strange	
		Clough in Sept 1982		
1974	21 July	Umslopogaas	D. Dinwoodie	
			R. A. Smith	
1974	Nov	Carmine Groove (W)	R. A. Smith	
			G. Stephen	
1977	29 Jan	The Dagger (W)	A. Nisbet	
			A. Robertson	
1977	30 Jan	Bodkin (W)	R. Renshaw	
		1PA, 1NA	G. S. Strange	
1977	11 July	Scalpel	D. Dinwoodie	
			G. S. Strange	
1978	May	Sgian Dubh	A. Nisbet	
		First pitch by A. Fyffe, M. Mowat,	Miss M. Bridges	
		R. Burnett, W. Forbes, Oct 1966		
		Direct route: pitch 1: N. Morrison,		
		D. Hawthorn, 26 July 1984; pitch 2:		
		J. Anderson, Miss L. Brown, 1979		
1980	18 May	Stanley	A. B. Lawson	172
			T. Ryan	
1980	8 Dec	Red Scar Route (W)	S. Kennedy	172
			N. Morrison	
			A. Nisbet	
1982	28 July	Sabre	S. Kennedy	
			C. McLeod	

1983	June	Scythe	B. Davison	
			R. F. Allen	
			S. Kennedy	
			G. P. Muhlemann	
			A. Nisbet	
1983	June	Delicatessen	A. Nisbet	
			R. F. Allen	
			B. Davison	
			S. Kennedy	
			G. P. Muhlemann	
1983	June	Henchman	M. Hamilton	
			R. Anderson	
1984	16 June	Crimson Cringe	B. T. Lawrie	
			N. Morrison	
1984	25 Aug	King Crimson	A. Ross	
			G. S. Strange	

LESSER CRAGS OF STOB COIRE ETCHACHAN/LOCH ETCHACHAN

1952	19 Aug	Bellflower Buttress	K. Winram	Vol. II
			G. C. Greig	
			M. Smith	
1953	15 Aug	Stag Buttress	A. Murray	Vol. II
			A. Imray	
			J. McLeod	
1954	4 April	Amphitheatre Edge	G. C. Greig	Vol. II
			G. H. Leslie	
1955	Sept	Lochside Chimney	M. Scott	Vol. II
			R. Ellis	
1962	28 Jan	Lochside Chimney (W)	H. Spencer	Vol. II
			M. Main	
1971	2 Jan	Bellflower Buttress (W)	D. Stuart	Vol. II
		1 PA	G. S. Strange	

Note: Sunday Crack is now worthless and The Slug does not have first ascentionists recorded

STACAN DUBHA

1954	1 Aug	Ribbon Ridge	T. W. Patey	Vol. I
			A. Watson	
1957	7 April	The Shuttle	G. Adams	Vol. I
			R. H. Sellers	
1969	20 Aug	Zigzag	B. Taplin	Vol. I
			D. Taplin	

CAIRN ETCHACHAN

| 1904 | July | Castlegates Gully | H. Stewart | Vol. I |
| | | | A. B. Duncan | |

1914	Easter	Castlegates Gully (W)	J. McCoss	Vol. I
			W. B. Meff	
			R. Clarke	
			W. Shepherd	
1952	24 May	Castle Gully	H. S. M. Bates	Vol. I
			K. A. Grassick	
			A. G. Nicol	
1952	Aug	False Scorpion	K. A. Grassick	Vol. I
			H. S. M. Bates	
			A. Q. Gardiner	
			A. Farquharson	
1952	6 Dec	Scorpion (W)	T. W. Patey	
		A remarkable first winter ascent on	J. M. Taylor	
		a big cliff	A. G. Nicol	
			K. A. Grassick	
1953	10 May	Scorpion	H. S. M. Bates	Vol. I
			T. Shaw	
1954	10 Aug	The Battlements	T. W. Patey	
		The start of Patey's explorations of	W. D. Brooker	
		the rock potential of this cliff		
1954	25 Sept	Boa	T. W. Patey	
			F. R. Malcolm	
			A. Thom	
1954	2 Oct	Equinox	T. W. Patey	Vol. I
			L. S. Lovat	
1954	2 Oct	Python	T. W. Patey	Vol. I
			L. S. Lovat	
1955	29 July	Crevasse Route	T. W. Patey	
		Variation by P. McDonald, G.	M. Smith	
		Johnstone, Sept 1967	A. Duguid	
1955	29 July	Eastern Approach Route	T. W. Patey	Vol. I
1955	7 Aug	Pagan Slit	G. Adams	Vol. I
			R. W. P. Barclay	
1955	13 Aug	The Guillotine	T. W. Patey	
			A. Duguid	
1956	12 Aug	Nom-de-Plume	R. W. P. Barclay	Vol. I
			R. H. Sellers	
1957	10 Feb	Route Major (W)	T. W. Patey	
			M. Smith	
1964	5 Jan	Castle Gully (W)	K. A. Grassick	
		Wrongly graded as V in Vol. I	D. Burnett	
1970	March	False Scorpion (W)	W. March	
			O. Ludlow	
1975	14 March	Sideslip (W)	A. Fyffe	
		Corresponds in part to Revelation	R. O'Donovan	
		Arete which fell down		
1977	5 March	Attic Rib (W)	R. J. Archbold	
			D. M. Nichols	

1977	29 May	Red Guard Lower chimney had possibly been climbed previously but this climb proved to be one of the best rock routes on the gully face	R. J. Archbold N. D. Keir	
1978	5 March	The Sword (W)	J. C. Higham D. Wright	169
1978	24 March	Red Guard (W) Tension traverse and 3PA Keir gets the first winter ascent of his own summer route The "dirty continuation groove" by G. S. Smith, R. Barton	N. D. Keir M. Freeman	
1978	11 July	Time Traveller Start of renewed interest in an unfashionable cliff	D. Morris A. Fyffe	
1978	12 July	Pythagoras	A. Fyffe S. Crymble	
1978	12 July	Poison Dwarf	A. Fyffe S. Crymble	
1978	July	Bastille	R. J. Archbold T. Syme	170
1979	4 Feb	Eastern Approach Route (W)	A. Fyffe A. Liddell	170
1979	4 Feb	The Guillotine (W)	A. Fyffe A. Liddell	170
1979	28 Feb	Siberia (W)	A. Fyffe T. Walker	
1980	27 Feb	Pagan Slit (W)	M. Fowler A. Strapcans	NR
1981	13 Jan	Crevasse Route (W) Start of a campaign by Nisbet	S. Kennedy A. Nisbet	172
1981	14 Feb	Equinox (W)	S. Kennedy A. Nisbet N. Morrison	
1981	15 Feb	Boa (W) Slings on an axe used once for aid	A. Nisbet S. Kennedy N. Morrison	172
1981	9 Dec	Python (W)	A. Nisbet P. Langhorne	174
1982	15 Jan	Bastille (W)	A. Nisbet S. Allan	174
1982	16 Jan	The Hairpin Loop (W)	A. Nisbet S. Allan	174
1982	23 Dec	Nom-de-Plume (W)	A. Nisbet P. Langhorne	174

SHELTER STONE CRAG

1904	July	Pinnacle Gully	H. Stewart A. B. Duncan	Vol. I

1907	16 June	Castle Wall	H. Raeburn	Vol. I
			F. S. Goggs	
1907	16 June	Raeburn's Buttress	H. Raeburn	Vol. I
		The pioneers were of the opinion that the climb was dangerous—it is still so. "A long stride on to a disintegrating shelflet of grass"	F. S. Goggs	
1912	July	Forefinger Pinnacle	H. G. Drummond	
			J. McCoss	
1947	27 Aug	Clach Dhian Chimney	W. S. Thomson	
		Route now followed by W. D. Brooker, J. W. Morgan, 1950	and party	
1953	14 May	Sticil Face	J. M. Taylor	Vol. I
			T. W. Patey	
1957	June	Postern	K. A. Grassick	Vol. I
		2PA	A. G. Nicol	
		Lower section by J. Y. L. Hay and G. Adams, September 1956	J. G. Lillie	
1957	27 Dec	Sticil Face (W)	K. A. Grassick	
		One of the more impressive routes in the pre-front-pointing era	A. G. Nicol	
1958	Aug	The Citadel	R. H. Sellers	
		The biggest fifties route in the area although 2PA at lower crux and several PA on upper FFA: unknown	G. Annand	
1962	8 June	The Needle	R. Smith	
		The first big "Modern" route on the cliff. A superb achievement and years ahead of its time	D. Agnew	
1968	Aug	The Pin	R. Carrington	
		1PA and 1NA The 1961 guide considered these slabs "manifestly impossible" FFA: B. Cambell-Kelly, M. Kosterlitz, early seventies	J. Gardner	
1968	Aug	Steeple	K. Spence	
		(2NA) Top pitches climbed in the rain	M. Watson	
			Pitches 1–6	
			J. Porteous	
			K. Spence	
			Pitches 7–9	
		FFA: J. Lamb , P. Whillance, May 1975	M. Watson	
1968	7 Sept	Thor	M. Rennie	Vol. I
		Originally A1 and A2 on pitches 2 and 3. The top pitch linking the dièdre with The Pin is still not free	G. S. Strange	
1969	Summer	West Ridge Route	W. March and party	Vol. I
1969	Aug	Snipers	G. Shields	
		2PA	R. Carrington	

1969	Aug	Postern Direct	J. Cunningham	
			W. March	
1969	Aug	Consolation Groove	J. Cunningham	
		3PA on the crux which is often greasy	W. March	
		FFA: unknown		
1970	31 Jan	Castle Wall (W)	B. S. Findlay	
			G. S. Strange	
1970	Summer	Threadbare	J. Cunningham	Vol. I
		Considerable aid used on pitch 3 and 2 PA below the roof	W. March	
1971	Feb	Raeburn's Buttress (W)	W. March	
			J. Hart	
1971	Summer	Haystack	R. Carrington	
		1PA	I. Nicolson	
		FFA: unknown		
		The hardest route in the area for a long time		
1972	4 Jan	Clach Dhian Chimney (W)	C. Butterworth	
			A. Frost	
1972	Feb	Quartz Gully (W)	A. Fyffe	
		Climbed in descent by T. W. Patey, Aug 1954	E. Fyffe	
1972	Feb	Garbh Gully (W)	A. Fyffe	
			E. Fyffe	
1976	Summer	Blockbuster	J. Jones	NR
			M. Burrows-Smith	
1977	12 March	Breach Gully (W)	M. Freeman	
			G. S. Strange	
1978	4 March	Blunderbuss (W)	J. C. Higham	
			D. Wright	
1978	March	Western Grooves (W)	A. Fyffe	
			R. D. Barton	
1978	27 May	Cupid's Bow	D. Dinwoodie	
		An impressive and much sought after route which eventually fell with 1PA in Thor dièdre and 3PA on the main pitch. Finally freed at its present grade by M. Hamilton, R. Anderson, 4 June 1982	R. Renshaw	
1979	March	Unknown Gully	A. Fyffe and party	NR
1980	5/6 Jan	Postern (W)	M. Hamilton	
		The first VI in this area. A bivouac was taken and the seconds jumared some pitches	K. Spence	
			A. Taylor	

1980	23 Feb	The Citadel (W) Second jumared some pitches The subject of many attempts. K. Spence and J. Porteous retreated from above the lower crux in 1969. Cunningham and March had to descend from higher after a benightment in 1971 The winter variation by A. Rouse, B. Hall in 1975	M. Hamilton K. Spence	
1981	Summer	The Missing Link The nearest thing yet to a free Thor	D. Cuthbertson D. Jamieson	
1982	5 May	The Spire	M. Hamilton R. Anderson	
1982	24 July	The Run of the Arrow Had previously repulsed some strong parties. The *in situ* wires are from a previous attempt	P. Whillance T. Furnis	
1983	27 July	The Harp	P. Whillance R. Parker	

HELL'S LUM CRAG

1950	Sept	Deep Cut Chimney	I. M. Brooker Miss M. Newbigging	
1952	12 April	Hell's Lum A semi-winter ascent as snow masked half of the big gully pitch and also covered several other sections	I. M. Brooker Miss M. Newbigging	Vol. I
1953	8 Aug	Kiwi Slab 3PA Original start was up the green buttress but it became more usual to follow the lower diagonal fault	R. Naylor M. W. Parkin	Vol. I
1955	30 Sept	The Escalator	A. G. Nicol T. W. Patey Miss E. M. Davidson	
1956	March	Hell's Lum (W)	G. McLeod and party	
1956	21 Oct	The Pothole	R. W. P. Barclay R. H. Sellers	Vol. I
1957	4 Aug	Devil's Delight The move onto the open faces shows the quality of climbing to be found here	R. H. Sellers G. Annand	
1958	14 Sept	Hellfire Corner Slings for aid at bulge	G. Annand R. H. Sellers	
1958	Oct	Brimstone Groove 1PA	G. Annand R. H. Sellers R. Reid	Vol. I
1959	Feb	Kiwi Slabs (W)	T. W. Patey V. N. Stevenson	

1960	Jan	The Escalator	J. Y. L. Hay	
			A. Thom	
1961	Sept	Hell's Lump	J. R. Marshall	
		Mistakenly called Hell's Lumps in Vol. I	J. Stenhouse	
1961	Sept	The Clean Sweep	R. Smith	
		A typical Smith find, probably the best route on the crag	G. Tiso	
1961	Sept	Hellfire Corner Direct Start	R. Smith	
		Now the normal start	G. Tiso	
1961	3 Sept	The Wee Devil	T. W. Patey	Vol. I
			J. M. Taylor	
1963	1 June	The Girdle	M. George	Vol. I
			D. Pyper	
1963	27 June	Sneer	A. McKeith	
1963	11 Oct	Auld Nick	G. Brown	
			I. Houston	
			I. Small	
1966	23 Jan	Sneer (W)	D. Haston	
			B. Robertson	
			J. Heron	
1968	31 Aug	The Vacuum	R. A. Croft	161
			J. R. Sutcliffe	
1969	24 June	Sic	G. Boyd	Vol. I
		A previously neglected part of the cliff begins to receive some attention	P. Kale	
1969	28 June	Puke	J. Bower	Vol. I
			P. Kale	
1969	29 June	Raw Mince	J. Bower	Vol. I
			R. Simpson	
1969	27 July	Styx	W. March	
			D. K. Mardon	
1969	12 Sept	Drop Out	W. March	
		Peg, nut and tension traverse eliminated in Summer 1982 by A. Fyffe and R. D. Barton.		
1969	12 Sept	Good Intentions	W. March	
		Aid nut eliminated soon afterwards	M. MacArthur	
1969	Nov	Sic (W)	J. Bower	Vol. I
			H. Pinkerton	
1969	28 Dec	The Gullet (W)	J. Bower	
			B. S. Findlay	
1970	Jan	Chancer (W)	J. Cunningham	
		4 ice-screws and a tension used but still the high point of "dagger" technique developed by Cunningham as the fore-runner of modern front-point technique	W. March	
1970?		Hell's Lum Direct	J. Cunningham	Vol. I
			W. March	

Year	Date	Route	Climbers	Vol
1970	14 Nov	Puke (W)	T. Anderson J. Bower	Vol. I
1970	27 Dec	Brimstone Groove (W) The first route to tackle the big ice-sheet	S. Docherty K. Spence	
1971	18 Sept	Big De'il 1PA FFA: unknown	G. S. Strange D. Stuart	
1971	18 Sept	Salamander	D. Dinwoodie J. Tweddle	
1971	17 Nov	Wee Devil (W)	D. Dinwoodie J. Mothersele	
1971	20 Nov	Auld Nick (W)	M. Freeman G. S. Strange	
1972	2 Jan	Kiwi Gully	W. March I. Nicholson	
1973	Feb	Salamander (W) Originally wrongly reported as an ascent of Hellfire Corner	J. Cunningham W. March R. O'Donovan	
1973	Feb	Devil's Delight (W) The bigest and best of the pure ice routes	J. Cunningham W. March R. O'Donovan	
1975	June	The Exorcist	A. Liddell R. Smith	
1975	13 Aug	Squirk	K. Schwartz Miss R. Morrow	167
1976	July	The Omen	A. Liddell M. Burrows-Smith	
1976	4 July	The Underworld	A. Fyffe R. D. Barton	168
1977	5 July	Devil Dancer	A. Fyffe R. D. Barton	
1978	4 July	Towering Inferno Barton and Fyffe also climb a VS Variation to pitch 3	R. D. Barton A. Fyffe E. Fyffe	
1978	Winter	Clean Sweep (W)	G. Smith A. Slater	
1979	Winter	Nobody's Fault (W) The present name reflects the history. Smith never officially recorded any of his ascents this winter so details are vague	G. Smith and party	
1981	1 Aug	The Devil's Alternative	A. Fyffe R. D. Barton	
1982	24 Jan	Boke	F. Burnton C. Dale A. Dytche A. Horner	
1982	3 Aug	Second Sight	R. D. Barton A. Fyffe	
1984	10 Aug	Prince of Darkness	R. D. Barton A. Fyffe	

| 1984 | 25 Aug | Damien | A. Liddell | |
| | | | M. Seaton | |

STAG ROCKS

1930	July	Serrated Rib	J. Nimlin and party	Vol. I
1949	17 July	Pine Tree Route	E. L. Smith	Vol. I
			R. Mennie	
1954	Aug	Triple Towers	T. W. Patey	Vol. I
			G. B. Leslie	
1955	Aug	Relay Climb	T. W. Patey	
		An impressive solo at that time.		
		Patey solved the problem of the		
		central bulge after works by others		
		Upper section: K. Winram, Aug		
		1953, Lower section: G. H. Leslie,		
		M. Smith, June 1954		
1955	14 Aug	The Tenements	G. H. Leslie	
			M. Smith	
			C. Petrie	
1956	Sept	Afterthought Arete	R. H. Sellers	
			M. Smith	
1956	Nov	Final Selection	R. H. Sellers	
			M. Smith	
1957	June	Quartz-Digger's Cave Route	R. H. Sellers	
			G. Adams	
			F. Henderson	
1960	May	Deception Inlet	A. Thom	Vol. I
			M. Smith	
			G. Annand	
1962	29 July	Wigwag	J. Stenhouse	
			G. J. Ritchie	
1962	Aug	Longbow Direct	D. Pyper	
			J. McArtney	
1962	Aug	Groove and Rib	R. Marshall	
			J. R. Marshall	
1962	Oct	The Sand-Pyper	D. Pyper	
		1 PA	C. A. Sands	
		FFA: unknown		
		Direct finish on 1 July 1972 by		
		M. G. Geddes and J. C. Higham		
1969	Jan	Stag Route (W)	J. T. Campbell	
		Direct version in March 1971 by W.	B. Findlay	
		March, J. Brailsford	N. D. Keir	
			G. S. Strange	
1969	6 Aug	Alb	B. Taplin and party	Vol. I
1969	7 Aug	Purge	B. Taplin	Vol. I
			D. Taplin	
1969	6 Sept	Longbow Direct (Alt. Start)	G. Shields	Vol. I
			S. Wilkinson	
1969	Nov	Afterthought Arete (W)	W. March	
1969	Nov	Triple Towers (W)	W. March	Vol. I

1969	Nov	Serrated Rib (W)	W. March	Vol. I
1969	Nov	Final Selection (W)	W. March	Vol. I
1970	Winter	C. M. Gully (W)	J. Cunningham W. March	
1970	7 Feb	Pine Tree Route (W)	J. Bower A. Morgan	
1971	17 Feb	Amphitheatre Gully (W) 1 PA	W. March J. Hart	
1971	18 Feb	Apex Gully (W)	W. March J. Hart	
1972	Aug	Addenda	A. Fyffe W. March	168
1972	3 Aug	Rodent Appears to be the same as Groove and Rib	A. Kimber D. Wearing T. Calvert	164
1977	Feb	Cascade A much eyed-up ice problem Several axe rests taken	W. March D. Alcock	
1977	July	Windchill	R. D. Barton A. Fyffe	
1977	13 Aug	Amphitheatre Wall	A. Fyffe E. Fyffe	
1978	10 July	Shotgun	A. Fyffe E. Fyffe	170
1978	27 Dec	Wigwag (W) Only loosely based on the summer route	G. Smith M. Fowler	NR
1979	Winter	Central Route (W)	G. Smith G. Ball	NR
1979	Winter	The Tenements (W)	G. Smith	NR
1979	Winter	Deception Inlet (W) A series of winter ascents by G. Smith none of which were properly recorded	G. Smith K. Gasely	NR
1981	Winter	Relay Climb	K. Spence R. Milne R. Anderson	

STAC AN FHARAIDH

1952	10 Aug	Rectangular Rib	J. Hansbury W. Rae	Vol. I
1969	Summer	Pushover The beginning of exploration of these slabs results in the more obvious lines being climbed by locally based climbers notably Cunningham and Shields Variation: W. March and party	J. Cunningham and party	
1969	Summer	Whispers	J. Cunningham G. Shields	

1969	1 July	Après Moi	J. Cunningham	
			G. Shields	
1969	July	Sermon	G. Shields	
			S. Wilkinson	
1969	24 July	Mack's Dilemma	G. Shields	
			S. Wilkinson	
1970	4 June	Shielden	W. March and party	Vol. I
1970	4 June	Linden	W. March and party	
1970	5 June	Jillden	W. March and party	Vol. I
1970	14 June	Pippet Slab	J. Cunningham	
			W. March	
1971	11 Aug	Throwover	K. Schwartz	172
		1 NA	D. Regan	
		Referring to the placement of the aid nut	Miss M. Horsburgh	
1971	11 Sept	Déjà-vu	A. Fyffe	
			D. S. B. Wright	
1971	18 Sept	Deluge	G. Shields	Vol. I
		1 PA	C. Norris	
			D. S. B. Wright	
1972	5 Jan	Rectangular Gully (W)	W. March	163
1975	Summer	Cherry	A. Liddell	168
			M. Burrows-Smith	
1978	17 June	Speakeasy	A. Fyffe	
			D. S. B. Wright	
1980	7 Dec	Après Moi (W)	K. Spence	
			R. Anderson	
1980	7 Dec	Hoite-y-Toity (W)	K. Spence	174
			R. Anderson	
1981	22 Feb	Rectangular Rib (W)	R. Anderson	174
			A. Russell	
1981	Summer	Nosey Parker	R. Anderson	174
			A. Taylor	

COIRE AN T-SNEACHDA

1904	1 April	Pygmy Ridge	H. Raeburn	
			W. A. Gordon	
			G. H. Almond	
			A. Roth	
1904	1 April	Central Gully (W)	T. E. Goodeve	
			A. W. Russel	
			A. E. Robertson	
1935	24 March	Aladdin's Couloir (W)	A. Henderson	
			E. M. Davidson	
1936	April	Original Route (Summer)	A. Henderson	Vol. I
			E. M. Davidson	
			J. Geddes	
			A. Gray	
1939	Easter	Jacob's Ladder (W)	A. Henderson	
			F. Mitchell	
1946	Easter	Aladdin's Mirror (W)	E. U. M. C. party	

1946	Easter	The Runnel (W)	E. U. M. C. party	
1946	Easter	Crotched Gully (W)	E. U. M. C. party	
1952	12 Aug	Fiacaill Buttress	W. Rae	Vol. I
			J. Hansbury	
1953	9 Aug	The Lamp Direct	R. Naylor	Vol. I
			M. W. Parkin	
1954	Sept	Finger's Ridge	D. Bennet	
1957	April	Western Rib	D. Bennet	Vol. I
1958	17 Jan	Fiacaill Couloir (W)	T. W. Patey	
		The start of a series of fine solo first ascents		
1959	Feb	Spiral Gully (W)	T. W. Patey	
1959	Feb	Original Route (Winter)	T. W. Patey	
1967	Feb	Broken Gully (W)	T. W. Patey	
			J. McArtney	
			J. Cleare	
1967	24 June	Broken Pillar	K. Schwartz	163
1969	4 Jan	Invernookie (W)	K. Spence	
			J. Porteous	
1969	19 Jan	Fingers Ridge (W)	J. R. Dempster	
			J. I. Wallace	
1969	Summer	Fiacaill Buttress Direct	G. Shields and party	Vol. I
1969	10 Aug	Damnation	D. Sharp	
		1 PA	B. Taplin	
		FFA: unknown		
1969	2 Sept	Goodgame	D. Sharp	Vol. I
			B. Taplin	
1972	Winter	Western Rib (W)	W. March	163
			R. Mansfield	
1972	12 Feb	Doctor's Choice (W)	W. March	
			N. Dilley	
1972	13 Feb	Original Route (Summer) (W)	W. March	Vol. I
			B. Manson	
1973	Winter	Fiacaill Buttress (W)	G. Adam	NR
		Possibly climbed in mid sixties by D. Duncan and partner	W. March	
1978	18 March	Fluted Buttress Direct (W)	A. Fyffe	
			S. Crymble	
1979	19 Feb	Belhaven (W)	A. Fyffe	
			K. Geddes	
1979	1 March	Rampart (W)	A. Fyffe	170
			T. Walker	
1980	8 Nov	Cruising (W)	K. Spence	174
			R. Anderson	
1981	16 May	Magic Crack	G. S. Strange	
		An excellent find, has the best rock pitch in the corrie	M. Ross	
			J. Wyness	
			D. Dinwoodie	
1984	9 July	Fingers Ridge Direct	A. Fyffe	
			M. Bagness	

COIRE AN LOCHAIN

1931	July	Central Crack Route	A. Harrison	Vol. I
		So named from the crack in the Great Slab which was originally climbed	L. St.C. Bartholomew	
1933	23 April	Ewen Buttress	J. Ewen	Vol. I
		Named after MMC member who was killed in the Alps	E. M. Davidson	
1934	14 April	Right Branch Y Gully (W)	R. F. Stobart	
			T. Stobart	
			Miss Harbinson	
1935	24 March	The Couloir (in descent) (W)	E. M. Davidson	
			A. Henderson	
1935	13 April	The Vent (W)	E. M. Davidson	
			R. F. Stobart	
			Miss Macbain	
			J. Geddes	
1945	17 July	Savage Slit	R. B. Frere	
			J. D. Walker	
1948	30 Oct	The Vent	F. F. Cunningham	Vol. I
			A. G. MacKenzie	
1949	May	Western Route	C. Ross	
			J. Brewster	
			D. Banks	
1949	4 Sept	Vent Rib and Traverse	H. Watt	Vol. I
			W. A. Russell	
1952	16 Nov	Left Branch Y Gully	T. W. Patey	
			A. G. Nicol	
			A. Wedderburn	
1957	21 April	Savage Slit (W)	G. Adams	
		1PA	J. White	
		Still stops competent parties	F. Henderson	
1958	2 Feb	Central Crack Route (W)	T. W. Patey	
1959	Feb	Ewen Buttress (W)	T. W. Patey	
			V. N. Stevenson	
1959	Feb	The Milky Way (W)	T. W. Patey	
			V. N. Stevenson	
			I. W. Armitage	
1959	Feb	Western Route (W)	T. W. Patey	
1963	31 Oct	Gaffer's Groove	T. W. Patey	
		Climbed in heavy rain	D. Whillans	
1964	17 May	Fall-out Corner	T. W. Patey	
		1PA	R. Ford	
		FFA: unknown	M. Stewart	
1964	7 Aug	Crow's Nest Crack	R. D. B. Stewart	Vol. I
			D. Lynn	
			D. C. Easson	
1968	31 Aug	War and Peace	G. Shields	
		2PA plus nuts for aid	W. Gorman	
		FFA in 1983, A. Nisbet, B. Davison		

1968	Summer	Nocando Crack Second unable to follow	G. Shields	Vol. I
1968	Summer	Ventricle Nuts for aid on pitch 1 and 1 PA on pitch 2	J. Cunningham G. Shields	
1968	Summer	Procrastination	J. Cunningham G. Shields	
1968	25 July	The Vicar Pegs and tension used for aid FFA: B. Davison, A. Nisbet, 29 Aug 1983	G. Shields S. Wilkinson	
1968	21 Aug	Bulgy 1 NA FFA: unknown	G. Shields R. Doig	Vol. I
1968	25 Aug	Daddy Longlegs 5 PA's and 6 NA's FFA: B. Davison, A. Nisbet, 29 Aug 1983	G. Shields B. Hall	
1968	24 Dec	Chute Route (W)	M. Harris D. Scott R. Shaw	
1969	Summer	Puffer	J. Cunningham and party	Vol. I
1969	5 July	Prone	G. Bradshaw B. Taplin	Vol. I
1969	23 July	Grumbling Grooves	G. Shields S. Wilkinson	Vol. I
1969	8 Aug	Auricle	J. Cunningham W. March	
1969	8 Aug	Never Mind "Make a controlled slide down the edge to gain a foothold" 2 PA's and a tension. Only the tension remains	J. Cunningham W. March	
1969	11 Sept	Oesophagus	B. Taplin D. Taplin	Vol. I
1969	31 Dec	Iron Butterfly	S. Docherty B. Gorman	Vol. I
1970	29 March	Ventilator (W)	D. J. Bennet A. Somerville	Vol. I
1970	19 Sept	Vagrant	M. G. Geddes H. M. Gillespie	162
1971	9 April	Oesophagus (W)	W. March and party	
1971	30 Dec	Andromeda (W)	R. D. Barton J. C. Higham	
1975	Feb	Glottal Stop (W)	J. Cunningham R. Baillie	
1975	Feb	Gaffer's Groove (W)	J. Cunningham A. Fyffe	
1976	June	Transformer	A. Fyffe R. D. Barton	168
1979	28 Dec	Procrastination (W)	M. Fowler A. Henderson	

1981	July	The Overseer	D. Lawrence	
			A. Nisbet	
1983	29 Aug	The Demon	B. Davison	
			A. Nisbet	
1983	10 Dec	The Overseer (W)	A. Nisbet	
			E. Clark	
1983	11 Dec	Sidewinder (W)	A. Nisbet	
			E. Clark	
1983	17 Dec	Grumbling Grooves (W)	S. Allan	175
			A. Nisbet	
1983	18 Dec	Crow's Nest Crack (W)	S. Kennedy	175
			C. McLeod	
1983	18 Dec	Sidewinder Direct (W)	S. Allan	175
			A. Nisbet	

LAIRIG GHRU (NORTHERN SECTION)

1950	7 July	Lairig Ridge	W. D. Brooker	Vol. I
			T. Shaw	
1965	23 Dec	North Gully	R. Campbell	
			F. Harper	
			Miss M. A. Thompson	
1970	4 March	Central Gully	O. Ludlow	
			B. Taplin	
1972	9 March	Window Gully	W. March	
			J. Cleare	
			J. Bradshaw	

GLEN FESHIE: COIRE GARBHLACH AND OTHERS

1932	5 Oct	Hermit's Ridge	D. Myles	Vol. I
			J. H. B. Bell	
1968	2 Nov	Hermit's Ridge (W)	B. S. Findlay	160
			G. S. Strange	
1977	Nov	Waterfall Gully (W)	E. Henderson	169
		The claim of six routes, grade III/IV, in the upper corrie seems unlikely due to the broken nature of the rock	A. Douglas	
1977	Dec	Coylum Crack, Creag na Caillich	E. Henderson	169
			A. Douglas	
1978	Jan	Cascade Cave, Creag na Gaibhre	E. Henderson	169
			A. Douglas	
1979	27 Jan	The Chasm, Creag na Gaibhre	I. Dalley	NR
			G. S. Strange	

Graded List of Climbs in Order of Difficulty

Notes: About 25% of the Very Severe and Hard Very Severe routes, and 50% of the Extremely Severe routes are apparently unrepeated (in their free state). It should therefore be obvious that this graded list might be inaccurate as well as subjective. There was however, an approximate agreement among those consulted, apart from the E5 Grade which was close to random. The bottom 20 routes in the list are considered Mild Very Severe.

E6	The Improbability Drive		The Pin
E5	Flodden		Steeple
	Run of the Arrow		Cayman
	Cannibal		Gulliver
	Slartibartfast		Snipers (2PA)
	Perilous Journey		Post Mortem
	The Naked Ape		Fraud Squad
E4	The Ascent of Man	E1	Falseface
	Cupid's Bow		The Sword of Damocles
	Sans Fer		Joker's Crack
	Dragon-Slayer		Rolling Thunder
	Voyage of the Beagle		The Vault
	The Skater		Tough–Brown Integral
	Iron in the Soul		Stiletto
	The Missing Link		Dubh Loch Monster
	The Israelite		Mort
	Range War		Vampire
E3	Bombadillo		Three Step
	The Spire		Gadd's Route
	Crazy Sorrow		Drop-out
	The Snake		Chindit Direct
	The Giant		Falkenhorst
	The Wicker Man		The Prowl
	Jezebel		Raptor
	The Outlands		High Step
	The Harp		Solitaire
	Culloden		Waterkelpie Wall
	Vampire Direct		The Grinder
	Henchman		Sous Les Toits (1PA)
	Black Spout Wall		Death's Head Route (2PA)
	The Empty Quarter		The Vicar
	King Crimson		Talisman Direct Start
E2	Haystack		King Rat
	Cougar		Medium-Rare
	Friends Essential		Vixen
	The Demon		Katsalana
	Scythe		The Stretcher
	Crimson Cringe		Mantichore
	Alice Springs		The Needle
	Masque	HVS	Sylph
	The Crow		Poison Dwarf
	Nevermore		Damien
	Drainpipe Crack		Goliath Eliminate

VS

Ivory Tower	Sheath
The Chancel	Pinnacle Grooves
Devil's Alternative	Cyclops
The Primate	Dinosaur/Pink Elephant
Mirage (variations)	The Strumpet
Nihilist	Gibber
Slochd Wall	Devil Dancer
Umslopogaas	Good Intentions
Pantheist	The Link (direct)
Blue Max	The Sand-Pyper Direct
Prince of Darkness	The Citadel
Time Traveller	Come Dancing
The Sting	Homebrew
Cutlass	Brodan's Dyke
The Bishop	Hot Toddy
Magic Crack	Tough-Guy
Never Mind (1 PA)	Hot Lips
Daddy Longlegs	The Last Oasis
War and Peace	Helter Skelter
Epitome	Postern Direct
Amethyst Pillar	Windchill
Quickstep	Longbow Direct
Limbo Dance	The Chebec
Consolation Groove	Koala
Ventricle	Mousetrap
Scalpel	Ghost Crack
Dragonfly	The Dagger
Catwalk	Scabbard
Klonedyke	Bloodhound Buttress
Tickled Pink	Vertigo Wall (1 PA)
The Omen	Black Mamba
Second Sight	Pythagoras
Hood Route	Finger's Ridge Direct
Pushover	Delicatessen
Crypt	Vulcan
Predator	Mack's Dilemma
The Scent	Big De'il
Sgian Dubh	Whispers
Goliath	The Hinmost
The Exorcist	The Clean Sweep
Damnation	Nomad's Crack
The Chute	Tough–Brown Ridge Direct
Nymph	Fallout Corner
Dogleg	Parallel Gully B
Fool's Rib	The Last Tango
Psyche	Hell's Bells
A Likely Story	Jewell–Kammer Route
Streaker's Root	Sundance
The Gowk	Indolence
The Tower of Babel	Djibangi
Bellows	Tearaway
Salamander	Carmine Groove

Après Moi
Speakeasy
The Carpet
Hackingbush's Horror
Sabre
Pinnacle Face

Bugaboo Rib
Hellfire Corner
Hourglass Buttress
Styx
Pink Dwarf
Lamina

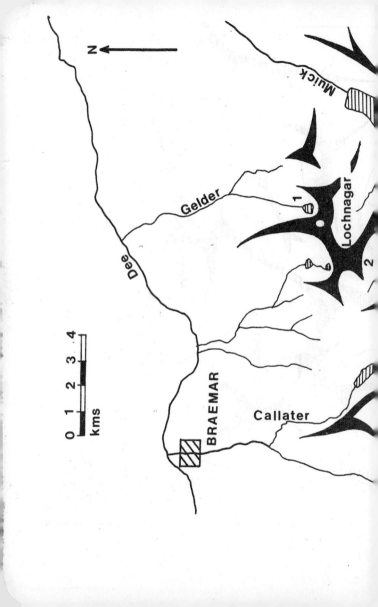